OXFORD THEOLOGICA

# OXFORD THEOLOGICAL MONOGRAPHS

# Ezekiel and the
# Ethics of Exile

ANDREW MEIN

OXFORD
UNIVERSITY PRESS

# OXFORD
### UNIVERSITY PRESS

Great Clarendon Street, Oxford, OX2 6DP
Oxford University Press is a department of the University of Oxford.
It furthers the University's objective of excellence in research, scholarship,
and education by publishing worldwide in

Oxford New York

Auckland Cape Town Dar es Salaam Hong Kong Karachi
Kuala Lumpur Madrid Melbourne Mexico City Nairobi
New Delhi Shanghai Taipei Toronto

With offices in

Argentina Austria Brazil Chile Czech Republic France Greece
Guatemala Hungary Italy Japan Poland Portugal Singapore
South Korea Switzerland Thailand Turkey Ukraine Vietnam

Oxford is a registered trade mark of Oxford University Press
in the UK and in certain other countries

Published in the United States
by Oxford University Press Inc., New York

© Andrew Mein 2001

The moral rights of the author have been asserted
Database right Oxford University Press (maker)

First published 2001
First published in paperback 2006

British Library Cataloguing in Publication Data
Data available

Library of Congress Cataloging in Publication Data
Mein, Andrew.
Ezekiel and the ethics of exile / Andrew Mein.
p. cm. – (Oxford theological monographs)
Includes bibliographical references and indexes.
1. Bible. O.T. Ezekiel–Criticism, interpretation, etc. 2. Ezekiel (Biblical prophet)–Ethics.
3. Jews–History–Babylonian captivity, 598–515 B.C. I Title. II. Series.
BS1545.52 .M45 2002      224'.406–dc21      2001036753

Typeset by Regent Typesetting, London
Printed in Great Britain
on acid-free paper by
Biddles Ltd, King's Lynn, Norfolk

ISBN 0-19-829992-3   978-0-19-829992-9
ISBN 0-19-929139-x (Pbk.)   978-0-19-929139-7 (Pbk.)

1 3 5 7 9 10 8 6 4 2

*To my parents*

# PREFACE

This book is the revision of a thesis for which the degree of D.Phil. in the University of Oxford was awarded in 1997. I am especially grateful to my supervisor, John Barton, who first suggested that I think about ethics in the Hebrew Bible, and guided me through my doctoral research with wisdom and constant encouragement. I would also like to thank Paul Joyce for reading my initial drafts and later revisions with great care, and for many invaluable discussions. I am grateful to David Chalcraft for his direction in matters sociological, and to Hugh Williamson and Ronald Clements for their helpful comments on earlier stages of the work. Thanks are also due to my family and friends, who have had to bear with me throughout the process of research, writing, and revision. This book is dedicated to my parents, Catherine and Renton Mein, without whose love and support it would never have been possible.

*Andrew Mein*
*Westcott House, Cambridge*

# CONTENTS

# LIST OF ABBREVIATIONS

| | |
|---|---|
| ATD | Das Alte Testament Deutsch |
| BETL | Bibliotheca ephemeridum theologicarum lovaniensum |
| BEvTh | Beiträge zur evangelischen Theologie |
| *BHS* | *Biblica Hebraica Stuttgartensia* |
| BHT | Beiträge zur historischen Theologie |
| BibS[N] | Biblische Studien (Neukirchen) |
| *BJRL* | *Bulletin of the John Rylands University Library of Manchester* |
| *BN* | *Biblische Notizen* |
| BWANT | Beiträge zur Wissenschaft vom Alten und Neuen Testament |
| *BZ* | *Biblische Zeitschrift* |
| BZAW | Beihefte zur Zeitschrift für die alttestamentliche Wissenschaft |
| CahRB | Cahiers de la Revue biblique |
| *CBQ* | *Catholic Biblical Quarterly* |
| EdF | Erträge der Forschung |
| *ETL* | *Ephemerides theologicae lovanienses* |
| *EvTh* | *Evangelische Theologie* |
| *ExpT* | *Expository Times* |
| FB | Forschung zur Bibel |
| FOTL | Forms of Old Testament Literature |
| FRLANT | Forschungen zur Religion und Literatur des Alten und Neuen Testaments |
| *HAR* | Hebrew Annual Review |
| HAT | Handbuch zum Alten Testament |
| HKAT | Handkommentar zum Alten Testament |
| HSM | Harvard Semitic Monographs |
| *HUCA* | *Hebrew Union College Annual* |
| ICC | International Critical Commentary |
| *IEJ* | *Israel Exploration Journal* |
| *Int* | *Interpretation* |
| *JAOS* | *Journal of the American Oriental Society* |
| *JBL* | *Journal of Biblical Literature* |
| JBLMS | Journal of Biblical Literature Monograph Series |
| *JNES* | *Journal of Near Eastern Studies* |
| *JSOT* | *Journal for the Study of the Old Testament* |

| JSOTS | Journal for the Study of the Old Testament, Supplement Series |
|---|---|
| *JTS* | *Journal of Theological Studies* |
| KAT | Kommentar zum Alten Testament |
| LXX | Septuagint |
| MT | Masoretic Text |
| NCB | New Century Bible |
| NICOT | New International Commentary on the Old Testament |
| OBT | Overtures to Biblical Theology |
| OTL | Old Testament Library |
| OTS | Oudtestamentische Studiën |
| *PEQ* | *Palestine Exploration Quarterly* |
| *RB* | *Revue Biblique* |
| RHPR | Revue d'histoire et de philosophie religieuses |
| SBB | Stuttgarter biblische Beiträge |
| SBLDS | Society of Biblical Literature Dissertation Series |
| SBLMS | Society of Biblical Literature Monograph Series |
| SBT | Studies in Biblical Theology |
| SJLA | Studies in Judaism in Late Antiquity |
| SOTS | Society for Old Testament Study |
| SSN | Studia Semitica Neerlandica |
| SVT | Supplements to *Vetus Testamentum* |
| *TDOT* | G. J. Botterweck, and H. Ringgren (eds.), *Theological Dictionary of the Old Testament* (Grand Rapids, Mich., 1974– ) |
| *ThZ* | *Theologische Zeitschrift* |
| *VT* | *Vetus Testamentum* |
| WMANT | Wissenschaftliche Monographien zum Alten und Neuen Testament |
| *ZAW* | *Zeitschrift für die alttestamentliche Wissenschaft* |
| *ZDMG* | *Zeitschrift der deutschen morgenländischen Gesellschaft* |
| *ZThK* | *Zeitschrift für Theologie und Kirche* |

# Introduction

The early sixth century BCE was a time of almost unparalleled crisis for the Jewish people, as successive Babylonian invasions left Judah devastated and Jerusalem in ruins. The book of Ezekiel forms a commentary on these events, and explains in lurid detail how the fall of Jerusalem and subsequent exile are the result of moral failure. The present work will demonstrate that many of the book's most distinctive ethical ideas can best be explained as a response to the experience of exile.

Ezekiel has always been a controversial figure: his book has provoked strong reactions from its readers, and this is nowhere clearer than in questions of morality. Some commentators have been straightforwardly critical of Ezekiel's ethics. The prophet's evident attachment to cult and ritual have been seen to obscure more genuine 'moral' issues,[1] and his bizarre visions, sign actions, and allegories often seem guaranteed to shock or revolt the reader.[2] Indeed, the sexually explicit, even perhaps pornographic, content of several oracles has led some recent critics to consider the book downright immoral.[3] Others have taken a more positive view, and there has been widespread agreement that Ezekiel represents an important milestone in the development of Israelite ethics. For the most part, this more positive interest has focused on one issue (the doctrine of individual responsibility) and one chapter (Ezekiel 18) in which that doctrine appears most clearly

---

[1] So e.g. R. H. Kennett, *Old Testament Essays* (Cambridge, 1928), 57; H. Wheeler Robinson, *Two Hebrew Prophets: Studies in Hosea and Ezekiel* (London, 1948), 102.

[2] One early exemplar of this trend is Voltaire, who expressed horror at God's demand for Ezekiel to eat cakes baked with dung, and concluded 'quiconque aime les prophéties d'Ezéchiel mérite de déjeuner avec lui': F. M. A. de Voltaire, *The Complete Works of Voltaire*, xxxv. *Dictionnaire philosophique, ii*, sous la direction de Christiane Mervaud (Oxford, 1994), 98.

[3] J. C. Exum, 'The Ethics of Biblical Violence against Women', in J. W. Rogerson, M. Davies, and M. D. Carroll R (eds.), *The Bible in Ethics: The Second Sheffield Colloquium*, JSOTS 207 (Sheffield, 1995), 248–71; F. van Dijk-Hemmes, 'The Metaphorization of Woman in Prophetic Speech: The Case of Ezekiel 23', in A. Brenner (ed.), *A Feminist Companion to The Latter Prophets* (Sheffield, 1995), 244–55.

stated. Antonin Causse is effusive: 'Cette nouvelle position du problème éthique et réligieuse . . . devait être la grand conquête du judaïsme.'[4] More recently some have questioned whether, in fact, individual responsibility is an important part of Ezekiel's message,[5] but the discussion of Ezekiel 18 has remained central. Indeed, one recent monograph devoted to Ezekiel's ethics concentrates entirely on this chapter as a 'point of entry into the book'.[6] While such attention to Ezekiel 18 is welcome, it can (perhaps accidentally) give the false impression that the rest of the book is less concerned with ethical issues. An important aim of this study, therefore, will be to take a broad view of the book's moral concerns and priorities, examining a range of different texts and issues.

However, before we can begin the detailed examination of the biblical text it will be necessary to deal with the more general problem of how to go about studying morality in ancient Israel and Judah. Much of the work which is done on ethics in the Hebrew Bible takes a very confessional and canonical view, and is primarily concerned with scripture as a resource for behaviour and the formation of community, whether Jewish or Christian. Less common is a more historical and sociological approach—the attempt to describe the moral systems of the ancient Israelites, the ways in which they made ethical decisions, and the social contexts in which they made them. It is this second task which will be the focus of this inquiry, and in the first chapter I shall attempt to provide a broad context for the more exegetical work that follows. Morality does not exist in a vacuum, but is anchored in the complex relations between individuals and groups that make up human society. In particular, the social circumstances of any human group are vital in determining the range of moral possibilities that is open to its members. Different groups of people have different economic resources and levels of political influence, different cultures and world-views, and as these vary so do ethical ideas and values, as well as the religious symbols which express those values. If we pay attention to the different moral worlds that

---

[4] A. Causse, *Du Groupe ethnique à la communauté réligieuse: le problème sociologique de la religion d'Israël* (Paris, 1937), 201.

[5] In particular, P. M. Joyce, *Divine Initiative and Human Response in Ezekiel*, JSOTS 51 (Sheffield, 1989).

[6] G. H. Matties, *Ezekiel 18 and the Rhetoric of Moral Discourse*, SBLDS 126 (Atlanta, Ga., 1990), 2.

are presupposed in biblical texts, we may contribute to a more complete picture of the moral life of ancient Israel.

In Chapter 2 I shall turn my attention to the book of Ezekiel, which is a particularly interesting example because of the unusual situation of exile in which the prophet's audience found themselves. The book of Ezekiel locates the prophet's activity in an enclave of exiles whom Nebuchadnezzar had deported from Judah to Babylonia in 597 BCE. Despite a number of attempts to challenge this setting, it remains the most likely context for his ministry and the formation of the book. As exiles these people belonged to two different moral worlds—two different realms of moral possibility. On the one hand, they were drawn from Judah's ruling élite, and, before their deportation, would have participated in decisions affecting major communal institutions like the temple and the army. But, on the other hand, their new status as a dominated minority within the huge Babylonian empire brought little or no political autonomy and posed serious threats to their communal identity. They were no longer able to participate in the main areas of political and religious life. Their moral world was sharply circumscribed, and it was really only in the spheres of family, business, and immediate community that they could take moral decisions. Ezekiel's oracles address both of these moral worlds, and the remainder of this work will examine some of the ways in which this makes itself felt in the book.

In Chapters 3 and 4 I shall examine some ways in which Ezekiel reflects the moral horizons of the Jerusalem élite, concentrating particularly on the content of the prophet's oracles of judgement. As Ezekiel predicts the destruction of Judah and Jerusalem, the moral judgements he condemns belong largely to the world of the communal institutions. While he does not ignore social justice, the prophet's special concerns are international politics and the correct maintenance of the state cult. In all of these areas Judah's leading citizens have failed to make the right moral decisions, and their sin on a grand scale will be answered by punishment on an equally grand scale. The combination of issues suggests that the moral world to which the majority of Ezekiel's oracles of judgement belong is that of the Jerusalem élite, a world which the exiles who formed his audience had only recently left behind.

In the final three chapters of the work I shall turn to the social context of exile, and investigate the effect of deportation on the community's moral concerns and priorities. As deportees to Babylonia the members of Judah's exiled élite immediately experienced a severe loss of status and serious threats to their communal identity. Elements in Ezekiel's ethics can be seen as mechanisms for survival among the exiles, providing significant impetus for social cohesion and the maintenance of a distinctively Jewish community. Ezekiel's ethical distinctiveness is seen perhaps most clearly in the high priority the prophet places on ritual, and the way that the language of cult dominates his analysis of past sin, present judgement, and future hope. Thus the rituals of the destroyed temple become the centrepiece of an ethical system which constantly looks back to the homeland for its symbolic coherence. At the same time, in those oracles which seem more directly addressed to the present concerns of the exiles an increasing 'domestication' of sin and virtue moves the focus of ethical interest from the institutions of state to the individual and the family. Furthermore, the book displays a movement from responsibility for judgement to passivity in the face of restoration that reflects the actual social circumstances of the exiles, who have moved from the world of power and influence in Jerusalem to the far more limited world of exile in Babylonia.

This study is an attempt to understand Ezekiel's ethics by setting them firmly in a particular historical and social context. It is primarily a historical-critical and exegetical work, but one whose questions and answers have been significantly influenced by a variety of social scientific sources, some more closely related to ancient Israel, some less so. As such, its aim is not so much to test one particular sociological theory as to find ways in which the combination of historical and sociological approaches can illuminate both this particular text and ethics in ancient Israel more generally. Of course an attention to social context will not explain everything. At the very least, Ezekiel's own background as a priest and use of earlier traditions are of enormous significance for his theology and the moral ideas with which he engages. Nevertheless, if moral worlds do have the close relationship with social worlds that I have proposed, then the characteristic uses of ethical material in Ezekiel's prophecy cannot properly be understood without reference to the distinctive social conditions of the Babylonian exile out of which they first arose.

# 1

# Moral Worlds: Ancient Israelite Ethics in a Social Context

It has often been said that ethics in the Hebrew Bible (for Christians, the Old Testament) is an under-represented area of Biblical Studies. Indeed, Brevard Childs wrote over thirty years ago that 'there is no outstanding modern work written in English that even attempts to deal adequately with the Biblical material as it relates to ethics', and, at least as far as the Hebrew Bible is concerned, progress has been painfully slow.[1] A flurry of publications on ethical matters in the past few years suggests that interest is growing, but it must be said that the subject is still relatively in its infancy. What is more, there is substantial disagreement between scholars about what the proper focus for the study of 'Hebrew Bible Ethics' or 'Old Testament Ethics' should be. We may easily agree with Robert Wilson, who has written that 'enough work has accumulated to suggest that the field is still in some disarray'.[2]

The subject of ethics in ancient Israel and the Hebrew Bible is a difficult one to enter for a number of reasons. For a start, by contrast with the literature of ancient Greece, the discipline of 'ethics' itself is quite alien to the Hebrew Bible. Although a great deal of its material is concerned with influencing behaviour and ideas, there is little or no detached reflection on the subject: nothing which we could describe as moral philosophy. Secondly, there is considerable uncertainty about what we mean when we use an expression like 'the ethics of the Hebrew Bible'. Are we interested in the beliefs of all or most ancient Israelites, the views of certain biblical authors, or indeed the ethical outlook of the whole Hebrew Bible?[3] Answering these questions is not helped by

---

[1] B. S. Childs, *Biblical Theology in Crisis* (Phil., 1970), 124.
[2] R. R. Wilson, 'Sources and Methods in the Study of Ancient Israelite Ethics', *Semeia*, 66 (1994), 55.
[3] We may also wish to view the Hebrew Bible/Old Testament in the context of the whole Christian Bible or, from a Jewish perspective, as it is supplemented by the Mishnah and Talmud.

*Moral Worlds*

the variety of competing voices in the text that demand obedience and action of the reader or hearer. As John Barton writes with some understatement, 'it is evident from the prophets, if it is indeed not obvious from common sense, that not all Israelites can have thought the same about at least some ethical issues'.[4]

Perhaps the most significant confusion which arises in the discussion does so because there are two distinct tasks which could both be described as 'the ethics of the Hebrew Bible'. We might broadly characterize the different approaches as 'descriptive ethics' and 'normative ethics'. The former seeks to uncover the moral norms and principles in biblical texts and their relationship to the culture of ancient Israel and Judah. The latter is also concerned to describe the ethical content of the Hebrew Bible, but it is driven by the fundamental question: 'How do we use the Bible as a source for moral guidance today?' In the history of Jewish and Christian biblical interpretation this task of 'normative' or 'constructive' ethics has been primary, and it remains so. Certainly it has been the aim of most of the recent monographs on the subject of ethics and the Hebrew Bible, whether they come from a conservative or liberal theological background. Walter C. Kaiser's *Toward Old Testament Ethics* is a comprehensive treatment of the subject from a very conservative evangelical viewpoint, which organizes the biblical material around the basic ideas of God's holiness and the demands which he has revealed in the Law.[5] Christopher Wright's *Living as the People of God*, which describes ethics within the Old Testament from the threefold perspective of theology, society, and economics, is nevertheless concerned to use the Old Testament as an authoritative source for moral thinking: 'if our aim is a coherent biblical ethic, then our final authority must be the completed text in its final form'.[6] From more liberal theological circles have come the works of Bruce Birch and of Waldemar Janzen, both of whom find in the genre of narrative the key for understanding the ethics of the Old Testament and for appropriating them to a Christian life.[7] In these and other such

[4] J. Barton, 'Understanding Old Testament Ethics', *JSOT* 9 (1978), 45; cf. also his recent work *Ethics and the Old Testament* (London, 1998).

[5] W. C. Kaiser, jun., *Toward Old Testament Ethics* (Grand Rapids, Mich., 1983).

[6] C. J. H. Wright, *Living as the People of God: The Relevance of Old Testament Ethics* (Leicester, 1983), 64.

[7] B. C. Birch, *Let Justice Roll Down: The Old Testament, Ethics, and Christian Life* (Louisville, Ky., 1991); W. Janzen, *Old Testament Ethics: A Paradigmatic Approach* (Louisville, Ky., 1994).

works we find widely differing approaches to the text, but nevertheless there is a common thread, as Douglas Knight points out: 'What all these types of appropriation have in common is the conviction, usually a religious conviction, that the Bible represents a source, and for some the final or—so they believe—the *only* source of moral direction.'[8]

Many of those who turn to the Hebrew Bible for ethical guidance have been heavily influenced by Brevard Childs's canonical criticism, and Childs himself has devoted considerable energy to the study of biblical ethics. For him the problem of ethics is the central problem of the Old Testament: 'knowing the will of God'. On the one hand, parts of scripture imply that God has made his will known clearly. There exist numerous clear injunctions to behave in a certain way. Yet, on the other hand, it is also clear that knowing God's will cannot be taken for granted, but must be sought after and discerned. Childs accepts that there can be tensions between different parts of the biblical material, both on this basic question of knowing the will of God and on more specific ethical questions. However, he rejects critical scholarship's concern with change and development in ethical behaviour and attitudes, preferring to see that the biblical tradition stressed the one unchanging will of God. Tensions can be accounted for by the different particular situations to which the words of God were addressed, but the basic movement is in one direction. When faced with any one ethical issue the task of the theologian is to examine the Bible for 'warrants' concerning the appropriate course of action:

First the Biblical theologian attempts to sketch the *full range* of the Biblical witnesses within the canonical context that have bearing on the subject at issue. Secondly, he seeks to understand the *inner movement* of the various witnesses along their characteristic axes when approached from within the context of the canon.[9]

This is a process which will allow different voices within scripture to be heard, and which need not come up with a definite solution to the problem in hand: 'The warrant does not function as an infallible rule of thumb, nor as an instance of an eternal principle,

---

[8] D. A. Knight, 'Introduction: Ethics, Ancient Israel, and the Hebrew Bible', *Semeia*, 66 (1994), 3.
[9] Childs, *Biblical Theology in Crisis*, 132.

but as a time-conditioned testimony to God's will in which word the Christian seeks to discern afresh his own obedient action in a new historical moment.'[10] Sometimes the search through the canon will produce one definitive answer, at other times it will be less directive, serving 'to delimit the area in which the decision must be sought', or even offering a variety of alternatives. It would be quite possible for Christians to disagree and be supported by biblical warrants on both sides of an argument.

Childs provides an attractive model for using the Hebrew Bible in ethics, but I believe that his approach suffers from a couple of quite serious flaws. First of all, since Childs ultimately provides no final arbiter of the different possible options in scripture, one is left to assume that whatever ethical decision is made will be made on other grounds than those found in scripture. This is in all likelihood the way in which most Christians in fact do make ethical decisions, as Cyril Rodd suggests:

It is highly improbable that the scriptures ever function as an absolute authority, over-riding all other motives. In practice the way everyone arrives at ethical decisions involves a wide range of attitudes, values, and internalized norms, as well as conscious decision. At most the Bible constitutes one factor in the adopting of ethical positions, and more often it is used to support attitudes which have been taken up on quite other grounds.[11]

If this is the case, it may be satisfactory for some, like Birch, who accept that scripture is one of a number of resources,[12] but rather makes a mockery of anyone who, like Childs himself, adopts a *sola scriptura* attitude to authority. One of the biggest problems with all the normative approaches to the Hebrew Bible is that we are left wondering whether it really is the Bible which has influenced a theologian's moral judgement, or something else. It is instructive to think that one commandment which is universally recognized in scripture by law, prophecy, and wisdom is the prohibition of usury and the taking of interest: a commandment equally universally ignored today.[13]

---

[10] Ibid. 134.

[11] C. S. Rodd, 'New Occasions Teach New Duties? 1. The Use of the Old Testament in Christian Ethics', *ExpT* 105 (1994), 101.

[12] Birch, *Let Justice Roll Down*, 34.

[13] Exod. 22: 25; Deut. 23: 19–20; Lev. 25: 35–8; Ezek. 18: 5–9; Ps. 15: 5; Prov. 28: 8; see Rodd, 'New Occasions', 100.

Equally problematic, as Robert Wilson points out, is the vehe-
mence with which some practitioners of normative ethics react to
the more historically or sociologically oriented treatments of
ancient Israelite ethics.[14] Childs, in particular, has dismissed the
kind of sociological approach proposed by authors like Wilson
and Barton: 'The route of a radical sociological approach will
never produce a normative ethic for the Christian faith, but will
only confirm the initial assumptions of cultural and theological
relativism'.[15] However, if it is not our aim to produce a normative
ethic for the religious faithful, why should we be bound by the
canonical approach? Far from being the case that the study of
biblical ethics is not theological enough, as Childs would have it,
I would suggest that it has been consistently too theological.
Wilson criticizes authors like Childs, Kaiser, and Birch for implying that 'historical description is in some sense irrelevant to the
theological use of the Bible's ethical material, whatever those
materials are finally determined to be'.[16] They are, in effect,
putting the cart before the horse, because the historical nature of
the biblical documents is one of the more important things that
make them so difficult to interpret in the first place. Here we
come upon what is probably the greatest stumbling block to any
normative use of scripture for ethics: the enormous culture gap
between our own experience and the experience of the communities who formed the Bible. Interpreters like Kaiser, Childs
and Birch seem to believe that by the adoption of the canonical
scriptures as an authoritative text we can somehow circumvent
that culture gap. To me, and I suspect to the majority of those
who favour a more descriptive approach to the ethics of the
Hebrew Bible, this is not at all straightforward. As Eckart Otto
makes plain at the beginning of his *Theologische Ethik des Alten
Testaments*: 'Die historische Distanz verbietet eine normative
Applikation alttestamentlicher Handlungsanweisungen auf die
heutigen Gesellschaften.'[17] We cannot even translate the plain
text of the Hebrew Bible without an awareness of the society
which formed it, and without first making the attempt to understand that society on its own terms.

---

[14] Wilson, 'Sources and Methods', 57.
[15] B. S. Childs, *Biblical Theology of the Old and New Testaments* (London, 1993), 676.
[16] Wilson, 'Sources and Methods', 60.
[17] E. Otto, *Theologische Ethik des Alten Testaments* (Stuttgart, 1994), 11.

A descriptive approach to the ethics of the Hebrew Bible is, as
I see it, primarily a historical and sociological task which relies
largely, but not exclusively, on the biblical record to examine
morality in ancient Israel. It is the study of the behaviour and
ideals for behaviour of a people far removed in time and place
from us and, like the study of ethics in ancient Greece or Egypt (or
for that matter modern Mongolia), need have no immediate cash
value for the Christian or Jewish ethicist. Of course the matter is
not that simple, but I think it is important to treat the Bible as a
resource for the study of ancient Israel with no more privilege
than we do Herodotus or the *Book of the Dead* as resources for
morals in Greece or Egypt. Thus an important aspect is the
separate study of the ethics of the individual biblical books or
authors, which come from a variety of periods and positions within the history of ancient Israel. To set these books in their proper
historical and social contexts is a necessary first step. However,
Douglas Knight takes this further as he describes a 'sociohistorical
construct' for biblical ethics, in which we approach the biblical
text not for its own sake nor that of our own moral decision
making, but with the primary aim of illuminating the moral life of
the historical communities that we now call ancient Israel:

> The final text, the preceding strata, and any hypothetical oral traditions
> need to be related, where plausible, to the communities, groups, and
> individuals that expressed in them their values and ideals . . . The focus
> falls on the morality not merely of texts but of the people's lives as they
> might have been played out in the real world. And significantly, the
> result amounts to a description of Israel's multiple moralities—not just a
> single unified 'orthodox' or dominant moral world but the full range of
> moral values evident in the people's behavior and in the economic and
> political systems throughout society.[18]

The Hebrew Bible provides us, then, with evidence from which
we can begin to draw a picture of the moral life of ancient
Israelites, the sorts of things that concerned them, and the ways in
which they solved ethical problems. It does not provide a complete picture: in about a thousand pages we have almost the entire
extant literary deposit of a society which lasted perhaps as many
years. Nor does it provide an entirely unified picture: although the

---

[18] Knight, 'Introduction', 4–5. A recent attempt by some social anthropologists to deal
with similar issues in (mostly) contemporary societies is the collection of essays in S. Howell
(ed.), *The Ethnography of Moralities* (London, 1997).

biblical authors clearly share much common ground on ethical matters, there is little coherence on many points. It is clear from the prophets or from Job that it was possible within ancient Israel to hold a variety of ethical positions, and it is often difficult to say whether a biblical author is outlining a generally held position or an idiosyncratic one. As John Barton writes: 'The Old Testament is evidence for, not coterminous with, the life and thought of ancient Israel; Old Testament writers may at times state or imply positions which were the common currency of ancient Israelites, but they may also propound novel, or controversial, or minority positions'.[19] We are not at liberty to assume that the evidence which has been preserved for us is in any way typical of the society. Indeed, it might be worth pointing out that one trend in recent scholarship has been to see the whole history of 'biblical Israel' as an ideological construct developed by scribal circles in the fourth century BCE or later.[20] This is to go too far, I am sure, but it is worth being reminded just how little we really know about ancient Israel. We must be careful not to assume that the ethics of any biblical author can be easily equated with those of his society, since the books of the Bible allow us only glimpses into the communities of ancient Israel and the moral ideas which were prominent there.

The work of scholars like Barton, Wilson, Knight, and McKeating has moved the study of ancient Israelite ethics forward significantly. On the one hand, they have made suggestions for a new method of examining morality in the Hebrew Bible that promises a richer and more realistic picture of the life of ancient Israel. On the other hand, in individual studies like McKeating's treatment of adultery or Knight's work on rights and privileges, they have provided fresh interpretations of individual ethical issues.[21] However, there has still been little work done which

---

[19] Barton, 'Understanding Old Testament Ethics', 46.

[20] So e.g. P. R. Davies, *In Search of 'Ancient Israel'*, 2nd edn., JSOTS 148 (Sheffield, 1995); K. W. Whitelam, *The Invention of Ancient Israel: The Silencing of Palestinian History* (London, 1996). G. N. Knoppers provides a good survey of the evidence (especially archaeological) and a response to such radicalism in his article 'The Vanishing Solomon: The Disappearance of the United Monarchy from Recent Histories of Israel', *JBL* 116 (1997), 19–44.

[21] H. McKeating, 'Sanctions against Adultery in Ancient Israelite Society, with some Reflections on Methodology in the Study of Old Testament Ethics', *JSOT* 11 (1979), 57–72; D. A. Knight, 'Political Rights and Powers in Monarchic Israel', *Semeia* 66 (1994), 93–117.

provides more comprehensive and sophisticated models to deal
with the complex and often troublesome evidence of the text of
the Hebrew Bible. Here some help may be sought from Wayne
Meeks's *The Moral World of the First Christians,* which can provide
a most helpful starting-point for our discussion.[22] This is a descriptive work which takes a broad historical and sociological
approach to the emerging Christian community, not simply concentrating on the more obvious ethical demands made in New
Testament texts. Meeks examines ethics 'from the bottom up',
and broadens the scope of ethical inquiry by asking not only *why*
a course of action is right or wrong, but also *who* it is that makes
the decision. To understand the moral formation of a group, we
must first understand something of their physical, social, and
symbolic world.

Meeks begins by describing the social and political world of the
Graeco-Roman cities and villages in which the first Christian
communities found themselves. He then presents some of the
most important ethical traditions which influenced moral decision
making within that social context: the schools of Greek philosophy
and the Jewish religion and scriptures. He goes on to discuss more
closely the social situations of the Christian communities themselves, and examines Christian texts not for their theological ideas
but to see how they are concerned to affect behaviour, and how
their authors adopt strategies from different traditions to achieve
this. Robert Wilson commends Meeks's approach to ethics as one
which interpreters of the Hebrew Bible should adopt: 'Ethical
decision making, then, should be understood not as mechanical
application of abstract laws or theological principles to a moral
dilemma but as the choice of a course of action in the light of the
various social and cultural components of an individual's moral
universe'.[23] In order to develop a more realistic understanding of
ethics in ancient Israel we require a more sophisticated analysis of
the ways in which ethical decision making relates to the society in
which the decisions are made. Moral agents do not act independently of the world in which they live, and the ways in which they
choose to act will be largely determined by the way they understand that world to work. We cannot overestimate the importance

---

[22] W. A. Meeks, *The Moral World of the First Christians* (London, 1986).

[23] R. R. Wilson, 'Ethics in Conflict: Sociological Aspects of Ancient Israelite Ethics', in
S. Niditch (ed.), *Text and Tradition: The Hebrew Bible and Folklore* (Atlanta, Ga., 1990), 195.

of communities in shaping the world-views of their individual members. The picture of the world that we have is largely determined by what we learn from others as we grow up. It is absolutely basic to our functioning as human beings and yet, as Meeks points out:

When we speak of 'their world' or 'the world of the Roman empire' . . . we betray a sense of something very odd about the concept 'world'. On the one hand, nothing is more objective to us than our world; it is simply *there* and we must relate to it. Yet if we compare our description of the objective world with, say, a Bushman's description, or the description by a monk of thirteenth-century Europe, we are driven to the conclusion that different people may have different worlds.[24]

Our worlds, which seem so objective to us, are in fact symbolized and socially learned versions of reality, substantially determined by the societies in which we live. And of course the world-view which we have will affect our behaviour. Meeks puts it simply: 'On a flat earth I will not sail west to get to the East Indies.'[25] There is a complex relationship between the material conditions in which people live and the ways they perceive and describe that world. This is of vital significance in shaping values and aspirations, as well as the symbols that represent them. Meeks draws on the association of ethos and world-view as examined in a classic essay by the anthropologist Clifford Geertz, who writes:

A people's ethos is the tone, character, and quality of their life, its moral and aesthetic style and mood; it is the underlying attitude toward themselves and their world that life reflects. Their world view is their picture of the way things in sheer actuality are, their concept of nature, of self, of society. It contains their most comprehensive ideas of order. Religious belief and ritual confront and mutually confirm one another; the ethos is made intellectually reasonable by being shown to represent a way of life implied by the actual state of affairs which the world view describes, and the world view is made emotionally acceptable by being presented as an image of an actual state of affairs of which such a way of life is an authentic expression. The demonstration of a meaningful relation between the values a people holds and the general order of existence within which it finds itself is an essential element in all religions, however those values or that order be conceived.[26]

---

24 Meeks, *Moral World*, 13.
25 Ibid. 14.
26 C. Geertz, *The Interpretation of Cultures* (NY, 1973), 127.

Thus Geertz sees religious symbolism as the perennial connection
between ethos and world-view. Symbols, myths, and rituals help
to sum up the way the world is and how to behave in it. This
suggests that as we attempt to describe the moral world of any
society we must pay attention to the symbols which it uses as well
as the material conditions which obtain. In both symbolic and
social worlds we will find evidence with which to fill out the context in which ethical decisions are made. This in turn will help us
understand moral reasoning and behaviour.

It may be possible at this stage to abstract from Meeks's work
and the above considerations some principles with which to begin
the study of the moral world of the ancient Israelites (or indeed
any other society). There are several tasks which we must attempt.
We must describe the explicit ethical content of biblical texts:
these texts themselves are our most important resource for ethics;
we should examine the injunctions they contain and the ethical
priorities which they address. As we examine the texts it will be
important to describe the symbolism which is used to present and
reinforce ethical ideas, and to relate this to those religious traditions of thought which influence decision making and behaviour.
We must also study the physical, economic, and political circumstances in which people lived in ancient Israel, so as to locate
those groups who produced the biblical literature on some kind of
map or model of their society.[27] Through attention to the social
and symbolic worlds which we find presupposed by ethical texts
we may be able to reach a synthesis, whereby we gain a clearer
understanding of what mattered to people and how decisions
were made in ancient Israel.

There are a number of difficulties with the method, which we
must take into consideration. Meeks's approach can be criticized
for failing to distinguish carefully enough between the different
groups within early Christianity which were responsible for
different New Testament texts. The different biblical authors may
well reflect quite different social circumstances, and it is misleading to treat them as representing too unified a society. If this is a
problem for New Testament ethics, it is even more of one when

---

[27] This will be a difficult task, given the paucity of evidence from outside the biblical
tradition, but it is, nevertheless, important to make some inroads into the political economy of ancient Palestine.

we approach the Hebrew Bible. A number of problems arise as Wilson recognizes:[28]

1. For source material we are compelled to rely almost exclusively on the evidence of the Hebrew Bible, which is often lacking in those areas we would most like to investigate. Evidence from elsewhere in the ancient Near East is of more questionable relevance to Israel than Graeco-Roman evidence is for the early Christians.

2. Israelites form a far less homogeneous group than the early Christians, and 'it may well be that the moral world of the king and the royal court was different from the moral world of the priesthood, which in turn was different from the moral world of the wealthy landowner or the slave. In any given period, then, a number of moral worlds have to be described in order to present a comprehensive picture of Israelite perceptions.'[29]

3. By contrast with the short period of the early church we have for the Hebrew Bible the thousand year span of Israelite culture in which religious and political traditions were developing continuously. We can expect moral ideas to change over time, and should be aware of developing traditions within ancient Israel.

4. Whereas the classical moral tradition and the Old Testament were more or less fixed influences on the early church, the canon of Jewish authoritative traditions was still growing for most of the period in which the Hebrew Bible was written. Especially since the dating and location of texts within the Hebrew Bible is so fraught with difficulties, it is often extremely difficult to trace influences with any certainty.

Wilson has begun the attempt to adapt Meeks's methods by suggesting some important components of ancient Israel's moral world. As Meeks looked to the classical moral tradition and the Old Testament as the two main components of the early Christians' moral world, Wilson proposes three major influences on Israelite ethical perceptions: traditional norms, law, and prophecy. Traditional norms were those generally accepted beliefs about behaviour which formed 'the primary ground for moral decision making'.[30] Because they were customary and often

---

[28] See Wilson, 'Ethics in Conflict', esp. 195–6.
[29] Ibid. 196.
[30] Ibid. 197.

accepted without question, there is little direct evidence for these norms, making them extremely difficult to study. However, it is possible to discover traces of them in the biblical literature, which reveals that there were probably never norms common to all Israelites. Wilson finds evidence that different groups had different sets of customary norms for behaviour, which came into conflict with one another:

The roots of these conflicts seem to lie not only in differing theological stances but also in fundamentally divergent views on the nature of reality and Israel's role within that reality. These differing perceptions must have issued in differing ideas on appropriate behaviour, although the details of these ideas are difficult to describe with any specificity.[31]

The traditional norms which Wilson describes here are not to be seen as a single tradition which holds some specific ethical content. Nor do we find here the deposit of one particular group. Rather we see one *method* of reaching an ethical conclusion: 'We do *x* because we always have done.' The same is true of Wilson's other two traditions, law and prophecy. The three components represent different ways of reaching a decision, different kinds of authority, and do not reflect three distinct social groups within Israel. There is room for conflict within all three traditions, and in fact different groups probably drew on all three.[32] It may be the case that some groups favoured one method or authority more than another, but Wilson does not go into specifics at all.

Wilson has made some valuable suggestions here about different kinds of moral reasoning in ancient Israel, but the work he has done is as yet too general to be tested. He has concentrated on the intellectual components of Israel's moral world, but has not yet adequately dealt with either the social world into which they fit or the specific ethical content of the different traditions. Any thorough attempt to understand ancient Israelite ethics must take these two factors into account as well.

---

[31] Wilson, 'Ethics in Conflict', 197.

[32] The possibility of different and competing styles of moral discourse and reflection within one society is highlighted by Caroline Humphrey in a fascinating study of the situation in Mongolia. She describes the distinction between commonly held 'rules' and more significant and personal human 'exemplars': C. Humphrey, 'Exemplars and Rules: Aspects of the Discourse of Moralities in Mongolia', in Howell (ed.), *The Ethnography of Moralities*, 25–47.

## Moral Horizons and Social Groups

When we compare people from widely differing cultures it is clearly the case that there exist different moral worlds: different ways of understanding the world and how to behave in it. For each moral world, we can think of a different range of actions which are possible and/or permissible, amounting to what we might call 'moral horizons'. By this I mean not only differences in the content of ethical demands (for example, whether or not incest is forbidden), but also differences of ethical scope: a tribal hunter-gatherer is unlikely to have within his moral horizons any sense of the way in which nation-states should relate to one another, and similarly a modern Western politician is unlikely to be aware of the problems of, say, the wrongful killing of sacred animals. There can be no question that the two inhabit different moral worlds. If this is true across a range of societies, it is also true of groups within a single society. Despite broad continuities of language and culture, there are often profound differences in ethical concern between different interest groups within society. This was the same in ancient Israel as in any other society, ancient or modern.

It is not new to draw attention to the importance of social group for understanding the ethics of the Hebrew Bible. As John Barton writes:

Even from an OT that has plainly been edited to express the attitudes of the official religious leadership in the post-exilic age, and to smooth out the evidence of dissenting voices, it is clear that in many periods there were sharp divisions of emphasis, and even straightforward disagreements, between different groups in Israel over many ethical issues.[33]

However, the identification and social location of these groups has proved more of a problem. The tendency among biblical scholars has been to equate social group with theological tradition and to stop there, without attempting to describe how those who belong to a particular theological tradition fit into the social world of ancient Israel. When such an attempt does occur, we often find a simple opposition of 'professional groups', as in McKane's antithesis of prophets and wise men, or Hanson's understanding of post-exilic theology being riven between the practitioners

---

[33] J. Barton, 'Approaches to Ethics in the Old Testament', in J. W. Rogerson (ed.), *Beginning Old Testament Study*, 2nd edn. (London, 1998), 118.

of theocratic legalism or apocalyptic eschatology.[34] The same
thing can happen as scholars search for the origins of a tradition:
people attempting to locate the origins of the Deuteronomistic
movement have tended to look to a range of professional groups:
northern Levites, northern prophetic circles, Jerusalem scribes,
and so on. All of these make sense in some respects, but none is
entirely convincing, and we must ask whether the proposals in fact
reflect anything like the social reality of monarchical Judah.
Patricia Dutcher-Walls finds that the lack of agreement among
scholars on the location of the Deuteronomists is symptomatic of
'a methodology that examines biblical texts without a sociological
understanding'. She continues: 'My proposal is that a model of
the social stratification and political culture of monarchic Israel
will allow a better understanding of where in the social structure
the Deuteronomists might have been located.'[35] This is a significant step for two reasons. First, we cannot successfully attempt to
place any ancient Israelite religious group without first having
some map or model of the society to which they belonged. We
should not deny either the existence or the importance of professional interest groups, but it is useful to have a broader framework into which we can place them. Secondly, the attempt to
locate groups within a social structure will draw attention to the
material and political interests which affect ethics, not just the
theological ones. Important as theology may be, it is far from the
only influence on moral decision making. As Henry McKeating
writes:

It is commonly assumed that for Israel religion was the decisive influence
in moral matters. On nearly every page the Old Testament appears to
confirm such a view. But allowances have to be made for the fact that
the Old Testament is a body of largely religious documents, edited and
put together (and in many cases produced) by people for whom religion
was a dominant interest. Of course Israel's ethic (like her history)
appears to cry out for a religious interpretation, but this is because, in the
documents at our disposal, it has already been given one . . . Were

[34] W. McKane, *Prophets and Wise Men* (London, 1965); P. D. Hanson, *The Dawn of
Apocalyptic: The Historical and Sociological Roots of Jewish Apocalyptic Eschatology*, 2nd edn. (Phil.,
1979).
[35] P. Dutcher-Walls, 'The Social Location of the Deuteronomists: A Sociological Study
of Factional Politics in Late Pre-Exilic Judah', *JSOT* 52 (1991), 80; I shall return to her work
below, in Chapter 3.

the principles by which real Israelites actually lived quite so closely determined by religious faith? It may be that they were, but we cannot without further ado assume so.[36]

We need to take a step back from theology and look at the constitution of society in ancient Israel before we can build a satisfactory picture of the moral worlds we will find there, and perhaps the most profitable first step will be to find a scheme into which we can place the different social groups which were responsible for the creation and preservation of the biblical literature. We can then move on to give further attention to the complex relationship between social stratification and ethics.

## A Model of Society in Ancient Israel

Gerhard Lenski begins his classic study of social stratification, *Power and Privilege*, with one question: 'Who gets what and why?'[37] With the development of agriculture and industry in human society an economic surplus is produced, and it is clear that at all times and in all places this surplus is unequally distributed among the population. Individuals and groups have different levels of access to the so-called 'scarce goods' of wealth, prestige, and power, and the study of social stratification is the attempt to measure and account for these distinctions in society. There has been considerable debate over which aspect of stratification is primary. In the Marxist tradition classes are defined on the basis of economic wealth. Ownership of the means of production is seen as the base upon which other aspects of cultures are built. Those who possess economic resources have the power to control others, and to create the cultural or ideological capital with which to distinguish themselves from others. On the other hand, in the sociological tradition deriving from Max Weber, a more multi-dimensional approach to stratification is evident. 'Weber wanted to argue that economic wealth was not the only criterion of social

---

[36] McKeating, 'Sanctions against Adultery', 70.
[37] G. Lenski, *Power and Privilege: A Theory of Social Stratification* (NY, 1966), title of first chapter. Dutcher-Walls has very helpfully proposed Lenski's work as a basis for understanding social stratification in Israel and Judah ('Social Location', 80–3). See also her more recent monograph, *Narrative Art, Political Rhetoric: The Case of Athaliah and Joash*, JSOTS 209 (Sheffield, 1996), esp. 143–6.

power and influence.'[38] In some circumstances distinctions of
prestige based on tradition, culture, or education were more
important for determining access to power and wealth. In *Power
and Privilege*, Lenski describes power itself as the most important
variable for measuring stratification. Although he begins with a
very broad definition of class he soon isolates power as the most
significant factor in stratification:

> *power* classes must be our chief concern. The distribution of privilege and
> prestige seem largely determined by the distribution of power, at least
> in those societies in which a significant surplus is produced . . . Power
> manifests itself in two basic forms, force and institutional power. The
> latter, in turn, can be subdivided into the power of position and the
> power of property.[39]

As we approach ethics in ancient Israel we should expect all these
elements of stratification: power, wealth, and prestige, to have
some effect in the shaping of groups and their moral worlds.

Lenski's work is extremely broad in its scope, and he analyses
stratification across a whole spectrum of societal types from the
primitive hunter-gatherer to the modern industrial. In each case
he derives a model—or, rather, a series of generalizations—from a
broad range of historical and sociological accounts. For our purposes the most interesting are what he calls 'agrarian societies'.[40]
These are societies which have achieved a fairly advanced level of
technology but no industrialization. Their efficient agricultural
systems produce a large economic surplus.[41] Advances in engi-
neering can use this surplus to build monuments like the medieval
cathedrals or the pyramids. By comparison with less advanced
agricultural societies we see developments in military technology:
the use of cavalry and chariots, and improvements in fortifications
and siege equipment. The increase in economic surplus is matched

---

[38] B. S. Turner, *Status* (Milton Keynes, 1988), 7. On Marx and Weber see also J. Scott,
*Stratification and Power: Structures of Class, Status, and Command* (Oxford, 1996), esp. chs. 2 and
3.

[39] Lenski, *Power and Privilege*, 75.

[40] As well as *Power and Privilege*, see also G. Lenski and J. Lenski, *Human Societies: An
Introduction to Macrosociology*, 4th edn. (NY, 1982), 169–217.

[41] Lenski's reliance on technology as the primary motive force behind social evolution
(cf. his discussion of the plough in *Human Societies*, 169–71) has recently been criticized by
S. K. Sanderson in *Social Evolutionism: A Critical History* (Oxford, 1990), 149–53. Nevertheless,
the model of stratification within (fairly static) agrarian societies that Lenski proposes
remains very useful.

by an increase in the power of the State, and ultimate power is normally concentrated in the hands of a single king or emperor. Agrarian societies are also marked by the growth of small urban communities, in which most of the power, influence, and affluence are concentrated. As the power of the State increases, the relations between State and religion become closer, reflecting the rulers' need for legitimacy. Examples of agrarian societies are to be found in most of the civilized societies of ancient and medieval Europe and Asia.[42] Lenski's model is drawn from a wide range of different societies, so we should not expect it to apply in every detail to the one society in which we are interested. Nevertheless, in broad terms this is the kind of society we see in ancient Israel, at least after the centralization of the State by David and Solomon.[43]

The most significant work on social stratification in ancient Israel has been that of Norman Gottwald, who draws inspiration from the work of Marx. In Marx's theory, different forms of society have different characteristic modes of economic production and forms of property: whereas in the classical world the economy was based on ownership of land and slaves, in modern industrial society ownership of capital has the primary role. Gottwald has characterized the pre-capitalist economic system operative in ancient Israel as a 'Tributary Mode of Production'.[44] A vast majority of the population worked on the land, producing basic goods, and the dominant class removed their economic surplus in the form of tribute or taxation:

Since technology and transport were not sufficiently developed to create a large consumer market for manufactured goods, the route to concentrating wealth or power in such circumstances was to gain control

---

[42] Two important comparative studies are S. N. Eisenstadt, *The Political Systems of Empires* (NY, 1963); J. H. Kautsky, *The Politics of Aristocratic Empires* (Chapel Hill, NC, 1982). Cf. also M. Mann, *The Sources of Social Power, i. A History of Power from the Beginning to AD 1760* (Cambridge, 1986); S. K. Sanderson, *Social Transformations: A General Theory of Historical Development* (Oxford, 1995), ch. 4.

[43] See the discussion in M. L. Chaney, 'Systemic Study of the Israelite Monarchy', *Semeia*, 37 (1986), 53–76. He writes: 'That the patterns of social stratification typical of agrarian monarchies manifested themselves in Israel and Judah is both certain and of an importance difficult to exaggerate' (55).

[44] N. K. Gottwald, 'Social Class as an Analytic and Hermeneutical Category in Biblical Studies', *JBL* 112 (1993), 5. This is, in effect, a renaming of Marx's own 'Asiatic' Mode of Production which Gottwald describes in 'A Hypothesis about Social Class in Monarchic Israel in the Light of Contemporary Studies of Social Class and Social Stratification', in his collection of essays *The Hebrew Bible in its Social World and Ours* (Atlanta, Ga., 1993), 139–64.

over agrarian and pastoral products, which the appropriators could themselves consume or assign to retainers at their discretion or convert into other valuables through trade and the acquisition of land.[45]

Under this tributary mode of production, ownership of the land is in the hands of the State, and state officials have the right to collect taxes on its behalf. This is the situation which Gottwald finds in monarchical Israel, admittedly in a weak form. Certainly under the monarchy the king controlled a very substantial proportion of the land, and could extract considerable tax, rent, and labour from his subjects. The speech attributed to Samuel in 1 Samuel 8 outlines (presumably with the benefit of hindsight) some of the less attractive aspects of the monarchy: forced labour, the confiscation of land, and the imposition of severe taxes:

These will be the ways of the king who will reign over you: he will take your sons and appoint them to his chariots and to be his horsemen, and to run before his chariots; and he will appoint for himself commanders of thousands and commanders of fifties, and some to plough his ground and to reap his harvest, and to make his implements of war and the equipment of his chariots. He will take your daughters to be perfumers and cooks and bakers. He will take the best of your fields and vineyards and olive orchards and give them to his servants. He will take the tenth of your grain and of your vineyards and give it to his officers and to his servants. He will take your menservants and maidservants, and the best of your cattle and your asses and put them to his work. He will take the tenth of your flocks, and you shall be his slaves.[46]

While it is difficult to assess the systems of ownership and taxation, it does appear that the State and its functionaries were the prime beneficiaries of any economic surplus. In ancient Israel, as in the rest of the ancient Near East, the powers of state were concentrated in the hands of the king.

Lenski begins his general analysis of ancient societies of this type at the top of the social ladder, where we find the ruler (almost a class in himself) and the governing classes. They form a tiny minority of the population of any state, but control a vast majority of its resources, both material and human. The composition of

---

[45] Gottwald, 'Social Class as an Analytic and Hermeneutical Category', 5.

[46] 1 Sam 8: 11–17. (Biblical quotations in translation are taken from the Revised Standard Version (RSV), unless otherwise noted.) It may be that the description of a king with much more limited power over his subjects that we see in Deut. 17 is the response of those who had suffered the injustices of the tributary system.

the governing class varies both within and between societies, but it can include those closest to the ruler, the highest officers of state, the most important civil and military officials, as well as the large-scale owners of land or of slaves. The people who form the ruling class are united by the opportunities open to them: 'To be a part of the governing class was to possess the right acknowledged by the supreme power in the land to share in the surplus produced by the peasant masses and urban artisans. This was their reward for upholding and enforcing the authority of the existing regime in general and the ruler in particular.'[47] There was a constant struggle between rulers and their governing classes, as each tried to get some advantage of power over the other. There were also struggles between different fractions of the ruling class, divided according to status group or party.[48] However, despite any differences, they clearly form a distinct stratum in any agrarian society.

Gottwald's Marxist framework leads him to propose a broadly twofold division of society: a dominant tribute-imposing class who control the means of production, and a dominated tribute-bearing majority who are the producers and taxpayers. At its most basic this is the distinction between the king (along with his closest family and associates) and everybody else. However, Gottwald is aware that the situation is more complex than this simple twofold division between rulers and ruled, and points out that, although ultimate power is in the hands of the ruler, there are many state functionaries who are also to be included within the governing class:

In my view, the state in its tribute-collecting function was the primary, and perhaps even exclusive, expropriator of the subject classes. Yet it would be ridiculous to contend that one person, the king, could be the sole beneficiary of such massive extraction of surplus labor value. Civil servants, military leaders, professional troops, artisans, and priests, in their capacities as state functionaries, were also beneficiaries of the extracted surplus. Themselves non-productive, except for the artisans, they lived off the village surplus product.[49]

All of these retainers were directly dependent upon the ruling élite for their livelihood, and, as Lenski points out, because of

---

[47] Lenski, *Power and Privilege*, 220.
[48] There is extensive discussion of the forms such conflict can take in Kautsky, *Aristocratic Empires*, esp. 169–266.
[49] Gottwald, 'A Hypothesis about Social Class', 155.

their dependence they provided a valuable base of support for the
ruler and governing classes. In particular, they were vital to the
distributive system, where they normally acted as middlemen
between the peasants and the ruling classes:

> It was the retainers who actually performed most of the work involved in
> effecting the transfer of the economic surplus from the producers to the
> political elite . . . Furthermore, because they were the intermediaries, the
> retainers deflected much of the hostility and resentment which otherwise
> would have been directed at the political elite.[50]

Thus retainers were very important in the maintenance of a
stable society. Although this is true collectively, as individuals they
were quite easily expendable since few possessed skills that could
not be easily acquired from others. They had little real bargaining
power, unless their skills were military and they could threaten the
use of force. Professional soldiers were a special case, and the
political élite had to be careful to reward them handsomely, for
fear that these retainers might use their force of arms to seize
control of the State. Despite the best efforts of rulers and their
retainers to monopolize the economic surplus, there were always
other groups that took a share. Of these the merchant classes
were the most successful, who could acquire considerable wealth
and prestige by their skilful trading and retain a certain degree of
independence.[51]

The next group Lenski discusses is the priestly class, which is
the one that perhaps varies most from society to society. In some
respects its position is similar to that of the retainers: its opportunities to amass wealth and prestige were largely tied to its
possessing the favour of the political élite. But it also occupied a
position of considerable strength and influence because the ruling
élites needed religious support to give their regimes legitimacy.

> For its part, the political elite badly needed the blessing of the priestly
> class. Only the latter could establish the legitimacy of a regime which
> constantly used its power to separate the common people from the major
> part of what they produced. The significance of this power to confer
> legitimacy is difficult to exaggerate.[52]

Because of this relationship, clashes between religious leaders
and rulers were common. The conflict between divine and royal

[50] Lenski, *Power and Privilege*, 246.     [51] Ibid. 255.     [52] Ibid. 260.

authority is familiar from many periods and cultures, and is certainly present in the Hebrew Bible. Across the whole range of agrarian societies we find widespread beliefs in supernatural powers or forces which could influence this world. The priests and other religious professionals were the intermediaries between the human and divine realms, so it was very much in the interests of rulers to have them on their staff. Keith Whitelam explains the need for this legitimation:

> The use of force was too costly and on the whole inefficient in maintaining royal power, giving rise to the heavy investment in means to propagate the royal symbolic universe. States could only survive if they attained legitimacy, often through the manipulation of religious symbols, since reliance upon coercion and force would destroy the very relationships upon which the ruling elite depended for their wealth and power.[53]

Despite the fact that much priestly effort was spent maintaining the present order of society, there were some whom the claims of their religion led to challenge tyranny and injustice, and to champion the cause of the weaker members of society. Lenski draws attention particularly to the western tradition of the justice of God, visible from Hammurabi to Muhammad and beyond: those who abuse justice do so against the will of a god who is quite capable of punishing the guilty. Religious figures who did speak out on behalf of the underclass were unique among the privileged classes in agrarian societies: 'In a type of society in which men of power saw to it that there was a massive flow of goods and services from the many to the few, some members of the priestly class managed to slow this movement and even to stimulate a small flow in the opposite direction.'[54]

However, this counterflow was never more than a trickle, and did little to improve the lot of the poor, who made up the huge bulk of population in any agrarian society. The backbone of these societies was made up of agricultural workers, the peasants, who were the actual producers of economic surplus. They led hard lives, rarely living at much more than subsistence level, and bearing the heaviest burdens of the State. Through heavy taxes on crops and land, as well as obligations of feudal service or

[53] K. W. Whitelam, 'Israelite Kingship: The Royal Ideology and its Opponents', in R. E. Clements (ed.) *The World of Ancient Israel: Anthropological, Sociological and Political Perspectives* (Cambridge, 1989), 121.

[54] Lenski, *Power and Privilege*, 266.

corvée, the peasants supported the ambitions and lifestyles of their superiors. Indeed, there was such a disparity of lifestyle between peasants and their betters that, as Lenski writes: 'Under such conditions the surprising thing is that some members of the privileged strata recognized the fact of their common humanity, not that the majority failed to do so.'[55] In the towns the artisans and semi-skilled labourers occupied a similar social position. Originally drawn from dispossessed peasants, they were collected in the towns where, for the most part, they worked for the merchants and received an income no greater than that of peasants. The lowest strata of society are what Lenski calls the 'expendables', which included beggars, outlaws, and underemployed itinerant workers: anyone who could not be sure of receiving even the minimal income of peasants or artisans.[56] The existence of such a class, which might comprise five or ten per cent of the population, was inevitable in societies where the birth rate outstripped the demand for labour.

Lenski has provided a general model which can be applied to a huge range of ancient and medieval societies, but as our concern is with the society of ancient Israel and Judah we should also be aware of more specific considerations. In her adaptation of his work to suit ancient Israel Dutcher-Walls points out the substantial influence of the temple and state religion, and would therefore place the high priests in the uppermost class.[57] Both she and Gottwald draw attention to the international situation, pointing out that the analysis of class is not limited to the individual state alone. Judah and Israel did not exist in a vacuum, but were constantly in contact with the great empires of Egypt and Mesopotamia. Assyria and Babylonia imposed severe tributes on the smaller states of Palestine and the Levant. When this was the case we can see the surplus of the Israelite peasantry being transferred ultimately to the ruling classes of Mesopotamia, while the Israelite state and ruling class served as functionaries of the Mesopotamians, collecting tribute and redirecting the surplus. In this case it is not unreasonable to include the foreign overlords as one subdivision of the governing classes in Judah and Israel. It is possible to draw up a tentative scheme of classes and class

---

[55] Lenski, *Power and Privilege*, 273; cf. also Chaney, 'Systemic Study', 56.
[56] Lenski, *Power and Privilege*, 281.
[57] Dutcher-Walls, 'Social Location', 84.

fractions in monarchical Israel, and Gottwald reproduces one
taken from an unpublished paper by Anthony Mansueto:

Social Classes and Social Fractions (sub-divisions of classes):
(a) ruling class groups: the Israelite royal houses, during the monarchic
    period, together with priestly sectors, dependent on taxes and corvées
    from the peasant communities; the metropolitan ruling classes of the
    various empires which dominated Israel, dependent on tributes levied
    on the population and collected by the indigenous ruling classes or by
    imperial administrators; and latifundaries, dependent on rents from
    more or less private estates.
(b) middle layers: craftsmen, functionaries, and lower clergy dependent
    on benefices which do not provide income sufficient to maintain an
    aristocratic style of life, and independent craftsmen and merchants.
(c) exploited classes: two principal kinds of peasantry
    • peasants protected by redistributional land tenure and other com-
      munity guarantees
    • tenant farmers on the estates of latifundaries; and marginated rural
      people who have no regular access to the land.[58]

In most respects this dovetails well with Lenski's more general
account of social stratification, and I think we have in the work of
Gottwald and Lenski the basis for a useful map of the social world
of ancient societies into which we can attempt to place the biblical writings.

Gottwald has consistently brought a Marxist approach to the
study of the Hebrew Bible, and uses economic class more or less
exclusively to determine the groups in ancient Israel: 'the most
illuminating way to understand wealth and power in the Bible—
as in all societies—is to understand the relation of groups of
people to the process of production of basic goods, which gener-
ates and replenishes human society in the perpetual flow of daily
life'.[59] However, we must question whether this is really enough to
explain the complex society of ancient Israel. There are too many
groups of people who share a similar level of wealth, but nevertheless form distinct groups with distinctive lifestyles and values:
two examples might be the priests and the military. The ancient
historian M. I. Finley, addressing himself to Greek and Roman
society, asks the same question about classification by relation to
the means of production:

[58] Gottwald, 'A Hypothesis about Social Class', 160.
[59] Gottwald, 'Social Class as an Analytic and Hermeneutical Category', 4.

Whatever the application of that classification in present day society, for the ancient historian there is an obvious difficulty; the slave and the free wage labourer would then be members of the same class, on a mechanical interpretation, as would the richest senator and the non-working owner of a small pottery. That does not seem a very sensible way to analyse ancient society.[60]

Finley is the first to point out the major differences between the economy of Greece and Rome and that of the ancient Near East, but his point remains valid for the latter too. The existence of these 'class fractions', which may have widely differing lifestyles, aspirations, and values, renders a strictly economic classification unhelpful. If, in our attempt to locate the moral worlds of ancient Israel, we distinguish a number of social worlds, we may be better served by the sociological concept of *status*, associated with the work of Max Weber.

Whereas for Marx all power groupings within society take the form of classes, and thus all conflict is class conflict, a more complex, and less strictly materialist, analysis of stratification is to be found in Weber. He describes different kinds of group within a society, and allows for a broader multidimensional picture of the conflicts between different interest groups to emerge. Typical of the Weberian approach to the problem is the distinction between class, status group, and party, as different kinds of interest group within a society. Weber was concerned to show that the distribution of economic wealth was not the only measure of power within a community: status is also fundamental. Status is not measured in terms of wealth but in terms of prestige or honour, and society is composed not only of classes but also of 'status groups' which, unlike classes, normally have a strong sense of community. Weber provides a definition of status situation: 'In contrast to the purely economically determined "class situation" we wish to designate as *status situation* every typical component of the life fate of men that is determined by a specific, positive or negative, social estimation of *honor*.'[61] He also distinguishes classes and status groups in economic terms: 'Classes are stratified according to their relations to the production and acquisition of goods; whereas status groups are stratified according to the principles of their *consumption* of

---

[60] M. I. Finley, *The Ancient Economy* (London, 1985), 49.

[61] M. Weber, *Economy and Society: An Outline of Interpretive Sociology* (Berkeley, Calif., 1978), ii. 932.

goods as represented by special "styles of life".[62] Thus status groups are united by common styles of life expressed in common patterns of consumption. These lifestyles reflect the honour in which the groups are held by other elements of the population. Conscious of their common position, members will tend to identify with one another, to adopt similar lifestyles, to intermarry, and so on:

> Weber was concerned to analyse the historical and social function of status groups or status communities which are collectivities enjoying a similar lifestyle, a unified moral system, a common language or culture, or religious differences. The result of these common cultural features is to produce separate, solidaristic communities which are organized to protect or advance their enjoyment of cultural and social benefits and privileges.[63]

Examples of status groups include racial and ethnic groups, religious, and even occupational groups, which we find taken to its extreme in the Indian caste system. Looking at ancient Israel, we may be able to rehabilitate the distinctions between prophets, priests, wise men, and apocalyptists, so beloved of biblical scholars, as examples of status groups. Certainly the priesthood, with its hereditary requirement for entry and distinctive lifestyle ordered around the maintenance of the temple, is a good candidate for a status group. In his own study of ancient Israel Weber wrote of the Levitical priests in Deuteronomic times as 'an exclusive status group', who 'claimed a monopoly in the employment of certain oracular formulae, priestly teaching, and priestly positions'.[64]

It is especially in traditional societies that we find stratification on the basis of status takes precedence over stratification on the basis of wealth.[65] Although it is theoretically possible to draw a sharp distinction between class and status group, it is often unnecessary to do so, because there is a tendency for classes to turn themselves into status groups; to organize themselves into culturally distinct units. Those who share a particular economic situation and recognize their common interests will develop a shared

---

[62] Ibid. 937.
[63] Turner, *Status*, 6.
[64] M. Weber, *Ancient Judaism* (NY, 1952), 171.
[65] Cf. Turner, *Status*, 20–1; Scott, *Stratification and Power*, 34–7.

culture, a shared world-view and ethos. Randall Collins comments:

From the Marxian viewpoint these classes were simply cloaking themselves in ideologies. Weber's theory agrees with this but with the added
proviso: the ideological or cultural side is absolutely necessary for a
group to become more than merely a set of persons with the same social
outlook, a shared social community.[66]

However, since status is based on the distribution of prestige or
honour not wealth, it is possible for those who share a similar economic position to be in quite different status situations 'which
refer to the evaluations which others make of them in terms of
prestige or esteem'.[67] Douglas Knight has argued that in ancient
Israelite village life, where there is a common economic position,
the distribution of power and political influence is set by 'status
and other traditional categories', including kinship relations, gender, age, profession, and property.[68] Moreover, status groups—
particularly racial, ethnic, and religious groups—can cut across
class divisions. So, for Weber the relationship between the elements of society is more complex than it was for Marx, as the
constant social conflict involves a range of different groups and
kinds of group. 'Classes become subdivided into status groups
and gain control of particular sectors of economic markets. A
secondary market for status attributes arises and this tends to blur
over the primary economic lines.'[69]

   Status groups are of particular interest from the point of view
of ethics. If we think of Weber's own example of the priesthood,
it is clear from the legislation in both Leviticus 21–2 and Ezekiel
44 that they form an exclusive hereditary group, not only carrying
out a distinct role in society, but also bound by different rules of
behaviour; for example, concerning marriage and bereavement.
The distinctions are maintained by means of the symbolic
language of holiness and purity. We can, therefore, see that moral
values and the symbols that represent them are a vital part of the
creation and maintenance of a distinctive group identity. They

---

[66] R. Collins, *Three Sociological Traditions* (NY, 1985), 88–9.
[67] D. Lee and H. Newby, *The Problem of Sociology* (London, 1983), 179.
[68] Knight, 'Political Rights and Powers', 107.
[69] Collins, *Three Sociological Traditions*, 90.

are an essential part of the culture and lifestyle that distinguishes one status group from another.

Weber's third kind of social group is the party. Parties are distinctive because they are rationally organized to achieve particular ends, and because they operate in the arena of the State, or other organizations. As Weber puts it, ' "parties" reside in the sphere of power'.[70] The members of parties are interested in influencing policy in a certain direction, which may be some particular cause, or merely personal advancement for themselves and their leaders. Often parties strive for both simultaneously. Although party interests may coincide to some degree with those of classes or status groups, this need not be the case:

In any individual case, parties may represent interests determined through 'class situation' or 'status situation', and they may recruit their following respectively from one or the other. But they need be neither purely 'class' nor purely 'status' parties. In most cases they are partly class parties and partly status parties, but sometimes they are neither.[71]

Parties are of considerable interest to us because they will often present their views in concrete, documented form. Morton Smith has helpfully pointed in this direction, suggesting that two religious parties dominated Israelite and Judaean politics before 587. Biblical texts provide evidence for the struggle between a minority 'Yahweh alone' party and the dominant 'syncretistic' party (with a heavy bias toward the former group), and members of each faction were drawn from a range of social backgrounds and occupations.[72] Since the parties themselves may represent different groups in society, so material produced by them can provide valuable insights into the world-view and ethical priorities of the groups they represent.

Throughout this survey we have argued that monarchical Israel and Judah, like all ancient agrarian states, were highly stratified societies. Conflict on the basis of social stratification is fundamental to the dynamics of any such society, and we can expect the distinct interests of social groups to be expressed in differences of

---

[70] Weber, *Economy and Society*, ii. 938. See discussion in Scott, *Stratification and Power*, 39‒45.

[71] Weber, *Economy and Society*, ii. 938. Weber himself describes parties in ancient Israel in *Ancient Judaism*, 274.

[72] M. Smith, *Palestinian Parties and Politics that Shaped the Old Testament* (NY, 1971), esp. ch. 2, 'Religious Parties among the Israelites before 587'.

ethos and world-view: in differences of moral horizon. However, to locate the appropriate groups within society is a complex task. The sociological analysis of class, status, and party can provide helpful insights as we attempt to determine what sort of social contexts are reflected in the moral horizons of biblical texts. In particular, the description of class fractions points us in the direction of a broader understanding of the operation of groups within Israelite society. Class fractions, like the latifundaries or upper-class priests, may form status groups within the ruling class which compete for prestige and influence. Such status groups may be based on heredity, as with the landowning families (or indeed priestly families), or they may be based on occupation or on other factors such as religious affiliation, in which case they may cut across the economic classes to some degree. All these groups may be represented by parties, who attempt to influence policy in line with the interests of various class fractions or status groups.

## Stratification and Moral Worlds

The above discussion of social stratification provides us with a model or map of the different social contexts out of which the biblical literature may come. It has become clear that the states of the ancient Mediterranean and Near East were, on the whole, highly stratified societies, and people's moral horizons varied tremendously with where on the social scale they found themselves. Wayne Meeks writes of the Roman Empire: 'The close stratification of the society profoundly affected the moral perceptions and moral choices of its members. The scope of an individual's power to affect events varied enormously with one's place in the scheme, and therefore the kind of moral issues about which one would be likely to think seriously varied widely, too.'[73]

This will have been equally true for Israel and Judah under the monarchy. Access to the power, privilege, and prestige (to the 'scarce goods' that result from economic surplus) is related to one's place in the social hierarchy, and largely determines the scope of actions for any individual or group. Class and status impose material constraints on the range of moral issues that are

---

[73] Meeks, *Moral World*, 35.

of relevance or importance to a group or individual. Equally important in the formation of moral worlds are the symbolic aspects of ethical thinking: the reasons that are given for certain beliefs or courses of action, the ways in which values and norms are expressed and given authority. However, we should guard against thinking of the groups we describe as enclosed, fully self-contained systems. The examination of stratification across the whole range of society makes it clear that social groups exist only in relation to other groups—there cannot be a ruling class without someone to rule—and, for the most part, the relationship between groups is one of conflict. As Bryan Turner writes of status divisions in society, 'status by its very character involves endless struggles over the allocation of scarce resources, especially scarce cultural resources'.[74] While these struggles may depend to some degree on the exercise of force or of material goods, we can also see the clash of different groups in society at the level of ideas and values.

As we examine social conflict at the level of ideas, morality, and religion, we find that the ruling class will tend to have the most powerful ideology, since it controls not only the material means of production but also what we might call the intellectual means of production. Control of education, literacy, and publication is largely in the hands of those in power, and can be used to support their ideas and programmes. These cultural means are necessary because the ruling class cannot rely upon force alone to ensure its continued domination, but must, at least to some degree, pacify the dominated groups and convince them that it is in their best interests to remain under the status quo. Bruce Lincoln describes how discourse is used to supplement force:

In the hands of élites and of those professionals who serve them . . . discourse of all forms—not only verbal, but also the symbolic discourses of spectacle, gesture, costume, edifice, icon, musical performance, and the like, may be strategically employed to mystify the inevitable inequities of the social order and to win the consent of those over whom power is exercised, thereby obviating the need for direct coercive use of force and transforming simple power into 'legitimate' authority.[75]

---

[74] Turner, *Status*, 9.
[75] B. Lincoln, *Discourse and the Construction of Society: Comparative Studies of Myth, Ritual, and Classification* (NY, 1989), 4–5.

Religious and ethical discourse is particularly important in the forming of consciousness, and in the persuasion of individuals to act in certain ways.

Max Weber, in his historical sociology, paid considerable attention to the religious ethics to be found in a wide variety of societies and religious traditions. He characterizes the ways in which competing classes and status groups normally approach religion and ethics. He compares the extent to which the religion is rationalized to produce a system, and the degree to which it is related to ethical behaviour. He asks whether a religious vision offers salvation from the present order of things or its preservation. His examination of the groups responsible for rationalization and the development of religious ideas—priests, prophets, and other holy men—is the foundation of this work. 'By analyzing the emergence of such groups, their changing position in the society, and their "material and ideal interests" the impact of ideas upon society becomes understandable'.[76] Weber considers that religion results from the attempt to find meaning in human existence and provides ways for people to make sense of the complexities of their natural and social environment. The answers which religions offer may reflect the underlying circumstances in which they live, and thus to some extent be determined by material conditions. But, importantly, Weber goes beyond Marx in arguing that religion does not only reflect material circumstances: it can act as a powerful force for social change, or provide the concepts by which social circumstances can be transformed. Weber sees the social role of religion in dynamic terms; the success or failure of religious ideologies may have significant consequences. Any religious ideology is unlikely to provide satisfactory solutions for all class or status groups within a society, and for some groups the dissatisfaction with prevailing religious orthodoxies may promote change. So we find that, for Weber, religious and ethical ideas must be seen in the context of competing status groups within society. These groups make constant efforts to preserve their distinctive style of life at both the cultural and the economic level. Weber's project is this:

In order to understand the stability and dynamics of a society we should attempt to understand these efforts in relation to the ideas and values

[76] R. Bendix, _Max Weber: An Intellectual Portrait_ (London, 1960), 87–8.

that are prevalent in the society; or, conversely, for every given idea or value that we observe we should seek out the status group whose material and ideal way of life it tends to enhance.[77]

To take an example from Weber's own work on ancient Judaism, he highlights the pacifist ethic of the patriarchs, who needed to co-operate with those among whom they lived in order to secure pasturage for their flocks and herds. He characterizes them as 'a stratum of powerless metics who as small stock breeders lived among military burghers'.[78] He goes on to contrast their ethic with the warrior code of the more organized and settled tribes, who could exercise control over significant areas of land. Relying as it does on the biblical scholarship of the late nineteenth century, Weber's reading of Genesis is inevitably dated, but the questions he was asking remain to be answered. His general approach is still an extremely profitable way into ethics in the Hebrew Bible, which is so obviously a collection of the religious ideals of a number of different groups within ancient Israelite society. When we find competing ethics and competing ideologies in the Hebrew Bible (as we do classically in the case of support for the monarchy or individual responsibility) we should think about the kind of groups in society that such ideas must represent. And when we determine the range of ethical possibilities allowed by individual texts we should again try to fit these moral horizons to a concrete social situation, as far as is possible.

## The Social Location of Biblical Literature

When we inquire about the social location of the biblical writings, it is probable that we should think in broad terms of the upper strata of society: the governing class and their favoured retainers, as well as the most important priests and other officials. Despite any possible early egalitarianism in Israel, the level of literacy required to create literature of this kind makes it unlikely that any of the lower orders were involved in its production. Moreover, there is a substantial amount of ruling-class ideology reproduced

---

[77] Bendix, *Max Weber*, 259. See M. Weber, *The Sociology of Religion* (London, 1965), esp. chs. 5, 6, and 7.

[78] Weber, *Ancient Judaism*, 51.

in the Hebrew Bible, particularly in royal texts like Psalm 72. In general, the protagonists of biblical literature are found in the upper portion of society. For example, both the Deuteronomistic and Chronicler's Histories focus on the actions of political and religious leaders. The standard which the Deuteronomists apply to the rulers of Israel and Judah is one which largely concerns their attitude towards the state cult and their relationships with other nations: these are clearly ruling-class issues.[79] Much prophecy is addressed to rulers, attempting to influence foreign and domestic policy. As was the case in the historical writings, the state cults in Jerusalem or Dan and Bethel are often the focus of attention. Although the Wisdom literature does not share the extravagant mythological imagery of the royal texts, recent work suggests that its authors also represent the upper echelons of society. Brian Kovacs has shown that the ethics of the book of Proverbs read most easily as those of literati and intellectuals: a scribal group who played an administrative role in society and developed its own codes of conduct as an 'in-group morality'.[80]

There is a considerable concern for social justice expressed in many parts of the Hebrew Bible, but this in itself is not enough to locate the origin of those ideas among the poor. We find a similar concern in the hymn which prefaces the code of King Hammurabi of Babylon, but the code itself contains different penalties dependent on social status in which the poor inevitably fare worse.[81] Thus the expressed desire to protect the poor need not interfere with the ruling classes' determined efforts to maintain control of the surplus which they produce, and may indeed be part of the mystifying discourse with which they persuade their subjects to remain loyal. Walter Houston, drawing inspiration from the work of Antonio Gramsci and Michael Walzer, writes that 'any enduring ideological expression of leadership will always

[79] See e.g. Dutcher-Walls's analysis of the account of Athaliah's reign in 2 Kings 11–12, which she understands as a story 'fashioned to express narratively the ideological concepts of a particular élite viewpoint' (*Narrative Art, Political Rhetoric*, 178); cf. also the discussion of political propaganda in K. W. Whitelam, 'The Defence of David', *JSOT* 29 (1984), 61–87.

[80] B. Kovacs, 'Is there a Class Ethic in Proverbs?', in J. L. Crenshaw and J. T. Willis (eds.), *Essays in Old Testament Ethics: J. Philip Hyatt In Memoriam* (NY, 1974), 171–89. So also J. D. Pleins, 'Poverty in the Social World of the Wise', *JSOT* 37 (1987), 61–78.

[81] A translation of the code can be found in J. B. Pritchard (ed.) *Ancient Near Eastern Texts Relating to the Old Testament*, 3rd edn. (Princeton, NJ, 1969), 163–80. For discussion see H. J. Boecker, *Law and the Administration of Justice in the Old Testament and the Ancient Near East* (London, 1980), 67–133.

carry with it concessions to the subordinate classes and in particular will contain moral ideas which are acceptable to them'.[82]

Nevertheless, I have no desire to put the whole of the biblical literature into an upper-class strait-jacket, and this is a passionate literature in which the conflict between the supporters of different ideologies is openly visible. Throughout the Hebrew Bible we find damning criticism of the nations' leaders, and what Gottwald calls 'dark' views of the ruling class.[83] While it is unlikely that such criticism comes directly from the peasantry, it is evidence of the moral and religious discourse of those who were dissatisfied with the status quo. To determine the identity of these dissenters we should probably return to the idea of status group and party. In particular, what we may be witnessing is the clash of different groups within the more economically secure classes who try to gain some influence over the State. These are groups who exist at some remove from the centre of political and economic power (and might therefore be considered 'disprivileged') but who, unlike those classes which are least privileged, have sufficient resources to be aware of their own distress.

There also exists within the Hebrew Bible a consistent emphasis on salvation and a connection between religion and ethics that Weber would have seen as alien to the ruling nobility. For him, some form of economic or other distress is required for the development of salvation religion:

Since every need for salvation is the expression of some distress, social or economic oppression is an effective source of salvation beliefs, though by no means the only source. Other things being equal, classes with high social and economic privilege will scarcely be prone to evolve the idea of salvation. Rather they assign to religion the primary function of legitimizing their own life pattern and situation in the world.[84]

Where there is an ethical religion found among privileged classes, the tendency will be for it to see the position of the individual as in some way merited from the religious point of view: the gods favour those who deserve favour, and religion is used to uphold

---

[82] W. Houston, ' "You Shall Open your Hand to Your Needy Brother": Ideology and Moral Formation in Deuteronomy 15: 1–8', in J. W. Rogerson, M. Davies, and M. D. Carroll R (eds.), *The Bible in Ethics: The Second Sheffield Colloquium*, JSOTS 207 (Sheffield, 1995), 297–8.
[83] Gottwald, 'Social Class as an Analytic and Hermeneutical Category', 9.
[84] Weber, *Sociology of Religion*, 107.

the present social order.[85] However, the biblical data very probably reflect even greater complexity than Weber allows. Some explanation of the inconsistency of the evidence may be found in the fact that the ruling élite that preserved the Bible—the post-exilic temple community—was not the ruling élite under which much of it was composed: the monarchies of Israel and Judah. And indeed there is ample evidence to suggest that those who did control post-exilic Jerusalem were the ideological successors of a pre-exilic opposition group that Morton Smith calls the 'Yahweh alone party'.[86]

## A Way Forward

It seems clear that morality is closely bound up with social circumstances. Different groups of people have different world-views and religious ideologies, different economic and political circumstances, and as these vary so do ethical ideas and values. This is true not only between different cultures but even within any one society, where a number of different interest groups compete for power, privilege, and prestige. In this respect ancient Israel was little different from anywhere else, as the biblical evidence makes plain. Within one society, of course, there are many similarities of outlook, particularly where the ruling élite have managed to use religion to legitimate their own status, but there are also considerable differences in religious and ethical ideas between the different status or class groups that exist. A conflict sociology such as Weber's, which 'conceived of society as an arena of competing status groups, each with its own economic interests, status honor, and orientation toward the world and man',[87] remains an extremely useful tool to understand the ways in which groups in society operate, and hence to discover the moral worlds in which they live.

The description of the moral worlds of ancient Israel looks like a very difficult task, since the society is so broadly defined and historically opaque. Nevertheless, it remains worth attempting, if we want better to understand biblical texts and the society that

[85] Cf. Ps. 37: 25, and the arguments of Job's comforters.
[86] For further discussion of factional politics in late pre-exilic Judah, see below, Ch. 3.
[87] Bendix, *Max Weber*, 262–3.

produced them. What is required is the application of this broad historical and sociological method to specific texts and settings. If we apply our method not to the whole of Israelite society but to more closely defined sections of it, and to smaller portions of the biblical text, we may begin to describe the moral worlds of groups within Israel. The task before us requires the detailed examination of a particular text within its social context, and the remainder of this work will therefore be taken up by a single extended case study: Ezekiel's ethics in the context of the Babylonian exile.

# 2

# Ezekiel and the Exiles

As we attempt to examine the shape of ancient Israelite moral worlds it is important to fix upon a specific period and specific texts to make the focus of our enquiry: this study will concentrate on the period of the Babylonian exile, and on the book of Ezekiel as representative of the community which experienced that exile. Nebuchadnezzar's deportation of a large number of people from Judah to Babylonia in 597 BCE has long been recognized as one of the most important events in the formation of Judaism, since it set a pattern whereby those living away from the land of Israel could maintain a distinct religious and cultural identity. Early socio-logical interpreters of the Hebrew Bible stressed the effect of this dramatic change in social circumstances upon the Jewish com-munity. For Max Weber it was a highly important factor in the transformation of the Jews from a national group into a 'pariah people': 'a guest people who were ritually separated, formally or *de facto*, from their social surroundings'.[1] In the development of ritual regulations for the ordering of life the Jews built up a barrier between themselves and the outside world that enabled them to keep together. Antonin Causse too found the experience of diaspora to be the most significant impetus that drove Judaism to become a religious rather than merely an ethnic community: 'Il s'agit d'une formation sociologique nouvelle qui ne sera ni une fédération de clans ni un peuple, mais une communauté réligieuse dont les destinées ne seron liées aux condition d'un groupe ethnique et aux destinées d'un État.'[2]

More recently, important research has been done by Daniel L. Smith, whose work *The Religion of the Landless* draws together com-parative material from ancient Mesopotamia and the sociology of

---

[1] Weber, *Ancient Judaism*, 3.
[2] A. Causse, *Du Groupe ethnique*, 194. Cf. also his earlier work, *Les Dispersés d'Israël: les origines de la Diaspora et son rôle dans la formation de Judaïsme* (Paris, 1929).

modern groups of exiles to illuminate the biblical exile.[3] Much of Smith's work, in particular that on the development of the *bet aboth* and structural changes within exilic society, bases its conclusions largely on materials describing the community of the restored exiles.[4] By contrast with Smith, my primary focus will be the first generation of exiles, those actually deported in 597 BCE and subsequent years. The historical data available about the life of the exiles is not abundant, so I will be forced to draw on earlier and later material in my reconstruction of events, but the primary source for the community in that period must be the book of Ezekiel.[5]

To claim that Ezekiel is a document produced among the first generation of exiles would not have been controversial a hundred years ago, and to a large extent is no longer controversial today. However, in the intervening years the book has been the subject of numerous theories of date, place and manner of composition that, if true, would severely limit its value as evidence about the exile. Therefore, as a preliminary to our main investigation of the social circumstances of the exile, it will be necessary to recapitulate some of this debate.

## Preliminaries: Ezekiel as a Prophet of the Babylonian Exile

The book of Ezekiel places the prophet among a group of Jewish exiles in Babylonia. The first verse of the book states that the prophet's vision appeared 'as I was among the exiles by the river

---

[3] D. L. Smith, *The Religion of the Landless: The Social Context of the Babylonian Exile* (Bloomington, Ind., 1989). He has recently, under his new surname Smith-Christopher, revisited some of the same areas, in an article, 'Reassessing the Historical and Sociological Impact of the Babylonian Exile (597/587–539 BCE)', in J. M. Scott (ed.), *Exile: Old Testament, Jewish and Christian Conceptions*, Journal for the Study of Judaism, Supplement Series, 56 (Leiden, 1997), 7–36.

[4] See Smith, *Landless*, 93–121.

[5] Historians who approach the period of the exile have to come to terms with both the huge importance given to the experience within the biblical literature and the fact that there is far less evidence for what actually happened than would be ideal. A significant debate about the problems involved in writing the history of the exilic period (and some possible solutions) has been recently set out in a collection of essays edited by L. L. Grabbe: *Leading Captivity Captive: 'The Exile' as History and Ideology*, JSOTS 278 (Sheffield, 1998); cf. also the essays in B. Becking and M. C. A. Korpel (eds.), *The Crisis of Israelite Religion: Transformation of Religious Tradition in Exilic and Post-Exilic Times*, OTS 42 (Leiden, 1999).

Chebar', and in 1: 3 this place is described as 'in the land of the
Chaldeans'. It is 'to the exiles, to your people', that YHWH sends
Ezekiel in 3: 11, and in 3: 15 these exiles are living at a place called
Tel Abib, again by the river Chebar.[6] The book is characterized
by a series of dates which also serve to place the prophet among
the exiles of 597, since they take that year as the beginning of the
dating system. Ezek. 1: 2 speaks of the 'fifth year of the exile of
King Jehoiachin', and 33: 21 of the 'twelfth year of our exile'.[7] The
majority of these dates belong to the first twelve years after the
deportation, and this ties in well with the content of the oracles
that are framed by them, which refer to the events of that period
which led up to the fall of Jerusalem.

Until the beginning of the last century there was an almost
unanimous consensus that the book of Ezekiel was the product of
this single prophet and of the age in which it is set. It was, thanks
to its distinctive style and structure, one of the last prophetic books
to undergo radical literary analysis. Indeed, as late as 1891 S. R.
Driver could sum up the position of most of his contemporaries:
'No critical question arises in connexion with the authorship of
the book, the whole from beginning to end bearing unmistakably
the stamp of a single mind.'[8]

The process of unravelling began with the work of Gustav
Hölscher, who struck out against the prevailing orthodoxy by
denying the vast majority of the book to the prophet Ezekiel.[9]

---

[6] The Chebar reappears in Ezek. 3: 23; 10: 15, 20, 22; 43: 3. For discussion of the exact
meaning of the phrase and its location see below, p. 62.

[7] Cf. also 40: 1, which equates this to the fourteenth year 'after the city was conquered'.
Other dates, in 8: 1; 20: 1; 26: 1; 29: 1; 29: 17; 30: 20; 31: 1; 32: 1; 32: 17; and 33: 21, follow
the same system without being so explicit about the starting-point. The very first date
reference 'in the thirtieth year', which is further defined as the fifth year of Jehoiachin's
exile (593 BCE), remains an unsolved puzzle, with perhaps the most plausible suggestion
being that it refers to Ezekiel's age in 593: so H. McKeating, *Ezekiel*, Old Testament Guides
(Sheffield, 1993), 63; L. C. Allen, *Ezekiel 1–19*, Word Biblical Commentary, 28 (Dallas, Tex.,
1994), 21. For fuller discussion of the dates see W. Zimmerli, *Ezekiel 1*, Hermeneia (Phil.,
1979), 9–11; McKeating, *Ezekiel*, 62–72; J. Finegan, 'The Chronology of Ezekiel', *JBL* 69
(1950), 61–6: K. S. Freedy and D. B. Redford, 'The Dates in Ezekiel in Relation to Biblical,
Babylonian and Egyptian Sources', *JAOS* 90 (1970), 462–85.

[8] S. R. Driver, *Introduction to the Literature of the Old Testament*, 2nd edn. (Edinburgh, 1891),
261.

[9] G. Hölscher, *Hesekiel: Der Dichter und das Buch* BZAW 39 (Giessen, 1924). There is not
space here for a complete review of Ezekiel research. For recent fuller treatments see
B. Lang, *Ezechiel: Der Prophet und das Buch*, EdF 153 (Darmstadt, 1981), 1–17; McKeating,
*Ezekiel*, 30–61; K. P. Darr, 'Ezekiel Among the Critics', *Currents in Research: Biblical Studies*, 2
(1994), 9–24.

Hölscher believed that only the poetic oracles in the book of Ezekiel formed a genuine kernel (147 verses out of 1,273). These poems were supplemented in prose by a Zadokite editor writing in the fifth century BCE. This work opened the floodgates of radical criticism, as it were, and, in the decades that followed, one could be forgiven for thinking that exegetes were trying to make up for lost time, so many and varied were the interpretations put on this hitherto clear and straightforward prophet. McKeating's comment is apt: 'So diverse were they that almost the only thing about Ezekiel on which scholars appeared to be agreed was that the book did *not* "bear the stamp of a single mind".'[10]

Perhaps the most extreme of all the critics of Ezekiel in this period was Charles Cutler Torrey who, in his book *Pseudo-Ezekiel and the Original Prophecy*, proposed that the exiled prophet Ezekiel was a late fiction.[11] The original prophecy described Jerusalem in the age of Manasseh, but was written by a late third-century pseudepigrapher. The detailed picture of Jerusalem is one drawn from the picture of Manasseh's reign we find in 2 Kings 21, and the 'thirtieth year' of Ezekiel 1: 1 actually refers to the thirtieth year of Manasseh.[12] A still later editor moved the scene from Jerusalem to Babylon, which is a setting found only in 'a series of brief and easily recognized interpolations'.[13] To support this late date of composition, Torrey finds in the prophecies references to Persia and to Alexander the Great (who is the prototype of Gog) and he finds the Hebrew of the book full of Aramaisms which betray a late date. This view that the book of Ezekiel is a late pseudepigraphon has continued to find a few supporters, the most recent of whom is Udo Feist, who reaches his conclusions largely on the basis of an extensive review of nineteenth- and twentieth-century scholarship.[14] Feist gives considerable importance to the

---

[10] McKeating, *Ezekiel*, 31–2.

[11] C. C. Torrey, *Pseudo-Ezekiel and the Original Prophecy*, Yale Oriental Series Researches, 18 (New Haven, Conn., 1930).

[12] Ibid. 64–9.

[13] Ibid. 44.

[14] U. Feist, *Ezechiel: Das literarische Problem des Buches forschungsgeschichtlich betrachtet*, BWANT 138 (Stuttgart, 1995). Other supporters of a pseudepigraphal approach include J. Smith, *The Book of the Prophet Ezekiel: A New Interpretation* (London, 1931); N. Messel, *Ezechielfragen* (Oslo, 1945); L. E. Browne, *Ezekiel and Alexander* (London, 1952); J. Becker, 'Ez 8–11 als einheitliche Komposition in einem pseudepigraphischen Ezechielbuch', in J. Lust (ed.), *Ezekiel and his Book: Textual and Literary Criticism and their Interrelation*, BETL 74 (Leuven, 1986), 136–50.

literary character of the book, arguing that it is a unity which can best be understood against the background of apocalyptic literature. For all proponents of the pseudepigraphal approach, however, it has proved difficult to sustain the idea that the book is so late. The linguistic evidence is ambiguous at best, and recent discussions of the language of the book suggest that it is best characterized as belonging to the 'transition' between Classical Biblical Hebrew and Late Biblical Hebrew, a finding entirely consonant with the traditional dating of Ezekiel to the sixth century.[15]

Whilst there are some connections between the book of Ezekiel and later apocalyptic literature, they are certainly no stronger than those which bind it to works which are more clearly prophetic, like Jeremiah. Feist himself admits that it is difficult to understand why this otherwise unknown figure, Ezekiel, should have been chosen as the figure behind which the pseudepigrapher hides.[16] Furthermore, although it is not inconceivable that the events of the sixth century that are described might be read as an elaborate code for the historical situation of the Hellenistic period, the book gives little in the way of explicit indication that it should be read so. Indeed, there is such a good fit between the events referred to in the book and what we know from biblical and cuneiform sources of the early sixth century (and particularly Jerusalem in the reign of Zedekiah) that for most interpreters it is unnecessary to seek a different historical context or set of political references. To deny Ezekiel to the sixth century would appear to be an example of what Hans Barstad has called 'the strange fear of the Bible' sometimes to the fore in contemporary scholarship.[17]

There does remain a problem about the book's consistent focus on Jerusalem, which interpreters have approached in a number of ways. Torrey found the book's consistency of address to Jerusalem an insuperable problem for anyone who wishes to place Ezekiel's hearers in Babylonia; the bulk of the oracles are directly addressed to Judah and Jerusalem; the most natural people to be the 'house of Israel', the 'rebellious house', would be the Hebrews of

[15] A. Hurvitz, *A Linguistic Study of the Relationship between the Priestly Source and the Book of Ezekiel: A New Look at an Old Problem*, CahRB 20 (Paris, 1982); M. F. Rooker, *Biblical Hebrew in Transition: the Language of the Book of Ezekiel*, JSOTS 90 (Sheffield, 1990).

[16] Feist, *Ezechiel*, 219, 223.

[17] H. M. Barstad, 'The Strange Fear of the Bible', in L. L. Grabbe (ed.), *Leading Captivity Captive: 'The Exile' as History and Ideology*, JSOTS 278 (Sheffield, 1998), 120–7.

Palestine: 'not merely because of the long standing use of these terms but also because any assemblage of "exiles" who could be addressed by an "exilic" prophet would be a very small fraction of the Israelite people'.[18] Moreover, to address Jerusalem would not be to address the needs of any exiled community: 'One would not expect prophets to attract any attention among recently departed exiles, especially if their oracles concerned far distant Jerusalem.'[19] Robert Carroll has recently proposed a similar line of argument, in which he suggests that, while the book's superscription gives it a setting amongst deportees, 'this is a piece of misdirection by the writer which gives rise to a misreading of the book'.[20] In fact the real interest of the book is Jerusalem and it is best read as 'a series of textual representations of Jerusalem life in terms analogous to living in a diaspora'.[21] There is no real connection with the experience of sixth-century deportees, but the book's notions of exile, deportation, and diaspora have more the character of a metaphor which expresses the current fears and aspirations of a group in Jerusalem/Palestine. Carroll does not speculate here about the date of composition, but broadly speaking he appears to follow Torrey's view that the book is pseudepigraphal.[22]

The argument that the book is too focused on Jerusalem is not solely the preserve of those who would see the prophet Ezekiel as the literary invention of a later age, but has also been adopted by scholars who believe that the book provides an accurate picture of the date and character of Ezekiel's ministry, but not its location. Thus Volkmar Herntrich argued that the Babylonian location was added by an editor to a collection of prophecies which were uttered in Jerusalem by a spectator of the dreadful events taking place.[23] The scenes in Jerusalem were not visionary, as the book presents them, but real. Like Torrey, he argued that the title 'rebellious house' was inappropriate for the exiles, and the full

---

[18] Torrey, *Pseudo-Ezekiel*, 24.

[19] Ibid. 35.

[20] R. P. Carroll, 'Deportation and Diasporic Discourses in the Prophetic Literature', in J. M. Scott (ed.), *Exile*, 80.

[21] Ibid. 81.

[22] Carroll is elsewhere concerned to rehabilitate Torrey's views on the history of the exile: see his chapter 'Exile! What Exile?' in L. L. Grabbe (ed.), *Leading Captivity Captive*, 62–79.

[23] V. Herntrich, *Ezechielprobleme*, BZAW 61 (Giessen, 1932). See also G. R. Berry, 'Was Ezekiel in the Exile?', *JBL* 49 (1930), 83–93; J. B. Harford, *Studies in the Book of Ezekiel* (Cambridge, 1935).

force of the prophecy was reserved for the inhabitants of Jerusalem.

This idea of a historical Jerusalem ministry proved very popular in the 1930s and -40s. A predictable modification was made by Bertholet, who argued that the prophet's ministry began in Jerusalem, that he moved from there to one of the Judaean towns some time before the fall of the city, and that he was finally exiled to Babylon shortly after 587.[24] Broadly speaking, chapters 1–24 and most of the oracles against the nations have a Palestinian setting, and chapters 33–48 belong to the exiles. Bertholet's theory is taken up by Robinson, and spawned still further variations.[25] Thus R. H. Pfeiffer and H. G. May both suggest a scheme whereby Ezekiel began in Jerusalem, was exiled to Babylon, and then finally returned to Jerusalem.[26]

The most recent expansion of Herntrich's theory is that proposed by William Brownlee, who believes not only that Ezekiel was a Palestinian prophet (all references to *golah* in the book are in fact corruptions of Gilgal, where the prophet lived), but also that the expression 'set your face against' is a formula for travel, so that Ezekiel actually went to all the places described to proclaim his oracles.[27] Thus he was to be found not just in Judah, but also in Ammon, Phoenicia, Egypt, and Edom, and Tyre. The one place where Brownlee believes the prophet never went is Babylon!

Despite the efforts of Herntrich, Brownlee, and others, there are a number of reasons why the hypothesis of a Jerusalem ministry has proved unsatisfactory. In the first place, the prophet's visions of Jerusalem are presented not as fact but as vision. The level of detail we find might have as much to do with a writer's fertile imagination as with historical verisimilitude. Moreover, as one who had been a priest in Jerusalem prior to his exile, Ezekiel would undoubtedly have had vivid memories of both city and temple which could provide the basis for his visions.[28]

---

[24] A. Bertholet and K. Galling, *Hesekiel*, HAT 13 (Tübingen, 1936).

[25] Robinson, *Two Hebrew Prophets*.

[26] R. H. Pfeiffer, *Introduction to the Old Testament*, 3rd edn. (NY, 1941), 531–41; H. G. May, 'The Book of Ezekiel', in G. A. Buttricke, *et al.* (eds.), *The Interpreter's Bible*, vi. (NY and Nashville, Tenn., 1956), 41–338.

[27] W. Brownlee, '"Son of Man Set Your Face": Ezekiel the Refugee Prophet', *HUCA* 54 (1983), 83–110. See also W. Brownlee, *Ezekiel 1–19*, Word Biblical Commentary, 28 (Waco, Tex., 1986).

[28] So J. W. Wevers, *Ezekiel*, NCB (Grand Rapids, Mich., and London, 1969), 25.

Secondly, it is not legitimate to suggest that just because the book is very interested in Jerusalem the prophet must have been there (or for that matter, *contra* Carroll, that the work must have been composed there). As we have seen, Ezekiel is placed in the context of a group of people who have only recently been exiled from Jerusalem, so it is hardly surprising that they should have retained an interest in events in their homeland. If the evidence of Jeremiah 29 may be relied upon it would appear that there was some measure of communication possible between the two communities, and it seems likely that the exiles felt that their future was very much bound up with that of the city.[29]

That oracles are addressed to the city is equally no guarantee that the prophet must have been in Jerusalem any more than the oracles against the nations in prophets like Amos or Isaiah must have been delivered in Damascus, Ammon, Assyria, or wherever. Indeed, such an approach with regard to Ezekiel reaches a kind of *reductio ad absurdum* in Brownlee's picture of Ezekiel as a 'refugee prophet', constantly on the move. Far more satisfactory is the explanation given by Moshe Greenberg for the prophet's interest in Jerusalem. As is the case in oracles against the nations:

> an exiled prophet's address to Jerusalem would really have been aimed at the ears of his proximate audience. In Ezekiel's case, little contrast would have been felt between the ostensible and the real audience, since the hearers of the prophet were, in fact, Jerusalemites who identified themselves with their fellow citizens in every way. If there is any anomaly in Ezekiel's addressing Jerusalem from the exile, it is no greater than the anomalous contemporaneity of two Jerusalemite communities hundreds of miles apart at this juncture of history.[30]

Such a position is now much more representative of the general views of Ezekiel scholars, and this reflects something of a consensus that has existed since the 1950s—and especially the work of

---

[29] Much of Jer. 29 stems from the editors of the book, but most commentators believe that a genuine letter sent by Jeremiah to Babylonia forms a core; it is therefore evidence for some degree of communication between Judah and exile after 597. See W. McKane, *Jeremiah XXVI–LII*, ICC (Edinburgh, 1996), pp. cxxxix–cxl; E. W. Nicholson, *Preaching to the Exiles: A Study of the Prose Tradition in the Book of Jeremiah* (Oxford, 1970), 98; W. L. Holladay, *Jeremiah 2*, Hermeneia (Phil., 1989), 139.

[30] M. Greenberg, *Ezekiel 1–20*, Anchor Bible, 22 (Garden City, NY, 1983), 17. Carroll has asserted that 'of course no biblical writer would have been a denizen of Jerusalem or Palestine *and also* have lived in Babylonia' ('Exile! What Exile?', 68). That, however, is exactly the position of the prophet Ezekiel as presented in the book.

Georg Fohrer and Walther Zimmerli, which provides a degree of
compromise between early traditionalism and the radicalism that
replaced it. Fohrer argued for the traditional understanding of the
date and place of Ezekiel's ministry, and that by far the larger part
of the book reflects this origin.[31] However, he also accepted that
there is a significant degree of interpretative addition. Zimmerli,
in his massive commentary and numerous studies, also accepted
that a substantial majority of the book could be traced back to the
sixth-century prophet, but spent more effort elaborating the way
in which the prophet's words were transformed into the present
book.[32] He posited the existence of an 'Ezekiel school', initially
formed from the prophet's disciples, who transmitted the text and
added to it in very much the same style as the original.

The analysis of redaction and stratification in Ezekiel has
remained the focus of interest for a substantial minority of
scholars,[33] and perhaps reached its most extreme form in the case
of Jörg Garscha. Garscha believes in Ezekiel the sixth century
prophet but limits his contribution to the book to a mere thirty
verses, and constructs an elaborate scheme of editions made during the next few centuries to account for the present text.[34] Most
recently in this vein, Karl-Friedrich Pohlmann's commentary
finds a small original deposit of the prophet's words worked into
an initial prophetic book, subsequently overlaid by two principal

---

[31] G. Fohrer, *Die Hauptprobleme des Buch Ezechiel*, BZAW 72 (Berlin, 1952); also his commentary, *Ezechiel*, HAT 13, 2nd edn. (Tübingen, 1955). Within the English-speaking world,
similar moves back towards a more traditional approach can be seen in C. G. Howie, *The
Date and Composition of Ezekiel*, JBLMS 4 (Phil., 1950); C. J. Mullo Weir, 'Aspects of the Book
of Ezekiel', *VT* 2 (1952), 97–112; H. H. Rowley, 'The Book of Ezekiel in Modern Study',
*BJRL* 36 (1953/4), 146–90. For a recent summary and restatement of the arguments for the
traditional understanding see T. Renz, *The Rhetorical Function of the Book of Ezekiel*, SVT 76
(Leiden, 1999), 31–8.

[32] W. Zimmerli, 'Die Eigenart der prophetischen Rede des Ezechiel: ein Beitrag zum
Problem an Hand von Ezech. xiv 1–11', *ZAW* 66 (1954), 1–26; id., 'The Special Form- and
Traditio-Historical Character of Ezekiel's Prophecy', *VT* 15 (1965), 515–27; id., 'Deutero-
Ezechiel?', *ZAW* 84 (1972), 501–16.

[33] See e.g. H. Schulz, *Das Todesrecht im Alten Testament: Studien zum Rechtsformen der Mot-
Jumat-Sätze*, BZAW 114 (Berlin, 1969); H. Simian, *Die theologische Nachgeschichte der Prophetie
Ezechiels: Form- und traditionskritische Untersuchung zu Ez 6; 35; 36*, FB 14 (Würzburg, 1974);
F. L. Hossfeld, *Untersuchungen zu Komposition und Theologie des Ezechielbuches*, FB 20 (Würzburg,
1977); K.-F. Pohlmann, *Ezechielstudien: Zur Redaktionsgeschichte des Buches und zur Frage nach den
ältesten Texten*, BZAW 202 (Berlin, 1992).

[34] J. Garscha, *Studien zum Ezechielbuch: eine redaktionskritische Untersuchung von Ez 1–39*,
Europäische Hochschulschriften, 23 (Bern and Frankfurt, 1974). Original verses are 1: 1, 3
and parts of 17: 2–10 and 23: 2–25.

redactional layers which belong to the Persian period.[35] He distinguishes an earlier '*golaorientierte Redaktion*' which emphasizes the special status of the 597 deportees and a later '*diasporaorientierte Redaktion*'. Thus, although there is a small sixth-century core to the book, its value as a historical or sociological resource for the period it purports to describe is hardly greater than if it were wholly a late and anonymous pseudepigraphon.[36] There is much in work like this that is plausible, but the proliferation of complex redactional models alongside the failure of any one of them to command widespread support has tended to put in question the value of the method.

Most vocal in his questioning of the redaction critical method has been Moshe Greenberg, who finds none of the criteria for redaction acceptable from a literary point of view, and finds nothing anachronistic within the book which would demand a date after 571 BCE.[37] He adopts a 'holistic' approach, concentrating on the literary artistry of the text, and the careful patterning of material. However, Greenberg almost certainly goes too far in denying any substantial redactional activity within the book. For one thing, it is by no means clear that the careful patterning he finds could not be the work of a redactor rather than the original author.[38] The question is made especially difficult because of the apparent coherence of the book. What is most noteworthy about the Ezekiel tradition (by comparison with, for example, Isaiah or Jeremiah) is its homogeneity. As Paul Joyce rightly points out, the book 'has proved notoriously resistant to any straightforward division into primary and secondary material', since 'secondary material (even where it can be identified) bears an unusually close "family resemblance" to primary'.[39] While it is undoubtedly true that Ezekiel's prophecies have undergone some process of editing

---

[35] K.-F. Pohlmann, *Der Prophet Hesekiel/Ezechiel Kapitel 1–19*, ATD 22/1 (Göttingen, 1996).

[36] So Feist, who of course believes it to be exactly such a pseudepigraphal work (see *Ezechiel*, 14).

[37] Greenberg, *Ezekiel 1–20*, esp. 18–27; also his 'What are Valid Criteria for Determining Inauthentic Matter in Ezekiel', in J. Lust (ed.), *Ezekiel and his Book*, 123–35.

[38] R. E. Clements, 'The Chronology of Redaction in Ez 1–24', in J. Lust (ed.), *Ezekiel and his Book*, 288–9.

[39] P. M. Joyce, 'Synchronic and Diachronic Perspectives on Ezekiel', in J. C. de Moor (ed.), *Synchronic or Diachronic? A Debate on Method in Old Testament Exegesis*, Oudtestamentische Studiën, 34 (Leiden, 1995), 115–28. See also Joyce's discussion in *Divine Initiative and Human Response in Ezekiel*, JSOTS 51 (Sheffield, 1989), 21–31.

or accretion, it is possible, and even likely, that this process began with the prophet himself.[40]

The vast majority of current Ezekiel research takes places somewhere on a spectrum between the cautious radicalism of Zimmerli and the conservatism of Greenberg. It is difficult to be more precise about the various 'camps' that scholars fall into. It is noteworthy that if we look at two recent attempts to set the scene, by Lang and by Duguid, both of whom are fairly conservative in their analysis of the text, we find that the work of some, such as Hossfeld, is seen as radical by one (Duguid), but moderate (*vermittelnde*) by the other (Lang).[41] Hence it is safer to speak of a 'spectrum' or 'continuum' of Ezekiel research where different studies can be located. The position taken in this study is that the book of Ezekiel is largely the work of the prophet himself and of his exilic editors, who lived and wrote in a social context not radically dissimilar to Ezekiel's.[42] The book therefore represents a genuine contemporary attempt to make sense of the events of the early sixth century, and remains one of our best sources for understanding the experience of the Jewish exiles in Babylonia.[43]

## Historical Background: The Context of Empire

The deportations to Babylonia have to be seen in the context of Judah's history over the preceding century and a half; this is, to a large extent, a history of relationship with the great regional empires of Assyria, Babylon, and Egypt.[44] From the re-emergence

---

[40] Zimmerli, *Ezekiel 1*, 71. Zimmerli himself has argued against such a radical redaction critical approach, in particular attacking Schulz's notion of a discrete priestly strand in the book: see especially his essay 'Deutero-Ezechiel?'. His critique of Garscha and other recent commentators can be found in the preface to the second volume of his commentary (*Ezekiel 2*, Hermeneia (Phil., 1983), pp. xi–xviii).

[41] I. M. Duguid, *Ezekiel and the Leaders of Israel*, SVT 56 (Leiden, 1994), 6; Lang, *Ezechiel*, 14. Feist provides a rather different and imaginative survey in which Lang and Greenberg manage to be at opposite ends of the spectrum (*Ezechiel*, 12–19).

[42] So Clements, 'Chronology of Redaction'.

[43] Besides Zimmerli and Greenberg, the majority of recent commentaries adopt this position towards the book: e.g. Allen, *Ezekiel 1–19*; *Ezekiel 20–48*, Word Biblical Commentary, 29 (Waco, Tex., 1990); W. Eichrodt, *Ezekiel: A Commentary*, OTL (London, 1970); J. W. Wevers, *Ezekiel*, NCB (London, 1969); J. Blenkinsopp, *Ezekiel*, Interpretation (Louisville, Ky., 1990).

[44] For a concise survey of this whole period from a Mesopotamian perspective see M. T. Larsen, 'The Tradition of Empire in Mesopotamia', in M. T. Larsen (ed.), *Power and*

of Assyria as a world power under Tiglath–Pileser III (745–727 BCE) to the fall of Jerusalem, Judah was perpetually in a state of vassalage to one or other of these, and was constantly caught up in the struggles between them.[45] After one hundred years of expansion and strong rule the Assyrian empire began to disintegrate during the second half of the seventh century, and as a consequence of this decline Josiah, king of Judah, was able briefly to assert the nation's independence (2 Kgs. 22–3). However, such independence was short-lived, as the Egyptians and Babylonians carved up the old Assyrian territories. By the end of the sixth century the Babylonians, under their king, Nabopolassar, had effectively taken over the whole of Mesopotamia, while Egypt was exerting influence over the Assyrians' former vassals in the West.[46] These small states of Syria and Palestine stood between the two

*Propaganda: A Symposium on Ancient Empires*, Mesopotamia, 7 (Copenhagen, 1979), 87–8. For more detail and full bibliography see D. J. Wiseman, 'Babylonia 605–539 B.C.', in J. Boardman, I. E. Edwards, *et al.* (eds.), *The Assyrian and Babylonian Empires and other States of the Near East, from the Eighth to the Sixth Centuries B.C.*, The Cambridge Ancient History, 2nd edn., vol. iii, pt. 2, (Cambridge, 1991), 229–51; A. Kuhrt, *The Ancient Near East c.3000–330 B.C.*, 2 vols. (London, 1995), ii. 589–97.

[45] The historical literature on Judah in this period is vast. The primary source material is largely in 2 Kings, for which see the historically oriented commentary of M. Cogan and H. Tadmor, *II Kings*, Anchor Bible, 11 (NY, 1988). For broad historical treatments see e.g. G. W. Ahlström, *The History of Ancient Palestine from the Palaeolithic Period to Alexander's Conquest*, JSOTS, 146 (Sheffield, 1993); H. Donner, 'The Separate States of Israel and Judah', in J. H. Hayes and J. M. Miller (eds.), *Israelite and Judaean History*, OTL (Phil., 1977), 435–88; J. A. Soggin, *An Introduction to the History of Israel and Judah*, OTL 2nd edn. (Valley Forge, Pa., 1993), 244–70; T. C. Mitchell, 'Judah until the Fall of Jerusalem (c.700–586 B.C.)', in Boardman, Edwards, *et al.* (eds.), *The Assyrian and Babylonian Empires*, 371–409. On Judah's subordination to Assyria in particular, see J. W. McKay, *Religion in Judah under the Assyrians 732–609 B.C.*, SBT, 2nd ser., 26 (London, 1973); M. Cogan, *Imperialism and Religion: Assyria, Judah and Israel in the Eighth and Seventh Centuries B.C.E.*, SBLDS 19 (Missoula, Mont., 1974); H. Spieckermann, *Juda unter Assur in der Sargonidenzeit* (Göttingen, 1982); B. Otzen, 'Israel under the Assyrians', in M. T. Larsen (ed.), *Power and Propaganda*, 251–61. Cogan has recently reviewed developments, in 'Judah under Assyrian Hegemony: A Reexamination of Imperialism and Religion', *JBL* 112 (1993), 403–14. Recent studies which concentrate on the last few years of Judah's existence include a number by A. Malamat: 'Jeremiah and the Last Two Kings of Judah', *PEQ* 83 (1951), 81–7; 'The Last Kings of Judah and the Fall Of Jerusalem', *IEJ* 18 (1968), 137–56; 'The Twilight of Judah in the Egyptian–Babylonian Maelstrom', in *Congress Volume: Edinburgh 1974*, SVT 28 (Leiden, 1975), 123–45; 'The Last Years of the Kingdom of Judah', in A. Malamat and I. Eph'al (eds.), *The World History of the Jewish People: Ancient Times*, iv. *The Age of the Monarchies*, i. Political History (Jerusalem, 1979), 205–21. See also the thorough examination in C. R. Seitz, *Theology in Conflict: Reactions to the Exile in the Book of Jeremiah*, BZAW 176 (Berlin, 1989).

[46] Such influence over Judah is seen in Pharaoh Necho's deposition of Jehoahaz, and appointment of Jehoiakim as king in his place (2 Kgs. 23: 31–5).

powers, and this region was the area in which the imperial show-
down took place. The balance of power shifted decisively with the
battle of Carchemish in 605 BCE, at which the Babylonian crown
prince, Nebuchadnezzar, routed the Egyptian army and, to all
intents, became the master of Syria and Palestine.[47] Succeeding
his father as king, he consolidated his power in the region over
the next couple of years, campaigning in order to receive tribute,
and receiving the homage of the king of Ashkelon and, in all
probability, of Jehoiakim, king of Judah. However, not long after
this Nebuchadnezzar overstretched himself by attacking Egypt
itself. As the Babylonian Chronicle reports:

The fourth year [601]: the king of Akkad mustered his army and
marched to Hattu.[48] He marched about victoriously in Hattu. In Kislev
[Nov./Dec. 601] he took his army's lead and marched to Egypt. When
the king of Egypt heard the news he mustered his army. They fought and
both sides suffered severe losses (lit. they inflicted a major defeat upon
one another). The king of Akkad and his army turned and went back to
Babylon.[49]

For the rulers of the buffer states between the two empires such a
defeat posed problems: Should they stay with Nebuchadnezzar
and risk the danger of an Egyptian resurgence, or revolt, believ-
ing that the Pharaoh would be a more secure overlord? At any
rate, it seems to be Nebuchadnezzar's defeat in Egypt that provoked Jehoiakim to revolt against Babylon (2 Kgs. 24: 1), but this
rebellion had disastrous consequences. After taking some time to
reorganize and re-equip his troops, Nebuchadnezzar returned to
Syria/Palestine to deal with the rebels. Late in 598 BCE he invaded
Judah and besieged Jerusalem, capturing the city on 16 March
597. The Babylonian Chronicle describes this action briefly:

The seventh year: in the month Kislev the king of Akkad mustered his
army and marched to Hattu. He encamped against the city of Judah,
and on the second day of the month Adar captured the city and seized

---

[47] I retain the traditional English spelling of Nebuchadnezzar. His Akkadian name
*Nabu-kudurri-uṣur* (probably to be translated 'O Nabu, protect my offspring') seems to be
better rendered by Nebuchadrezzar. See D. J. Wiseman, *Nebuchadrezzar and Babylon*
(Oxford, 1983), 2–3.

[48] The normal Babylonian name for Syria/Palestine.

[49] Babylonian Chronicle: from the translation of A. K. Grayson, *Assyrian and Babylonian
Chronicles* (Locust Valley, NY, 1975), 101.

its king.[50] A king of his own choice he appointed in the city and taking the vast tribute he brought it into Babylon.[51]

Although the Babylonian account gives no names, we learn from 2 Kings that Jehoiakim had died by the time of the capture of the city, and it was his young son Jehoiachin who surrendered himself to Nebuchadnezzar. It was at this point, in the spring of 597, that a large proportion of the upper classes of Judah (including Ezekiel) and the treasures of the temple were taken into captivity.

The king that Nebuchadnezzar appointed was a man called Mattaniah, apparently another of Josiah's sons. He received the throne name Zedekiah from the Babylonian king, and promised allegiance (2 Kgs. 24: 17). Zedekiah did not fulfil the promise, but rebelled in the ninth year of his reign. The Babylonian response was another lengthy siege, and the city finally fell in the summer of 587 BCE.[52] At the end of the siege, the fleeing Zedekiah was captured and taken to Nebuchadnezzar at Riblah, where the rebel king was forced to watch his family slaughtered, before himself being blinded and led in chains to Babylon, where he was imprisoned (2 Kgs. 25: 1–7). At this point we lose track of him; we must assume he died in prison. This time the Babylonian retribution was more severe; the city and temple were thoroughly sacked and another group of people taken into exile (2 Kgs. 25: 8–21). A governor was appointed, and Judah was incorporated into the administrative structure of the Babylonian empire (2 Kgs. 25: 22–4). With the destruction of Jerusalem in 587 the state of Judah ceased to exist as an independent political entity, and a new and important phase in Jewish history began.

---

[50] Wiseman comments: 'The insertion of a precise date for the capture of Jerusalem indicates the importance of this event in Babylonian eyes' ('Babylonia 605–539 B.C.', 232).

[51] Grayson, *Assyrian and Babylonian Chronicles*, 102.

[52] The date of the fall of Jerusalem is a matter of some debate, because of the difficulty of establishing an exact chronology which fits all biblical and extra-biblical sources. The year 587 is perhaps the more popular of the two possibilities and has been recently defended by, e.g., H. Cazelles, '587 ou 586?', in C. L. Meyers and M. J. O'Connor (eds.), *The Word of the Lord Shall Go Forth: Essays in Honor of David Noel Freedman in Celebration of his Sixtieth Birthday* (Winona Lake, Ind., 1983), 427–35; J. Hughes, *Secrets of the Times: Myth and History in Biblical Chronology*, JSOTS 66 (Sheffield, 1990), 158–231; E. Kutsch, 'Das Jahr der Katastrophe: 587 v. Chr.', *Biblica*, 55 (1974), 520–45. The alternative, 586, is preferred by Malamat, 'Last Kings of Judah' and 'Twilight of Judah'; Cogan and Tadmor, *II Kings*, 323; J. H. Hayes and P. K. Hooker, *A New Chronology for the Kings of Israel and Judah* (Atlanta, Ga., 1988), 95–8. Certainty is probably impossible.

## The Deportations from Judah

I now turn my attention away from the land of Judah and towards the exiles, amongst whom the priest Ezekiel was numbered. The use of deportation as a political and economic tool had been common for a long time in the Near East, but was put to particular effect by the Neo-Assyrians from the time of Tiglath-Pileser III (745–727 BCE), and by their Neo-Babylonian successors.[53] Assyrian deportations had already had a significant impact on Israel and Judah. With the fall of the northern kingdom, the Assyrian king, Sargon, had taken its leading citizens, bringing in a new ruling class from Mesopotamia. Judah had also suffered some instances of deportation during Sennacherib's campaign of 701. Nebuchadnezzar was responsible for two (or three) major deportations: the first, and probably largest, followed Jehoiachin's surrender in 597; the second came after the sack of Jerusalem in 587; and Jeremiah records a third group taken in 582.[54] When Jehoiachin surrendered in 597, the Babylonians did not bring in foreign leadership to control Judah, but they nevertheless effectively removed the military and administrative heart from the Davidic state. The king's palace officials and administration, the soldiers, and the craftsmen of Judah were removed, as is described in 2 Kings:

> And Nebuchadnezzar king of Babylon came to the city, while his servants were besieging it; and Jehoiachin the king of Judah gave himself up to the king of Babylon, himself, and his mother, and his servants and his princes, and his palace officials. The king of Babylon . . . carried off all the treasures of the house of the LORD . . . He carried away all Jerusalem, and all the princes, and all the mighty men of valour, ten thousand captives, and all the craftsmen and the smiths; none remained, except the poorest people of the land. And he carried away Jehoiachin to Babylon; the king's mother, the king's wives, his officials, and the chief men of the land, he took into captivity from Jerusalem to Babylon. And the king of Babylon brought captive to Babylon all the men of valour, seven thousand, and the craftsmen and the smiths, one thousand, all of them strong and fit for war.[55]

---

[53] The most important study is B. Oded, *Mass Deportations and Deportees in the Neo-Assyrian Empire* (Wiesbaden, 1979).

[54] Jer. 52: 30.

[55] 2 Kgs. 24: 14–16. The evidence of Jeremiah (esp. ch. 29) and Ezekiel would suggest that religious leaders such as prophets and priests were also deported at the same time.

The population of Jerusalem and Judah which was taken into exile was largely drawn from the upper strata of society, which was in accordance with the normal deportation policy of these Mesopotamian empires.

There is some confusion about how many people were actually deported. The 10,000 captives of 2 Kings 24: 14 is contradicted by the 7,000 men of valour and 1,000 craftsmen and smiths of verse 16. Moreover, a considerable discrepancy exists between the figures in this account and the 3,023 Judaeans of Jeremiah 52: 28. Kings does not give exact figures for the second deportation but implies that a large number of people were taken, while Jeremiah describes two more deportations and a total number of exiles of 4,600. A number of attempts have been made to combine these figures and arrive at a definite conclusion,[56] but it is probably more satisfactory to agree with Robert Carroll that: 'Such discrepancies are better not harmonized but accepted as evidence for the lack of definitive evidence available to the editors of the biblical stories.'[57]

More problematically, we are not sure how many people in total are implied by the figures: we can certainly assume that the men were taken with their families—Assyrian inscriptions and reliefs suggest that this was the norm—but it is unclear whether the figures in Kings and Jeremiah refer to everyone deported or just to the male heads of households.[58] There is no real problem in principle with taking a higher rather than a lower number; Bustenay Oded estimates that as many as 4,500,000 people were the victims of forced resettlement from the eighth to the sixth centuries, and, for example, the Assyrian Sennacherib claims to have moved more than 200,000 at a time.[59] From Kings and Jeremiah we can only draw the conclusion that a significant proportion of the élite of Judah, probably numbering several thousands, were

---

[56] See e.g. Malamat, 'Twilight of Judah', 133–4. Smith-Christopher has recently argued, on the basis of the degree to which Jerusalem was destroyed, that 'the numbers of exiles must have been larger than the estimates of the book of Jeremiah, and closer to the estimates in 2 Kings 24' ('Reassessing', 17).

[57] R. P. Carroll, *Jeremiah: A Commentary*, OTL (London, 1986), 869; cf. also the discussion in H. M. Barstad, *The Myth of the Empty Land: A Study of the History and Archaeology of Judah During the 'Exilic' Period*, Symbolae Osloenses Fasciculi Suppletorii, 28 (Oslo, 1996), 33–4.

[58] On the deportation of families see Oded, *Mass Deportations*, 23–4.

[59] Oded, *Mass Deportations*, 20. It appears that the Neo-Babylonians were more selective in their choice of exiles.

exiled to Babylonia.[60] It is very difficult to fathom exactly the numbers involved, especially in the absence of any corroborating Babylonian evidence, and perhaps the final judgement of Daniel Smith is the only possible one: 'But once it is granted that a body of people were exiled large enough to form large "communities" of disaster and exile victims, then the specific numbers become less relevant.'[61]

At the beginning of the last century C. C. Torrey suggested that the exile was 'in reality a small and insignificant affair', and went so far as to claim that 'Hebrew Literature contains no "exilic" elements.'[62] This kind of scepticism about the exile has recently been revived by writers like Robert Carroll and Thomas Thompson. Carroll argues that we should treat the exile primarily as myth. The concept need have no historical referent and, even if it did, we lack sufficient evidence to provide a reconstruction of events. To speak of exile favours a later, Jerusalem-oriented viewpoint.[63] Thompson argues in a similar fashion that exile is a metaphor that expresses the piety of the biblical writings far more than it connects with any historical circumstances. There is a problem of continuity, a gap between stories of deportation and stories of return which raises 'the question of whether any such historical event of the past is in fact the reference of the traditions we do have'.[64] For Thompson and others, it is not just the exile that comes under suspicion. Their scepticism is part of a thoroughgoing scepticism about the whole history of Israel prior to the Persian period, and is combined with the view that more or less the whole of the biblical tradition is the invention of a 'post-exilic' élite.[65]

It is certainly true that the notion of exile, along with that of

---

[60] It is equally difficult to know exactly what proportion of the population was taken, since estimates of the whole population of Judah around 600 BCE vary between about 100,000 and 250,000 and for Jerusalem from about 20,000 to 250,000. For discussion see J. Blenkinsopp, 'Temple and Society in Achaemenid Judah', in P. R. Davies (ed.), *Second Temple Studies*, JSOTS 117 (Sheffield, 1991), 22–53 and Smith-Christopher, 'Reassessing', 17–18.

[61] Smith, *Landless*, 32; cf. also Soggin, *History of Israel and Judah*, 262.

[62] C. C. Torrey, 'The Exile and the Restoration', in his *Ezra Studies* (Chicago, Ill., 1910), 285, 288.

[63] Carroll, 'Exile! What Exile?', esp. 67, 78–9.

[64] T. L. Thompson, 'The Exile in History and Myth: A Response to Hans Barstad', in Grabbe (ed.), *Leading Captivity Captive*, 111.

[65] For a fuller presentation of the thesis see esp. Davies, *In Search of 'Ancient Israel'*.

exodus, takes on a significant amount of theological or mythological colouring within the biblical tradition, and it is also true that it is used with particular rhetorical power by the élites of the Persian period. However, this in itself is not enough to deny the exile any historical referent. In the first place, we know that communal deportation was an important part of Assyrian and Babylonian policy in the region. Secondly, the assumption that biblical literature contains no useful historical information is as flawed as the opposite assertion that it is wholly reliable. Writing in the same volume as Carroll and Thompson, Lester Grabbe provides a balanced treatment of the problem. He has demonstrated that it is not unreasonable on the basis of comparative evidence to assert that communities of deportees did (if rarely) manage to retain their ethnic identity, and that in a few cases we have parallel accounts of exiled communities which returned to their original homeland. The problem of continuity may, therefore, be more imagined than real. The biblical account of the deportations is at the very least plausible, and, our source in 2 Kings is largely confirmed by comparison with contemporary Babylonian sources.[66] Moreover, as we have seen in discussing the location of Ezekiel's ministry, it is hardly surprising that those among the deportees who held on to their Jewish identity retained Jerusalem, the city they had left behind, at the centre of their interest.

What, then, of the relationship between communities in Jerusalem and Babylonia after the deportations of 597 and 587? Whilst the biblical material can give the impression of almost total depopulation of the land, and the removal of 'all Israel' to exile in Babylon, it does seem very unlikely that this was the case. Martin Noth, for one, believed that the community in Babylonia was 'just an outpost'.[67] Recently Hans Barstad has argued along similar lines that the Babylonian invasions left Palestine much less devastated than is commonly thought, and that we should think of a considerable continuity of population and institutions in Palestine.[68] But, while these scholars are right to point out that the

---

[66] L. L. Grabbe, 'The Exile under the Theodolite: Historiography as Triangulation', in Grabbe (ed.), *Leading Captivity Captive*, 87–90.

[67] M. Noth, *A History of Israel* (London, 1958), 296.

[68] Barstad, *The Myth of the Empty Land*; cf. also Robert Carroll's earlier article of the same title: R. P. Carroll, 'The Myth of the Empty Land', *Semeia*, 59 (1992), 79–93.

vast majority of Judaeans did not go into exile (perhaps 90 per cent remained), the significant issue for us is the social status of those who were deported. More important than the sheer numbers involved are the social groups from which the exiles were drawn. An important aspect of imperial policy was to deport the upper strata of society—the political, religious, and economic leaders—and thus to render the conquered territory more easily governed.

This is indeed the picture that Kings presents. King Jehoiachin and his family were deported, and along with them the chief officials of the State, the military leaders, and the craftsmen and smiths formed the bulk of the exiles. In our examination of social stratification in late pre-exilic Judah, we have seen that these were precisely the groups who were involved in the political arena of ancient Judah.[69] Those who were left behind may well have been the majority but they were the 'poorest people of the land' (2 Kgs. 24: 14).[70] Those who returned from exile, who are largely responsible for the final contours of the Hebrew Bible, have powerfully presented themselves as the genuine continuation of the State, so that a historian like Oded is drawn into saying: 'Actually, the main centre of the people of Israel between the fall of Jerusalem and their return under Cyrus . . . was located in Babylonia and was concentrated around the exiled royal family.'[71] Numerically speaking it is absurd to think that Babylon could have been the centre of the people of Israel, when the vast majority of the population remained in Judah, but such an assessment is eloquent testimony to the effective self-presentation of those Jews who returned from Babylon.[72] It was, I believe, significant for the survival and development of Judaism that it was the parts of Judaean society with the highest degree of education and political involve-

[69] See above, Ch. 1; also below, Ch. 3.

[70] As Richard Coggins points out, Ezekiel's quotation of those remaining after 587 is testimony to their numbers 'we are many—surely to us is given the land as a possession' (Ezek. 33: 24): R. J. Coggins, 'The Origins of the Jewish Diaspora', in R. E. Clements (ed.), *The World of Ancient Israel: Sociological, Anthropological and Political Perspectives* (Cambridge, 1989), 166. Barstad comments that 'we should keep in mind that members of the peasant proletariat, the non-landowning families, despite being a majority, probably did not count as "people" at all' (*The Myth of the Empty Land*, 31).

[71] B. Oded, 'Judah and the Exile', in J. H. Hayes and J. M. Miller (eds.), *Israelite and Judean History*, OTL (Phil., 1977), 481.

[72] See Coggins, 'Jewish Diaspora', 165–6.

ment who formed the bulk of the exiles.[73] Even after the loss of their material prosperity they retained the intellectual and symbolic apparatus with which they could make sense of their experience and maintain their ethnic identity.

## The Life of the Exiles in Babylonia

What did the exiles do in Babylonia? Here we have to admit that the evidence is very limited, but we can draw on Assyrian and Babylonian records as well as the Hebrew Bible to build up a general outline of the policy of deportation and of the conditions of the Jewish exiles.[74] The movement of large populations was, as Smith describes it, 'propaganda by the deed'.[75] The Neo-Assyrians were experts at imperialist propaganda; they set up numerous statues and royal inscriptions as symbols of power and domination in areas that were conquered or that had rebelled against the central authority.[76] The removal of large sections of the community to places far away was the most powerful way to demonstrate the power of the empire to its subjects. But deportation had other practical benefits: the removal of an entire leadership stratum left whoever the Assyrians or Babylonians installed as new leaders with fewer enemies to worry about, and these dangerous elements of the conquered populations were usefully redeployed as soldiers, construction workers, or farmers, in the service of the empire.[77] We would expect this to have been the fate

---

[73] This was recognized by Causse, who writes: 'Mais cette minorité représentait l'élite, l'élite par l'influence sociale et aussi par la science et par la piété. Et maintenant au sein de la grande épreuve, le petit troupeau s'affermit et s'épure encore' (*Les Dispersés*, 27).

[74] Again, there is a substantial literature on the history of the exilic period. Important studies include: E. Janssen, *Juda in der Exilzeit*, FRLANT 69 (Göttingen, 1956); P. R. Ackroyd, *Exile and Restoration*, OTL (London, 1968); id., 'The History of Israel in the Exilic and Post-Exilic Periods', in G. W. Anderson (ed.), *Tradition and Interpretation* (Oxford, 1979), 320–50; T. C. Mitchell, 'The Babylonian Exile and the Restoration of the Jews in Palestine', in Boardman, Edwards, *et al.* (eds.), *The Assyrian and Babylonian Empires*, 410–60; E. Bickerman, 'The Babylonian Captivity', in W. D. Davies and I. Finkelstein (eds.), *The Cambridge History of Judaism*, i (Cambridge, 1984), 342–58.

[75] Smith, *Landless*, 29.

[76] On Assyrian imperial ideology, see M. Liverani, 'The Ideology of the Assyrian Empire', in Larsen (ed.), *Power and Propaganda*, 297–317; also J. Reade, 'Ideology and Propaganda in Assyrian Art', in Larsen (ed.), *Power and Propaganda*, 329–43.

[77] See Oded's chapter 'Aims and Objectives of Mass Deportation', in *Mass Deportations*, 41–74.

of the majority of exiles from Judah and Jerusalem who arrived in Babylonia in 597 and later.

We are best informed about the position of the exiled king Jehoiachin, who seems to have been kept hostage at the Babylonian court. The release of the king from prison is reported in 2 Kings 25: 27, and his prominent place at the table of Evil-Merodach (Amel Marduk). We have some information about the conditions of his imprisonment: his name appears on ration lists found in the royal palace in Babylon. Four such lists have been discovered, one of which is dateable to 592 BCE.[78] 'They mention groups and individuals of various nationalities. As regards Jews they mention apart from the king (who is once designated as *mar šarri*, i.e. "the crown prince") and his five sons, eight anonymous and five named Jews.'[79] His royal status seems to have been acknowledged, since he is given the title 'Prince of Judah' on the lists. Albright and others have drawn the conclusion that Jehoiachin was well treated, and lived perhaps in what we might call a 'gilded cage'.[80] However, it is impossible to determine how many people were in his retinue and therefore whether the allocation of rations is generous or not.[81] Albright also suggested that seals found at Tell Beit Mirsim bearing the inscription 'Eliakim servant of Jehoiachin' implied that the king still held land in Judah after his exile.[82] However, recent studies have shown that the seals in question are of the wrong style and from an earlier period, so Albright's suggestion cannot be sustained.[83] There is nevertheless some evidence that he remained the leader of the Jewish commu-

---

[78] The texts were first published by E. F. Weidner, 'Jojachin, König von Juda, in babylonischen Keilschrifttexten', *Mélanges Syriens offerts à Monsieur René Dussaud*, ii (Paris, 1939), 923–35.

[79] R. Zadok, *The Jews in Babylonia during the Chaldean and Achaemenian Periods according to the Babylonian Sources* (Haifa, 1979), 38. On diplomatic hostages under Nebuchadnezzar see Wiseman, *Nebuchadrezzar*, 81–4.

[80] W. F. Albright, 'The Seal of Eliakim and the Latest Preexilic History of Judah, with Some Observations on Ezekiel', *JBL* 51 (1932), 77–106. Kuhrt comments on the large quantities of oil supplied to Jehoiachin and his retinue (*Ancient Near East*, ii. 608). Block suggests that the image of a vine successfully transplanted, in Ezekiel 17, points towards favourable conditions (*Ezekiel 1–24*, 541).　　　　[81] So also Smith, *Landless*, 35.

[82] Albright, 'Seal of Eliakim', esp. 78–84, 102–3; followed by, e.g., Oded, 'Judah and the Exile', 481–2.

[83] N. Avigad, 'New Light on the Na'ar Seals', in F. M. Cross (ed.), *Magnalia Dei: Essays on Bible and Archaeology in Memory of G. Ernest Wright*, (Garden City, NY, 1976), 294–300; D. Ussishkin, 'Royal Judean Storage Jars and Private Seal Impressions', *Bulletin of the American Schools of Oriental Research*, 223 (1976), 1–14; H. Weippert, *Palästina in vorhellenistische Zeit*, Handbuch der Archäologie, Vorderasien II, Band i. (Munich, 1988), 678.

nity in exile: it may be significant that Ezekiel's careful and regular dating system begins from Jehoiachin's exile, suggesting that the prophet (or his editors) considered him still to be the legitimate ruler of Judah. Moreover, the prominent position of his descendant Zerubbabel in the restoration community suggests some continuity of at least symbolic power.[84] Under whatever conditions he was held, it looks as if Jehoiachin remained the titular head of the Jewish community, and the Davidic house remained the focus of many people's hope for the future.[85]

In any case, the treatment of Jehoiachin will not have been typical of the experience of the rest of the Jewish exiles. Certainly he may have had some sort of retinue, but that is likely to have comprised only his family and personal retainers. Of the other exiles we are less well informed. Those who had valuable skills were probably allowed to continue using them: thus we may expect the craftsmen to have been deployed in cities on the building works that were so characteristic of Nebuchadnezzar's reign.[86] Indeed, in one of his inscriptions he explicitly describes the use of deportees in the rebuilding of the Etemenanki temple in Babylon,[87] and there are also some names of craftsmen that appear on the palace ration lists published by Weidner. It was common practice for deported soldiers to be absorbed into the armies of the conquering empire, and, although there is little direct evidence for this in the case of the exiles of 597 or 587, it is likely to have been the fate of at least some of the soldiers.[88] There

---

[84] That Zerubbabel was Jehoiachin's grandson seems clear, but sources are divided over whether he was the son of the exiled king's first son Shealtiel (Ezra 3: 2, 3; Hag. 1: 1) or his third son Pedaiah (1 Chr. 3: 19). It is far less clear that the other prominent leader of the exiles, Sheshbazzar, was a member of the Davidic family at all: see H. G. M. Williamson, *Ezra, Nehemiah*, Word Biblical Commentary, 16 (Waco, Tex., 1985), 17.

[85] Davidic hopes are evident, for example, in Ezek. 34 and Jer. 33. For further discussion of Ezekiel's rather muted Davidic hopes see below, Ch. 7.

[86] See Wiseman, *Nebuchadrezzar*, 51–80, on his numerous large-scale building projects throughout the empire. Most famous is said to have been the Hanging Gardens of Babylon, one of the wonders of the ancient world. However, in a recent article Stephanie Dalley has argued that these gardens were in fact built by the Assyrian kings in Nineveh: S. Dalley, 'Nineveh, Babylon and the Hanging Gardens: Cuneiform and Classical Sources Reconciled', *Iraq* 56 (1994), 45–58.

[87] The text is published in F. H. Weissbach, *Das Hauptheiligtum des Marduk in Babylon* (Leipzig, 1938), 46–7; see also D. L. Smith, 'The Politics of Ezra', in P. R. Davies (ed.), *Second Temple Studies*, JSOTS, 117 (Sheffield, 1991), 79.

[88] Oded, 'Judah and the Exile', 483–4. Stephanie Dalley describes the striking example of Samarian cavalry in the Assyrian army: S. Dalley, 'Foreign Chariotry and Cavalry in the Armies of Tiglath-Pileser III and Sargon II', *Iraq*, 47 (1985), 31–48.

is also evidence that the last king of Babylon, Nabonidus (555–539 BCE), may have deployed Jewish garrisons at some of the oases of northern Arabia.[89] But it seems likely that the majority of the exiles were settled in agricultural communities and put to work on the land and on the canals which watered the grain fields of Mesopotamia.[90] The redirection of manpower, the most important economic resource in any agrarian society, had been one of the most important functions of deportation policy from the beginning.

For the period of the early exile we rely on the evidence of the books of Ezekiel and Jeremiah. Ezekiel is said to be among the exiles at Tel Abib on the נהר כבר. While it is impossible to identify this with complete certainty it is likely that the phrase נהר כבר is the Hebraization of the Akkadian *naru kabaru* that is referred to twice in the Murashu archive.[91] It is likely that this canal was not the 'great canal' that supplied Babylon, passing by Nippur on its way to rejoin the Euphrates at Uruk and often identified with the modern *šaṭṭ en-nil*.[92] It is referred to as near Nippur rather than running through it, so is more likely to be a smaller canal which was tributary to the larger one.[93] Attempts to specify the exact location remain speculative, but we can be confident that Ezekiel's community was located somewhere 'within the commercial orbit of Nippur'.[94] Despite the book's remarkable silence about the occupations of its protagonists, it seems that, since they lived among the canals, it is most likely that they were engaged in agricultural work of some kind.

That sizeable communities of Jewish exiles did settle in the region of Nippur is confirmed by the records of the Murashu banking family which have been discovered there.[95] These cunei-

---

[89] C. J. Gadd, 'The Harran Inscriptions of Nabonidus', *Anatolian Studies*, 8 (1958), 31–92; Mitchell, 'Babylonian Exile', 421–2.

[90] Mitchell, 'Babylonian Exile', 422.

[91] Ibid. 421.

[92] So e.g. G. A. Cooke, *A Critical and Exegetical Commentary on the Book of Ezekiel*, ICC (Edinburgh, 1936), 4–5; Zimmerli, *Ezekiel 1*, 112; Soggin, *History of Israel and Judah*, 267.

[93] Greenberg, *Ezekiel 1–20*, 40.

[94] Mitchell, 'Babylonian Exile', 421.

[95] The most recent thorough examination of this archive is M. W. Stolper, *Entrepreneurs and Empire: The Muraŝû Archive, The Muraŝû Firm, and Persian Rule in Babylonia* (Istanbul, 1985). On Jews in the Murashu documents see especially M. D. Coogan, 'Life in the Diaspora: Jews at Nippur in the Fifth Century BC', *Biblical Archaeologist*, 37 (1974), 6–12; also his *West Semitic Personal Names in the Muraŝu Documents*, HSM, 7 (Missoula, Mont., 1976); Zadok, *Jews in Babylonia*.

form tablets from the fifth century BCE detail contracts involving farmers, shepherds, and fishermen in the region outside the city of Nippur. Bickerman summarizes the activity of this family firm:

The house of Murashu in Nippur loaned money, held mortgages, leased and subleased land, collected taxes and rents, and was engaged in other operations related to the management of land property, the mainstay of the Babylonian economy; the Murashu only exceptionally deal with real estate in the city, and we learn nothing from them about the Jews in the City of Nippur itself.[96]

Among the names of people involved in the contracts are some which are obviously Jewish, containing theophoric elements with *yaw* or *yahu* (i.e. YHWH); for example, Yahunatan, Tobyaw, Padayaw, Banayaw, and Zabadyaw.[97] On the basis of this onomastic evidence, it is possible to conclude that there was a Jewish minority in the region that made up perhaps 3 per cent of the population.[98] The Murashu tablets date from the second half of the fifth century BCE, and, although this is long after the initial deportations, they remain one of the most important sources of information for the life of the early Diaspora.[99]

The ancient city of Nippur does seem to have absorbed an unusually large number of foreign exiles under the Neo-Babylonians. Place names from the Murashu archive suggest that there were groups of Anatolians, Syrians, Phoenicians, Egyptians, and others settled in communities in the city's agricultural hinterland.[100] Most telling is the place name *ᵃˡgalatu*, which simply means 'exile', and, as Eph'al says, 'clearly testifies to the foreign origin of its inhabitants, and the circumstances of their arrival in Babylonia'.[101] That Nippur was such a centre for deportation seems to have its roots in the conflict of empires in the seventh century. Nippur remained loyal to the Assyrians longer than most of

---

[96] Bickerman, 'Captivity', 345.
[97] Coogan, *Personal Names*, 49–53, 119–21; also his 'Life in the Diaspora', 7–9.
[98] Zadok, *Jews in Babylonia*, 78.
[99] It is significant that there appears to have been no major shift of population or change of administrative pattern in the region as it moved from Babylonian to Persian control. See Kuhrt, *Ancient Near East*, ii. 603.
[100] See esp. I. Eph'al, 'On the Political and Social Organization of the Jews in Babylonian Exile', *ZDMG* suppl. 5 (1980), 107–8: the places from which the settlements' names were drawn fit fairly well with our knowledge of Nebuchadnezzar's campaigns in the West.
[101] Eph'al, 'Political and Social Organization', 109.

the cities in Babylonia, and passed into Nabopolassar's hands only after some struggle.[102] It is likely that he confiscated a great part of the city's territory, and that therefore his son Nebuchadnezzar was in a position to settle deportees on this new crown land.[103] Eph'al believes that the information of the Murashu documents, combined with Ezekiel's evidence, gives the impression of 'masses of people brought to the Nippur region (and perhaps also to other areas in Babylonia) as part of an extensive effort to rehabilitate that region, which had suffered severely during the Assyro–Babylonian wars in the seventh century B.C.'.[104] Rehabilitation is also suggested by the element *Tel* (mound) in Ezekiel's Tel Abib, and the names of other places where the exiles lived. These may have been ruined settlements in need of replanting and redevelopment.[105]

Jeremiah's letter to the exiles also appears addressed to people engaged in agriculture: 'Build houses and live in them; plant gardens and eat their produce' (Jer. 29: 5).[106] Certainly the Jews who feature in the Murashu tablets are, for the most part, small landholders, farming plots along the banks of the canals in the region of Nippur. We can easily imagine them as originally part of Nebuchadnezzar's reconstruction plans. Other Jews in the Murashu documents are found as shepherds and fishermen, working (sometimes alongside Gentiles) in the canals and waterways. Some ethnic groups are known to have formed a kind of corporation, called a *hatru*, which served as the intermediary between individual tenants and the government.[107] It is possible that Jewish corporations like these existed, as Albertz suggests, but the evidence of the archive does not allow us to say this with any certainty.[108] A small number of Jews are minor officials, but noth-

---

[102] See J. Oates, 'The Fall of Assyria (635–609 B.C.)', in Boardman, Edwards, *et al.* (eds.), *The Assyrian and Babylonian Empires*, 174–7. It appears that the city was under siege from 620 BCE until its final surrender in 616. Cf. also S. W. Cole, *Nippur in Late Assyrian Times, c.755–612 BC*, State Archives of Assyria Studies (Helsinki, 1996), 79–80.

[103] Bickerman, 'Captivity', 344–5.

[104] I. Eph'al, 'The Western Minorities in Babylonia in the 6th–5th Centuries BC: Maintenance and Cohesion', *Orientalia*, 47 (1978), 81–2.

[105] Oded, 'Judah and the Exile', 482–3; Ezra 2: 59 mentions Tel Melah and Tel Harsha. Cf. also Mitchell, 'Babylonian Exile', 422.

[106] Although much of Jer. 29 stems from the editors of the book, it seems likely that at least vv. 5–7 are genuine and reflect the period after 597: cf. Nicholson, *Preaching to the Exiles*, 98; also Holladay, *Jeremiah 2*, 139.

[107] For full discussion of the *hatru*, see Stolper, *Entrepreneurs and Empire*, 70–103.

[108] R. Albertz, *A History of Israelite Religion in the Old Testament Period*, ii (London, 1994), 373. The Assyriologist M. Dandamaev believes that these *hatru* organizations were not formed

ing suggests that, as an ethnic group, the Jews were particularly successful in the Achaemenid administration. The evidence of the Murashu documents would suggest that a large number of the deported Jews were settled in the countryside around Nippur, where they engaged in low-status occupations in agriculture and food production. One further statistic that may be significant is that Jews made up a surprisingly large proportion of Nippur's interpreter-scribes, which suggests that their ancestors had come from literate backgrounds and had managed to pass their skill down the generations.[109]

It is true that the Murashu archive represents only one group of Jewish exiles, and there must have been some Jews who retained a higher status during the exile. We have already mentioned the craftsmen who will have been put to work in the cities of Babylonia and may well have prospered there. Josephus talks of the rich Jews who refused to leave their property at the time of the restoration, and Ezra 2: 64–6 portrays a returning community of considerable affluence, who have entertainers, slaves, mules, and camels.[110] Ezra 1: 6 also details the wealth provided for the returning Jews by their neighbours, although it is most likely that these neighbours were Gentiles.[111] Hugh Williamson points out that the picture 'contrasts sharply with Hag 1', and conjectures that 'the wealth of those returning rapidly evaporated because of a succession of bad harvests'.[112] It is, however, equally possible that the picture of enormous wealth represents a certain amount of wishful thinking on the part of the author of Ezra. Eph'al finds it hard to think that the poor farmers of Nippur could be related to the upper classes of the first deportation, but it is unclear that a large number of deportees were drawn from the lower classes.[113] We should remember that it was largely the upper echelons of society who were deported, and it was part of the Babylonian policy to

until the Persian period, so they are irrelevant as regards Ezekiel's community: M. Dandamaev, 'Babylonia in the Persian Age', in W. D. Davies and I. Finkelstein (eds.), *The Cambridge History of Judaism*, i (Cambridge, 1984), 334.

[109] R. Zadok, 'Onomastic, Prosopographic and Lexical notes', *BN* 65 (1992), 52. He suggests that as many as one third of such scribes were Jews.

[110] Josephus, *Ant. Jud.*, 11. 3; cf. Zadok, *Jews in Babylonia*, 88–9.

[111] Williamson argues that here we have an allusion to the motif of the 'despoiling of the Egyptians' seen in Exod 3: 21–2; 11: 2; 12: 35–6 (*Ezra, Nehemiah*, 16).

[112] Williamson, *Ezra, Nehemiah*, 38.

[113] Eph'al, 'Political and Social Organization', 110.

neutralize the political efficacy of urban élites by resettling them as farmers or labourers. Moreover, we should not underestimate the devastating effect of such a drop in status; on the whole I find Lemche's picture compelling:

> It was impossible for the deported élite to maintain their social position in exile . . . They were in large part the leadership class, but, in the eyes of the Babylonians they could be put to little use within the complicated administrative system then in use in Mesopotamia. For one thing, the Judaeans were not educated so as to be able to undertake important administrative jobs (for which knowledge of cuneiform and Sumerian, the 'Latin' of the day, was essential); for another, there would always be doubts as to the loyalty of the group. It appears that to begin with the leadership stratum were reduced to the lot of peasants who farmed plots of land which had been assigned to them by the Babylonian state.[114]

It is not difficult to think that within a few generations these once proud families would be reduced to the level of the farmers, shepherds, and fishermen of the Murashu documents.

### The 'Captivity' and the Maintenance of Community

It seems that, although there is much talk of the Babylonian 'captivity', the vast majority of exiled Jews were not prisoners nor were they enslaved.[115] Despite the inevitable pressure to assimilate that living in Babylonia must have produced,[116] they were clearly allowed some personal freedom and some degree of communal organization. The elders seem free to assemble at Ezekiel's house, and there is evidence for the activity of anti-Babylonian prophets in both Ezekiel 13 and Jeremiah 29; they must have had some public space in which to deliver their oracles. One of the most important features of the Babylonian exile was the success of at least some Jews in retaining their communal and ethnic identity. It is seen most clearly in the fact of the return itself: there remained the degree of communal organization to let this second great movement of people happen.

[114] N. P. Lemche, *Ancient Israel: A New History of Israelite Society* (Sheffield, 1988), 180.

[115] M. A. Dandamaev, *Slavery in Babylonia from Nabopolassar to Alexander the Great (626–331 B.C.)* (DeKalb, Ill., 1984), esp. 563–4.

[116] This pressure is perhaps most evident in the Jewish adoption of Babylonian names some of which, like Mordechai, contain Babylonian theophoric elements. See Coogan, 'Life in the Diaspora', 10–11.

A number of factors influenced this successful resistance to the pressures of assimilation; many of these come from within the Jewish community itself, particularly the traditions of ritual and purity which were adapted from the Jerusalem temple for life in the Diaspora. One external factor, however, is vital, and that is the substantial difference in deportation policy between the Neo-Assyrians and their Neo-Babylonian successors.[117] As opposed to the traditional Assyrian policy, the Babylonian kings appear to have settled their deportees in groups. Eph'al writes of a 'conceptual dichotomy of deportation' between the Babylonian and Assyrian kings: 'The latter considered enforced 'mingling' of the exiles, and their 'Assyrianization', as one of the foundation stones of their empire, whereas the former sought to utilize the economic potential of the exiles, avoiding interference in their social and religious lives.'[118] Eph'al's study of toponyms in the Murashu archive suggests to him that there were a number of ethnic minorities in sixth–fifth century Babylonia, and that groups such as Egyptians and Tyrians, as well as Judaeans, were able to remain living in communal groups, and maintain some sense of national identity in the face of the many pressures of living in a new environment. It has to be said, however, that the Jews were particularly successful at this community maintenance, and my study seeks to examine some ways in which they made the best of the situation they found themselves in.

Communal leadership remained in some forms at least. Although from prison his power could only be symbolic, it is likely that the knowledge that Jehoiachin was alive and well sustained the hopes of some Jews. Ezekiel associates more than once with a group referred to as the elders, who approach him for advice, and seem to be representatives or leaders of the community (Ezek. 8: 1; 14: 1; 20: 1, 3). In the absence of the political institutions of state, it appears that the elders retained some of their previous status. It is possible that they even increased their importance. Eph'al comments:

The *immediate* change in status of the 'elders' in exile is apparent in the list of those whom Jeremiah addressed in a letter from Jerusalem, some-

---

[117] D. L. Smith tends to downplay the differences in policy in the interests of a more oppressive picture of the processes of empire, whoever the rulers are. See Smith, *Landless*, 30–1; also Smith-Christopher, 'Reassessing'.
[118] Eph'al, 'Western Minorities', 87.

time after Jehoiachin's deportation: 'to the elders of the exiles, and to the priests, the prophets, and to all the people whom Nebuchadnezzar had taken into exile from Jerusalem to Babylon'. The 'elders'' name leads all the rest.[119]

Ezekiel's interaction with the elders also suggests that public space of some kind was available in which it was possible to debate the religious and political issues that concerned the community.[120] This does seem to be the implication of prophetic activity among the exiles—not only Ezekiel's, but that of the prophets he condemns in 13: 1–16 and that of prophets like the Ahab and Kolaiah mentioned in Jeremiah's letter. Just how public this public space was is not so clear.

Perhaps more surprisingly, the priests also managed to remain together in groups. The return of a powerful priestly class at the restoration implies that, despite the destruction of the temple and their distance from Jerusalem, the priestly families maintained a continuity of tradition and office over the fifty years of exile.[121] We may also note that in the following century Ezra knew he could find a group of cultic officials living together in exile at the place Casiphia (Ezra 8: 17).[122] It seems that the Jews were free to associate together, and to engage in business, to marry and to retain some control over their social and religious affairs.

When we think of this freedom of association and of some degree of organization, it is important to remember that exile meant that such freedom was much more limited than had been the case in Judah and that any communal autonomy was severely restricted. It is important to recognize ways in which the domination of the Babylonian empire would have made itself felt. In the first place, they had been forced to move, and there can be no doubt that the experience of defeat and deportation itself will have left a considerable psychological mark on those who went through

---

[119] Eph'al, 'Political and Social Organization', 112.

[120] That this should be the case is inevitable. Even in the most dominated of slave populations, there are numerous ways in which the subordinates will manage to communicate with one another and make some form of communal resistance to their oppressors: see J. C. Scott, *Domination and the Arts of Resistance: Hidden Transcripts* (New Haven, Conn., 1990).

[121] Ezra 1: 4–6.

[122] Williamson comments that the suggestion that there was a sanctuary or other cult centre there is supported by the repeated use of the word מקום in these verses (*Ezra, Nehemiah*, 117.)

it, even if it is now difficult for us to quantify or evaluate it. For a start, the experience of military defeat and the long journey to Babylonia will have reminded the Jews of their subject status. Secondly, they were not allowed to leave, and as aliens the Jewish exiles lacked the basic political rights of even the poorest free-born Babylonian citizen.[123] Moreover, it is more than likely that whatever work they were doing was forced labour of some kind.[124] It is clear that these exiles felt a deep sense of loss and dislocation. This is put most obviously in Psalm 137:

> By the waters of Babylon, there we sat down and wept,
> when we remembered Zion.
>
> .    .    .    .    .    .    .    .    .    .    .
>
> For there our captors required of us songs, and our tormentors
>   mirth, saying:
> 'Sing us one of the songs of Zion!'
> How shall we sing the LORD's song in a foreign land?

The psalm is eloquent testimony to the distress, anger, and powerlessness felt by the deported community.[125] A similar sentiment can be seen in two of the quotations we find put in the mouth of Ezekiel's audience. 'The fathers have eaten sour grapes, and the children's teeth are set on edge' (Ezek. 18: 2) speaks of present suffering for which the exiles try to blame the previous generation. More despondent still is Ezekiel 37: 11: 'Our bones are dried up, and our hope is lost; we are clean cut off.' In both cases the implication is that the community's assessment of its own position is very negative.[126] Furthermore, in the hopeful conclusion to chapter 34 we find the image of exile as a place of hard labour and imprisonment, from which YHWH must free his people: 'and they shall know that I am the LORD, when I break the bars of their yoke, and deliver them from the hand of those who enslaved them' (34: 27). Similar images of bondage and forced labour are found in Second Isaiah (esp. 42: 7; 47: 6; 49: 9), and among the anti-Babylonian oracles of Jeremiah 50–1 the passage in 51: 34–5

---

[123] See Dandamaev, 'Babylonia in the Persian Age', 330–1, for discussion of the place of aliens in the Babylonian social structure.

[124] See e.g. Smith-Christopher, 'Reassessing', 24–5.

[125] See e.g. Albertz, *History of Israelite Religion*, ii. 412–13. Other psalms may reflect the situation of exile, but none is so explicit as this; for discussion see Ackroyd, *Exile and Restoration*, 225–6.

[126] Ackroyd, *Exile and Restoration*, 32.

draws attention to Nebuchadnezzar's harsh treatment of Judah.[127] These and other biblical sources witness to the difficulty of the exiles' life, whatever small freedoms they might have had, and whatever small degree of communal organization was left to them. As Smith writes: 'In sum, exile was a punishing experience, more effective than any symbol left in the homeland, which unavoidably reminded Jews that they were conquered.'[128]

While Smith accepts the widely held view that the exiles were not technically slaves, he nevertheless sees the category of slavery as a useful one for describing the threat which they faced. He uses a definition of slavery provided by Kopytoff: 'The slave begins as a social outsider and undergoes a process of becoming some kind of insider. A person, stripped of his previous social identity is put at the margins of a new social group and is given a new social identity within it.'[129] Such a removal of identity has also been described as 'social death', and this choice of metaphor seems appropriate to the exiles since it is given graphic representation in Ezekiel's vision of the valley of dry bones (37: 1–14).[130] The destruction and recreation of identity also fits well both with the relocating of the erstwhile Jerusalem élite in positions of powerlessness on the margins of Babylonian society, and with the policy of changing names that marked Nebuchadnezzar's treatment of Mattaniah/Zedekiah, and may have been more widespread.[131] Smith describes the exiles' situation:

Both the policy of name changing and constant reassurances by the prophets that it was Yahweh who willed the exile and not the power of foreign gods, seem to reflect an awareness of the symbols of power that

---

[127] See Smith, 'Politics of Ezra', 77–8; Causse, *Les Dispersées*, 27. J. L. Wilkie, in discussion of the passages in Second Isaiah, argues that treatment of the Jews worsened during the reign of Nabonidus: 'Nabonidus and the Later Jewish Exiles', *JTS*, NS, 2 (1951), 36–44. Smith-Christopher describes the increase in the language of chains, bonds, and imprisonment in exilic literature and comments that 'the metaphor of imprisonment, and references to places of imprisonment, do not grow more plentiful during the exile by pure chance, especially noting its foreignness to the Israelite judicial system. Contemporary assessments of the exile must not simply dismiss this imagery as purely metaphorical with no historical basis' ('Reassessing', 30–1). [128] Smith, *Landless*, 31.

[129] Ibid. 37, quoting Igor Kopytoff, 'Slavery', in A. R. Beals, B. Spiegal, and S. Fyler (eds.), *Annual Review of Anthropology* (Palo Alto, Calif., 1982), 209.

[130] O. Patterson, *Slavery and Social Death* (Cambridge, Mass., 1982); see Smith, *Landless*, 39–40.

[131] Smith also draws attention to Daniel and the three young men in Dan 1: 6–7, but, since this story is to be dated long after the period it purports to describe, it is questionable whether it can be used as evidence for the early exile.

the exiles had to live with and struggle against. Slavery is a point on a 'continuum of domination'. The Babylonian exiles may not have been slaves, but evidence suggests they were most assuredly in this continuum.[132]

How are we to evaluate the experience of domination and its repercussions in the life of the community? We have argued that the moral world in which a group conducts its affairs is substantially affected by its material and social conditions, so it would be surprising if the exiles' moral world was not affected by their experience of exile. Clearly relations of domination are ubiquitous in human society, taking an enormous number of different forms and provoking a vast range of possible responses. Nevertheless, comparative studies may be helpful, since there do appear to be common patterns that emerge. As James Scott writes in the preface to his book, *Domination and the Arts of Resistance: Hidden Transcripts*: 'What I do wish to assert . . . is that to the degree structures of domination can be demonstrated to operate in comparable ways, they will, other things being equal, elicit reactions and patterns of resistance that are also broadly comparable.'[133] He continues:

Thus, slaves and serfs ordinarily dare not contest the terms of their subordination openly. Behind the scenes, though, they are likely to create and defend a social space in which offstage dissent to the official transcript of power relations may be voiced. The specific forms (for example, linguistic disguises, ritual codes, taverns, fairs, the 'hush-arbors' of slave religion) this social space takes or the specific content of its dissent (for example, hopes of a returning prophet, ritual aggression via witchcraft, celebration of bandit heroes and resistance martyrs) are as unique as the particular culture and history of the actors in question require.[134]

As we have already noted, Ezekiel's oracles and actions presuppose some public space or other for their performance, even if that space is the prophet's own house. Moreover, we may note that while Ezekiel (by comparison with Jeremiah or Second Isaiah) is remarkably free of direct threats to the Babylonian authority, his theology which makes YHWH responsible for all that has befallen

---

[132] Smith, *Landless*, 41. More recently he has reasserted this, drawing attention to Babylonian inscriptions which attest the forced nature of deportees' labour (Smith-Christopher, 'Reassessing', 23–5).

[133] Scott, *Hidden Transcripts*, p. xi.

[134] Ibid. p. xi.

the community is, by providing an alternative explanation, subversive of a Babylonian interpretation of events which might place the responsibility with Nebuchadnezzar or with Marduk. And although he does not explicitly predict the fall of Babylon, some such political outcome is implicit in all of his promises of restoration. Thus even Scott's brief outline is suggestive of the situation of Ezekiel and the exiles.

As well as considering the general effects of domination on a community, it is also possible to draw attention to comparative studies of groups whose situation is broadly similar to that of the exiles. This is the burden of Daniel Smith's work, which compares the experience of the Babylonian exiles with that of a number of exiled groups in more recent history. These groups are ones which suffered forced migration, but which did resist outside pressure and retain their identity, as must also have been the case for the community in which the exilic biblical texts were produced. Smith's starting-point is that the experience of a crisis like exile affects what he calls people's 'mazeway'—the sense one has of meaning and order in the world.[135] Different people and groups respond in different ways to the crisis, some give in and reformulate their patterns of belief and behaviour according to the dominant ideology, others resist and attempt to maintain their identity. He describes his project:

But what we are most interested in is conceptualizing the process of restructuring identity in conditions of crisis and the challenge to the 'mazeways'. 'Mechanisms' can be seen at work in conditions of social crisis and interaction. One can assume, therefore, that an analysis of such mechanisms would be a most significant tool for understanding the nature of, and response to, a social crisis.[136]

In a comparative sociological examination of the modern and biblical communities Smith describes a number of strategies or patterns of activity which act as 'mechanisms for survival'. In fact Smith, in *The Religion of the Landless*, pays far less attention to Ezekiel than he does to other biblical texts,[137] but as we examine

---

[135] The expression is drawn from A. F. C. Wallace; see e.g. 'Revitalization Movements', *American Anthropologist*, 58 (1956), 264–81.                                        [136] Smith, *Landless*, 52.

[137] In 'Reassessing the Impact of the Babylonian Exile', the same author—now called Smith-Christopher—makes the intriguing suggestion that passages about Ezekiel's abnormal behaviour might effectively be read 'in the light of recent work on Post-Traumatic Stress Syndrome' (19 n. 39).

the Ezekiel material we shall discover connections with at least two of the mechanisms he proposes: (i) an increase in concentration on ritual and purity, especially where the continued existence of a minority group is under threat; and (ii) the development of a folk literature focused on stories of heroes who overcome the threats facing the oppressed community, and on the hope of a deliverer.

Smith uses a variety of exilic and post-exilic biblical texts to build up a strong case for seeing the exiled Jews as one of these 'dominated minorities', who successfully resisted the external pressures of the crisis and preserved their ethnic identity. However, in this welcome concentration on the exiles' subordinate status in Babylonia, there is one aspect of their experience to which he pays too little attention, and which is particularly important for an examination of the first generation of exiles: that is their previous experience as members of a political élite in Judah. As we have seen, the exiles of 597 and later were drawn substantially from the upper social strata of Judah and Jerusalem—they were the people who would have had power and influence under the Davidic monarchy, whether in politics, religion, or the economy. On being taken to Babylonia and settled there in small agricultural communities, their experience will have been marked overwhelmingly by the drop in status they suffered as they moved from being a ruling minority in a position of power to being a disempowered and dominated minority at the service of the Babylonian state. But the change in their material surroundings could not unmake these people totally, and they must have retained at least some of the intellectual and cultural elements of their former status.

## Ezekiel and the Ethics of Exile

In the remainder of this study I intend to work through in detail the ethical interests we find in Ezekiel, and concentrate on illuminating the extraordinary dual status of the exiles. It is my hypothesis that there are, as it were, two different moral worlds addressed in the book of Ezekiel—that of the Jerusalem élite and that of the exiles. But because the exiles were drawn from the Jerusalem élite they can be one and the same people, to whom both sets of circumstances are appropriate. It is important to recognize the different kinds of moral possibilities within these two social settings.

If Ezekiel's exiles are drawn from the upper classes of Jerusalem society, as the evidence suggests, we should expect the moral concerns of a political élite to loom large in their understanding of the city and its fate. Many of them prior to their exile would have been familiar, to a greater or lesser extent, with Judah's main communal institutions, such as the royal bureaucracy, the temple, and the military. Thus when Ezekiel predicts the destruction of Judah and Jerusalem, we should not be surprised that the moral judgements he condemns involve principally such national and institutional interests as international politics and state religion. Where the fate of Jerusalem is concerned, sin, virtue, and responsibility are to be seen on this large national and international stage: sin on a grand scale is answered by punishment on an equally grand scale. In providing this explanation of YHWH's anger the prophet offers a rationale for events which operates within the symbolic world with which his hearers were familiar, but in fact his analysis demonstrates the end of that world.

Of course, for his audience, their physical involvement with the world of Judah is already at an end. With their deportation and resettlement the exiles no longer have access to the political and religious life of Jerusalem. The moral world that they inhabit from day to day is more constrained, and the claims of family, business, and the immediate community are likely to press harder than affairs of state. The different shape of the community will imply different communal concerns: as a dominated minority in a foreign environment, questions of assimilation or the retention of a distinctive group identity are likely to be prominent. We should therefore examine Ezekiel's ethics for evidence of this new moral world of exile, and for elements that might provide impetus for social cohesion and communal survival. We shall find that the prophet's distinctive emphasis on ritual provides one such element, enabling the destroyed temple to remain a focus for the community's ethical system. Another aspect of accommodation to exilic conditions is what we might call the 'domestication' of ethics—the shift in moral interest from state institutions to individuals and families in oracles that do not directly concern Jerusalem. A final area for examination will be the dramatic movement from responsibility for judgement to passivity in the face of restoration that we find in the book. This movement can be seen to mirror the actual social circumstances of the exiles, who have gone from being people of some importance with a wide range of moral possibilities open to them to being small-time servants of Babylonian agricultural policy.

There can be no question that a social group which had possessed all the privileges their society could offer now began to suffer from severe loss of privilege. This change, and the associated experience of status inconsistency on a grand scale, produced one of the most fruitful crises in the history of ideas, as people attempted to explain what had happened to them, to maintain the identity of their group, and eventually to hope for the future. As we examine the book of Ezekiel we shall see many signs which suggest that he was coming to terms with these problems, using familiar symbols to find a way through a new and strange world.

# 3

# The World of Politics

Ezekiel's oracles of judgement proclaim the fall of Jerusalem and the destruction of all the familiar institutions of Jerusalem society. This is, in effect, to predict the destruction of the actual and symbolic world in which his audience would have lived as members of that society. The oracles explain the destruction of Jerusalem as the result of sin: the sins of the 'house of Israel' have built up to such a level that YHWH has no choice other than to leave his temple and city to a certain doom. The vast majority of the material which we most easily call 'ethical' is to be found in these oracles of judgement, and it will be an important part of this study to examine them. What are the sins which Ezekiel finds responsible for the fall of Jerusalem? What are the areas of moral competence to which they belong? What are the social contexts which such actions and decisions presuppose? We may build up a picture of the moral world of the book by examining the kinds of action which are important in this condemnation. We have already seen that the majority of the exiles of the first deportation belonged to Judah's upper classes. If these are the people whom Ezekiel addresses, then we should expect to find in the oracles of judgement an explanation of events which is in line with the moral possibilities which were open to these people, at least prior to their deportation.

What are the sins that bring about the fall of Jerusalem? In broad terms Ezekiel reiterates the typical concerns of his prophetic predecessors—a deadly concoction of political faithlessness and cultic irregularity has brought the situation to its shocking climax. On the political side, Ezekiel does not ignore social justice, but his dominant concern is foreign policy. This is most visible in a series of elaborate allegories in chapters 16, 17, 19, and 23, all of which are critical of Judah's relationships with foreign powers. At least as significant in Ezekiel's explanation of events is Judah's cultic apostasy, which is presented in most detail in the temple vision of chapter 8, but is also prominent elsewhere in the book. These areas which Ezekiel outlines as responsible for the fate of Jerusalem belong largely (if not exclusively) to the moral concerns of Jerusalem's political élite. Behaviour within individual and family relationships plays a less prominent role than moral failure in the affairs of state. Sin and virtue in Jerusalem have a grand scale, and serious consequences.

## Ethics and Factional Politics in Late Pre-Exilic Judah

As we saw in Chapter 1, it is clearly the case that there exist different moral worlds: different ways of understanding the world and how to behave in it. For each moral world, we can think of a different range of actions which are possible and/or permissible—what we might call 'moral horizons'. Despite broad continuities of language and culture, there are often profound differences in ethical concern between different interest groups within society. Among the most important divisions within a society are those of class and status, where people who have substantially different resources and styles of life also have a widely different range of moral possibilities open to them. There are areas of action which require the exercise of substantial political power, and these include such things as war and foreign policy, as well as policy about major state institutions like temples. Decisions in these areas can only be taken by people with some degree of political power: in ancient Israel, by members of the small ruling class.[1] These rather broad areas of policy provide considerable scope for disagreement and conflict between individuals and groups within the upper class. Their conflicts may well reflect the constant struggle for control of the State that takes place between the ruler and the governing classes, as well as between different factions within the political élite who wanted to support, influence, or oust the present ruler.[2] That not just Ezekiel but the Hebrew Bible as a whole contains so much polemical writing about state religion and the conduct of foreign policy is an indication that such factional politics were not lacking in ancient Israel and Judah.

It is no new thing to suggest that there were different parties or

[1] See D. A. Knight, 'Political Rights and Powers', esp. 100–5.
[2] See above, Ch. 1.

factions operating in late pre-exilic Judah. Max Weber, despite arguing strongly for the independence and religious motivation of the prophets, also admits: 'Whether the prophets wished it or not they actually always worked in the direction of one or the other furiously struggling inner-political cliques, which at the same time promoted definite foreign policies: Hence the prophets were considered party members.'[3]

Often biblical scholars have identified political factions with the producers of the various genres of biblical literature. Thus we see prophets, priests, and wise men ranged against one another in the political struggle.[4] However, while it may have been the case that there was a predominance of one such group in any faction, it is too simplistic to see the factions in Judah in this way. It is more likely that they drew their members from across a range of professional interest groups. Morton Smith's discussion of religious parties among the Israelites before 587 BCE points in this direction. He describes a 'Yahweh alone' party, for whom YHWH was the only god whom Israelites should worship. This faction opposes the dominant 'syncretistic' party, and both groups draw on a broad range of people from different social backgrounds: prophets, priests, and people might belong to one or the other. The 'Yahweh alone' party drew support from a number of places:

There were circles in the Judaean court and the Jerusalem temple, among the followers of the prophets, and in isolated sects (the Rekabites). These groups and others whose existence is presumable (e.g. among the Levites) sometimes had in common only their exclusive devotion to Yahweh. This state of affairs is reflected by the 'party's' literature, which evidently derives from groups not closely related.[5]

If anything, Smith places too much importance on the religious beliefs of the 'Yahweh alone' party, and does not consider the material factors which might have influenced their formation as a party. The fact that the Hebrew Bible is largely religious in its

---

[3] Weber, *Ancient Judaism*, 274. His views are echoed by Bernhard Lang, who writes: 'Prophecy is an institution that belongs to the land-owning upper classes and which constantly plays its part in the mastery of political problems. If one looks at the position of prophecy in the social structure it appears as a channel whereby the nobility can advance its right of a say in public affairs. Structurally, prophecy serves as one of its means of political expression in public' (*Monotheism and the Prophetic Minority: An Essay in Biblical History and Sociology* (Sheffield, 1983), 68).

[4] See above, Ch. 1.

[5] Smith, *Palestinian Parties*, 31.

orientation leads us in this direction, but we might be better to read it at least in part as the symbolic vision or ideology of a party with decidedly this-worldly aims.[6] There may be less of an opposition between religion and politics than is sometimes imagined. Smith does, however, usefully show how people from different professional backgrounds could unite in the service of a common religious and political end.

Probably the most well known of the factions to be found in Judah around the end of the seventh century are the Deuteronomists, whose distinctive hand and ideology permeate so much of the biblical literature. These ubiquitous Deuteronomists have, nonetheless, proved notoriously difficult to locate. Numerous attempts to find them among a variety of professional interest groups, including prophets, Levites, and scribes, have proved unsatisfactory. Patricia Dutcher-Walls bases her attempt to find them on a sociologically informed reading of parts of Kings and Jeremiah.[7] She adopts the basic model of stratification proposed by Lenski,[8] and adds to his discussion of élite factions by drawing on the work of the ancient historian T. F. Carney, who explores the use of social-scientific models for understanding ancient societies.[9] His work concentrates on divisions within the governing class and thus fits quite neatly with that of Lenski. Using the Roman Empire as the primary source of his data, Carney describes the dynamics of ruler and governing élite: 'Relationships between the emperor and his bureaucrats have the feel of a zero-sum game: what one side won the other side lost. So the autocrat's prime concern was to control his ministers.'[10] A ruler does this in a variety of ways, all of which seek to make the possession of office dependent on loyalty to him, or to make sure that powerful members of the aristocracy are excluded from his inner circle. The élites in government have their own strategies for survival and self-aggrandizement. Normally drawn from the landed gentry, they are concerned to limit the influence the ruler has over their estates and the revenue which these produce. The govern-

---

[6] On this point cf. also McKeating, 'Sanctions against Adultery', 70.

[7] Dutcher-Walls, 'Social Location'; cf. also her chapter 'Sociological Analysis', in *Narrative Art, Political Rhetoric*, 142–79.

[8] See above, Ch. 1.

[9] T. F. Carney, *The Shape of the Past: Models and Antiquity* (Lawrence, Kan., 1975).

[10] Carney, *Shape of the Past*, 55.

mental élites fall into different categories, and Dutcher-Walls summarizes: 'The three large sectors which the ruler confronts are the military, with its power of organized force, the administration, who have the power to block actions, and the ecclesiastical structures, which have the power to confer legitimacy. By wielding these powers successfully, these sectors can limit, control, and even depose the ruler.'[11] To wield their powers successfully the members of the political élite cannot act alone, but must form coalitions and factions, and such factions will often cut across different sectors of the governing class: military, administrative, and ecclesiastical.[12]

We may imagine that the pattern of struggle in Israel and Judah under the monarchy was not too dissimilar to that found elsewhere, but should allow for some factors in which they do appear different. Dutcher-Walls draws attention to the particularly important position of the state religion and temple in Jerusalem. Because of this we should give a more prominent social position to the high priests of the Jerusalem temple: 'in a society where religion is a state affair, and the temple the king's sanctuary, the high priests must be ranked in power and prestige in the uppermost class'.[13] We should also pay attention to the fact that Judah's political and economic situation was constantly influenced by the actions of the large empires which surrounded it, demanded tribute of it, and ultimately conquered it.[14] We can, therefore, expect any political factions within Judah to have something to say about the temple, and also about the policy which the State ought to adopt towards the great empires.

Dutcher-Walls begins her study of the biblical texts by looking at the account of Josiah's reform, the first occasion on which a

---

[11] Dutcher-Walls, 'Social Location', 84.

[12] So also Kautsky, *Aristocratic Empires*, 237–8.

[13] Dutcher-Walls, 'Social Location', 81; cf. also Lenski, *Power and Privilege*, 208–9, 257, where he practically makes the modification himself.

[14] Dutcher-Walls, 'Social Location', 81. A similar point is made by Marvin Chaney, who writes: 'Long before they were able to dominate these states outright, [the regional superpowers] never ceased meddling in the affairs of their smaller neighbours, who occupied the land bridge where superpower interests met and clashed. Under these circumstances Egyptian, Mesopotamian, and other foreign diplomats sought influence with various factions of the Israelite and Judahite élites': see M. L. Chaney, 'Debt Easement in Israelite History and Tradition', in D. Jobling, P. L. Day, and G. T. Sheppard (eds.), *The Bible and the Politics of Exegesis: Essays in Honor of Norman K. Gottwald on his Sixty-Fifth Birthday* (Cleveland, Ohio, 1991), 128.

recognizably Deuteronomistic party emerges. She then goes on to examine some of the stories about Jeremiah, which help to show factions in operation. Josiah's reforms described in 2 Kings 22–3 seem to reflect clearly both a religious and a political agenda.[15] YHWH's reinstatement as the only national god is combined with a new independence in foreign policy. The evidence of Kings suggests that Josiah's supporters came from across a range of different groups within the upper class, including figures like Shaphan the scribe, Hilkiah the high priest, and Huldah the prophetess, who was married to one of the King's attendants.

Using our model to reflect upon this narrative and the social roles mentioned in it, it is clear that the reform is carried out in and by the highest and most powerful class. The king and some of his closest advisors are involved. But it is also evident that the reform supporters are spread across various social stations—priests, a prophetess, the king's servants, scribes, and nobles are all a part of the action. Although the apologetic nature of the narrative can only display unanimity across the top officials, our model helps us be aware that what is portrayed here is most likely a faction at work supporting the king and its policies.[16]

It is important to notice that the kinds of people who are involved in the political faction Dutcher-Walls describes are exactly the kinds of people whom Nebuchadnezzar deported: the military, administrative, and religious leaders of the community. The moral issues of Jerusalem politics which are so central to the book of Ezekiel (especially the conduct of foreign policy and the state cult) are the issues which would have been highly relevant to these members of the élite classes.[17]

[15] See Soggin, *History of Israel and Judah*, 255–8; also N. Lohfink, 'The Cult Reform of Josiah of Judah: 2 Kings 22–23 as a Source for the History of Israelite Religion', in J. M. Miller, P. D. Hanson, and S. D. McBride (eds.), *Ancient Israelite Religion: Essays in Honor of Frank Moore Cross* (Phil., 1987), 459–75.

[16] Dutcher-Walls, 'Social Location', 85. Dutcher-Walls carries on by examining five passages from Jeremiah, in which the conflict between the prophet and his opponents reflects a later period when the Deuteronomistic faction has fallen out of favour. Here too she concludes: 'There is not one faction of priests versus prophets, or gentry versus king's officials. Rather, each faction seems to include the full range of elite social roles—prophets, officials, priests and gentry—in its circle of influence and power . . . The divisions thus lie between political ideologies, not between roles, status levels or occupations among the elites' ('Social Location', 92).

[17] Dutcher-Walls provides a parallel example in her study of Athaliah's rise and fall. She highlights the propagandistic value of the narrative in 2 Kings 11–12, and emphasizes that this propaganda is addressed not to the whole community, but only to the political élite. She comments 'only elites have the power to concern themselves with the story's evident

### Ezekiel and the Political Community

There has been a tendency in Ezekiel scholarship over the last century or so to read the prophet apolitically.[18] This goes back in part to those in the nineteenth century who saw Ezekiel as a *Schreibtischprophet*, unconnected with the life of the people. For Ewald and many who followed his example the prophet's work was a 'leises inneres Selbstgespräch zwischen Jahwe und dem Propheten ohne lebendige Rücksicht auf das Volk'.[19] Early in the twentieth century J. Herrmann, who did much to correct the picture of Ezekiel as an uninvolved author, nevertheless did not acknowledge a political aspect to the prophet's message: 'In politischen Fragen hat Ezechiel nicht eingegriffen, so ist seine Verkündigung im wesentlichen eine rein religiöse.'[20] A similar position is to be found in much of the most influential recent work on Ezekiel: Fohrer, Eichrodt, and Zimmerli all find that the pastoral role of the prophet in his community far outweighs his active political role. The position is well summarized by Zimmerli: 'He did not live in a place where the rightness of political decisions could be fought over, but outside such a sphere, in exile where he formulated the harsh and final prophetic message of judgement without any direct contact with the decisions of the inhabitants of Jerusalem.'[21]

Ezekiel is seen by these interpreters principally as a theologian, as one who explains the disaster and who offers hope in repentance and a return to YHWH, seen largely in religious terms. In more recent work this tendency to read Ezekiel as not involved in politics is evident in Ellen Davis's *Swallowing the Scroll*, which presents the prophet as more interested in the creation of a written work and its implied audience than in the real conflicts of political struggle.[22] More surprisingly, even in Iain Duguid's

---

interests, things like royal succession and the temple's upkeep. And their interest in these matters would be keen, as the working out of the royal ideology could have a practical impact on their livelihood and power positions in society' (*Narrative Art, Political Rhetoric*, 173).

[18] For a full discussion see Bernhard Lang, *Kein Aufstand in Jerusalem: Die Politik des Propheten Ezechiel*, SBB (Stuttgart, 1978), 152–66.

[19] H. Ewald, *Die Propheten des Alten Bundes*, ii (Stuttgart, 1841), 326.

[20] J. Herrmann, *Ezechiel*, KAT 11 (Leipzig, 1924), 84.

[21] Zimmerli, *Ezekiel 1*, 177.

[22] E. F. Davis, *Swallowing the Scroll: Textuality and the Dynamics of Discourse in Ezekiel's Prophecy*, JSOTS 78 (Sheffield, 1989).

recent book *Ezekiel and the Leaders of Israel* we find a prophet who is not really politically engaged. In this study, which 'represents an attempt to clarify one area of the prophet's thought, namely his attitude towards the various leadership groups within Judean society', the author undertakes a detailed examination of these groups and believes that Ezekiel has a vision of a radically re-structured society.[23] He does not, however, examine the degree to which Ezekiel's vision represents the interests of any one group in society, nor does he provide any sense of the social context in which political ideas such as these were to be discussed.

Bernhard Lang has presented a most salutary corrective to all attempts to read Ezekiel apolitically. In his book *Kein Aufstand in Jerusalem*, he examines the use of political propaganda in the book and shows the connections between the political situation it presupposes and the common ways of going about international politics in the ancient Near East. A large part of the book's message is addressed to Zedekiah's government and its folly. From exile the prophet attacks his policy of rebellion against Babylon and predicts dire consequences: he is engaged in a genuinely polit-ical activity at all points.[24] In another essay, Lang writes of the symbolic actions:

> Performed on the eve of an anti-Babylonian revolt, they challenged public opinion by visualizing the inevitable consequences of such an inconsiderate, foolish protest. What Ezekiel wanted to sound was a note of warning to make the king and the people abandon that policy. Only an immediate and radical change of the political course could prevent a national disaster.[25]

One might argue that those who were in exile would rapidly lose interest in a political life they were no longer able to influence. However, it seems more likely that they would have retained a keen interest in events at home, especially in the years prior to the fall of Jerusalem. As long as the city stood they could have believed that Judah would recover from the crisis of 597 and that they would soon be restored to their former state. It certainly appears that political controversies were current among the exiled élite, although we must question the effect which their debates will

---

[23] Duguid, *Leaders*, 1.
[24] Lang, *Kein Aufstand*, passim.
[25] B. Lang, 'Street Theater, Raising the Dead and the Zoroastrian Connection in Ezekiel's Prophecy', in Lust (ed.), *Ezekiel and his Book*, 301.

have had on the actual formation of policy in Jerusalem.[26] Jeremiah 29 suggests not only that letters could be sent between the two communities, but that there were among the prophets and priests in exile active supporters of the anti-Babylonian party. Ezekiel 13: 1–16 suggests that he had prophetic opponents whose predictions of peace (13: 10) implied that Zedekiah's foreign policy would be successful. Ezekiel's response to any such hopes is consistently and unequivocally negative. Moreover, by delivering oracles which seem to implicate his listeners in the sins of Judah, the prophet forces them too to accept responsibility for the present and coming disaster. As I have suggested, he offers a rationale for events which operates within the symbolic world with which his hearers were familiar, but in fact his analysis demonstrates the end of that world.

### Ezekiel and Foreign Policy

Like his prophetic predecessors Ezekiel condemns the alliances made between Judah and foreign powers.[27] This condemnation is most vivid in the historical allegories of chapters 16 and 23, where Jerusalem is portrayed as a woman whose voracious sexual appetite drives her to take lovers from among the nations. In Ezekiel 16: 26–29 she is said to have acted promiscuously with Egyptians, Philistines, Assyrians, and Babylonians. The woman 'Jerusalem' must here be a figure for Judah's political leadership; as Allen writes, 'Jerusalem, as the centre of royal administration and responsibility, could reasonably be held responsible'.[28] The adulterous allegory in Ezekiel 23 is more consistently focused on foreign policy, and seems also to be more directly related to the events of the late seventh and early sixth centuries. The order in which Oholibah (Jerusalem) takes lovers—Assyrian, Babylonian, then Egyptian—reflects the changing balance of power in Syria/Palestine during the years leading up to the fall of Jerusalem. Just which pharaoh is involved is unclear. Allen suggests that the

---

[26] See Lang, *Kein Aufstand*, 138–9; Smith-Christopher, 'Reassessing', 15–16.

[27] Most notably Isaiah and Jeremiah in Jerusalem, and Hosea in the North. For a full survey of political themes in the prophets see N. K. Gottwald, *All the Kingdoms of the Earth: Israelite Prophecy and International Relations in the Ancient Near East* (NY, 1964).

[28] Allen, *Ezekiel 1–19*, 240.

sexual potency ascribed to the Egyptians, 'whose members were like those of asses and whose ejaculation like that of horses',[29] is a reference to 'the dynamic Hophra who came to the Egyptian throne early in 589 B.C.'.[30] On the other hand, Julie Galambush finds a reference to his predecessor Psammeticus II in 23: 36–45, which details the entry of Oholibah's lovers into the temple itself. In 592 Psammeticus had made a tour of Palestine, together with an entourage which included priests, and his likely aim was to gain the support of local rulers like Zedekiah:

> If the Egyptians had entered the temple or temple complex along with their priests in 592 in conjunction with their inciting Zedekiah to revolt, this could be the event described in 23: 36–45 as people's entering the temple 'to profane it.' The 'men from afar,' received for an adulterous liaison with Oholibah, would then be Egyptians.[31]

This is an attractive suggestion, although it is necessary to acknowledge that the exact details referred to in these allegories remain rather obscure. What is clear from chapter 23, however, is that Ezekiel is condemning not only alliances in general, but also the specific relationship with Egypt that Zedekiah fostered.

Judah's relationship with Egypt was the most pressing political problem of Zedekiah's reign: Should the king remain loyal to Babylon or submit to pressure from the other regional superpower, Egypt? For a time under Josiah, Judah had possessed a measure of political autonomy and domestic issues could come to the fore, as the waning strength of Assyria left a power vacuum in the region. However, with the rise of Babylonia the small states of Syria/Palestine once again found themselves in the front line of struggle between Mesopotamia and Egypt.[32] Thus it is no surprise that foreign policy was at the heart of the problems facing the rulers of Jerusalem, and in 597 the young King Jehoiachin paid a severe penalty for the policy of rebellion which he inherited. Rainer Albertz, drawing largely on the evidence of the book of Jeremiah, describes the political situation after the first deportation:

---

[29] My translation of Ezek. 23: 20: אשר בשר חמורים בשרם וזרמת סוסים זרמתם.
[30] Allen, *Ezekiel 20–48*, 47.
[31] J. Galambush, *Jerusalem in the Book of Ezekiel: The City as Yahweh's Wife*, SBLDS 130 (Atlanta, Ga., 1992), 122.
[32] See discussion above, pp. 50–3.

After Nebuchadnezzar had appointed Zedekiah, another of Josiah's sons, vassal king of the rump state of Judah, as early as 594 there was a renewed anti-Babylonian conspiracy in which several small states in the region took part. Here for the first time we can certainly detect a national religious party which could not accept the political reality created by Babylonian superiority, and argued for a revision of it by the speediest possible military alliance with Egypt. This party was headed by the temple priesthood under the leadership of the chief priest Seraiah, a grandson of Hilkiah: it found spokesmen in a series of temple prophets like Hananiah in Jerusalem (Jer. 28) or Zedekiah, Ahab (29: 21f.) and Shemaiah (29: 31) among the exiles. Its political arm consisted of a group of court officials in Jerusalem to which the Malikyah (Jer. 21: 1; 38: 1, 6) and Shelemiah (Jer. 37: 3, 13; cf. 36: 26) families were particularly prominent; we may assume that this group also found sympathizers among members of the upper class who had been deported. The opposition to this influential national religious party was made up of the rest of the reform party under the leadership of the Shaphanids, and this also included the prophets Jeremiah and Ezekiel. This party in principle had a pro-Babylonian attitude.[33]

Thus it appears that the issues addressed in chapter 23 (and, as we shall see, in other parts of the book) will have been precisely those which most exercised the minds of the Jerusalem élite in the period of Zedekiah's rule. In this respect the prophet is undoubtedly participating in the political debates of this Jerusalem élite. It is important to point out that outside the ruling class it is unlikely that there would be much interest in these decisions taken at the top level. From the point of view of any of the sections of society whose taxes supported the ruling class, the question to whom tribute was paid would have been irrelevant: to the peasantry one overlord is much like another. As Lenski writes: 'It is no great exaggeration to say that the outcomes of all the countless struggles between rulers and governing classes had almost no effect on the living conditions of the common people, except as these struggles sometimes led to violence and destroyed their very livelihood.'[34] Thus the political debates upon which Ezekiel's oracles focus would have had relevance only within a very limited section of society.

The most explicitly political oracle in the book of Ezekiel is the

---

[33] Albertz, *History of Israelite Religion*, i. 237. Cf. also Dutcher-Walls, 'Social Location', 85–90.
[34] Lenski, *Power and Privilege*, 241.

extended allegory of the eagles and the vine in chapter 17. This allegory is widely accepted as the authentic voice of the prophet: even Jörg Garscha, who limits Ezekiel's contribution to the book to a mere thirty verses, finds the original prophet here.[35] Together with the interpretation which follows, this oracle presents a neat summary of the main problems of foreign policy facing the rulers of Judah in the last years before the fall of Jerusalem. The allegory describes a great eagle who removes the topmost shoot of a tall cedar of Lebanon and plants a new seed in its place. The seed becomes a vine which first flourishes then turns away towards another great eagle, who transplants it. The question is asked: 'Behold, when it is transplanted, will it thrive [הֲתִצְלָח]? Will it not utterly wither when the east wind strikes it—wither away on the bed where it grew?' (17: 10). The second part of the chapter provides the interpretation for this allegory: the first eagle is the king of Babylon, and the second the king of Egypt.[36] The topmost shoot represents Jehoiachin, and the indecisive vine his successor Zedekiah.[37] The interpretation concentrates on the oath of loyalty to Babylon which Nebuchadnezzar made Zedekiah take, and on the disastrous consequences of breaking this oath: 'Will he succeed [הֲיִצְלָח]? Can a man escape who does such things? Can he break the covenant and yet escape?' (17: 15). Ezekiel makes the astonishing claim that in breaking his covenant with Nebuchadnezzar, Zedekiah has in effect broken his covenant with yhwh himself. 'As I live, surely *my* oath which he despised, and *my* covenant which he broke, I will requite upon his head' (17: 19). As Norman K. Gottwald writes: 'The severity of Ezekiel in condemning Zedekiah's breach of the vassal oath is unparalleled in prophecy.'[38]

How does this relate to ethics? We should pay attention to the general area of activity in which decisions are taken, the specific courses of action recommended or criticized, and the symbols

[35] Garscha, *Studien zum Ezechielbuch*, 286.
[36] Most commentatators think of Psammeticus II here rather than his successor Hophra. See e.g. M. Greenberg, 'Ezekiel 17 and the Policy of Psammetichus II', *JBL* 76 (1957), 304–9; Zimmerli, *Ezekiel 1*, 362.
[37] This is clear despite the fact that he is not named; indeed Zedekiah is never named in the book of Ezekiel. See the discussion in Lang, who concludes 'das Fehlen des Eigennamens von König Zidkija erklärt sich aus dem Zeitbezug des prophetisches Wortes; als es gesprochen wurde, wußte jedermann, wen der Prophet meinte' (*Kein Aufstand*, 25–7).
[38] Gottwald, *All the Kingdoms*, 306.

which are used to express these. The first of these is clear: the general issue is the king of Judah's foreign policy. Moreover, that he has made a wrong decision in Ezekiel's eyes is obvious. The logic of the allegory is that to turn away from the first eagle is a practical mistake resulting in disaster. However, in the interpretation that follows the issue is theologized and the question of oath breaking takes precedence.[39] The fact that the oath of vassalage was sworn in YHWH's name seems to be the issue, and we arrive at a matter of YHWH's honour: never far from the view of our prophet.[40] This stress on the person of YHWH has led some commentators to play down the political content of the oracle, and this can be seen in Iain Duguid's comment: 'The prophet is not concerned with practical politics—the arguments in favour of or against siding with Egypt or Babylon—but rather with the inevitable consequences of disobedience.'[41] The implication is that it is Zedekiah's oath breaking that is the moral issue rather than his political faithlessness. Certainly Ezekiel's argument operates at the theological level and he highlights the wrongness of oath breaking: an oath taken in the name of YHWH the national god is the most potent symbol of the king's commitment to a particular course of action. But of course his breaking the oath is not something abstract, but is defined as the act of 'sending ambassadors to Egypt, that they might give him horses and a large army' (Ezek. 17: 15). The moral decision taken is simultaneously a religious one and a practical one.

Moreover, the combined issue of loyalty to Babylon and to YHWH is not something that involves the king alone. It is right that Zedekiah should be the principal focus of attention, since the king has the final authority to make decisions about Judah's allegiance, and he is the person who has the most to lose. However, he is not the only person for whom international politics is a live issue. Albertz has outlined two distinct political factions within the Jerusalem upper class; it is clear that the members of these factions had a keen interest in the political situation, and a certain degree of influence over the king. Indeed it is commonly stated

---

[39] The condemnation of Zedekiah as חלל 'unhallowed' in 21: 25 may also refer to the oath breaking described in chapter 17. Duguid writes that 'he has committed sacrilege by profaning a holy oath: thus he is named *ḥalal* godless' (*Leaders*, 37).

[40] The centrality of YHWH's honour in Ezekiel's theology is well described by Joyce, *Divine Initiative*, ch. 6.

[41] Duguid, *Leaders*, 34–5.

that Zedekiah was a weak monarch who relied to an enormous extent on his advisers.[42] A close reading of the oracle in chapter 17 would suggest that Ezekiel is concerned with the behaviour of all those who have a stake in the political decision. The vassal treaty to which he refers has a broader impact than is sometimes recognized. Important here is the interpretation of 17: 13:

ויקח מזרע המלוכה ויכרת אתו ברית ויבא אתו באלה ואת אילי הארץ לקח

That is: 'And he took one of the royal seed and made a covenant with him, and put him under oath, and the chief men of the land he took.'[43] The key phrase here is ואת אילי הארץ לקח ('and the chief men of the land he took'), which is often understood as referring to the first deportation and seen as unconnected with the covenant and oath which immediately precede it. Greenberg writes: 'The last clause of vs. 13 . . . seems to belong before the last clause of vs. 12 (cf. 2 Kings 24: 15) ; placed there it would chiastically close the sentence concerning the deportation: *wyqḥ. . . lqḥ*.'[44] However, it is also possible that the phrase connects the 'leaders of the people' with the covenant and oath which Zedekiah entered into, as Zimmerli suggests: 'In its present position v 13b$\beta$ is only intelligible if it forms a constituent part of the covenant making.'[45] Bernhard Lang believes that this oracle is concerned to address a Jerusalem ruling class who were themselves partners to the treaty with Nebuchadnezzar: 'Der Terminus *nahm* (*laqaḥ*), muß sich nicht auf die Deportierten beziehen (wie v. 12), sondern kann v. 13 bedeuten: der Großkönig "nimmt" bestimmte Leute des besiegten Landes und macht sie zu seinen Vertragspartnern.'[46] Hossfeld also suggests that לקח here has a sense of taking into a covenant, drawing attention to the parallel usage in 2 Chronicles 23: 1.[47] A further piece of evidence in favour of this reading might be that both לקח and בוא seem to be used differently in verses 12 and 13. In verse 12 both verbs are used literally: 'he took [ויקח] her king . . . and brought [ויבא] them to Babylon'. In verse 13 they are used in a more metaphorical sense: ויבא is clearly so since it is followed by באלה, and so a similar shift in the focus of לקח is also plausible.

[42] See e.g. Soggin, *History of Israel and Judah*, 263; Noth, *History of Israel*, 284.
[43] My translation.
[44] Greenberg, *Ezekiel 1–20*, 314; so also Wevers, *Ezekiel*, 106.
[45] Zimmerli, *Ezekiel 1*, 365.
[46] Lang, *Kein Aufstand*, 56.
[47] Hossfeld, *Untersuchungen*, 78: so also Allen, *Ezekiel 1–19*, 252.

Ezekiel 17: 14 would then refer to the purpose of the covenant made with Zedekiah and the leaders of Judah, 'that the kingdom might be humble and not lift itself up, and that by keeping the covenant it might stand'. Submission to Babylon is the price of national survival. For Lang, this oracle is largely addressed to Jerusalem; the prophet is trying to influence events there from a distance. Zimmerli, with some justification, makes the suggestion that some of the exiles were in a precarious position as hostages, their future dependent on Zedekiah's loyalty:

Thus the conjecture of Ehrlich, which has in mind here the hostages taken from the sons of nobles through whose deportation the treaty with Zedekiah was to be sanctioned, must be considered more seriously and outlined more sharply in the light of recent knowledge. This shows us differences among those deported in 597 B.C.: (1) The small circle of the rulers who were directly guilty of a harmful policy and who were held in the city of Babylon in close proximity to the Babylonian king; (2) the larger circle of those carried off as hostages and settled away from the capital along with others in Tel Abib (provisionally?), to which the prophet himself belonged.[48]

If there were such hostages among Ezekiel's community the immediate concern with Zedekiah's policy is highlighted. If the decisions made in Jerusalem can affect the lives of the exiles, it goes a long way to explaining why they retained such an interest in politics at home.

Whether the proposal of Lang or of Zimmerli is correct, we can still see that Ezekiel's oracle belongs to the realm of upper-class political discourse. His community in exile may no longer be able to influence policy, but they are familiar with the moral issues of foreign-policy making, and appear to have been divided into rival groups supporting different policies. They are to some extent implicated in the political decisions that are made, and this is why the term 'rebellious house', with which Ezekiel addresses his audience at the beginning of the interpretation of his allegory, is an appropriate one for both his audience and the protagonists of events in Jerusalem. Chapter 17 makes it clear that, from the point of view of the prophet, rebellion against Babylon is a serious error of political judgement. More than that, it is rebellion against YHWH, who guaranteed the oath of loyalty himself. Not only the

---

[48] Zimmerli, *Ezekiel 1*, 365.

king, but his advisers and other members of the ruling élite are
included in Ezekiel's condemnation. The rebellious house is not
just the house of David, but includes a wider political stratum
within the society of ancient Jerusalem.

The term, בית מרי ('rebellious house') is frequently used in the
book of Ezekiel, most prominently in chapter 2 where the prophet
receives his initial commission from YHWH. Here the tendency
among scholars is to read מרי in a theological or 'theopolitical'
sense. Greenberg describes the people's sin as 'rebellion against
their divine Lord and King'.[49] Often the address is seen as referring to the past history of Israel as much as the present situation.
Zimmerli finds in the term a counterpart to the term 'house of
Israel' which has a historical focus, and Wevers too thinks of a
history of sin: 'Israel is for Ezekiel a generic term comprising all
Israel from its inception onwards, as is clear from verse 3b. So too
Israel can be termed rebellious, since its history has been one of
sinful rebellion against Yahweh. The exiles are part of that Israel
and share in its guilt corporately, even though themselves not
rebellious'.[50] Our reading of chapter 17 would suggest that a more
present and mundane act of rebellion is at the centre of Ezekiel's
interest, and that attitudes among the exiles might well be called
rebellious. Chapter 17, however much it reinforces the theopolitical understanding of the phrase, nevertheless also brings the
straightforwardly political into play. Moral decision is at the level
not just of abstract theologizing, but of the practical choices of
policy-making, and, as we have seen, this affects the ruling classes
as well as King Zedekiah.

The involvement of the upper classes with the fate of the king
is further highlighted by another passage in which the term בית מרי
arises, chapter 12. Here the prophet performs a sign-action; carrying the baggage of an exile he vividly portrays the impending fate
of 'the prince who is in Jerusalem and all the house of Israel who
are in it' (12: 10). Lang emphasizes the fact that Ezekiel's signs of
exile are addressed to both people and King, and draws attention
to Assyrian policy:

Vielleicht darf man auch hier den auf Vollständigkeit bedachten
Systematiker am Werk sehen. Überdies ist die Parallelität von

---

[49] Greenberg, *Ezekiel 1–20*, 63.
[50] Wevers, *Ezekiel*, 49; cf. Zimmerli, *Ezekiel 1*, 133–4.

Königsschicksal und Volksgeschick in Vorderasien seit langem eine politische Realität. Die Assyrer drohten ihren Vasallenkönigen und deren Volk von jeher gleich harte Strafen an; nicht nur ein untreuer Vasallenkönig allein wird bestraft, wenn es zu Aufstand kommt; das Volk ist mitverantwortlich.[51]

The Babylonians continued this policy, and we should remember that those who bore the brunt of Nebuchadnezzar's displeasure in 597 were the Jerusalem élite. Therefore the threat of exile in the sign-action refers to the consequence of a political act of rebellion against Nebuchadnezzar. In chapter 17 Ezekiel made explicit criticism of the political decisions being taken in Jerusalem; a similar criticism may be implicit here in chapter 12. While I doubt that Ezekiel was much able to influence the conduct of policy in Jerusalem, it is, nonetheless, an area of action and moral decision with which his exiled audience would have been familiar, and with which they could make sense of events at home.

Another political allegory is to be found in the dirge of chapter 19, which again is widely accepted as the genuine voice of the prophet.[52] It is described as a lamentation for the נשיאי ישראל, the 'princes of Israel'. The term נשיא is one that Ezekiel tends to use of the kings of Judah, and especially of Zedekiah. In its usage in the oracles of judgement and the oracles against the nations, it tends to refer to rulers 'with less political and territorial clout' than those who are designated מלך (typically Nebuchadnezzar and Pharaoh are called מלך).[53] In 19: 1–9 we meet two lion cubs who grow up to terrorize their neighbourhoods and both suffer exile as a penalty. Much of the scholarly discussion has centred on the identification of the two lions.[54] The first is obviously Jehoahaz, son of Josiah, who was removed to Egypt by Pharaoh Necho after a reign of only three months (2 Kgs. 23: 33). The second is less

---

[51] Lang, *Kein Aufstand*, 21. So also D. I. Block, who writes: 'The capture of the king becomes a symbol of the captivity of the nation' (*The Book of Ezekiel: Chapters 1–24*, NICOT (Grand Rapids, Mich., 1997), 374).

[52] Fohrer, *Ezechiel*, 104–6, Zimmerli, *Ezekiel 1*, 396; Lang, *Ezechiel*, 5.

[53] Seitz, *Theology in Conflict*, 124; cf. Zimmerli, *Ezekiel 1*, 209, on 7: 27a. נשיא must refer to the king of Judah in 12: 10, 12; 21: 30; 34: 24; 37: 25. On the term נשיא more generally see E. A. Speiser, 'Background and Function of the Biblical *Nāśî*', *CBQ* 25 (1963), 111–17; P. J. Budd, *Numbers*, Word Biblical Commentary, 5 (Waco, Tex., 1984), 11; S. S. Tuell, *The Law of the Temple in Ezekiel 40–48*, HSM 49 (Atlanta, Ga., 1992), 103–15.

[54] A very thorough discussion and bibliography is found in C. T. Begg, 'The Identity of the Princes in Ezekiel 19: Some Reflections', *ETL* 65 (1989), 358–69.

certain; all three of Jehoahaz's successors, Jehoiakim, Jehoiachin, and Zedekiah, have been proposed. Of these the least likely is Jehoiakim, since he was never taken into exile, and therefore the allegory would not connect with historical reality.[55] Perhaps a majority of recent commentators have favoured Jehoiachin, and taken the past tenses of the lament as referring to events which have already taken place.[56] However, I think he is a less likely candidate than Zedekiah, the current ruler. In the first place, as Allen points out, there is every possibility that a prophetic lament like this is predictive in intent, and the fate of Jehoahaz serves as a model for what will befall Zedekiah.[57] Secondly, the lament makes much of the lioness who bore the two cubs, and Zedekiah did in fact share the same mother as Jehoahaz, the queen mother Hamutal.[58] Moreover, the language of snare, net, and deportation used in 19: 8–9 seems highly appropriate to Zedekiah, since Ezekiel uses similar language to describe his fate in 12: 13 and 17: 20.[59] More generally, it is Zedekiah who is the constant focus of prophetic outrage, while Jehoiachin hardly features in Ezekiel's criticism. Indeed, Jehoiachin is, by contrast with Zedekiah, dignified with the title מלך (1: 2; 17: 12).[60]

Again the tendency to read Ezekiel too theologically makes interpreters underplay the political content of this oracle, and to some extent the identification of the second lion with Jehoiachin fits in with this. Thus Duguid, who sees the principal sins of the monarchy as oppression and injustice, finds nothing in chapter 19 suggestive of foreign policy as an issue important in the minds of the rulers and significant for the fall of Jerusalem. Its reference is 'no longer now the political sins of chapter 17 but the moral sin of oppressing their people'.[61] The violence of the lion who 'devoured

---

[55] Supported by Noth, 'The Jerusalem Catastrophe of 587 BC and its Significance for Israel', in *The Laws in the Pentateuch and Other Essays* (Edinburgh, 1966), 273–4; Stalker, *Ezekiel*, 166; Begg, 'Identity', 368; Block, *Ezekiel 1–24*, 605–6.

[56] See e.g. Wevers, *Ezekiel*, 112–13; Zimmerli, *Ezekiel 1*, 394–5; May, 'Ezekiel', 165; Cooke, *Ezekiel*, 204–5; Gottwald, *All the Kingdoms*, 309–10; Duguid, *Leaders*, 35–6.

[57] Allen, *Ezekiel 1–19*, 288.

[58] This identification is recently supported by I. Kottsieper, '"Was ist deine Mutter?" Eine Studie zu Ez 19, 2–9', *ZAW* 105 (1993), 444–61. Also Fohrer, *Ezechiel*, 106: Eichrodt, *Ezekiel*, 253–6; Lang, *Ezechiel*, 102–3.

[59] Seitz, *Theology in Conflict*, 137.

[60] For more discussion of the contrast between Zedekiah and Jehoiachin in Ezekiel see Seitz, *Theology in Conflict*, 122–3, 130–1.

[61] Duguid, *Leaders*, 36.

men' (19: 6) is paralleled by the accusation made against the נשיאם in 22: 25:

> Her princes in the midst of her are like a roaring lion tearing the prey; they have devoured human lives; they have taken treasure and precious things; they have made many widows in the midst of her.[62]

Domestic oppression may be an element in the oracle of chapter 19, but the language of destruction might equally refer to military defeat, and Judah certainly suffered most because of her ruler's failure to avoid war. If we accept the identification of the second lion cub with Zedekiah, then the statement that he 'prowled among the lions' can be seen as an allusion to the king's dealings with Egypt, and another political event of 594, when the king assembled a meeting of the western kings to plot rebellion (Jer. 27: 1–11).[63] The oracle looks to Zedekiah's arrogant foreign policy as a source of the disaster which will overtake him and his city. We have seen that such political concerns belong to factions within the ruling class. These are the people whom Nebuchadnezzar deported, and we find in Ezekiel's oracles evidence that the community in Babylon was made up of people for whom these upper-class political debates were an issue. In short, the political content of the book of Ezekiel reflects the concerns of that portion of society which 2 Kings described as comprising the exiles.

## Domestic Politics: Social Justice

Even if social justice is not the principal focus of Ezekiel 19, the book does contain a number of oracles where injustice is seen as responsible for the fall of Jerusalem. In particular, the leaders of society, the king and ruling classes, are attacked for their greed and violence, which is normally described in fairly general terms. Typical is chapter 7, which is addressed to 'the land of Israel' and opens with a twice-repeated announcement of imminent disaster, a sign of the divine wrath and punishment of 'all your abominations'. These are filled out in verses 10–11:

---

[62] Zimmerli comments: 'in substance we are reminded of the crimes of the king in 2 Sam. 11 and 1 Kings 21, as well as of Jer 22: 17' (*Ezekiel 1*, 468).

[63] Allen, *Ezekiel 1–19*, 208; Brownlee, *Ezekiel 1–19*, Word Biblical Commentary, 28 (Waco, Tex., 1986), 302. Brownlee also considers v. 7a to refer to foreign rather than domestic policy.

Behold, the day! Behold, it comes! Your doom has come, injustice[64] has blossomed, pride has budded. Violence has grown into a rod of wickedness; none of them shall remain

The chapter ends with a further prediction of doom and national bewilderment prefaced by another general attack on violence in society (7: 23–4):

Because the land is full of bloody crimes and the city is full of violence, I will bring the worst of nations to take possession of their houses

Most of Ezekiel's references to social wrongdoing are as general as this; they tend not to single out any specific abuse but use words like 'violence', 'injustice', or 'bloodshed' to conjure up a picture of lawlessness and disorder. The word for 'violence', חמס, which appears in 7: 11, 23; 8: 17; 12: 19 (cf. also 28: 16; 45: 9), is fairly common in the Hebrew Bible, and reasonably spread throughout all sorts of literature.[65] However, the use of דמים ('bloodshed'), as a metaphor for social evils is one which Ezekiel makes more his own. It is probably the most common designation in Ezekiel for all those sins not already covered by idolatry (see e.g. 7: 23; 9: 9; 18: 13; 22: 2; 24: 6, 9).[66]

A few oracles of judgement do take social justice as their main theme, most notably in chapters 11, 22, and 34. Ezekiel 22 provides the most extensive treatment of social injustice. The chapter addresses the 'bloody city' Jerusalem, and condemns a wide range of offences. The catalogue of sins in 22: 6–12 contains a wide range of social, sexual, and cultic crimes,[67] and the first wrongdoers on the list are the נשיאי ישראל, the 'princes of Israel', who 'have been bent on shedding blood' (22: 6). This probably refers to the royal house, Zedekiah and his family, and possibly also to his predecessors.[68] In the latter part of the chapter (22: 25–9) a range of society's leaders are attacked for failing to fulfil their responsibilities. One

---

[64] Reading הַמַּטֶּה ('injustice, perversion'; cf. 9: 9) for MT הַמַּטֶּה ('the rod'): so Fohrer, *Ezechiel*, 43; Zimmerli, *Ezekiel 1*, 196; Wevers, *Ezekiel*, 63; Allen, *Ezekiel 1–19*, 100.

[65] See H. Haag, 'חמס', *TDOT*, iv. 478–87.

[66] The language is drawn from the priestly sphere; I shall discuss it in more detail in Chapter 5, below.

[67] There are close parallels between 22: 6–12 and 18: 5–18, where themes of social justice are also raised. However, the context in 18: 5–18 is not an oracle proclaiming the downfall of Jerusalem, but a series of test cases which serve to define the righteous and the wicked. I shall examine 22: 6–12 in more detail as part of my discussion of Ezekiel 18 below, Chapter 6.

[68] See e.g. M. Greenberg, *Ezekiel 21–37*, Anchor Bible, 22A (NY, 1997), 454.

of the main criticisms Ezekiel makes is that people are not doing their jobs properly. In 7: 26–7 the perplexity of prophet, priest, elders, and king comes as a result of YHWH's judgement, but in 22: 23–31 they themselves are responsible: the princes violent, priests profane and prophets false, while the people of the land imitate their leaders in robbery, extortion, and oppression.[69]

Elsewhere in the book the leaders are also at fault. Ezekiel 11: 1–13 describes Ezekiel's vision of twenty-five men, who are 'the men who devise iniquity and give wicked counsel in this city', and appear to be members of the political élite. They include the named individuals 'Jaazaniah the son of Azzur' and 'Pelatiah the son of Benaiah', who are described as שרי העם ('princes of the people'), implying their membership of the ruling class, if not some official position.[70] These men are charged with making the statement לא בקרוב בנות בתים ('the building of houses is not near'). This expression is difficult to interpret, but one possibility is that they may not need to build houses because they have already been seizing those belonging to other people.[71] They are further accused in verse 6: 'You have multiplied your slain in this city, and filled the streets with your slain.' A number of recent commentators see this as referring to acts of violence on the part of the accused men, perhaps judicial murder. So, for example, Rainer Kessler writes: 'Es ist also wohl an den Vorwurf zu denken, daß die Beamten, sei es durch Justizmord, sei es durch nackte Gewalttaten, eien erheblich Zahl von Menschenleben auf dem Gewissen haben.'[72]

Ezekiel 34 is an extensive allegory which uses the imagery of sheep and shepherd to represent the affairs of Judah. The first part of the oracle (34: 1–6) attacks the 'shepherds of Israel' and accuses them of fattening themselves at the expense of their sheep and of ruling harshly. It is likely that these shepherds are the kings of Judah, past and present.[73] The image of the king as a shepherd

[69] Cf. Block, *Ezekiel 1–24*, 727.

[70] Wevers, *Ezekiel*, 76; cf. also Duguid, *Leaders*, 110; Block, *Ezekiel 1–24*, 331.

[71] My translation and interpretation follows Fohrer, *Ezechiel*, 59–60; Allen, *Ezekiel 1–19*, 117, 160.

[72] R. Kessler, *Staat und Gesellschaft im vorexilischen Juda vom 8. Jahrhundert bis zum Exil*, SVT 47 (Leiden, 1992), 99; see also Cooke, *Ezekiel*, 122; Wevers, *Ezekiel*, 77; Allen, *Ezekiel 1–19*, 161.

[73] Allen, *Ezekiel 1–19*, 161; Duguid, *Leaders*, 39–40. Greenberg includes not only Jehoiachin and Zedekiah, but also their 'advisors and officials, all in disgrace' (*Ezekiel 21–37*, 694–5).

who protects his people is a common one in the ancient Near East.[74] There is, moreover, a close parallel between this passage and Jeremiah 23: 1–2, which is often believed to be about Jehoiakim and Zedekiah.[75] On the other hand, the reference to exile as the fate of the sheep who 'were scattered all over the face of the earth' may suggest that Ezekiel is condemning his contemporaries. In that case the prophet would have had in mind not only Zedekiah himself, but also the whole leadership stratum of Judah.[76] A second part of the oracle addresses conflict between different members of the flock, and attacks the economically privileged 'fat sheep' who have 'abandoned the traditional responsibility of the upper class for the social well-being of the other classes'.[77]

The claim is often made that the prophets suppressed their own class interests in order to defend those less fortunate than themselves. Thus Albertz writes: 'the strength of their religious motivation makes it clear how much they could detach themselves from the interest and views of their classes. Their religious impulse set them at a distance from themselves and their origins.'[78] In all these oracles Ezekiel stands up for the rights of poorer members of Judaean society, and it might be argued that when he does this he is no longer participating in a moral discourse that is restricted to the political élite. Certainly it is true that those members of subordinate classes who were adversely affected would have had some way of voicing their grievance, and might well have expressed themselves in language similar to Ezekiel's. Moreover, issues of social justice are far less clearly tied to state institutions, like the temple or the army, than are the issues of foreign policy that we discussed earlier in the chapter. But, on the other hand, it would be wrong to assume that a moral debate about social justice is out of place among the political élite. As was mentioned in the discussion of Israelite society in Chapter 1, it was important for rulers to present themselves as just and benign, in order to achieve their aims with the minimum of coercion. Throughout

---

[74] For discussion see Zimmerli, *Ezekiel 2*, 213–14; Block, *Ezekiel 25–48*, 279–82.

[75] McKane, *Jeremiah I-XXV*, 555, 559.

[76] Kessler, *Staat und Gesellschaft*, 112–13; Fohrer, *Ezechiel*, 192. Carroll makes the same point about the Jeremiah passage (*Jeremiah*, 444).

[77] Duguid, *Leaders*, 122.

[78] Albertz, *History of Israelite Religion*, i. 164.

the ancient Near East kings proclaimed the just way they treated
their subjects; this was seen as a sign of divine favour, and therefore a legitimation of their rule. In the Hebrew Bible the relationship between social justice and royal power is probably clearest in
Psalm 72, where we find juxtaposed:

> May all kings fall down before him, all nations serve him!
> For he delivers the needy when he calls, the poor and him who
>     has no helper.
> He has pity on the weak and the needy, and saves the lives of the
>     needy.
> From oppression and violence he redeems their life; and precious
>     is their blood in his sight.
> Long may he live, may Gold of Sheba be given to him!
>
> (Ps. 72: 11–15a)

The king's political power and right to receive tribute are expressly justified by his care for the poor. If such a psalm, which has its
original context within the royal cult, places such a high premium
on justice, then we have no cause to assume that a critique like
Ezekiel's comes from anywhere other than élite circles.[79] Moreover, if rulers used images of social justice and harmony to express
their political legitimacy, it is not surprising that their opponents
would attack them on the same grounds. An intriguing example
is drawn from Ugaritic literature. In the epic of Keret an ambi-
tious prince challenges his father's right to govern, and it is
significant that this takes the form of an accusation of injustice to
the poor:

> You have been brought down by your failing power.
> You do not judge the cause of the widow,
> You do not try the case of the importunate.
> You do not banish the extortioners of the poor,
> you do not feed the orphan before your face
> (nor) the widow behind your back.[80]

King Keret's failure to act in these ways is seen as responsible for
the shaking of the moral order in the land; his neglect of the poor

---

[79] On Ps. 72 see e.g. K. W. Whitelam, *The Just King: Monarchical Judicial Authority in Ancient Israel*, JSOTS 12 (Sheffield, 1979), 29.
[80] J. C. L. Gibson, *Canaanite Myths and Legends* (Edinburgh, 1978), 102.

has undermined his right to rule. Significantly for our point of view, the accusation of injustice which challenges Keret's right to rule is made not by one of those who are suffering, but by his son, another member of the political élite.

Admittedly this is legend rather than history, but I believe that we are justified in suggesting that social criticism may form part of a political debate that takes place within élite circles. Given the degree to which Ezekiel's political opinions about foreign policy show him to be operating within such an élite moral world, it is most plausible to see the social criticism which he addresses to Jerusalem as part of that same moral world. As in the case of foreign policy, it is unlikely that Ezekiel was actually attempting to advise on specific courses of action; most of his criticism is too general for that to be the case. The prophet's invective builds up a picture of Jerusalem and its rulers as so corrupt that total destruction is the only option left to YHWH.

While social justice is an important theme in Ezekiel's message, it is not as prominent as international relations. We can see from the preceding survey that international politics is one area in which moral decisions that affect the future of the people of Israel can be taken. Ezekiel is clear that in Judah's relations with its foreign neighbours, and especially with the great empires, we find one of the roots of YHWH's anger, and his decision to destroy his nation. While Ezekiel goes further than any of his predecessors in equating Nebuchadnezzar's treaty with YHWH's covenant, the area of moral engagement here is one familiar to us from other prophets. As in Isaiah and Jeremiah, we find that a concern to influence foreign policy forms a substantial part of the prophet's message. This is an activity which is most relevant to a ruling élite which has some stake in the decisions to be made. Isaiah and Jeremiah can be seen as participants in a political struggle within the ruling classes of Judah; as we have seen, political factions tend to be drawn from different occupational groups within the political classes, and in the work of the prophets we may see an attempt to provide religious legitimation for their political platform. This is true of Ezekiel: as prophet and priest he is primarily a 'religious' rather than a 'political' figure, but the effect of his prophecy is to provide religious legitimation for those who are opposed to revolt. He is less influential because of his distance from those active in policy-making.

In this context we must not underestimate the importance of religious legitimation in ancient agrarian societies like Judah.[31] The care of the gods was as fundamental to the ordering of society as one's domestic policies and foreign relations. In particular, the state cult was organized to bring blessing and prosperity to a nation (or at least its ruling élite). Thus theology itself can become a political issue, and the politics of religion are as important a part of the debates of pre-exilic Judah as the rest of policy-making. It is therefore not surprising that theological and cultic issues feature so prominently in Ezekiel's oracles, and it is to his treatment of the politics of cult that I shall turn in the next chapter.

[31] See e.g. Lenski, *Power and Privilege*, 260.

# 4

# The Politics of Cult

There can be little question that Ezekiel, of all the prophets, is most concerned with matters of cult, and his priestly background is often invoked as the source of numerous features of the book. Among the most central of these is the idea that YHWH's presence in his temple at Jerusalem is the guarantee of safety and prosperity for his people; thus the god's abandonment of his dwelling-place in chapters 8–11 marks the beginning of the end for his people. I have suggested that in thinking about Ezekiel's ethical distinctiveness it is useful to apply the notion of a dual moral world. Ezekiel's audience in Babylonia are members of the Jerusalem political élite, who in the experience of exile are suffering a substantial loss of status and identity. These two moral worlds are ones in which substantially different kinds of moral decision are open to members of the community, and this is as true of cult as it is of the rest of life. It is highly significant that the language of cult and ritual dominates the prophet's analysis of past sin, present judgement, and future hope. The Jerusalem temple, even after its destruction, remains the central symbol around which the community can order its life in exile.[1] In this chapter I propose to examine the cult in the book of Ezekiel, but to continue thinking about the Jerusalem side of the exiles' experience, their participation in the moral world of the Jerusalem élite.

I have argued in the previous chapter that Ezekiel's treatment of foreign policy belongs to the moral world of those members of the Jerusalem political élite whom Nebuchadnezzar exiled in 597 BCE. I shall argue here that Ezekiel's attitude to the cult also shows the prophet to be operating within this moral and political world. Despite the general nature of much of his criticism, whenever he provides detailed examples of cultic apostasy to explain the fall of Jerusalem it is not the 'popular' religion of the masses that he attacks, but a failure to maintain the state cult correctly. These

[1] I shall discuss this at length in my next chapter, 'Ritual and Ethics'.

lengthy diatribes show a concern with the two aspects of religious policy most associated with the Deuteronomic reform: idolatry and cult centralization. His positive attitude to cult centralization evident in chapters 6 and 20 draws heavily on the theological and political programme of the Josianic reform. His cultic *pièce de résistance*, chapter 8, attacks the pollution of the state cult by non-Yahwistic and foreign influences. Furthermore, in the extended allegories of chapters 16 and 23 we find the combination of sin in foreign policy and cultic irregularity paraded with an obscene thoroughness. Moreover, we find that if specific individuals or groups of people are mentioned as responsible for the cultic improprieties, they too are normally drawn from the political élite. Although his theological and political programme is not identical to that of the Deuteronomists, his concentration on similar issues suggests that Ezekiel is participating in the same world of upper-class moral and political discourse as he was in the case of foreign policy.

## Cult and Politics in Judah

As we saw in our introductory discussion of moral worlds and Israelite ethics, ancient Israel and Judah can be classified as 'agrarian societies', and in all such societies religion was a very important part of social life and of the state machinery.[2] An appeal to higher authority provided much of the legitimacy which was vital for any regime to rule successfully and to maintain peaceful relations with its own people. John Kautsky makes a useful generalization: 'The legitimacy and authority of the aristocracy rests on claims of divine sanction and on tradition—and tradition itself is usually inextricably interwoven with religious elements in aristocratic empires . . . Those who maintain and propagate religion, then, play an important part in maintaining aristocrats in power.'[3]

Not only do the religious authorities provide authority for those who are in power, they also form part of the administrative machinery of state, as temples provide convenient places to collect

[2] See above, Ch. 1.
[3] Kautsky, *Aristocratic Empires*, 159; see also Eisenstadt, *Political Systems of Empires*, 140–2; Lenski, *Power and Privilege*, 260.

taxes, keep records of population, and perform other administrative tasks.[4] Moreover, in a society like ancient Israel, where little or no distinction is made between the state and its religion, the line between religion and politics is inevitably blurred. We should not be surprised to see religious leaders participating in the same political factions as their secular counterparts:[5] debates about religion have an inevitable political significance. John S. Holladay, jun., writes:

The dominant religious structure within any nation-state of the Iron II period in the general Syro-Palestinian setting almost certainly paralleled the political structure of the state, confirming and complementing the overtly political state governments with the stipulations, sanctions, and blessings of the true rulers of the universe.[6]

Like decisions about taxation, about the army, or about foreign policy, decisions about the state cult fell into the range of moral possibilities open to the political élite. The other side of this coin is, of course, that religious heterodoxy, especially where it concerns the state cult, must be seen in the context of upper-class factional politics. 'As a parallel apparatus to the purely political organization, such a religious structure could no more suffer "political", that is to say, religious, heterodoxy than could the political apparatus.'[7] The differing religious and political ideologies of groups within the ruling élite can be expected to have practical consequences in the ordering of the cult. This is indeed what we find in the Hebrew Bible. In particular, throughout the books of Kings, cultic reforms are associated with changes of government in both the northern and southern kingdoms. It is often pointed out that the interests of Kings are much more religious than political, and it is clearly true that much more space is given to matters of cult than to economy or even foreign policy.[8] However, the dichotomy between the religious and the political is a false one: 'From start to finish, the official religion

---

[4] For full discussion of this phenomenon in ancient Israel and Judah, see G. W. Ahlström, *Royal Administration and National Religion in Ancient Palestine* (Leiden, 1982).

[5] See above, Ch. 3.

[6] J. S. Holladay, jun., 'Religion in Israel and Judah under the Monarchy: An Explicitly Archaeological Approach', in Miller, Hanson, and McBride (eds.), *Ancient Israelite Religion*, 266.

[7] Ibid. 266.

[8] See e.g. J. A. Soggin, *Introduction to the Old Testament*, 3rd edn. (London, 1989), 226; G. von Rad, *Old Testament Theology* (Edinburgh, 1965), i. 343.

of Judah legitimated royal political claims and expressed royal interests. Cult reforms—in Judah always led by kings—also were intended to serve the social-political interests of the monarchy.'[9]

A few examples should suffice: Jeroboam's most significant action, from the point of view of the Deuteronomistic historian, was to set up alternative shrines to Jerusalem: the new state requires its own state religious apparatus (1 Kgs. 12: 25–33). Jehu's prophetically inspired reform involved the removal of the worship of Baal and Asherah from Israel, and its replacement by a purer cult of YHWH: his new regime is given legitimacy by the revitalized YHWH religion (2 Kgs. 9–10). In Judah the removal of Queen Athaliah is accompanied by the destruction of her temple of Baal and the execution of its priest (2 Kgs. 11). The kings of Judah whom the Deuteronomists praise most highly, Hezekiah and Josiah, are those who pursued a policy of national independence accompanied by extensive cultic reforms.[10] Lohfink has argued convincingly that the account of the reform in 2 Kings 22–3 contains genuine historical information, and he accepts the general picture of the reform it gives.[11] Two religious issues dominated this reform. The first was the centralization of the cult in the Jerusalem temple, and the second the removal of all forms of idolatry, both native and foreign. It is important to recognize that Josiah's reign was a time when Judah could reassert its political independence, and the reforms were part of a revival of nationalism:

Josiah's deuteronomic reform was not an act of political rebellion . . . Rather it was the core of a post-imperial cultural revolution by which the monarch sought to create a nationalist consciousness fitting Judah's newly independent status. Political independence from Assyria had already occurred via the demise of imperial power in the west. Josiah's reform sought cultural independence as well.[12]

It has often been argued that the reform account was written as propaganda for Josiah: its presentation of the king acting according to YHWH's revealed will supports the religious and political

[9] R. H. Lowery, *The Reforming Kings: Cults and Society in First Temple Judah*, JSOTS 120 (Sheffield, 1991), 210.

[10] We should probably also think of Manasseh's changes to the cult as religious and political reforms; see Ahlström, *Royal Administration*, 67–9, 75–81.

[11] Lohfink, 'Cult Reform', 459–76.

[12] Lowery, *Reforming Kings*, 216.

aims of the reform.[13] But for whom was this propaganda written? Not the mass of the population whose lives will have been little changed by any decisions made at the top, but the political élites upon whose support Josiah depended for the peace and security of his kingdom. Thus the issues and arguments which surrounded Josiah's reforms were clearly of interest to Judah's upper classes, who were the only people with the influence to affect the royal policy.

If we turn to Ezekiel's world—Jerusalem after the death of Josiah—what would we expect to be the main religious-political issues of the day? The main political issue remained the problem of imperial domination. The independence of Josiah's reign proved to be short-lived, and, as we have seen, during the years between his death in 609 BCE and the fall of Jerusalem in 587 Judah once again became a pawn in the power struggle between Egypt and Mesopotamia, this time represented by the Babylonians.[14] Josiah's successors did not continue with his policy of political independence, and it is likely that many of his religious reforms lapsed as well.[15] There is enough evidence in Kings, Jeremiah, and Ezekiel to suggest that opponents of the Deuteronomists became the holders of political power, and we should expect that they made changes or reforms to the cult that they inherited. These opponents could easily have said that YHWH 'was angry at Josiah's "apostasy", at his suppression of the high places and the like'.[16] Thus it appears very likely that the issues of the Josianic reformation continued to set the religious side of the political agenda.

## Cultic Apostasy and the Fall of Jerusalem

Ezekiel's condemnation of cultic apostasy certainly focuses on similar religious issues to those associated with the reform of the state cult. His interests and emphases are not identical to those of

---

[13] Lohfink, 'Cult Reform', 469, following F. M. Cross, *Canaanite Myth and Hebrew Epic: Essays in the History of the Religion of Israel* (Cambridge, Mass., 1973), 274–89; R. D. Nelson, *The Double Redaction of the Deuteronomic History*, JSOTS 18 (Sheffield, 1981).

[14] See above, Ch. 2.

[15] A matter of considerable debate, which I shall discuss more fully at the end of this chapter.

[16] M. Smith, 'The Veracity of Ezekiel, the Sins of Manasseh, and Jeremiah 44: 18', *ZAW* 87 (1975), 14.

the Deuteronomists, but there are enough areas of overlap to suggest that he is a participant in very similar debates. What is now required is a closer examination of the cultic improprieties against which Ezekiel rails. What are they? Who performs them? What is their political or cultural significance? I propose to concentrate on Ezekiel's treatment of the two main issues of the Josianic reform: idolatry and cult centralization. I shall begin by examining some of the condemnations of cultic apostasy throughout the book, then go on to examine the most extensive selection in chapter 8.

Ezekiel's oracles of judgement powerfully condemn the people of Judah for their failure to worship YHWH correctly in his holy city, and, indeed, cultic apostasy is perhaps the most important reason that the prophet gives for the fall of the city.[17] Often Ezekiel's oracles simply predict destruction for the people and city, without specifying the crimes being punished. Only in chapter 5 do we begin to receive more detail about the actions of Judah which have provoked YHWH's fierce anger:

Thus says the Lord GOD: This is Jerusalem; I have set her in the centre of the nations, with countries round about her. And she has wickedly rebelled against my ordinances more than the nations, and against my statutes more than the countries round about her, by rejecting my ordinances and not walking in my statutes. (Ezek. 5: 5–6)

This failure to observe statutes and ordinances is very characteristic of Ezekiel's more general complaints, and certainly includes the failure to observe correct cultic practice. Although Jerusalem is compared unfavourably to the nations this does not mean that the nations are guiltless. The statutes and ordinances of the nations may refer to 'all religious and moral precepts and rules',[18] but where the nations are condemned in the Hebrew tradition it is often for their cultic failures, especially within literature influenced by the Deuteronomic reform. The criticism of Jerusalem in 5: 7–8 is followed in verse 11 by another complaint which, while still fairly general, begins to flesh out what Ezekiel finds so objectionable about his people's behaviour that immediate judgement is called for:

---

[17] Von Rad, *Old Testament Theology*, ii. 224.
[18] D. M. G. Stalker, *Ezekiel: Introduction and Commentary* (London, 1968), 72.

Wherefore as I live, says the Lord GOD, surely because you have defiled my sanctuary with all your detestable things and with all your abominations, therefore I will cut you down: my eye will not spare, and I will have no pity.

'My sanctuary' is, of course, the Jerusalem temple. The 'detestable things' (שִׁקּוּצִים) are almost certainly idols of some kind, and although the word 'abomination' (תּוֹעֵבָה) sometimes has a broader significance, it too can refer to idols. Michael Fishbane has described the general complaints of 5: 6 and 11 concerning rebellion against the laws and defilement of the sanctuary as 'the two topics which recur with similar generality or greater specificity throughout Ezekiel's oracles'.[19] Thus the cult is always at the centre of the prophet's interests.

The connections between Ezekiel and priestly tradition are very strong, and Clements expresses a popular opinion when he writes: 'Whereas all the theological connections of the book of Jeremiah are with the Deuteronomic movement, those of Ezekiel are to be found in the work of the emergent Priestly school.'[20] Here, in 5: 6, the words for 'statutes' and 'ordinances', חֻקּוֹת and מִשְׁפָּטִים, have their closest parallels in priestly literature. Notably, the form חֻקּוֹת is favoured by the Holiness Code (and Ezekiel), whereas Deuteronomy tends to use חֻקִּים.[21] That there is a particularly close relationship between Ezekiel and the Holiness Code is undisputed, but the precise nature of that relationship has proved difficult to define.[22] Henning Graf Reventlow has examined the numerous connections between the two, and suggested that there is no direct dependence of one upon the other, but both have a shared background in a priestly liturgy of covenant renewal.[23] However, his speculation about a common cultic origin cannot be demonstrated, and perhaps a more likely

---

[19] M. Fishbane, 'Sin and Judgment in the Prophecies of Ezekiel', *Int* 38 (1984), 133.

[20] R. E. Clements, 'The Ezekiel Tradition: Prophecy in a Time of Crisis', in R. J. Coggins, A. Phillips, and M. Knibb (eds.), *Israel's Prophetic Tradition: Essays in Honour of Peter Ackroyd* (Cambridge, 1982), 126.

[21] See Matties, *Ezekiel 18*, 176–8. חֻקּוֹת appears in conjunction with מִשְׁפָּטִים in Lev. 18: 4, 5, 26; 19: 37; 20: 22; 25: 18; 26: 14–15, 43; Ezek. 5: 6–7; 11: 20; 18: 9, 17; 20: 11, 13, 16, 19; 37: 24; 44: 24; חֻקִּים in Deut. 4: 1, 5, 8, 14, 45; 5: 1, 31; 6: 1, 20; 7: 11; 11: 32; 12: 1; 26: 16, 17.

[22] For discussion see K. W. Carley, *Ezekiel Among the Prophets: A Study of Ezekiel's Place in Prophetic Tradition*, SBT, 2nd ser., 31 (London, 1975), 62–5; Matties, *Ezekiel 18*, 11–13; Allen, *Ezekiel 1–19*, 92–6.

[23] H. G. Reventlow, *Wächter über Israel: Ezechiel und seine Tradition*, BZAW 82 (Berlin, 1962).

proposal is that Ezekiel had access to an earlier version of H than is found in the present book of Leviticus.[24] Zimmerli considers the influence to be reciprocal, and suggests that 'the circles which must have given H its (pre-P Document) form must not be sought too far from the circles which transmitted the book of Ezekiel'.[25] Whatever the exact relationship, what seems clear is that many of Ezekiel's moral opinions are 'plainly based on a tradition of covenant law'.[26] From the point of view of our study of moral worlds, however, the precise nature of the influence is less important than the general level of culture to which the traditions belong. If their source was the Jerusalem temple—Judah's state cult—then we may be confident that the language is at least as appropriate as Deuteronomistic language for Ezekiel to condemn cultic apostasy among Judah's élite.

As Ezekiel's criticism of Judah takes shape, both idolatry and cult centralization are to the fore. As has been pointed out before, much of Ezekiel's religious polemic is very general in nature, but idolatry (often alongside bloodshed) takes pride of place in his generalizations about the state of the nation. More than worship outside the central sanctuary, idolatry is the sin which provokes the prophet's anger. In 22: 3 he attacks the 'city of blood': 'A city that sheds blood in the midst of her, that her time may come, and that makes idols to defile herself!' In 36: 18 he summarizes the reasons for the fall of Jerusalem: 'So I poured out my wrath upon them for the blood which they had shed in the land, for the idols with which they had defiled it.'

Ezekiel attacks idolatry in all sorts of contexts. It appears not only in criticism of the present state of the city, but in all of the prophet's extensive historical retrospects (chapters 16; 20; 23). The two allegories of Jerusalem as an adulterous wife stress idolatry alongside failure in foreign policy as leading to the city's downfall, and it takes pride of place in the long account of Israel's failings in chapter 20. Here the prophet accuses the whole community of being apostate even at the time of the exodus from Egypt, when they did not forsake the idols of Egypt (20: 8). Their disobedience continues through the wilderness period and the occupation of the land, right up to Ezekiel's present audience in exile. The oracle contains quite general language concerning the failure to obey

---

[24] Allen, *Ezekiel 1–19*, 96.       [25] Zimmerli, *Ezekiel 1*, 52.
[26] Carley, *Ezekiel Among the Prophets*, 65.

statutes and ordinances and the more specific critique of sabbath breaking alongside the condemnation of idolatry, but it would appear that the prophet conceives of idolatry as the root sin. It is the first sin mentioned, and is given priority in 20: 16 at least: 'they rejected my ordinances and did not walk in my statutes, and profaned my sabbaths; *for their heart went after their idols*'. Idolatry would appear to be the sin that explains the others.

Idolatry is not only a communal crime but also figures in the more individualistic contexts of chapters 14 and 18. In many of the more general cases it is difficult to see exactly what the idolatry involves, what were the particular cultic offences which so outraged the prophet. In cases like chapters 14 and 18 it is easy to see the problem as one of individual or private religious practice. But it is significant that in these particular chapters idolatry is not specifically connected with the fall of Jerusalem.[27] Elsewhere it is not private idolatry, nor even the expression of popular religiosity, but the correct maintenance of the state cult which forms the focus of Ezekiel's concern. Those passages that describe the idolatry in some detail are all concerned with negative aspects of the state cult.

As well as the removal of idolatry, Josiah's religious reforms limited sacrificial worship to one place: the altar in the sanctuary of the Jerusalem temple. This theology of the central sanctuary is fundamental to both Deuteronomistic and priestly understandings of worship, and so it is no surprise that we should find it in Ezekiel, although the motif is certainly less prominent than idolatry in the prophet's explanations of the present disaster. In Ezekiel it appears in 5: 5: 'This is Jerusalem: I have set her in the centre of the nations, with countries round about her.' Although the language is different, we are reminded of the Deuteronomistic refrain 'the place YHWH chose to put his name'.[28] The city's centrality is made even clearer in Ezekiel 38: 12 which speaks of the land as the 'navel of the earth'.[29] The place of Jerusalem at the centre of the nations implies its divine election; it is YHWH's action which has given Jerusalem her status. Zimmerli argues that the

[27] See discussion below, Ch. 6.

[28] See esp. Deut. 12; cf. Wevers, *Ezekiel*, 58; Zimmerli, *Ezekiel 1*, 174–5; Block, *Ezekiel 1–24*, 197–8.

[29] Heb: טבור הארץ. Specific reference to the navel as the centre of the earth is common throughout the theologies of the ancient Near East and Greece; see Zimmerli, *Ezekiel 2*, 311; Stalker, *Ezekiel*, 71.

word שמתיה ('I have set her') in 5: 5 implies that Jerusalem's pre-
eminent position is not natural but 'rests on divine affirmation'.[30]
And certainly the vision of Ezekiel 9 in which the destroyers are
commanded to 'begin from my sanctuary' shows the disastrous
consequences of failing to recognize the significance of YHWH's
choice of Jerusalem. Zimmerli goes on to suggest that the analogy
for the choice of Jerusalem is the election of the Davidic
monarchy: 'We are tempted to speak of an adoptionist motif
which appears here, similar to that in Ps. 2: 7 affirming the divine
sonship of the Davidic kings.'[31] This is surely correct: in both cases
we are moving in very similar social worlds and indeed thought
worlds. The legitimation of royal dynasty and royal sanctuary are
so closely tied together that it is no surprise to find that they share
common theological concepts.

This kind of theology does not provide the main thrust of the
Deuteronomistic treatment of the central sanctuary, where there
is a greater concentration on the condemnation of shrines outside
Jerusalem which contravene the proposed legislation. Perhaps the
most significant part of Deuteronomistic religious polemic (at least
in Kings) is the attack on the *bamoth*: 'high places'. Such condemnation is also present in the book of Ezekiel, if not to quite the
same degree as in Deuteronomistic literature.

Ezekiel 6 is a judgement addressed to the 'mountains of Israel',
which is first of all a designation for the whole land of Israel, but
also alludes to those places where illegitimate cultic activity went
on. Ezekiel, like the Deuteronomists, rejects utterly worship at
the so-called 'high places'. The allusion is made plain in 6: 3b:
'Behold I, even I, will bring a sword upon you, and I will destroy
your high places.' The bulk of the prophet's criticism is levelled at
the idolatrous worship of these sanctuaries, but the text also hints
at a concern with the central-sanctuary legislation.

What were these high places that caused so much offence to the
biblical authors? The word *bamah* seems to imply elevation of
some sort, and the main suggestions have been that it originally
refers either to a hill-top shrine or to a shrine whose principal
feature was some kind of raised platform for an altar.[32] However,

---

[30] Zimmerli, *Ezekiel 1*, 175.       [31] Ibid.

[32] See R. de Vaux, *Ancient Israel: Its Life and Institutions* (London, 1961), 284–8; P. H.
Vaughan, *The Meaning of 'bamâ' in the Old Testament: A Study of Etymological, Textual and
Archaeological Evidence*, SOTS Monograph Series, 3 (Cambridge, 1974).

neither of these derivations is able fully to explain the use of the term in the Hebrew Bible. 'Known usage of the word *bama* suggests that it refers to built constructions of urban provenance and without a noticeable locational preference for high ground.'[33] Richard Lowery describes them as follows: 'In deuteronomic literature, "high place" describes sanctuaries that are illegitimate and inferior, that is, all sanctuaries other than the Jerusalem temple.'[34] Despite the picturesque language of high hills and green trees, it is likely that the *bamoth* were not principally popular open-air sanctuaries but part of the official religious establishment of the state of Judah.[35] In Kings we discover that Solomon was accustomed to sacrifice at הבמה הגדולה at Gibeon (1 Kgs. 3: 4), and Jeroboam's state sanctuary at Bethel is also called a *bamah* (2 Kgs. 23: 15; cf. 1 Kgs. 13: 31–2).[36] It is, therefore, reasonable to suppose that these shrines were royal sanctuaries outside Jerusalem, which were 'an integral part of the First Temple system'.[37]

Such royal sanctuaries will have had a number of functions. Their principal purpose will have been to perform ritual service for the king's god YHWH. 'The high place represented the religious-political authority of the royal house and of its god Yahweh.'[38] Not only ritual service, but also the very presence of a public building helps to cement the link between State and God. Lowery argues further that the royal sanctuaries were also part of the administrative system of the State, serving as points for tax collection:

Deuteronomy's relatively elaborate discussion of tithe payment in a deuteronomic state without high places implies that, before the deuteronomic reform, people paid their tithes at the local high place. Echoes of this pre-deuteronomic system may be discerned in Deuteronomy's instructions to store the triennial tithe 'within your gates'.[39]

Thus we can see that any reform of the *bamoth* would have wide-ranging implications for the position of the royal house in the eyes of the people, and for their ability to raise taxes, without which they could neither finance their own luxurious lifestyles, nor pay

---

[33] W. B. Barrick, 'High Place', *Anchor Bible Dictionary*, iii. 197.
[34] Lowery, *Reforming Kings*, 78.
[35] Ahlström, *Royal Administration*, 66.
[36] We should possibly also think of royal cultic installations not mentioned in the Bible, such as those excavated at Arad and Kuntillet 'Ajrud (Ahlström, *Royal Administration*, 40–2).
[37] Lowery, *Reforming Kings*, 79.     [38] Ibid. 79.     [39] Ibid. 114.

the tribute demanded by Mesopotamian or Egyptian overlords. Moreover, their prominence in the cultic reforms of Hezekiah, Manasseh, and Josiah testify that the *bamoth* were a significant religious-political issue in late pre-exilic Judah.

Ezekiel here predicts destruction for the shrines and for their altars, whose worship he considered illegitimate: 'Your altars shall become desolate, and your incense altars shall be broken; and I will cast down your slain before your idols' (6: 4). The presence of altars indicates that the *bamoth* were places of sacrifice, which in the Deuteronomic reform was restricted to the temple in Jerusalem. Ezekiel also condemns what are called חמנים, which appear to be incense altars or incense burners placed on or near an altar: equally, there is no place for offering incense outside the central sanctuary.[40] There is substantial evidence, mostly Deuteronomistic, to suggest that the *bamoth* were in fact places of Yahwistic worship rather than that of other deities,[41] but Ezekiel here firmly associates them with idolatry. This is the first occurrence in the book of the word גלולים, which is Ezekiel's most characteristic term for 'idols' (39 out of 48 biblical occurrences), by which we should probably think of divine images or statues of some sort.[42] Outside Ezekiel the term appears most commonly in Kings, where it tends to refer to the idols worshipped by bad kings or removed by good ones (1 Kgs. 15: 12; 21: 26; 2 Kgs. 21: 11, 21; 23: 24). Zimmerli comments that 'since it is used in the book of Ezekiel without any closer definition, Ezekiel must have taken it up as a term already coined. Was it formed in the period of the reform?'[43] This seems very reasonable, and we should see Ezekiel's adoption of the language of the reform as evidence for his commitment to the religious and political debates of the Jerusalem political élite.

The grim punishment of the *bamoth* is to be concluded with the desecration of these 'holy' places, by the bodies and bones of the worshippers being scattered around the broken altars and

---

[40] See Eichrodt, *Ezekiel*, 94; Zimmerli, *Ezekiel 1*, 186; Greenberg, *Ezekiel 1–20*, 132. Block argues that the word חמנים actually means 'chapels' or some other kind of cultic buildings, in which case the connection with the central sanctuary law would be even clearer (*Ezekiel 1–24*, 225–6).

[41] See e.g. de Vaux, *Ancient Israel*, 288.

[42] Zimmerli, *Ezekiel 1*, 187: the usage in both Lev. 26: 30 and Jer. 50: 2 seems to make this explicit.

[43] Zimmerli, *Ezekiel 1*, 187; echoed by Greenberg, *Ezekiel 1–20*, 132.

impotent idols (6: 5–6), and the whole of the passage 6: 3–6 is reminiscent of Leviticus 26: 30 ff.:

And I will destroy your high places [במות] and cut down your incense altars [חמנים] and cast your dead bodies upon the dead bodies of your idols [גלולים]; and my soul will abhor you. And I will lay your cities waste and I will make your sanctuaries desolate, and I will not smell your pleasing odours

It is very likely that the threats in both Ezekiel and Leviticus come from the same circle, and that this condemnation of the *bamoth* as idolatrous is more influenced by priestly than Deuteronomistic theology. Where allusions to the Deuteronomic central-sanctuary law are found, commentators have often supposed these to be editorial additions. In 6: 13, we read:

And you shall know that I am the LORD, when their slain lie among their idols round about their altars, upon every high hill, on all the mountain tops, under every green tree, and under every leafy oak, wherever they offered pleasing odour to all their idols.

The similarity of this language to Deuteronomistic and Jeremian formulations about worship on the high places has led Zimmerli and others to pronounce this verse a later addition.[44] The other passage in Ezekiel which is particularly tied to polemic against the *bamoth* appears in 20: 27–9. Towards the climax of an oracle which recounts Israel's disobedience from the Egyptian bondage to the present, the prophet focuses on the sins of the recent past. As was the case in 6: 13 we find apparently Deuteronomistic language used of the Israelites in the land: 'wherever they saw any high hill or any leafy tree, there they offered their sacrifices and presented the provocation of their offering' (20: 28). This is followed by an aetiological pun (20: 29):[45]

ואמר אלהם מה הבמה אשר אתם הבאים שם ויקרא שמה במה עד הים הזה

Because of the pun here and the Deuteronomistic language preceding it commentators have often considered this passage secondary. Thus Zimmerli dismisses it as 'a piece of later exegetical elaboration' which concentrates 'in a Deuteronomistic

---

[44] Zimmerli, *Ezekiel 1*, 191; Fohrer, *Ezechiel*, 39–40.
[45] Greenberg offers the punning translation 'I said to them "What is the high-place you hie to?"—and it is called high-place to this day' (*Ezekiel 1–20*, 362).

manner' on the high places as Israel's most significant sin in the land.[46]

However, even if these two references to high place worship as contravening the central-sanctuary regulation are additional, there is further evidence that it mattered to Ezekiel himself, and not only his editors. The same condemnation of idolatry and high-place worship is also found in chapter 16, the first allegory of Jerusalem as an unfaithful wife. YHWH's speech, which reaches a climax with the humiliation and death of the woman, begins with the insulting accusation or reminder that Jerusalem's origins were Canaanite: 'your father was an Amorite, and your mother a Hittite' (16: 3). He goes on to describe how he found the child abandoned, cared for her, and finally married her, giving her lavish gifts of clothing, jewellery, and food. The terms which are used here are not only suggestive of opulence, but also serve to draw an analogy between the woman Jerusalem and the temple itself. Julie Galambush summarizes the points of contact:

> In fact, the woman is clothed in material (*tḥš*) mentioned elsewhere only as the covering for the tabernacle and its cultic paraphernalia (e.g., Exod 25: 5; 26: 14; 35: 7, 23; Num. 4: 6, 8, 10). Jerusalem's clothing includes *rqmh* and *šš* (v 10) . . . Outside of Ezek. 16: 10, the two roots are used together exclusively to describe the materials and furnishings of the tabernacle (Exod 26: 36; 27; 16; 28: 39; 35: 35; 36: 37; 38: 18, 23; 39: 29). The woman who is 'fit to be queen' (v 13) is adorned with the same materials that adorn Yahweh's holy place and is fed *slt* and *šmn* (v 13), offerings prescribed for the tabernacle.[47]

However, Jerusalem's response to this generosity is to turn away from YHWH to other lovers (vv. 15 ff.). Both here and in chapter 23 Ezekiel uses the most graphic imagery of prostitution and adultery. It is unlikely that actual cultic prostitution is at issue

---

[46] Zimmerli, *Ezekiel 1*, 412. Stalker, *Ezekiel*, 173; Cooke, *Ezekiel*, 220; J. Pons, 'Le Vocabulaire d'Ez 20: Le prophète s'oppose à la vision deutéronomiste de l'histoire', in Lust (ed.), *Ezekiel and his Book*, 225–6.

[47] Galambush, *Jerusalem in the Book of Ezekiel*, 95. In a note she points out that this association between the clothing of YHWH's wife and her symbolic identity as the temple/tabernacle is made explicit in the Targum: 'I clothed you in embroidered garments . . . and I put costly shoes upon your feet. And I consecrated priests from among you that they may serve before me in linen headgear, and the high priest in colorful vestments . . . And I placed my tabernacle in your midst, set with gold and silver and a curtain of linen and colored cloth and embroidery (S. H. Levey (tr.), *The Targum of Ezekiel*, The Aramaic Bible, 13 (Wilmington, Del., 1987), 50).

here: although this imagery using the verb זנה dominates the two extended allegories in chapters 16 and 23, it is rare in Ezekiel outside these two chapters. Zimmerli writes: 'It clearly does not belong to the widely used vocabulary of the prophet, but is wholly dependent on the simile of the unfaithful wife, which reached Ezekiel from Hosea and Jeremiah.'[48] Verses 16–20 take the gifts which YHWH gave to Jerusalem and show how she used each in turn for the service of her prostitution. Her first sin recalls the legislation against the high places as (in verse 16) she uses the garments she was given (in verse 10) to make 'gaily decked shrines' (במות טלאות). The woman's finery, representative of the furnishings of the temple, is used to decorate a different, and therefore illegitimate, site of worship. Greenberg draws a comparison with the adulteress in Proverbs 7: 16ff.:[49]

> I have decked my couch with coverings,
>   coloured spreads of Egyptian linen;
> I have perfumed my bed with myrrh, aloes, and cinnamon
> Come, let us take our fill of love till morning.

In Ezekiel 16 the *bamoth* take the place of the bed, as Jerusalem offers herself to all comers. In verses 24f. and 31 the words גב and רמה also recall the high places, and the idea of building these places 'in every square' and 'at the head of every street' is reminiscent of the Deuteronomistic 'on every high hill and under every green tree' as well as Jeremiah 11: 13: 'For your gods have become as many as your cities, O Judah; and as many as the streets of Jerusalem are the altars you have set up to shame, altars to burn incense to Baal.' In this case there is no clear literary dependence upon Deuteronomistic models, as there seems to have been in 6: 13 and 20: 27. More likely, we are dealing with the same theological idea expressed slightly differently. Given the close parallels between Ezekiel 6 and Leviticus 26 it seems reasonable to deduce that Ezekiel's polemic is taken from the milieu of priestly rather than Deuteronomistic theology, but in both cases the centrality of the Jerusalem sanctuary is an immovable datum of the religion. And if it is the case that the desire for centralized worship was fundamental to Ezekiel's theology, then perhaps we should not be

[48] Zimmerli, *Ezekiel 1*, 342.
[49] Greenberg, *Ezekiel 1–20*, 280.

so hasty to excise the more obviously Deuteronomistic passages in
6: 13 and 20: 27.[50]

Not only the *bamoth* are at issue: Jerusalem's faithlessness also
takes the form of idolatry. As in the previous verse she turned the
garments into shrines, in 16: 17 she takes the gifts of gold, silver,
and jewels which YHWH had given her and makes from them
צלמי זכר ('images of men' or 'male images') with which she pro-
ceeds to prostitute herself.[51] How important is the maleness of the
images? A popular suggestion has been that they represent
phallic symbols of one sort or another drawn from the so-called
'Canaanite fertility cult'.[52] Eichrodt supports this idea, saying that
the images of men 'may well suggest phallic images, as large
statues are unknown in Canaanite worship'.[53]

However, we are more likely to be dealing here with full representative images of gods than with phallic symbols, particularly
because of the description of the clothing and feeding of these
images. Although such a description is unique in the Hebrew
Bible, these activities formed an important part of the daily
temple service in Mesopotamia and Egypt, where the images of
the gods were elaborately cared for.[54] It may be that only male
gods like Baal or Molech are intended, but it is equally possible
that all other gods, male and female, are intended by this passage,
and the maleness of the imagery is just a result of the adultery
motif of which it forms a part.

The combination of *bamoth* and idolatry we have already seen
to be characteristic of the cultic concerns of the Josianic reformation, and perhaps here in chapter 16 Zimmerli is right to ask 'are

---

[50] There are numerous other points of contact between Ezekiel and Deuteronomistic
literature; for discussion see Carley, *Ezekiel Among the Prophets*, 57–62; Joyce, *Divine Initiative*,
119–24; Matties, *Ezekiel 18*, 13–17. Joyce makes the attractive suggestion: 'Whilst still in
Jerusalem, Ezekiel imbibed at least some of the concerns and style of the deuteronomistic
movement. These elements were reinforced both through an awareness of the Jeremiah
tradition and through the influence of deuteronomists active in the Babylonian exile'
(*Divine Initiative*, 123).

[51] The motif of using gold or jewellery to make idols is not uncommon in the Hebrew
Bible; in Ezekiel we find it again in 7: 20: 'Their beautiful ornament they used for vainglory, and they made their abominable images (lit. "images of their abominations") and
their detestable things of it.'

[52] Wevers, *Ezekiel*, 98; Stalker, *Ezekiel*, 143; Eichrodt, *Ezekiel*, 207; Galambush, *Jerusalem
in the Book of Ezekiel*, 66; D. J. Halperin, *Seeking Ezekiel: Text and Psychology* (University Park,
Pa., 1993), 147, 149.

[53] Eichrodt, *Ezekiel*, 207.

[54] Cf. Greenberg, *Ezekiel 1–20*, 280.

we to think of the age of Manasseh?'.[55] Moreover, we are again reminded of Manasseh as the description of Jerusalem abusing YHWH's gifts reaches its climax in 16: 20–1 with the sacrifice of children:

And you took your sons and your daughters whom you had borne to me and these you sacrificed to them [the images of men] to be devoured. Were your harlotries so small a matter that you slaughtered my children and delivered them up as an offering by fire to them?

Both Manasseh and his predecessor Ahaz are condemned by the Deuteronomists for 'offering up their children by fire' (2 Kgs. 16: 3; 21: 6), which is most naturally understood as a reference to sacrifice. A similar royal villain is Mesha, king of Moab, who in a time of military crisis 'took his eldest son who was to reign in his stead, and offered him for a burnt offering upon the wall' (2 Kgs. 3: 27). That the issue was of importance to royal reformers is seen from the account in 2 Kings 23: 10 of Josiah's action: 'And he defiled Topheth, which is in the valley of the sons of Hinnom, that no one might burn his son or daughter as an offering to Molech [למלך].'[56] The success of this attempt to purify the cult may be doubted, since condemnation of the offering of children למלך reappears in Jeremiah (32: 35; cf. also 7: 31; 19: 5).

The appearance of child sacrifice in the second extended allegory of the book (23: 37, 39) has often been dismissed as a late and imitative addition. It is interesting to notice that those people who sacrificed their children did not consider it incompatible with the worship of YHWH. Ezekiel 23: 39 reads: 'For when they had slaughtered their children in sacrifice to their idols, on the same day they came into my sanctuary to profane it.' That people thought not only that such a practice was compatible with the worship of YHWH, but that he had actually commanded it, is hinted at by the extraordinary passage in Ezekiel 20: 25–6:

---

[55] Zimmerli, *Ezekiel 1*, 344.

[56] The precise sense of the phrase למלך has been debated. Eissfeldt disputed the common idea that it referred to a god, Molech, by reference to the Phoenician *molk*, which appears to be a term for a type of offering. Although this suggestion proved popular the most recent treatments of the subject have rejected it in favour of the traditional rendering of the term as a divine name, most probably a royal title 'king' which has taken on the vocalization of בשת 'shame': for full discussion see G. C. Heider, *The Cult of Molek: A Reassessment*, JSOTS 43 (Sheffield, 1985); J. Day, *Molech: A God of Human Sacrifice in the Old Testament*, University of Cambridge Oriental Publications, 41 (Cambridge, 1989).

Moreover I gave them statutes that were not good and ordinances by which they could not have life; and I defiled them through their gifts in making them offer by fire all their first-born, that I might horrify them.

Ezekiel appears to make an explicit reference to the law of the first-born in Exodus 34: 19f., which contains the same phrase: כל פטר רחם לי ('all that opens the womb is mine'). He suggests that this law demands the sacrifice of first-born sons, and indeed the treatment of the first-born in Exodus 22: 30 does sound fairly absolute: 'The first-born of your sons you shall give to me.' However, Exodus 13 and 34 both provide for the redemption of sons. The polemic against child sacrifice in Deuteronomy and Jeremiah suggests that at least some people believed that YHWH demanded it. In 20: 25ff. Ezekiel must be describing the mis-application of this law of the first-born. Unique to the passage here is the combination of the first-born law with the language of burning children, typical of the Molech cult, which results in the 'unprecedented and incredible charge that Israelites regularly offered up every firstborn as a sacrifice—a manifest exaggeration'.[57] A further problem arises about the recipient of these alleged sacrifices: verses 25–6 clearly make YHWH the object of such worship, whereas verse 31 seems to connect the child sacrifice with idols: 'When you offer your gifts and sacrifice your sons by fire, you defile yourself with all your idols to this day.'

There is clearly some confusion about what exactly was going on in these rites. In his discussion of Jeremiah 7, Carroll argues that polemical writing like this need not be taken literally, adding that writings containing Deuteronomistic influence 'have a tendency to substitute abuse for argument and contempt for description'.[58] However, the biblical and extra-biblical evidence gathered by Heider and Day suggests that such sacrifices did take place in ancient Palestine, and the Deuteronomistic author of Kings certainly makes them part of a royal responsibility. Thus we can see that where Ezekiel joins in the chorus of outrage against this idolatrous practice he is again raising a moral issue which concerned the Jerusalem élite in the final decades of the state of Judah.

We have examined a number of oracles in which the disastrous fate of the nation is blamed on failures in matters of cult. The

---

[57] Greenberg, *Ezekiel 1–20*, 370.     [58] Carroll, *Jeremiah*, 222.

principal failings have all fallen within the major concerns of the Deuteronomistic reformers: cult centralization, idolatry, and the sacrifice of children. Thus we have seen that the main issues for Ezekiel were not those of individual or popular religion but those concerned with the correct maintenance of the state cult. As I have suggested, sin on a grand scale evokes punishment on an equally grand scale, and this is very true of the one section of Ezekiel's cultic criticism which remains to be discussed: the vision of abominations in the temple. If we have found hints that Ezekiel's cultic polemic is as intimately tied to the moral concerns of the Jerusalem élite in our discussion of chapters 6, 16, 20, and 23, we shall find our suspicions confirmed when we turn to the temple vision of chapter 8.

## The Temple Vision of Ezekiel 8

The most comprehensive portrayal of idolatry in the book is in chapter 8, where at the beginning of his vision of the temple in Jerusalem Ezekiel is shown all the abominations practised there. This is a very important part of the book: it is after the description of these abominations that the glory of YHWH abandons his temple to its grim fate at the hands of destroying angels. The actual practices described must be particularly heinous; clearly together they represent the complete failure of the people of Judah to remain loyal to YHWH even in that place which was particularly singled out to be his dwelling. Zimmerli considers that, as the number four expresses the totality of an event or sphere, by these four sins Ezekiel is shown the fullness of sin in Jerusalem.[59] However, both individually and taken together the sins here remain difficult to elucidate. To what cultic practices, illegitimate in Ezekiel's eyes, do they refer? In many respects they are unique, and, while parallels have been drawn in part from elsewhere in the Hebrew Bible, they remain tenuous. A number of scholars have questioned the assumption that they reflect actual sins in Jerusalem in the last days of the monarchy. These writers have drawn attention to the very different picture of the nature of Judah's cultic apostasy found in the contemporary

---

[59] Zimmerli, *Ezekiel 1*, 252.

Jeremiah and Lamentations.[60] I am not sure that the supposed closeness to events of these texts makes as much difference to their value as historical sources as some would want. It is quite conceivable that it is Ezekiel who presents something which approximates more closely to the real events than the other texts, which tend to be more governed by Deuteronomistic ideology. Although the abominations of chapter 8 have a very exotic feel to them, they must have been convincing enough for Ezekiel to address them to his contemporaries, who would have had as much (or as little) information about the situation in Jerusalem as he did.

Perhaps the first question to ask is whether the four quite different rites depicted here reflect aspects of one single ceremony. Thus T. H. Gaster attempted to explain the chapter as relating to a whole agricultural festival, using as a source the Ugaritic poem about the birth of the gods Shahar and Shalem.[61] But the impression given by the chapter, with its distinct groups of people, is that unrelated rites are being described, and, on the whole, these attempts to interpret Ezekiel 8 have not found support; Zimmerli speaks for by far the majority of commentators when he writes that 'we must give up trying to find behind the four abominations of Ezekiel 8 a comprehensive cultic event and endeavor to understand each act for itself'.[62] Such connections as are to be found between them are more likely to reflect aspects of a general religious movement or perhaps only a collection of scenes drawn from Ezekiel's imagination. We are unlikely to reach any conclusion unless we examine chapter 8 itself in more detail, looking at each of the cultic abuses Ezekiel describes.

---

[60] So e.g. Y. Kaufmann, *The Religion of Israel* (London, 1961), 406–9; M. Greenberg, 'Prolegomenon', in C. C. Torrey, *Pseudo-Ezekiel and the Original Prophecy, and Critical Articles* KTAV edn. (NY, 1970), pp. xxii–xxiii; Fishbane, 'Sin and Judgment', 134–5.

[61] T. H. Gaster, 'Ezekiel and the Mysteries', *JBL* 60 (1941), 289–310. Other recent advocates include H. G. May, 'The Departure of the Glory of Yahweh', *JBL* 56 (1937), 309–21; M. Nobile, 'Lo sfondo cultuale di Ez 8–11', *Antonianum*, 58 (1983), 185–200.

[62] Zimmerli, *Ezekiel 1*, 238; Ackerman, *Under Every Green Tree*, 52–3.

## The 'Image of Jealousy'

At the beginning of Ezekiel's visionary journey he is set down beside the first of the abominations he is to be shown: the סמל הקנאה, usually translated 'image of jealousy' (8: 3, 5).[63] What is this סמל הקנאה? Albright suggested that it represents a carved orthostat or guardian figure, but this has not been widely accepted.[64] Most commentators are agreed that it is a statue of some sort.[65] The word סמל appears in Phoenician inscriptions with the meaning 'statue', and this sense fits all of its five occurrences in the Hebrew Bible.[66] The word קנאה is commonly translated 'jealousy', referring to YHWH's passionate outrage at being supplanted. An alternative reading emphasizes lust rather than jealousy: the New English Bible (NEB) translates 'the image of Lust to rouse lustful passion'.[67] This idea of lust is taken to its extreme in the recent work of David Halperin, who suggests that Ezekiel's vision was of an actual act of coupling.[68] While such a reading surely goes beyond the evidence, Halperin is right to draw attention to the note of sexual jealousy that is sounded throughout the book. The tradition of YHWH's jealousy is an old one in the Hebrew Bible, and in Ezekiel קנאה most often refers to the god's wrath: 'a designation for the jealous anger of YHWH against anything hostile to him'.[69] This is the most natural way to understand the gloss in verse 3b, normally translated 'which provokes jealousy'. Moreover, in both the Decalogue and the Deuteronomistic traditions YHWH's jealousy is especially related to the production of graven images, such as the one we have here in Ezekiel.[70]

Some commentators are unwilling to identify the statue,[71] but those who do almost uniformly accept that it was of the goddess Asherah.[72] According to 2 Kings 21: 7 Manasseh set up a פסל of

---

[63] So RSV ad loc; Zimmerli, *Ezekiel 1*, 217–18.

[64] W. F. Albright, *Archaeology and the Religion of Israel* (Baltimore, Md., 1956), 165–6.

[65] e.g. Greenberg, *Ezekiel 1–20*, 168; Fohrer, *Ezechiel*, 50–1; Wevers, *Ezekiel*, 68; Cooke, *Ezekiel*, 92; Eichrodt, *Ezekiel*, 122.

[66] Aside from Ezek. 8: 3, 5, it is found in Deut. 4: 16; 2 Chr. 33: 7, 15. See S. Ackerman, *Under Every Green Tree: Popular Religion in Sixth Century Judah*, HSM 46 (Atlanta, Ga., 1992), 56–7.

[67] Also Eichrodt, *Ezekiel*, 105.     [68] Halperin, *Seeking Ezekiel*, 121.

[69] Zimmerli, *Ezekiel 1*, 238.     [70] Ackerman, *Under Every Green Tree*, 60.

[71] Cooke, *Ezekiel*, 92; Wevers, *Ezekiel*, 68.

[72] Greenberg, *Ezekiel 1–20*, 168; Fohrer, *Ezechiel*, 50–1; Eichrodt, *Ezekiel*, 122–3; Allen, *Ezekiel 1–19*, 142. H. C. Lutzky, in a recent article has argued not only that the text refers

Asherah in the temple, and in the parallel passage in Chronicles (2 Chr. 33: 7, 15) this image is called פסל הסמל, apparently making the identification with Ezekiel 8.[73] The Asherah that Manasseh built and Josiah removed was undoubtedly set up inside the temple, as part of the state cult (2 Kgs. 21: 7; 23: 6). Our identification of the סמל הקנאה as an image of Asherah may be strengthened by the Hebrew text, which appears to place it too inside the temple area. The Hebrew of verse 3 reads: אל־פתח שער הפנימית הפנה צפונה. The Hebrew is awkward but its most natural translation does seem to be 'at the entrance of the northern gate of the inner court'. Some commentators remove הפנימית on the grounds that it is not represented in the Septuagint.[74] Thus, with the removal of the reference to the inner court, Zimmerli does not accept that Ezekiel is set down so close to the heart of the temple, and sees here a reference to the gate of the city.[75] However, Eichrodt and Greenberg both consider the reference to be to the entrance of the inner court of the temple, and this is the more satisfactory solution.[76] Thus the סמל stands in the outer court that is mentioned in 10: 3, 5 as well as in the descriptions of the future temple (40: 17 ff., 23 ff.) and the late pre-exilic temple (2 Kgs. 21: 5; 23: 12). If, as Greenberg suggests, in verse 5 שער המזבח is to be understood as 'altar gate' this would help confirm the location as this outer court, since the gate would be so called because it was opposite the great altar of sacrifice in the inner court.[77] Although in some ways

---

to Asherah, but that סמל הקנאה originally read 'image of the creatress', deriving קנאה from קנה rather than קנא, and making the connection with Asherah's title at Ugarit, *qnyt ilm*: H. C. Lutzky, 'On "the Image of Jealousy" (Ezekiel viii 3, 5)', *VT* 46 (1996), 121–5.

[73] Ackerman points out that *asherim* were frequently erected by Israelites and normally in Jerusalem. That, there, such a statue should have been part of the state religion is quite conceivable, given the goddess's place as queen and consort of the high god El in the Ugaritic pantheon, as well as the recent evidence from Kuntillet 'Ajrud that in at least some Israelite circles she may have been worshipped as YHWH's consort. (See e.g. S. Olyan, *Asherah and the Cult of Yahweh in Israel*, SBLMS 34 (Atlanta, Ga., 1988), esp. 74; also the discussion in J. Day, 'Asherah in the Hebrew Bible and Northwest Semitic Literature', *JBL* 105 (1986), esp. 406–8.)

[74] Zimmerli, *Ezekiel 1*, 217; Fohrer, *Ezechiel*, 47; Wevers, *Ezekiel*, 67; Ackerman, *Under Every Green Tree*, 39, 53–5.

[75] Zimmerli, *Ezekiel 1*, 237; supported by Ackerman, *Under Every Green Tree*, 53–5; and Duguid, *Leaders*, 112.

[76] Eichrodt, *Ezekiel*, 122; Greenberg, *Ezekiel 1–20*, 168; Cooke, *Ezekiel*, 101. One should perhaps also point out that the reading of the Greek is dependent only on the textual tradition of the Codex Vaticanus. The Codex Alexandrinus, followed at this point in Rahlfs' edition of the LXX, contains the reading ἐπί τὰ πρόθυρα τῆς πύλης τῆς ἐσωτέρας τῆς βλεπούσης πρὸς βορρᾶν. [77] Greenberg, *Ezekiel 1–20*, 168.

the Greek text provides a more logical progression, especially as understood by Zimmerli and Ackerman as a progression from outside the city to inside the temple, we should remember that this is a vision and we cannot necessarily expect everything to be supremely logical.[78] Also, if we are correct in making the association between the image of jealousy and a statue of Asherah, then the temple complex is the most likely place to find this. It is where *asherim* have been placed before in Jerusalem, particularly by Manasseh, and we have in Chronicles an early understanding of Ezekiel which seems to confirm this.

What are the moral and political implications of this statue of Asherah, placed inside the temple compound? With which people is such cultic activity most commonly associated? In the Deuteronomistic history we find that the Asherah is connected with the cultic reforms of Manasseh and Josiah. In 2 Kings 21: 7 Manasseh's placing of an Asherah in the temple court is reported. According to 2 Kings 23: 6, however, this statue was removed and ground into dust by King Josiah, so if Ezekiel 8 refers to such a statue, this may reflect the sins of the earlier generation: it is certainly one of the major religious symbols of the old order that Josiah attempted to sweep away. It is also quite possible that an image had been restored by one of Josiah's successors, perhaps in the attempt to put ideological distance between himself and the reforming king.[79] The continuing polemic against aspects of the cult which we find in the Deuteronomists and Ezekiel suggest that these issues were still alive. The presence of the Asherah in the temple is a powerful symbol of the failure of the Deuteronomistic party to make progress in the reign of Zedekiah. So, who are the people responsible for this abomination? I do not believe that we have here an example of so-called 'popular' religion, if by that is meant the religion of the ordinary inhabitants of Jerusalem, and, despite Ackerman's claim to be examining popular religion, she does not attempt to show how the Asherah fits into popular culture. In the Deuteronomistic presentation of the last decades of Judah the Asherah is regularly connected with the religious policy of monarchs, and here in Ezekiel it appears in the context of the Jerusalem temple. We are dealing with the incorrect maintenance

[78] Becker, 'Ez 8–11 als einheitliche Komposition', 142; Duguid, *Leaders*, 67–8.
[79] Eichrodt accepts a restored statue of Asherah and links this with the worship of the 'queen of heaven' described in Jer. 7: 18; 44: 17–19, 24 (*Ezekiel*, 122–3).

of the state cult: the temple which is at one and the same time the national sanctuary and the King's private chapel. So the criticism, even if it is not explicit, must be of those with the power to affect change in the state cult: the king and his associates, members of that same Jerusalem élite from which the exiles in Babylon were drawn.

## The Elders and their Pictures

The second abomination (8: 7–12), although obscure in detail, makes plain the concerns of the prophet. The crime is one of idolatry, performed by a group of Judah's leading citizens. The vision begins strangely as Ezekiel is instructed to dig through a wall in the temple compound. Thereupon he is confronted by the extraordinary and unparalleled picture of seventy elders offering incense to pictures or engravings on the wall of a room. There has been a great deal of discussion about what cultic practice is being described and how historically possible such a scene is. The first things described are (8: 10):

והנה כל־תבנית רמש ובהמה שקץ וכל־גלולי בית ישראל
מחקה על־הקיר סביב סביב

That is: 'and there, portrayed upon the wall roundabout, were all kinds of creeping things, and loathsome beasts, and all the idols of the house of Israel.' The rare word מחקה (only here, Ezek. 23: 14, and 1 Kings 6: 35 in the Hebrew Bible) appears to mean 'relief work', or 'carvings', and this relief work is defined as 'detestable creatures and all the idols of the house of Israel'. The phrase תבנית רמש ובהמה is lacking in the LXX, and draws on phrases from Deuteronomy 4: 17–18. Nevertheless, most scholars believe that, although it is a later gloss, it has correctly interpreted the scene, which is one of animal images. Greenberg points out that it:

interrupts the expected sequence *kol šeqeṣ* 'every detestation', as though to guarantee the reading *šeqeṣ* for the graph, which when elsewhere combined with *gillul* (as here) is read *šiqquṣ* 'loathsome thing'—always an idol. Here on the contrary the sense is 'detestable animals', as in Lev. 11:10–42, where *šeqeṣ* is the term for creatures (e.g. vermin) forbidden as food.[80]

[80] Greenberg, *Ezekiel 1–20*, 169.

Zimmerli notes that part of the logic of Leviticus 11 is to legislate against hybrid creatures which do not conform to the accepted pattern of what an animal, bird, or fish should be. Such creatures are on the wall receiving incense from Israel's representatives.[81]

Ackerman, on the other hand, does not accept that the gloss correctly interprets the scene. She argues that שֶׁקֶץ refers not to unclean animals which are depicted, but to unclean food which is eaten. She sees, therefore, a double abomination, the elders are eating unclean food and worshipping idols: this is, she claims, the characteristic activity of a *marzeaḥ* association.[82] The *marzeaḥ* is a religious institution known of throughout the West Semitic world. A god would be honoured by an association who held celebration which 'centered around feasting and especially around drinking'.[83] Members of the *marzeaḥ* association were drawn from the upper classes of their society, and the association itself often owned fields, vineyards, and a central meeting house. It is the meeting of such an association that Ackerman finds in Ezekiel 8: 10–12, and its sin is not so much the existence of the association as its idolatrous worship. If she were right that this is a *marzeaḥ*, it would certainly support our case that Ezekiel is addressing the moral concerns of the upper classes.

However, our knowledge of the *marzeaḥ* institution in ancient Israel is extremely limited, since there are only two biblical references to such a thing (Amos 6: 7 and Jer. 16: 5). Both of these emphasize the centrality of eating and drinking rather than worship, whereas here in Ezekiel 8 there is no mention of drink, and the idea of feasting is only present if we accept Ackerman's translation of שֶׁקֶץ as 'unclean food' rather than the more natural 'unclean animals'. The main focus of Ezekiel 8 is on the offering of incense as the main activity of the group. Incense formed an important part of the cult of YHWH and a very powerful offering: Deuteronomy 33: 10 places it in parallel with whole burnt offerings on the altar.[84] Not surprisingly it was also part of the cult of idols, as we read in Jerermiah 19: 13 (burning incense on rooftops to all the host of heaven) and Isaiah 65: 3 (burning incense on bricks). Although it is quite bad enough for the elders

---

[81] Zimmerli, *Ezekiel 1*, 240. Also Wevers, *Ezekiel*, 69; Cooke, *Ezekiel*, 94.
[82] Ackerman, *Under Every Green Tree*, 68–71.
[83] Ibid. 72.
[84] Cf. also Korah's rebellion in Num. 16, where the use of incense is at issue.

to be participating in the worship of detestable images in any way, there may be a comparison to be drawn between this passage and 2 Chronicles 26: 19, where Uzziah, by burning incense (to YHWH) intrudes upon privileges which were properly priestly.[85] To introduce the notion of a *marzeaḥ* feast only adds unnecessary complication to a scene which is difficult to understand as it is, and distracts attention from the main crime. The worship of animal images is condemned both in the Decalogue and in Deuteronomy 4, and is quite bad enough on its own to merit Ezekiel's condemnation.

What is the significance of all this clandestine cultic activity, performed by seventy elders? Who are the elders? The appearance of the number seventy does suggest that some sort of official body is intended here. As Duguid comments, 'Their actions provide a shocking contrast to the JE stratum of the Pentateuch in which seventy of the *ziqne yiśra'el* received the unique privilege of seeing God (Exod. 24: 1–11) and were endowed with the same spirit as Moses (Num. 11: 16–30).'[86] Ezekiel emphasizes the corruption at the very top of Judaean society. The mention of 'Jaazaniah the son of Shaphan' may also be significant. If he were the son of the same Shaphan who was King Josiah's scribe, then we see that the family is still involved at the highest level, but this son, at least, has joined the opposition to his father's reforms.[87] The picture is clearly one of the Jerusalem aristocracy at prayer.

The precise nature of their worship remains obscure, especially because the provenance of such animal images is uncertain. Greenberg is perplexed by the scene, and allows for the possibility of either Babylonian or Egyptian influence.[88] It is worth noting that in its details this abomination has no obvious connection with the sins of Manasseh, as even Greenberg is forced to admit.[89] Nevertheless, it appears to be defiantly anti-Yahwist, or at least anti-Deuteronomic. Perhaps here again Ezekiel attempts to show the religious activities of those whom he opposed politically. And

---

[85] See Zimmerli, *Ezekiel 1*, 241; Klein, *Ezekiel: The Prophet and his Message*, Studies on Personalities of the Old Testament (Columbia, SC, 1988), 55.

[86] Duguid, *Leaders*, 113.

[87] Ibid., 114. Other members of Shaphan's family are mentioned in Jer. 29: 3; 36: 12: cf. Dutcher-Walls, 'Social Location', 85–7, 92.

[88] Greenberg, *Ezekiel 1–20*, 169.

[89] Greenberg writes that 'the secret rites of vss. 10–12 are another story and may have been practised in Ezekiel's time' (*Ezekiel 1–20*, 202).

indeed there is a possible connection with foreign policy. Cooke argues that a Babylonian source for the rite is most likely, particularly because of the worship of Tammuz and of the sun which Ezekiel is shown later in the vision, and Block suggests as a prototype the animal figures on Babylon's Ishtar Gate.[90] For Eichrodt the 'creeping things' and 'beasts' are clear evidence of Egyptian prototypes: 'In Egypt more than anywhere we find gods in animal shape, whether as crocodiles, snakes and dung beetles, or as oxen, sheep, and cats.'[91] Evidence from Babylonia cannot compare with this, and, as additional proof, he quotes H. Schmidt's observation with approval: 'at that period of Jerusalem's history Babylonian gods did not need to go into hiding'.[92] The clandestine nature of the cult vouches for its Egyptian provenance. Eichrodt accepts that here we have Egyptian religious influence, and he puts a political slant on his interpretation, seeing in the seventy elders not the current Jerusalem officialdom (of Zedekiah) but members of the old ruling class, whose hopes were centred on alliance with Egypt. The clandestine Egyptian cult was 'little more than an alternative way of expressing their political programme'.[93] It is extremely difficult to judge which interpretation is most likely. However, as Ezekiel presents it, these members of the aristocracy have given up their allegiance to YHWH and are indulging in illicit cultic activities within the very gate of the temple, the royal sanctuary and home of YHWH. Despite the difficulty of knowing exactly what is condemned, we are clearly again in the domain of the state cult and the moral world of the political élite.

## The Women Weeping for Tammuz

The third abomination Ezekiel is shown, the women weeping for Tammuz, is clearer than either of the previous ones in both place and activity. At least we can be certain that at this stage in Ezekiel's vision we have reached the temple area proper: the 'entrance of the north gate of the house of the LORD' (8: 14) is most likely the entrance to the inner court of the temple. Tammuz is the young fertility God of Mesopotamia (the Sumerian Dumuzi), and the consort of Ishtar (Inanna). In the mythology, Ishtar, after

---

[90] Cooke, *Ezekiel*, 94; Block, *Ezekiel 1–24*, 291.
[91] Eichrodt, *Ezekiel*, 124.          [92] Ibid. 124.          [93] Ibid. 125.

first giving him up to death as a substitute for herself, travels down to the underworld to rescue him. As his cult spread he took on the characteristics of a vegetation deity, particularly representing the dying of plant life in the summer heat. In this capacity he was lamented by his worshippers every year and the fourth month of the Babylonian calendar (June–July) became named Tammuz after him. Thorkild Jacobsen describes the cult: 'In the cult drama of the death of the god and lament for him, celebrated at the end of spring, the loss of god, the waning of power for new life in nature, is counteracted by mourning and lament.'[94] In both the mythology and the mourning rituals women played a prominent part, and Meindert Dijkstra sensibly suggests that the women here in Ezekiel 8: 14 are professional cultic personnel:

> They may have belonged to the class of the קדשים—priesthood that was also responsible for the cult of Asherah. Up to the time of Josiah this caste possessed quarters in the Temple area where women weaved for the Asherah (2 Kgs 23: 7), so why not wailed over Tammuz?[95]

In this case again, we are not dealing with a spontaneous expression of popular religiosity, but the public ordering of the state cult.

What is this East Semitic fertility god doing inside the Jerusalem temple complex in the early sixth century? Perhaps it is as a result of the gradual encroachment of Mesopotamian religious culture in Palestine over the centuries of Assyrian and Babylonian dominance. The books of Kings describe how Ahaz succumbed to this pressure by building an altar under the influence of the king of Assyria (2 Kgs. 16: 10–18). It has often been argued that the Assyrian vassals like Ahaz and Manasseh were compelled to introduce Assyrian elements into the Jerusalem cult. Martin Noth provides a representative example: 'So long as Judah was a tribute paying Assyrian vassal . . . the official Assyrian religion had a place alongside the traditional worship of Yahweh in the state sanctuary in Jerusalem.'[96]

However, more recently the work of Cogan and McKay has

---

[94] T. Jacobsen, 'Toward the Image of Tammuz', *History of Religions*, 1 (1962), 212.

[95] M. Dijkstra, 'Goddess, Gods, Men and Women in Ezekiel 8', in B. Becking and M. Dijkstra (eds.), *On Reading Prophetic Texts: Gender-Specific and Related Studies in Memory of Fokkelien van Dijk-Hemmes*, Biblical Interpretation Series, 18 (Leiden, 1996), 98.

[96] Noth, *History of Israel*, 266.

called this into question.[97] On the one hand, there is insufficient Assyrian evidence to prove that religious obligations were made part of the treaties between the kings of Assyria and their vassals, and, on the other hand, both these scholars have argued that many of the cults attributed to Ahaz and Manasseh were actually native rather than foreign. Thus it is possible that the wailing for Tammuz represents not so much a Babylonian incursion into Israel's religious life as the renaming of a cult already known and practised in the native Canaanite culture.[98] The Phoenician god Adonis fulfils a very similar role, and it is also possible that Baal might have been assimilated to Tammuz. Baal of Ugarit is quite clearly a god who dies and then returns to life, although it is less clear that he should be thought of as a 'vegetation deity'. In the Baal cycle his death is followed by scenes of mourning by his sister-consort Anat and then the high god El. The Baal of the Hebrew Bible is clearly connected with fertility, and, although it is nowhere explicitly stated that he dies and rises, the Bible does contain possible allusions to this. Ackerman draws attention to three texts which seem to imply that Baal was worshipped with mourning rites:[99] 1 Kings 18, where the prophets of Baal seek to rouse the storm god by gashing themselves; Hosea 7: 14, which she reads as condemning those who gash themselves[100] 'for (want of) grain and wine'; and Zechariah 12: 10, which describes the mourning for Hadad-Rimmon in the vale of Megiddo.

This cult of Baal is again one of the aspects of religion in Judah most fiercely condemned by the Deuteronomists. In their history of the kingdom of Judah we find that the worship of Baal appears not in connection with popular culture but with palace intrigue and the religious policy of the ruling élite. The story of Queen Athaliah's overthrow in 2 Kings 11 describes the destruction of a Baal temple in Jerusalem. The new regime is solemnized by a covenant between YHWH, king, and people. This covenant is the prelude to the destruction of Baal's temple and its priest Mattan, who is probably best viewed as the chief religious officer of Athaliah's outgoing administration. The cultic reform is an act

---

[97] Cogan, *Imperialism and Religion*; McKay, *Religion in Judah under the Assyrians*.
[98] This view would be compatible with Block's view that 'the Tammuz' is less likely to be the god himself than 'a special genre of lament' (*Ezekiel 1–24*, 294–5).
[99] Ackerman, *Under Every Green Tree*, 86–91.
[100] 'Reading the root *gdd* with G for MT *yitgoraru*' (Ackerman, *Under Every Green Tree*, 89).

'symbolizing the downfall of Athaliah and the end of Omride political influence in Judah'.[101] Such an attack on Baal worship is firmly within the moral domain of the ruling élite.

Manasseh also is said to have built altars for Baal, which the account of Josiah's reform places inside the temple itself. Kings presents these altars for Baal, like his Asherah, as one aspect of the wicked king's religious policy, ultimately undone by Josiah. Although it is normally assumed that these cults were indigenous ones, it is possible that they were in fact only indigenous names given to Assyrian deities, and this suggestion is supported by the unusual appearance of the name Tammuz here in Ezekiel. For our purposes, it is not particularly important which view is correct. More important is that the worship of Baal in Jerusalem and the temple was an important issue of policy for groups like the Deuteronomists and their opponents. We do not find exactly the same picture in Ezekiel as in Kings, but we are clearly moving in the same moral world.

## The Sun Worship in the Temple

The fourth and last abomination Ezekiel is shown is the most serious: men worshipping the sun inside the inner court of the temple (8: 16). The place they have chosen for this abominable worship is 'between the porch and the altar'. This area appears to be especially holy within the court since it is here, according to Joel 2: 17, that the priests pray to YHWH on a fast day. *Mishnah Kelim* 1. 9 ranks its sanctity only less than that of the sanctuary proper, the eighth of ten degrees of sanctity.[102] The men here have turned their backs on the sanctuary to worship the sun; Ezekiel considers this the most appalling expression of contempt for YHWH.[103]

Who are the men involved in this cult? Zimmerli wonders whether their position between porch and altar suggests a 'specifically priestly circle, analogous to the circle of seventy elders', and asks: 'Was then the avoidance of the title "priest"

---

[101] Lowery, *Reforming Kings*, 108.

[102] Greenberg, *Ezekiel 1-20*, 171.

[103] The expression והנם שלחים את־הזמורה אל־אפם (8: 17bβ), which RSV translates 'Lo they put the branch to their nose', and which forms part of the climax to this scene, is obscure and not well understood. It is perhaps most likely that it refers to some manner of 'insulting physical gesture' (Block, *Ezekiel 1-24*, 299; cf. Zimmerli, *Ezekiel 1*, 244-5).

intended polemically?'.[104] This is possible but by no means demanded by the text. Iain Duguid makes the suggestion that the sun worshippers are not priests but elders, part of Judah's lay leadership. He argues that they are identical with the

אנשים הזקנים אשר לפני הבית

That is: 'elders who were before the house' (9: 6), who are the first to die in the destruction of Jerusalem. They are not only 'old men' but 'elders', holders of political office.[105] This ties in well with Eichrodt, who gives the scene a political interpretation, as he did with the second abomination. Whereas in that scene the seventy elders were representatives of the old guard hiding their allegiance to Egypt, the men in verse 16 are the new ruling class, who are supporters of Babylonia.[106]

What is the meaning and source of this solar worship? Although there can be no doubting the importance of the sun god in Egyptian religion, it seems unlikely that there is direct Egyptian influence here.[107] More promising is the Mesopotamian cult of Shamash, perhaps introduced under Assyrian influence by the loyal Assyrian vassals Ahaz and Manasseh. Sun worship is an aspect of the cult purged by Josiah: 2 Kings 23 describes Josiah's removal of 'the horses that the kings of Judah had dedicated to the sun' and 'chariots of the sun' (23: 11), as well as the 'idolatrous priests' who 'burn incense to Baal, to the sun, and the moon, and the constellations, and all the host of heaven'. Cooke believes that these were a Mesopotamian incursion into the religious life of Judah, and that there was a resurgence of such worship after the death of Josiah, 'with the hope of propitiating one of the chief Babylonian deities'.[108] He is echoed by Eichrodt: 'They are most probably representatives of "Zedekiah's proletarian government" (H. Schmidt), who are showing their loyalty to Babylon by engaging in her state cult, the worship of Marduk-Šamaš.'[109]

However, as Ackerman points out, 'there is no mention in the Bible of a solar cult *per se* introduced under the influence of Judah's Assyrian overlords'.[110] There is much to be said for the view of McKay and Cogan that the Assyrians did not force religious duties upon their vassals, but tolerated whatever native

[104] Zimmerli, *Ezekiel 1*, 243.          [105] Duguid, *Leaders*, 113–14.
[106] Eichrodt, *Ezekiel*, 127.          [107] *Contra* Fohrer, *Ezechiel*, 52.
[108] Cooke, *Ezekiel*, 99.          [109] Eichrodt, *Ezekiel*, 127.
[110] Ackerman, *Under Every Green Tree*, 95.

forms of cult were already in place. Both these authors argue that despite some inevitable Mesopotamian influence the sun cult is a part of indigenous West Semitic religion.[111] Most recently J. Glen Taylor has drawn together archaeological and biblical evidence to argue that a close relationship exists between YHWH and the sun:

In at least the vast majority of cases, biblical passages which refer to sun worship in Israel do not refer to a foreign phenomenon borrowed by idolatrous Israelites, but to a Yahwistic phenomenon which Deuteronomistic theology came to look upon as idolatrous.[112]

In the case of Ezekiel 8, Taylor's discussion echoes that of Zimmerli, who also thinks that the offenders here are indulging in a solarized YHWH worship and stresses that for Ezekiel the main sin would appear to be not the sun as a second god, but the turning away from YHWH's temple. It may ultimately be the case that, as with Tammuz, both Mesopotamian and local traditions could be held together in the cult without difficulty. Cogan, while he believes that the Assyrians did not impose religious obligations on Judah, nevertheless argues that cult objects like the horses for the sun represent Assyrian supplements to the native cult. Over the period of Assyrian domination Judah was culturally overwhelmed by her more powerful neighbour:

In a word, the diminutive Judahite state was buffeted on all sides by the cultural patterns dominant in the Assyrian empire. Although Assyria made no formal demands for cultural unity among its subjects, one of the by-products of political and economic subjugation was a tendency toward cultural homogeneity. Involved as it was in imperial affairs, Judah was faced with the problem of the assimilation of foreign norms on a national scale, for the first time in its history.[113]

Josiah's reforms were part of a nationalistic reaction to this assimilation which aimed at political, religious, and cultural renewal, and it seems highly likely that a number of native practices were to be swept away along with the foreign. Perhaps in the case of YHWH and the sun the accretion of Mesopotamian elements was felt to compromise or taint the cult too much to retain it. In the

---

[111] McKay, *Religion in Judah under the Assyrians*, esp. 32–6. Cogan, *Imperialism and Religion*, 84–8; cf. Ackerman, *Under Every Green Tree*, 98.

[112] J. G. Taylor, *Yahweh and the Sun: Biblical and Archaeological Evidence for Sun Worship in Ancient Israel*, JSOTS, 111 (Sheffield, 1993), 257.

[113] Cogan, *Imperialism and Religion*, 95.

end, the provenance of these cults is of less importance than their significance within the debates of Judah. What is not in doubt is Ezekiel's (and the Deuteronomists') disapproval of any solar cult. To them YHWH worship and sun worship are incompatible, and it is significant that it is another of the parts of the state cult which was removed by Josiah. Whatever its origin, it belongs to the religious symbols of those whom the Deuteronomists and their like opposed, and Ezekiel appears to suggest that there has been a return to the pattern of the period before the reform. As Zimmerli comments: 'In the period of the weakening and relaxation after the reform these tendencies must have reasserted themselves, whether we think of them as established from the Assyrian period or trace them back to Solomon, or even beyond this to reckon them as influences of the Canaanite Baal religion.'[114]

Such a conclusion raises one of the most vexed questions in the study of the temple vision: that of veracity. Does Ezekiel's picture of rampant idolatry in the state cult genuinely reflect the situation in Jerusalem in the time of Zedekiah? Although it is not always easy to work out exactly what is meant, it would have been far simpler for his original hearers to make sense of than for us, more than two and a half thousand years later. On the simplest reading one might be impressed by the wealth of detail: 'Normally one would be inclined to weight Ezekiel's specific report more heavily than the silence of Jeremiah, Kings and Lamentations.'[115] However, a number of scholars have argued that Ezekiel is an unreliable witness. It is sometimes proposed that the description of cultic sin in Ezekiel better fits the age of Manasseh than Zedekiah, and it is certainly true that in our analysis we have often pointed out where some cultic impropriety seems closely related to one of the things which Josiah reformed. If Josiah had removed idolatry and the *bamoth* from the state cult, at what point did they creep back in? Yehezkel Kaufmann and Moshe Greenberg both argue that Josiah's reforms were enduring, and that therefore Ezekiel's visions of sin in Jerusalem must look back to the age of Manasseh. They base their case on the evidence of Kings, Jeremiah, and Lamentations, seeing these as closer to the events than Ezekiel. Given the importance of the *bamoth* theme in Kings prior to Josiah,

---

[114] Zimmerli, *Ezekiel 1*, 243.　　[115] Smith, 'Sins of Manasseh', 13.

it is noteworthy that the last chapters of Kings know neither of any rebuilding of these shrines nor of a return to idolatry:

> It is obvious that the author of Kings would not have invoked the sins of Manasseh as the cause of the fall had he known of like outrages committed by Jehoiakim or Zedekiah. Nor does the author of Kings mention a recurrence of the high-place cults. His silence on this point, after carefully reckoning this sin against all the kings from Solomon to Josiah, can mean only that the high places were not rebuilt.[116]

But it must be said in response that Kings is no more reliable a witness than Ezekiel, and the Deuteronomistic author may have had his own reasons for highlighting the sin of Manasseh at the expense of the sins of later generations. He had to explain not only the fall of the city but also the rather ignominious death of Josiah. 'It was chronologically impossible to place the blame for the death of Josiah on any post-Josianic king: a pre-Josianic ruler had to be held responsible. Manasseh, Josiah's idolatrous predecessor, was the obvious candidate, and he was consequently blamed for the twin evils, the death of Josiah and the fall of Jerusalem.'[117] And, although the final chapters of Kings do not recount a rebuilding of the *bamoth* or lapse into idolatry, we should note that all four kings are said to have 'done what was evil in the sight of the LORD'. Torrey may have dismissed this as a stereotype with no serious evidential value,[118] but it is precisely a stereotypical description of religious apostasy for the kings of both North and South. So when we read that Jehoahaz, Jehoiakim, Jehoiachin, and Zedekiah 'did what was evil in the sight of the LORD' the implication is that 'like Solomon, Rehoboam, Manasseh, Amon, and all the kings of Israel they committed what was in the eyes of the Deuteronomists religious apostasy, that is, they allowed the reforms of Josiah to lapse'.[119]

So much for the evidence of Kings. Kaufmann and Greenberg also argue that Jeremiah, a prophet much closer to the events than Ezekiel, does not mention the collapse of the Josianic reforms among the sins of Judah. The kings are not blamed for polluting the cult, and, more importantly:

---

[116] Kaufmann, *Religion of Israel*, 406; cf. Greenberg, 'Prolegomenon', p. xxi.
[117] Ackerman, *Under Every Green Tree*, 49; see also Smith, 'Sins of Manasseh', 14.
[118] Torrey, *Pseudo-Ezekiel*, 59.
[119] Ackerman, *Under Every Green Tree*, 50.

it is crucial that in all his visits to the Temple, Jeremiah never once comes upon any of the abominations seen there by Ezekiel. The apostasy for which Jeremiah reproaches the people goes on outside the Temple (7: 9 f.), in the street, and on rooftops (7: 17f.; 11: 13; 19: 13), in unofficial private cults that were practiced throughout Israel's history. But Jeremiah does not (like Ezekiel) depict the temple as a desecrated, god-forsaken sanctuary: he never calls for its cleansing.[120]

But again the evidence is far from conclusive. The book of Jeremiah contains numerous references to idolatrous behaviour, and it is not possible to argue that all of them represent only private religious activities. Ackerman lists some of the places:

Jer. 44: 17, 21 imply that the cult of the queen of heaven was a part of the religion of the monarchy; it may therefore have been a part of the religion of the monarch's private chapel, the temple. Similarly, the host of heaven was worshiped on the rooftops of the people and on the rooftops of the palace (Jer. 19: 13); the participation of the monarchy again may implicate the temple cult. Elsewhere in Jerusalem, the Tophet, the site of child sacrifice destroyed by Josiah (2 Kings 23: 10) was rebuilt and thrived (Jer. 7: 30–34; 19: 1–13; 32: 35). The *bāmôt* sanctuaries also were re-established, and worship resumed there (Jer. 13: 27; 17: 1–4). The sabbath law was violated. Surely all these data do not suggest that the Josianic reform endured in Jerusalem.[121]

On the whole, it seems safest to conclude that there is a fair measure of veracity in Ezekiel's reports of non-Josianic cult practices. This is only what we should expect, given the dramatic change in policy undertaken by Josiah's successors. The kings who followed Josiah did not continue his programme of religious, cultural, and political independence, but were forced to become vassals first of Egypt, then Babylon. As Jehoiakim reversed Josiah's political policy, it is no surprise that he should have made changes in the state cult, and the same will have been true of Zedekiah. Given the close connection between politics and cult, it would be far more surprising if the Josianic reforms had endured.

[120] Greenberg, 'Prolegomenon', p. xxi.
[121] Ackerman, *Under Every Green Tree*, 50–1.

## Conclusion

We have seen that throughout the history of Israel and Judah the
state cult is a major focus of ruling-class political debate and
action: as one political faction is ousted and another takes power,
a different religious ideology becomes dominant, and changes in
religious ideology imply changes in the practice of the state cult.
Thus, if Ezekiel is to address the political concerns of the
Jerusalem élite, we should expect him to have plenty to say about
the state cult, and this, of course, is very much the case. In the
oracles we have examined, all of which seek to explain the fall
of Jerusalem, the prophet consistently attacks idolatry inside the
Jerusalem temple, and condemns as idolatrous the worship
offered outside the central sanctuary. Thus the twin concerns of
the Josianic reformation, idolatry and cult centralization, are at
the centre of Ezekiel's theological vision, and it is the corruption
and the pollution of the state cult which evoke the wrath of YHWH.
When Ezekiel blames cultic apostasy for the disasters of the
present, he is working within an established framework of moral
and political discourse, which would have been familiar and
meaningful to his audience in exile, drawn as they were from the
upper strata of Jerusalem society.

# 5

# Ritual and Ethics

That Ezekiel is both priest and prophet is a commonplace, and it has long been recognized that by contrast with the pre-exilic prophets he places an almost overwhelming importance on matters of cult and ritual. As von Rad comments, 'the world of ideas in which he lives, the standards which he applies, and the categories according to which he sees Israel's existence ordered before Jahweh, are expressly those of a priest'.[1] In the last chapter we examined some of the prophet's more explicit cultic concerns, and saw how his condemnation of apostasy, especially within the Jerusalem temple, was conducted in terms belonging to the moral discourse of the Jerusalem élite. However, the prophet's attachment to the cult is not limited to the content of cultic apostasy, nor is his audience's moral view limited to the world of Jerusalem politics. In this chapter I shall continue the analysis of Ezekiel's cultic interests, but turn my attention to the second principal area of their experience: the far more restricted moral world of exile. In particular, I shall examine the concepts associated with ritual and purity which dominate so much of the prophet's moral discourse. While we might explain this development simply in terms of the prophet's priestly background, there is evidence to suggest that Ezekiel's concern for purity is particularly appropriate to the social context of exile in which he and the community he addresses found themselves. We must ask why these ritual concepts, drawn originally from the regulations of the temple in Jerusalem, appear to have struck such a chord with an audience of exiles, and thereby to have helped maintain a distinctively Jewish community. In the book of Ezekiel, which is directly and explicitly addressed to the crisis of exile, we see the first steps towards a Judaism in which the rituals of the destroyed temple

---

[1] Von Rad, *Old Testament Theology*, ii. 224.

become the centrepiece of an ethical system which constantly looks back to the homeland for its symbolic coherence.[2]

## Ritual, Resistance, and the Moral World of the Exile

The recognition that cult, ritual, and purity are at the heart of Ezekiel's theology has not always led to a deeper understanding of the ethical thought of the book. Some scholars, noting the cultic emphases, have been content to castigate the prophet for his failure to be a good Protestant. H. Wheeler Robinson writes:

You cannot put ritual and moral demands on the same level without tending to assimilate their value which means, for most people, the externalization of the moral demands into an outward obedience at most; and, for some people, the exaltation of the ritual into something of intrinsic worth . . . Some of the admitted weaknesses of later Judaism (as also of Christianity) can be already seen in Ezekiel's failure to discriminate in the evils he denounces.[3]

Robinson's hostility towards the juxtaposition of ritual and moral demands in Ezekiel is typical of the negative attitude towards ritual found throughout modern Western culture in general, and biblical scholarship in particular.[4] But this negativity is short-sighted. As Mary Douglas and other anthropologists have pointed out, ritual is not just 'a bad word signifying empty conformity'.[5] At the most basic level rituals, which can be sacred or secular, are actions which carry meaning within specific social context, expressing and symbolizing the relationships between human actors. As such they are a necessary and important part of human existence: 'It is impossible to have social relations without symbolic acts.'[6] Shared rituals symbolize the moral values that a

---

[2] This is, of course, the situation of all Judaism after 70 CE. For discussion see J. Neusner, *The Idea of Purity in Ancient Judaism*, SJLA 1 (Leiden, 1973); on the parallel between the destruction of first and second temples see also Coggins, 'Jewish Diaspora', 173.

[3] Robinson, *Two Hebrew Prophets*, 102.

[4] See the survey by F. H. Gorman, jun., 'Ritual Studies and Biblical Studies: Assessment of the Past; Prospects for the Future', *Semeia*, 67 (1994), 13–36. Also M. Douglas, *Natural Symbols: Explorations in Cosmology*, 2nd edn. (London, 1973), 19–21; R. Wuthnow, *Meaning and Moral Order: Explorations in Cultural Analysis* (Berkeley, Calif., 1987), 97–8.

[5] Douglas, *Natural Symbols*, 19. A recent and thorough study of the whole area is C. Bell's book *Ritual: Perspectives and Dimensions* (NY and Oxford, 1997).

[6] M. Douglas, *Purity and Danger: An Analysis of Concepts of Pollution and Taboo*, Paperback edn. (Harmondsworth, 1970), 78.

group holds in common, and express the members' commitment to one another. Indeed, Bruce Lincoln goes so far as to argue that 'society is constructed from nothing so much as sentiments'.[7] People form or maintain social groups to the degree that they feel affinity for the members of the group and/or estrangement from those outside the group. Commonly held myths and rituals have the power to create and express these affinities. 'Like myth, ritual is best understood as an authoritative mode of symbolic discourse and a powerful instrument for the evocation of those sentiments out of which society is constructed.'[8]

Religious rituals, in particular, serve to confirm the connection between a group's religious and moral vision, and their understanding of the world around them; to use Geertz's terminology, their ethos and world-view. Geertz specifically addresses sacred rather than secular ritual:

For it is in ritual—that is, consecrated behaviour—that this conviction that religious concepts are veridical and that religious directives are sound is somehow generated. It is in some sort of ceremonial form—even if that form be hardly more than the recitation of a myth, the consultation of an oracle, or the decoration of a grave—that the moods and motivations which sacred symbols induce in men and the general conceptions of the order of existence which they formulate for men meet and reinforce one another. In ritual, the world as lived and the world as imagined, fused under the agency of a single set of symbolic forms, turn out to be the same world.[9]

Now, it is clear that some societies or social groups are more concerned with ritual than others, and it is important to ask what are the conditions for a high or increased level of ritual behaviour. Robert Wuthnow further suggests that ritual becomes more important in situations of social uncertainty, where there is doubt about the constitution or boundaries or the group: 'Other things being equal as far as the resources and freedom for engaging in ritual are concerned, the greater the uncertainty that exists about social positions, commitments to shared values, or behavioral options likely to influence other actors, the greater the likelihood that behavior will take on a ritual dimension of significance.'[10]

---

[7] Lincoln, *Discourse and the Construction of Society: Comparative Studies of Myth, Ritual, and Classification* (NY, 1989), 20.      [8] Ibid. 53.

[9] Geertz, *Interpretation of Cultures*, 112.

[10] Wuthnow, *Meaning and Moral Order*, 120.

Thus to increase the importance of ritual is typical of social groups
which perceive some threat to their continued existence: dissenting minorities, whether religious, ethnic, or political.

Such a view complements Douglas's theory that where we find
a high level of anxiety about purity and pollution we also find
considerable pressure to maintain group boundaries, and indeed
anxiety about maintaining such boundaries. In her book *Natural
Symbols* the prime example of such a community is the London
'Bog Irish': traditionalist Catholic immigrants who persist in ritual
abstinence from meat on Fridays, despite opposition from the
church hierarchy, who would prefer less 'external' spiritual disci-
plines. For these poor Irish in exile, the ritual may have lost much
of its original significance as an act of personal mortification (as
the clergy point out), but it has taken on a new significance in providing continuity between the old world and the new. 'No empty
symbol, it means allegiance to a humble home in Ireland and to a
glorious tradition in Rome. These allegiances are something to be
proud of in the humiliations of the unskilled labourer's lot'.[11] Such
a picture is highly suggestive of the situation of the Jews in
Babylon, and Douglas herself draws the analogy between the Bog
Irish Friday abstinence from meat and the Jewish avoidance
of pork.[12] It is important to stress here that there is a two-way
relationship between ritual codes and social circumstances. A
high degree of ritual behaviour does not merely arise out of the
experience of a closely knit group, but is also instrumental in
creating the conditions which allow that group its continued
distinctiveness, and indeed its existence.[13]

Daniel Smith has applied Douglas's work to the Babylonian
exile, arguing that the exilic redactors of the priestly legislation
served their community by providing them with cultic regulations
which could be used as identity markers in the minority context of
exile. He has confirmed her insights in a survey of groups of

---

[11] Douglas, *Natural Symbols*, 59.

[12] Ibid. 60–4.

[13] C. Bell writes more generally: 'Some evidence suggests that the very practices that
generate and maintain the systemization of ritual—processes of hierarchization, centralization, replication, marginalization, and the like, can be powerful forces in politics,
regional identity and interregional relations, economics, social stratification, philosophical
speculation, and theological abstraction. As such, the systemization of ritual would not
simple relate to other social and cultural phenomena as much as it would help constitute
them' (*Ritual*, 177).

forced migrants in the modern world whose position is similar to that of the Babylonian exiles, in that they too were moved in groups largely as a result of state intervention. In particular, Smith notes the increased use of ritual as a form of symbolic resistance among the Zionist Bantu churches of South Africa; the Japanese interned in camps by the US government during the Second World War; and groups of African slaves in the American South. Smith concludes that 'the role of ritual in minority, dominated contexts may play an important functional role in the preservation and symbolic resistance of the group in question'.[14] He goes on to interpret the priestly legislation as such a ritual response to the experience of domination, noting the extensive use of purity language in exilic metaphors for the behaviour of social groups. The aspects of P that Smith highlights as most significant are the concern for pure categories, the fear of transfer of pollution, and the problem of mixed marriages. He largely ignores Ezekiel, although he does draw attention to chapter 8, of which he writes: 'The entire chapter of Ezek. 8, which deals with the defilement of the temple during the exile, is another example, reflecting the horror of impurity among the exiles themselves and their cultic concerns.'[15]

Thomas Renz has recently drawn attention to Smith's hypothesis about the value of ritual in exile, but argues that it does not apply to the book of Ezekiel.[16] For Renz, Ezekiel's concern for purity is more oriented to the future restoration than to the present experience of the exiles, and more concerned with internal than external boundaries. He notes Ezekiel's awareness of the difficulty of maintaining complete purity in an unclean land (4: 12–15) and concludes: 'The response to this impossibility found in the book of Ezekiel does not seem to be to reinforce ritual boundaries, but to uphold the expectation of the return to the land where purity can again be put into practice.'[17] Renz is right to stress the importance of purity in Ezekiel's vision of the future, but he may have underestimated the prevalence of ritual concerns throughout the book and thereby also their potential importance for the maintenance of community and identity in exile.

The episode in Ezekiel 4 to which Renz refers is an ideal place to start, since it contains the first mention of purity in the book.

---

[14] Smith, *Landless*, 84.
[15] Ibid. 145.
[16] Renz, *Rhetorical Function*, 49–52.
[17] Ibid. 52.

Within the sign-action of 4: 9–17, whose overt message is one of scarcity of food and impending doom and exile for Jerusalem,[18] is embedded an intriguing exchange between YHWH and his prophet. Ezekiel is asked to prepare cakes baked with human dung, which are explicitly related to the uncleanness of life in exile (4: 13). He refuses, claiming that since his youth he has never defiled himself by eating unclean food (4: 14).[19] YHWH relents to the extent that Ezekiel is allowed to cook with cows' dung, and since he complains no further we may assume that the prophet is satisfied with this solution (4: 15). It is a surprisingly practical outcome, since Ezekiel is apparently offered a compromise which will allow him to maintain his purity even in exile. Indeed, Meindert Dijkstra goes so far as to argue that in this episode we see an early example of Halachic interpretation, which 'deals with the problems of preparing and eating clean and unclean food in exile'.[20] Dung of any kind was not a normal fuel in Palestine, but was an essential for life in Babylonia, and the compromise of cooking with cows' dung represents an accommodation of purity legislation to exilic conditions. This is an attractive interpretation, and, if it is correct, we should note not only that purity legislation might be adapted to suit the Babylonian context, but also that distinctively Jewish questions about distinguishing clean from unclean continue to set the agenda for Ezekiel's community of exiles.

Beyond this example, perhaps the most obvious place to look for ritual in Ezekiel is in chapters 40–48, where we are shown the shape of the restored temple and provided with detailed regulations for its cultic service.[21] The vision may be one of future

[18] This appears to be the symbolism of the 'siege rations' Ezekiel is commanded to prepare and eat: see e.g. Zimmerli, *Ezekiel 1*, 168–9; Allen, *Ezekiel 1–19*, 69.

[19] Margaret Odell notes the strength of Ezekiel's objection, commenting that 'his objection to eating food cooked over dung is his only expression of personal will or desire in the whole book' (M. S. Odell, 'You Are What You Eat: Ezekiel and the Scroll', *JBL* 117 (1998), 239).

[20] M. Dijkstra, 'The Valley of Dry Bones: Coping with the Reality of Exile in the Book of Ezekiel', in B. Becking and M. C. A. Korpel (eds.), *The Crisis of Israelite Religion: Transformation of Religious Tradition in Exilic and Post-Exilic Times*, OTS, 42 (Leiden: 1999), 126. A number of recent commentators, including even the normally conservative Greenberg, consider this passage a secondary insertion (*Ezekiel 1–20*, 125–6). Dijkstra relates it to Pohlmann's *golaorientierte Redaktion*, but seems rather more confident than Pohlmann that it reflects the experience of the early exilic community.

[21] Chapters 40–48 are among those whose authenticity has been most questioned, but a majority of modern commentators accept that at least a substantial core of the material

restoration rather than present reality, but it nevertheless gives us some access to the ideals and priorities of those for whom it was written. The focus on ritual is intense: indeed, the duty of Israel is conceived almost wholly in ritual terms. One might go as far as to say that ethics has been subordinated to (or even subsumed within) ritual.[22] As has often been pointed out, Ezekiel 40–48 is closely related to the priestly legislation, and it is therefore not surprising that we find some of the same concerns here that Smith found in P. And, as in Smith's understanding of P, it is not just the fact that there is a great deal of material about ritual, but also that this goes alongside a highly developed concern to protect the boundaries of the community.[23]

The concern for pure categories is clear in one of the principal tasks given to the priests in 44: 23: 'They shall teach my people the difference between the holy and the common, and show them how to distinguish between the clean and the unclean.' This almost exactly mirrors the injunction in Leviticus 10: 10, and in Ezekiel, as in P, the purpose of such careful distinctions is to ensure that what is unclean or common does not cross over into the realm of the holy. For Ezekiel, that was the great mistake of the past, and it is certainly plausible to see much of chapters 40–48 as a counter example to the horrors of chapters 8–11, showing how the temple might be ordered to be a fit dwelling place for YHWH. That this is indeed the prophet's concern is confirmed by YHWH's own words as he enters the new temple: 'The house of Israel shall no more defile my holy name' (43: 7). YHWH's perpetual presence in the sanctuary depends upon its purity, and

goes back to the original prophet. The most influential work has been that of H. Gese, *Der Verfassungsentwurf des Ezechiel (Kap. 40–48) traditionsgeschichtlich untersucht*, BHT 25 (Tübingen, 1957); cf. also Wevers, *Ezekiel*, 207. It is likely that the prophet's words may have been supplemented by later editors, but, as is the case elsewhere in the book, there is such a degree of homogeneity both of theme and language that it is very difficult to judge what is original and what is not (cf. Joyce, 'Synchronic and Diachronic', 118–22). It seems likely, given this considerable continuity, that the bulk of the material in these chapters, along with the rest of the book, was completed by the time of the return or, at the latest, during the early post-exilic period. It is appropriate, therefore, to treat 40–48 as an 'exilic' phenomenon.

[22] It is worth noting that even such material about social justice as appears in these chapters (45: 9, 10–12) focuses on weights and measures, and is immediately followed by instructions concerning the appropriate size for offerings!

[23] Renz argues that the use of בדל in Ezekiel 'does not reflect "xenophobic concerns"' (*Rhetorical Function*, 52), but the overall context in which this language appears is undoubtedly one where ritual distinctions are seen as a means of protecting the community from external threat.

so Ezekiel offers his audience the vision of a perfectly ordered temple. The sacrificial system, described in detail in chapters 43–6, has as its primary purpose the removal of impurity from the sanctuary. Kalinda Rose Stevenson has noted that within Ezekiel's design there are two most holy locations: the holy of holies and the altar; one the symbolic dwelling place of YHWH, the other the place of purgation. Significantly, it is not the holy of holies which is the exact centrepiece of the temple complex, but the altar:

This focus on the Altar expresses the understanding that societal and cosmic well-being needs more than the presence of YHWH. There is also need for a means of cleansing the society and cosmos from the effects of impurity. This is the function of the Altar and the concentric center of the Holy Place, the Portion, and the land. Israel in exile is suffering the results of impurity which drove YHWH into exile. The solution is to cleanse the impurity of society and cosmos by means of the Altar.[24]

This concern to prevent the transfer of impurity to the sanctuary is very much in line with Smith's understanding of P, and it is matched by Ezekiel's concern to protect the boundaries of the new community.

Unlike a number of the examples Smith cites (especially from Ezra/Nehemiah), Ezekiel 40–48 is not much concerned with mixed marriages. Nevertheless, it is concerned to prevent foreigners from entering the temple precincts. Ezekiel 44: 6–8 describes the past sin of admitting foreigners, 'uncircumcised in heart and flesh' into the sanctuary and thereby profaning it. Ezekiel 44: 9 provides the solution: no foreigners will henceforth be permitted to enter. The responsibility for ensuring that this is carried out will fall to the Levites, who will act as temple guards, overseeing the gates. The 'fortress mentality' we can discern here is given physical shape in the dimensions of the temple revealed earlier to the prophet. The new temple is conceived in the form of a walled city (40: 2), and one aspect of this is that the walls and gates of the temple are substantial defensive fortifications like those of a city. Stevenson points out that only here in the Hebrew Bible (40: 5; 42: 20) is the word הומה used to denote temple walls rather than city walls.[25] Ezekiel gives it a ritual role: 'to make a

---

[24] K. R. Stevenson, *The Vision of Transformation: The Territorial Rhetoric of Ezekiel 40–48,* SBLDS 154 (Atlanta, Ga., 1996), 40–1.      [25] Ibid. 44.

separation between the holy and the common' (42: 20). Equally a feature of Ezekiel's temple which distinguishes it significantly from the descriptions of both Solomon's temple and the wilderness tabernacle is the size and prominence of its gates. Such gates are nowhere else associated with temple structures, but only cities, and, again, their purpose is to defend the holy by controlling access to it. They are the 'first line of defense against unauthorized access',[26] protecting the temple and the community it serves. Katheryn Pfisterer Darr points out that even the more mythical themes we find towards the end of the Temple Vision are far from universalistic in application: a 'wall around paradise' limits the benefits of the renewed land to YHWH's community. Even in the wonderful vision of chapter 47 no transformation takes place beyond the perimeter of Israel's territory.[27]

A brief look at Ezekiel 40–48, then, suggests that these chapters contain a rather similar set of concerns to those that Smith found in P. The text promotes ritual codes of behaviour that protect the community from the threat of impurity, and sets the whole ritual system inside the impregnable fortress of the new community. On Smith's model, this looks very much like the appropriate response of an exiled community to the threat of domination. Ezekiel 8 and 40–48 present two opposing cultic pictures, one of utter and unforgivable desecration, the other of the prophet's ideal ritual system in operation. However, the examples we have examined so far by no means exhaust the commitment to ritual that is evident in the book. There is much more to be said about the relationship between the prophet's dominating cultic interests and the social experience of the deported Judaeans.

It is not only in the content of his oracles that the prophet's priestly background is evident, but also in his constant and striking use of cultic language. As McKeating puts it: 'Where the Ezekiel tradition differs markedly from earlier prophetic literature is not in the sins specified, but in the language in which they are spoken of. The book uses for preference the priestly/cultic language of defilement.'[28] Even when the sins described are not in themselves ritual, Ezekiel will often use cultic language to describe them. This 'ritualization' of sin and ethics in Ezekiel's prophecies

---

[26] Ibid. 45.
[27] K. P. Darr, 'The Wall Around Paradise: Ezekielian Ideas About the Future,' *VT* 37 (1987), 271–9. [28] McKeating, *Ezekiel*, 86.

sets him at some distance from earlier prophets, whose criticisms of the cult leave little room for a positive assessment of ritual. This is not to say that Ezekiel is alone in using the image of uncleanness to describe ethical states.[29] In sources outside priestly law it can be used as an image of divine rejection, as in Lamentations 4: 14–15 or Isaiah 35: 8. It is quite commonly used in connection with idolatry: in Genesis 35: 2 foreign gods are presented as defiling, and Jeremiah 2: 23 suggests that Baal worship and uncleanness are synonymous. The idea of the pollution of the land is present in Deuteronomy where a hanged corpse (21: 23) and a divorced wife who returns to her former husband (24: 4) are both described as defiling the land. Hosea used the image of an unclean land to describe the northern kingdom (Hos. 5: 3; 6: 10), and Jeremiah 2: 7 makes the strong statement: 'But when you came in you defiled my land, you made my heritage an abomination.'

However, these references to defilement hardly compare with the systematic ways in which Ezekiel uses the images of cultic wrongdoing and impurity to describe the sins of Judah and the state to which those sins have brought the nation. The degree to which the temple holds centre stage in the book is matched by the ways in which cult and purity dominate the prophet's ethical interests. In the rest of this chapter I shall examine some of the principal ways in which the cult makes itself felt throughout the book. More than any other prophet his vocabulary reflects priestly concerns, the two most significant terms being טמא and חלל. His principal image for social injustice and guilt is blood, a substance central in the priestly system. Moreover, he uses the image of unclean menstrual blood to symbolize the state of Jerusalem. There is no escape from ritual in the book of Ezekiel, and this ritual is part of the exiled community's attempt to define itself against a hostile outside world. Ezekiel's innovative response to the crisis was to revitalize the old institution of the temple by extending its symbolic language beyond the strictly priestly sphere. In the exiled situation in which there was no temple, the use of regulations for purity which have their significance only within the context provided by the temple—one of the most powerful symbols of nationality and identity—has the purpose of providing stability and a focal point for resistance.

---

[29] Cf. Neusner, *Idea of Purity*, 13–15.

## Images of Sin: Uncleanness and Profanation

Ezekiel shares with the priestly code the idea that the task of a priest is to 'teach my people the difference between the holy and the common, and show them how to distinguish between the clean and the unclean' (Ezek. 44: 23; cf. 22: 26; Lev. 10: 10). These two pairs of opposite concepts provided a general framework within which the life of the cult could be carried on. 'The presence or lack of a dynamic quality distinguishes the opposites from one another: profaneness is the lack of holiness, and purity is the lack of impurity.'[30] These concepts, and particularly the notions of impurity and defilement, are absolutely fundamental to the way Ezekiel describes the sins of the nation, and represent one of his most distinctive contributions to the development of Hebrew prophecy. The language has its origin in the cult of the pre-exilic temple, and, as Ezekiel broadens its application, condemning the people of Judah for their defilement and profanation of all that is clean and holy, he is acting in such a way as to keep the temple at the centre of his hearers' symbolic and moral worlds.

Most characteristic of Ezekiel's description of the sins of Judah is the term טמא. This root, which signifies concepts connected with impurity, uncleanness, defilement, and pollution, occurs approximately 280 times in the Hebrew Bible. Of these, some 182 occurrences are in the priestly work in Leviticus and Numbers. It is found 44 times in the book of Ezekiel, which represents approximately 15.5 per cent of all uses. This is substantially more than in any other prophetic book (it appears, for example, 6 times in Isaiah and 5 in Jeremiah). Ezekiel uses טמא to refer to a wide range of situations, from sexual intercourse to the defilement of sanctuary, people, and land.

What is the significance of impurity? At its most basic, purity is the state which is required for access to the cult, and if people or things become impure they are denied that access.[31] An unclean person must wait a period of time, then normally undertake some

---

[30] D. P. Wright, 'Holiness (OT)', *Anchor Bible Dictionary*, iii. 246; cf. also his 'Unclean and Clean', *Anchor Bible Dictionary*, vi. 729–41; J. Barr 'Semantics and Biblical Theology—A Contribution to the Discussion', in *Congress Volume: Uppsala 1971*, SVT 22 (Leiden, 1972), 15–16; P. P. Jenson, *Graded Holiness: A Key to the Priestly Conception of the World*, JSOTS 106 (Sheffield, 1992).

[31] W. H. Gispen, 'The Distinction between Clean and Unclean', *OTS* 5 (1948), 190; L. L. Grabbe, *Leviticus*, Old Testament Guide (Sheffield, 1993), 49.

act of ritual cleansing and make an offering in reparation for their
state.[32] The laws of Leviticus and Numbers detail the forms of
uncleanness which could affect Israelites, and describe the appropriate remedy for each case. Most serious is uncleanness associated
with death and corpses (e.g. Num. 19: 11–22), and indeed it has
been suggested that death is the prototype of all causes of defilement: all major pollutants are in some sense symbolic of death,
which has transgressed the boundary of life and encroached into
an area to which it does not belong.[33] Other causes of pollution
include childbirth (Lev. 12); the disease צרעת, usually translated
'leprosy' (Lev. 13–14); the various forms of genital discharge,
including menstruation (Lev. 15); and contact with unclean animals (Lev. 11). In most cases no ethical opprobrium attaches to the
unclean person because of these simple forms of defilement: 'That
is to say a woman in her menses or a man suffering a flux is not . . .
held in the priestly law code to be ethically or morally impure.
That a man is impure means only that there are certain things he
must not do, others that he must in order to return to a state of
purity.'[34] That he should return to a state of purity is important
because as long as he is impure he is both excluded from participation in the benefits of the cult and, in the case of major pollutions
such as corpse-defilement and צרעת, extremely contagious. Nevertheless, impurity is not the same as sin, and transgression of a rule
of purity does not have to carry any moral implications.[35]

There is some debate about whether this extremely contagious
and often dangerous 'substance' is an active force which works
against God or simply a state or condition. For example, Yehezkel
Kaufmann argues that Israelite monotheism had no room for the
presence of such dynamic forces:

[32] Even if that person was unlikely to participate in the cult in the near future, the
priestly laws give the impression that it was highly undesirable to remain in a state of
impurity.

[33] Cf. E. Feldman, *Biblical and Post Biblical Defilement and Mourning: Law as Theology* (NY,
1977), 31; J. Milgrom, 'Rationale for Cultic Law: The Case of Impurity', *Semeia*, 45 (1989),
106.

[34] Neusner, *Idea of Purity*, 11.

[35] T. Frymer-Kensky points out that some of the actions that cause impurity, such as
sexual intercourse and childbirth, are not morally neutral, but positively necessary for
human society to continue: see her 'Pollution, Purification, and Purgation in Biblical
Israel', in C. M. Meyers and M. J. O'Connor (eds.), *The Word of the Lord Shall Go Forth: Essays
in Honor of David Noel Freedman in Celebration of his Sixtieth Birthday* (Winona Lake, Ind., 1983),
403.

In spite of its belief in the substantiality of impurity, the Bible does not accord to it the status of a primary, demonic force. There is no tension of powers between the holy and the impure. Impurity is no more than a condition, one might almost say a religious-aesthetic state. All power and activity is concentrated in the realm of the holy; the domain of impurity is a shadow. In contrast to the pagan conception impurity is in itself not a source of danger; its divine-demonic roots have been totally destroyed.[36]

However, there is in P and other parts of the Hebrew Bible a sense that impurity might get out of control, that too much impurity will threaten YHWH's presence in his sanctuary and even Israel's occupation of the land.[37] Other scholars have found enough evidence that impurity is seen as a dangerous force in the Hebrew Bible to understand it as active and dynamic. Thus Baruch Levine can characterize it as 'the actualized form of evil forces operative in the human environment'.[38] It is probably going too far to represent impurity as demonic: for the most part it is human actions and conditions which cause it, and there is none of the fear of demons in Israel that is a feature of so much ancient Near Eastern religion. It is almost as if humans have replaced the demons as the threat to YHWH: 'This is one of the major contributions of the priestly theology: man is demonized. True, man falls short of being a demon, but he is capable of the demonic. He alone is the cause of the world's ills. He alone can contaminate the sanctuary and force God out.'[39] Thus impurity does seem to be more than just a state: it is an active (if not personal) force inimical to YHWH and his holy things, which is activated by human actions and conditions.[40]

Where impurity is seen as a serious threat the distinction between ritual and ethics begins to break down. The language of purity can be used metaphorically to express ethical rather than ritual categories: to express approval or disapproval of certain

---

[36] Kaufmann, *Religion of Israel*, 103.

[37] The logic is similar to that outlined by Koch in his theory of the relationship between act and consequence. See esp. his discussion of Hosea in 'Is There a Doctrine of Retribution in the Old Testament', in J. L. Crenshaw (ed.), *Theodicy in the Old Testament* (London, 1983), 64–9.

[38] B. Levine, *In the Presence of the Lord: A Study of Cult and Some Cultic Terms in Ancient Israel*, SJLA 5 (Leiden, 1974), 78. Cf. also H. Ringgren, *Israelite Religion* (London, 1966), 142.

[39] J. Milgrom, 'Israel's Sanctuary: The Priestly "Picture of Dorian Gray"', in his *Studies in Cultic Theology and Terminology*, SJLA 36 (Leiden, 1983), 82.

[40] Milgrom describes impurity as 'a physical substance, an aerial miasma which possessed magnetic attraction for the realm of the sacred' ('Israel's Sanctuary', 77).

actions. A good example is Isaiah 1: 16: 'Wash yourselves, make yourselves clean; remove the evil of your doings from before my eyes.'[41] Isaiah compares the moral state of the people to a ritual state of uncleanness. Most commonly Ezekiel's use of טמא refers to the state of the people of Judah, who have defiled themselves by their actions. For example, in the oracle of restoration in 20: 32–44, the people will look back at what caused their exile and recognize their mistakes: 'And there you shall remember your ways and all the doings with which you have polluted yourselves' (20: 43). This notion of a defiled people or city is widespread (also 22: 15; 24: 13; 36: 17; 36: 25, 29; cf. 20: 7, 18, 30, 31; 22: 3, 4; 23: 7, 30; 37: 23), and is used by Ezekiel as an image for their rejection by God. In the oracle of the corroded cauldron in chapter 24 we find it expressed plainly: 'Because I would have cleansed you and you were not cleansed from your filthiness, you shall not be cleansed any more till I have satisfied my fury upon you' (24: 13). It is also noteworthy that a number of the references to the people's defilement are in passages oriented towards their restoration. The image of cleansing or purification is used; thus in Ezekiel 36: 25 we read: 'I will sprinkle clean water upon you, and you shall be clean from all your uncleannesses, and from all your idols I will cleanse you.'[42]

Sometimes the ways in which the people have defiled themselves are left unspecified, or described in general terms: the concept is linked more generally with transgressions (פשעים) in 14: 11, 37: 23, and 39: 24. But when there is a specific cause, it is normally idolatry. Typical is the combination of idolatry and bloodshed in 22: 4: 'You have become guilty by the blood you have shed and defiled by the idols you have made.' The theme of the people's defilement by idols is prominent in chapter 20 (20: 7, 18, 30, 31) and elsewhere (22: 3, 4; 23: 7, 30; 37: 23). Ezekiel also uses טמא to refer to the sexual act, which might in itself be morally neutral.[43] However, he does this only in cases where he discusses sexual immorality: intercourse with a neighbour's wife (18: 6, 11,

---

[41] Neusner, *Idea of Purity*, 11–15. Other examples include Pss. 18: 20; 24: 3–5; 51: 6–9; Isa. 35: 8; Jer. 33: 8.

[42] Cf. also Ezek. 36: 33; 37: 23.

[43] Neusner comments: 'To say "he defiled her" may have been a euphemism for sexual relations, nothing more' (*Idea of Purity*, 14). It is not, however, commonly used with such a neutral sense: possibly Deut. 24: 4 or (less possibly) Gen. 34: 5, 13, 27.

15; 33: 26); incest (22: 11); and the relations of Oholibah with the Babylonians (23: 17). There appears to be a connection here with the Holiness Code, where, at the end of the list of prohibited sexual relationships in Leviticus 18, we read:

Do not defile yourselves by any of these things, for by all these the nations I am casting out before you defiled themselves; and the land became defiled, so that I punished its iniquity, and the land vomited out its inhabitants (Lev. 18: 24–5).

Here in Leviticus we find a logical connection between the defilement of the people and the defilement of the land itself, which is the prelude to elimination. The same logic seems to be in operation in Ezekiel, but the range of actions which have brought about the defilement is different, not only sexual abomination but also bloodshed and idolatry:

When the house of Israel dwelt in their own land, they defiled it by their ways and by their doings . . . So I poured out my wrath upon them for the blood they had shed in the land and for the idols with which they had defiled it (36: 17–18)

The people of Israel's actions have defiled not only themselves and their land, but also YHWH's sanctuary (5: 11; 23: 38) and his holy name (43: 7). Ezekiel 23: 38–9 condemns Oholibah for entering YHWH's temple in a state which will defile the sanctuary because of the grave sins she has committed:

Moreover this have they done to me: they have defiled my sanctuary on the same day and profaned my sabbaths. For when they had slaughtered their children in sacrifice to their idols, on the same day they came into my sanctuary to profane it.

Although most commonly in Ezekiel YHWH's holy name refers to his reputation, in 43: 7 it appears to act more as a cipher for his cultic presence, which has been defiled by the burial of kings and the idolatrous cult.[44] Like the defilement of the land, the defilement of sanctuary and of holy things are for Ezekiel serious sins which call down a severe judgement on the people. Ezekiel 5: 11 in fact summarizes his message on this point quite neatly:

---

[44] Milgrom has pointed out that YHWH's name is itself one of the sancta upon which it is possible to trespass, and thereby incur guilt requiring the *asham* sacrifice (*Cult and Conscience: The Asham and the Priestly Doctrine of Repentance*, SJLA 18 (Leiden, 1976), 19).

Wherefore, as I live, says the Lord GOD, surely, because you have defiled my sanctuary with all your detestable things and with all your abominations, therefore I will cut you down; my eye will not spare, and I will have no pity.

As we have seen, ritual purity is the precondition for access to the cult, and, for Ezekiel, access to the cult is fundamental to the relationship between YHWH and his people. The logic of the oracles of judgement is that the widespread defilement of people, land and sanctuary is enough to sever the relationship between the god and his dwelling place, with disastrous consequences for the nation. With language like this Ezekiel has moved beyond the metaphorical: sin causes its own kind of moral impurity which, like physical impurity, can taint YHWH's possessions. Milgrom believes that both are accounted for in the priestly rituals for the Day of Atonement. 'The חטאת which purges the sanctuary of its physical impurity (Lev. 16: 16) is also prescribed for the elimination of moral impurity (Lev. 16: 21).'[45] Perhaps a connection is to be found in the notion of holiness which includes both ritual and ethical demands within its scope. Also, since ethical and ritual demands are made by the deity, this tends to make both absolute and blur the distinctions. Karel van der Toorn suggests that the analogy of etiquette may aid discussion of ritual purity:

It has been argued that etiquette introduces the notion of pleasure as a norm of behaviour. Now when the pleasure of the gods is at stake it can easily be seen why the religious etiquette received a central place in the speculations of the ancients. To them there was no higher standard than the pleasure of the gods, since also the moral precepts were ultimately validated by the same notion.[46]

Milgrom has further analysed the system in which impurity represents a substantial and physical threat to YHWH's occupation of his sanctuary, and has shown that his sanctuary could be defiled not only by the presence of impurity within the temple, but also from a distance.[47] Certain sins and impurities are described as contaminating the sanctuary, notably Molech worship (Lev. 20: 3), the impurity from touching a corpse (Num. 19: 20, 13), and genital discharges (Lev. 15: 31). We have seen that although the

---

[45] Milgrom, 'Rationale for Cultic Law', 103.
[46] K. van der Toorn, *Sin and Sanction in Israel and Mesopotamia: A Comparative Study*, SSN 22 (Assen, 1985), 27.          [47] Milgrom, 'Israel's Sanctuary'.

name of Molech does not feature in Ezekiel, the sacrifice of children which formed that deity's worship is one of the crimes that Ezekiel condemns a number of times.[48] In Ezekiel 9: 7 the instruction to begin killing in the sanctuary is phrased using the language of defilement: 'Defile the house, and fill the courts with the slain.' It is presumably the corpses that cause the defilement.[49] And the discharge of menstrual blood is another of the most striking images which the prophet uses to express the unclean state of the people.[50] Milgrom's work is based on the priestly legislation, but it serves well to explain some of the imagery of the book of Ezekiel. He describes the graded power of impurity that culminates in wanton, unrepented sin, which 'not only pollutes the outer altar and penetrates to the shrine but . . . pierces the veil to the holy ark and *kapporet*, the very throne of God'.[51] He relates this to *The Picture of Dorian Gray*: 'On the analogy of Oscar Wilde's novel, the priestly writers would claim: sin may not leave its mark on the face of the sinner, but it is certain to mark the face of the sanctuary, and unless it is quickly expunged, God's presence will depart.'[52] Of course YHWH's departure would spell disaster for his people, so the temple sacrifices and the annual Day of Atonement ceremonies serve to cleanse the sanctuary of its impurity. But there remains a sense that the impurity caused by severe crimes is a serious and constant threat: it is possible that it might reach a level at which YHWH would have no choice but to leave. This is exactly the situation of the book of Ezekiel, where the prophet graphically describes the progress of the glory of YHWH away from his temple (chapters 8–11), and Milgrom is right to suggest that the system of sancta contagion underlies much of the prophet's theology.[53]

Tikva Frymer-Kensky supports Milgrom's idea that the impurity caused by sin is not simply to be seen as a metaphorical use of the word, but is a different order of pollution from the simple forms of Leviticus 11–16: 'Biblical Israel had two separate sets of what anthropologists would consider "pollution beliefs": a set discussed extensively as pollutions in the Priestly laws, since the

---

[48] See above, Ch. 4.
[49] Compare Josiah's desecration of the Bethel altar in 2 Kgs. 23: 15–16, 20; Allen, *Ezekiel 1–19*, 149.
[50] I shall return to the discussion of female blood later in this chapter.
[51] Milgrom, 'Israel's Sanctuary', 78.
[52] Ibid. 83.
[53] J. Milgrom, *Leviticus 1–16*, Anchor Bible, 3 (NY, 1991), 982.

priests were responsible for preventing the contamination of the
pure and the Holy; and a set of beliefs we might term "danger
beliefs".[54] These concerned actions forbidden by the deity, such as
murder, adultery, or eating blood, and for which there was no
ritual purification. These 'wanton sins' are said to defile not only
the sanctuary but also the people and even the land itself. To
Frymer-Kensky such defilement of people and land is more serious
than defilement of the sanctuary because no ritual purification can
be performed which will cleanse them. The accumulation of
pollution will have catastrophic results: since Israel's possession
of the land is dependent on its purity, if the land becomes too
polluted the people will lose it.[55] Pollution is an important image
which was used to describe the state of the land and people,
and which helped to provide a theoretical explanation of Israel's
history and particularly the destruction of the state of Judah.[56]

The second term which forms a distinctive part of Ezekiel's
description of sin in cultic terms is חלל ('to profane'). We find a
high concentration of forms of this verb in the book of Ezekiel—
31 of 79 biblical occurrences.[57] Ezekiel also includes 4 of the 7
occurrences of the adjective חל. These words, חל and חלל, are
applied to the distinction between the holy and the common or
profane. Again one of the pair of opposites (the holy) is active and
contagious, whereas the other (the profane) is the more neutral
basic state. The active and rather threatening power of holiness is
evident in rules which aim to keep it firmly inside the sanctuary;
for example, Ezekiel 44: 19 (cf. 46: 20):

And when they go out into the outer court to the people, they shall put
off the garments in which they have been ministering, and lay them
in the holy chambers; and they shall put on other garments, lest they
communicate holiness to the people with their garments.

---

[54] Frymer-Kensky, 'Pollution', 404.

[55] Ibid. 406–9.

[56] D. P. Wright suggests another distinction between kinds of impurity, thinking of
'tolerated' and 'prohibited' impurities. The former are the often unavoidable simple forms
of impurity while the latter are 'impurities arising from sinful situations' which Neusner
would consider as largely metaphorical. Wright sees the two kinds of impurity as intimately
related, and the experience of tolerated impurities serves as a reminder for the community
of the dangers of the more serious prohibited ones: see his 'The Spectrum of Priestly
Impurity', in G. A. Anderson and S. Olyan (eds.), *Priesthood and Cult in Ancient Israel*, JSOTS
125 (Sheffield, 1991), 150–82.

[57] There are 16 occurrences in Leviticus, mostly concentrated in the Holiness Code:
again compare 1 occurrence in Isa., 2 in Jer.

It is thus a serious offence to bring something which should be holy into the sphere of the profane. Ezekiel uses the symbolic language of profanation to describe Israel's offences and the effect these have on temple and God. Among the holy things that are profaned in the book the most prominent are probably the temple and its sanctuary and paraphernalia; the institution of the sabbath; and, most shocking, YHWH's name and person.

Since the priestly language of sacred and profane has its origin in the temple cult, it is not surprising that the profanation of the sanctuary is used as an image of sin. In 23: 39 the murderous Oholibah enters it with blood on her hands and thereby profanes it.[58] Besides profaning the sanctuary itself Ezekiel condemns priests who 'profane my holy things' (22: 26), which could include all things related to the cult.

In 7: 21–4 YHWH declares that he will give his 'precious place' into the hands of foreigners for destruction:

I will turn my face from them, that they may profane my precious place; robbers shall enter it and profane it, and make it a desolation. Because the land is full of bloody crimes and the city is full of violence, I will bring the worst of nations to take possession of their houses; I will put an end to their proud might, and their holy places shall be profaned. (7: 22–4)

Although it is possible that צְפוּנִי ('my precious place') refers to the land of Israel or the city of Jerusalem,[59] most commentators favour understanding it as the temple, or, even more specifically, the holy of holies.[60] In this case YHWH's turning away from his people represents his rejection of them which indirectly profanes his temple by allowing in outsiders to pillage it. The image is even more shocking in 24: 21, where it is YHWH himself who profanes his sanctuary: 'Behold I will profane my sanctuary, the pride of your power, the delight of your eyes, and the desire of your soul.' The language used to describe the temple in these oracles expresses its importance in the minds of Ezekiel and the exiled

[58] Cf. also Ezek. 44: 7. In the case of the sanctuary it seems that the language of profanation and defilement is almost interchangeable (cf. the usage in Ezek. 23: 38–9). One notable difference (at least in Ezekiel) is that the people do not *profane* themselves, only other things, whereas they are capable of *defiling* themselves by their actions. This testifies to the idea that profaneness is the neutral state while impurity is a more active force or substance.

[59] Greenberg, *Ezekiel 1–20*, 154.

[60] Cooke, *Ezekiel*, 82–3; Eichrodt, *Ezekiel*, 104; Zimmerli, *Ezekiel 1*, 212; Wevers, *Ezekiel*, 65.

community. Since it was so central to the prophet's thought, it
will have been most important for him to think through YHWH's
rejection of the temple, and it is significant that when he does this
he uses the priestly language of profanation.[61]

Of the things holy to YHWH which the people profane in
Ezekiel, the commonest is the sabbath (20: 13, 16, 21, 24; 23: 38,
39; cf. also 22: 8, 26). The sabbath commandment is present in all
Israelite legal traditions (Exod. 20: 8–11; 23: 12; 31: 12–17; 34: 21;
35: 2; Lev. 19: 3, 30; 23: 3; 26: 2; Deut. 5: 12–15) and it is probably
a very ancient part of Israel's religious and social tradition.[62] On
its appearance in Ezekiel there is a tendency for some scholars to
leap to the conclusion that as 'one of the few cultic practices which
could be observed without the paraphernalia of the Jerusalem
Temple', it became during the exile a significant marker of Jewish
identity.[63] This is certainly the impression given by Ezekiel 20,
where we read not only of the profaning of sabbaths but of the
sabbath's establishment 'as a sign between me and them, that they
might know that I the LORD sanctify them' (20: 12). This is closely
parallel to the priestly ideology of the sabbath presented in
Exodus 31: 12–17: it has become, like circumcision, one of the
distinguishing marks of the people of Israel:

You shall keep my sabbaths, for this is a sign between me and you
throughout your generations, that you may know that I, the LORD,
sanctify you. You shall keep the sabbath, because it is holy for you; every
one who profanes it [מְחַלְלֶיהָ] shall be put to death; whoever does any
work on it, that soul shall be cut off from among his people. (Exod. 31:
13–14)

But this understanding of the sabbath as a Jewish identity marker
does not work nearly so well for other occurrences of the sabbath
in Ezekiel, where it appears in parallel with aspects of the pre-
exilic cult. Thus in Ezekiel 23: 38 the accusation of profaning
sabbaths stands alongside that of defiling the sanctuary; in 22: 8

---

[61] Cf. T. M. Raitt, *A Theology of Exile: Judgment/Deliverance in Jeremiah and Ezekiel* (Phil., 1977), 68.

[62] On the origin of the sabbath and its place in Israelite religion see e.g. A. Phillips, *Ancient Israel's Criminal Law: A New Approach to the Decalogue* (Oxford, 1970); G. F. Hasel, 'Sabbath', *Anchor Bible Dictionary*, v. 849–56; H. A. McKay, *Sabbath and Synagogue: The Question of Sabbath Worship in Ancient Judaism*, Religions in the Graeco-Roman World, 122 (Leiden, 1994), 11–42.

[63] Wevers, *Ezekiel*, 117; cf. also Zimmerli, *Ezekiel 1*, 410.

sabbath and holy things are paired, and in 22: 26 the priests are accused of disregarding YHWH's sabbaths among a variety of other cultic offences. Moreover, as Eichrodt points out:

when he names the commandments by observing which one can confess one's adherence to Yahweh even in an unclean land (18: 6 ff.), Ezekiel passes over that same sabbath commandment, nor does he mention it in his enumeration of the sins of Jerusalem (24: 6 ff.) and of the sins of those who remained in the land after the deportation (33: 25 and also cf. 5: 11; 7: 23; 9: 9; 11: 6).[64]

It is possible to argue, on the basis of passages like Isaiah 1: 3, Hosea 2: 13, and 2 Kings 4: 23 and 16: 17, that the sabbath belonged to the calendar of the pre-exilic cult: 'a day of rest, a joyful feast day on which men visited sanctuaries or went to consult a "man of God" '.[65] Lamentations 2: 6 contains the line 'the LORD has brought to an end in Zion appointed feast and sabbath', and Albertz comments: 'Thus the pre-exilic sabbath was largely part of the official cult and had come to an end with the destruction of the Jerusalem temple.'[66] The appearance of the sabbath in Ezekiel 22 and 23 seems rather closer to this idea than to that of the covenantal sign. Even in the vision of the restored city in 40–48, where the keeping of the sabbath will form part of the new order, it is tied closely to the temple cult (44: 24; 45: 17; 46: 3, 4, 12).

What are we to make of this? Commentators are at sixes and sevens. Cooke, not normally given to dismissing sections of the book as late, argues that the emphasis on the sabbath in chapter 20 is 'so disproportioned as to suggest the handiwork of a later scribe, zealous for the Law'.[67] But other interpreters, including Wevers and Zimmerli, are less inclined to consider the references to the sabbath an interpolation.[68] It is possible that the whole

[64] Eichrodt, *Ezekiel*, 263; cf. also the discussion by Renz, who comments that 'even if the sabbath increased in prominence during the exile, the potential for boundary maintenance inherent in sabbath observance was not fully exploited in the book of Ezekiel' (*Rhetorical Function*, 51). [65] De Vaux, *Ancient Israel*, 482.

[66] Albertz, *History of Israelite Religion*, 408. Heather McKay (*Sabbath and Synagogue*, esp. 15–24, 41–2) has recently argued that the evidence of the Hebrew Bible suggests that the sabbath was kept as a day of rest rather than of worship, except in priestly circles (to which, of course, Ezekiel belonged). Even if it is to be seen more as a day of rest than a day of worship, it still seems to have belonged to a recognized calendar of holy days, alongside various others, most notably the new moon.

[67] Cooke, *Ezekiel*, 217; so Eichrodt, *Ezekiel*, 263–5.

[68] Wevers, *Ezekiel*, 117; Zimmerli, *Ezekiel 1*, 410.

chapter is a late addition to the book, as Hölscher and May suggest.[69] Perhaps unsurprisingly, Greenberg suggests the possibility that allegiance to the sabbath regulations was a mark of the true Yahwist as early as the time of Manasseh.[70] This would make the references to the sabbath in chapter 20 more compatible with the rest of the book, but unfortunately Greenberg does not provide any real evidence for his claim.

This is a very awkward problem, but I would offer as a tentative solution the possibility that the two different attitudes to the sabbath in the book of Ezekiel are reflective of the two different moral worlds the exiles inhabit. Ezekiel 22 and 23 are part of the prophet's condemnation of Jerusalem, which we have seen elsewhere to be associated with the moral world of the Jerusalem élite, therefore it is unsurprising that references to the sabbath still imply that it is part of the state cult. On the other hand, in chapter 20 we may see the first steps towards the use of the sabbath as an important marker of Jewish identity. In this context, it may be significant that chapter 20 is explicitly addressed to the elders of Israel who are in exile along with Ezekiel (20: 1), whereas chapter 22, at least, is specifically addressed to Jerusalem (22: 2).[71] Like the language of profanation itself, which was originally drawn from the world of the Jerusalem temple, sabbath observance may be an example of Ezekiel's reapplication of elements of the cult for life in exile.

The religious perspective of the book of Ezekiel is so uncompromisingly theocentric that it is no surprise to find YHWH's own name and person among the holy things that are profaned. In the first place the sinful actions of the people are said to provoke this result. Thus in 20: 39 the prophet proclaims 'my holy name you shall no more profane with your gifts and your idols'. W. Dommershausen's comment about the expression in Amos 2: 8 is equally relevant to Ezekiel: 'The name of Yahweh stands here for the person of Yahweh; there may be overtones of the idea that Israel's inhuman conduct implicates the name of Israel's god, so that other nations cease to respect it.'[72] This is the same conception

[69] May, 'Ezekiel', 167; Hölscher, *Hesekiel*, 108–10.

[70] Greenberg, *Ezekiel 1–20*, 367.

[71] Chapters 44–6 are, of course, part of Ezekiel's vision of a restored state cult, where the sabbath again has its place in the temple calendar.

[72] W. Dommershausen, 'חלל I', in *TDOT*, iv. 410.

which we find in all the uses of חלל שם in the Holiness Code (Lev.
18: 21; 19: 12; 20: 3; 21: 6; 22: 2, 32), where human actions which
trespass cultic regulations are at fault.[73] Within this context Ezekiel
also describes the profanation of YHWH himself, by the false
prophetesses (13: 19), and as a result of the cultic failures of the
priests (22: 26). In all of these cases Ezekiel is drawing upon cultic
images: 'in diesem Gedankenspiel zwischen heilig (*qdš*) und profan
(*ḥll*) ist das charakteristische kultische Denken erkennbar'.[74]

However, by contrast with H, there is another way in which
YHWH's holy name is profaned; not as a result of the people's
offences but because of their final destruction.[75] In the historical
summary of chapter 20 YHWH refrained from destroying Israel for
her sin 'for the sake of my name, that it should not be profaned
among the nations' (20: 9, 14, 22). After the disaster has struck, 36:
20–3 makes it clear that YHWH's name has been profaned by the
exile of his people: 'But when they came to the nations, wherever
they came, they profaned my holy name, in that men said of
them, "These are the people of the LORD, and yet they had to
go out of his land." ' (36: 20). Since the preservation of YHWH's
honour and reputation is fundamental to all his action in the book
this is a grave situation and one which he must rectify (cf. 36:
22–38). Paul Joyce writes of YHWH's motive:

What aspect of Yahweh's reputation is particularly in mind? The profanation of the divine 'name' appears to consist essentially in the casting
of doubt upon Yahweh's power and effectiveness . . . The nations have
misinterpreted Israel's defeat as a sign of Yahweh's weakness. He must
now (even at the cost of waiving the rigour of his judgment) act to correct
this misconception and vindicate his reputation as a powerful god.[76]

Zimmerli comments that a concern for YHWH's name is visible in
the intercessory prayers of Moses after the golden calf incident
(Exod. 32: 12) and that of the spies (Num. 14: 13 ff.).[77] This is not
quite accurate: at issue in Moses' prayers is the possibility that

---

[73] Outside H and Ezekiel the expression occurs only at Jer. 34: 16 and Amos 2: 8. It is
interesting to note that this expression never occurs in P, but only in H. P tends to use the
term מעל ביהוה to express the desecration of the divine name; see J. Milgrom, 'The Priestly
Doctrine of Repentance', *RB* 82 (1975), esp. 188–90.

[74] G. Bettenzoli, *Geist der Heiligkeit: Traditionsgeschichtliche Untersuchung des QDŠ-Begriffes im
Buch Ezechiel*, Quaderni di Semitistica, 8 (Florence, 1979), 202; cf. also 90.

[75] Dommershausen, 'חלל I', 410.

[76] Joyce, *Divine Initiative*, 102–3.

[77] Zimmerli, *Ezekiel 1*, 409.

YHWH will destroy his chosen people, and the response that this will provoke from the Egyptians. While these prayers do refer to YHWH's reputation among foreigners, neither the expression חלל שם nor even the word שם is used. Therefore the use of this language to describe YHWH's state as the result of his people's destruction would appear to be Ezekiel's innovation.

We should note the rather paradoxical situation that Israel's destruction (and hence YHWH's profanation) is something that the god himself brings about. Such paradox is characteristic of the prophet's thinking: in Ezekiel 8–9 YHWH's reaction to a series of progressively more defiling abominations is to announce the destruction of Jerusalem with the words 'Defile the house'. Most notorious are the 'statutes which were not good, and ordinances by which they could not have life' of 20: 25, which are again a reaction to persistent wrongdoing. It is almost as if YHWH's response to sin is to answer it with more in kind, and thereby to let it build up to such an intolerable level that disaster is inevitable.

Ezekiel uses the term חלל in a number of different contexts to express the sins of Judah. The profanation of YHWH's sabbaths, holy things, and sanctuary are offences for which Israel is held responsible. Moreover, the people profane YHWH's holy name by their sins and by the humiliation which their punishment has brought upon him. In contrast to his use of טמא, Ezekiel tends not to extend the concept of חלל outside the realm of the sacred, and does not use it to describe the state of the people themselves. Nevertheless, the extent to which he does use these cultic categories of sacred and profane provides a clear indication of the vital place which the temple and its ritual holds in the prophet's thought.

## The Symbol of Blood

Another of the most significant ways in which Ezekiel shows his attachment to cultic and ritual concerns is his use of imagery and concepts connected with blood. Blood is his principal metaphor for violence in society and the guilt of the house of Israel, and unclean female blood also provides an image for the wrongs of the nation. In all these cases Ezekiel draws on cultic traditions, and this use of language and imagery can be seen as part of his ritualization of ethical ideas. Blood is not the only such ritual image he uses to describe social and political sins, but it is unquestionably the dominant one.

Even a cursory reading of Ezekiel's oracles of judgement will make plain the prophet's concern with blood. Of approximately 360 occurrences of the word דם in the Hebrew Bible some 54 are in Ezekiel; only Leviticus with its elaborate details for the manipulation of sacrificial blood has more (84). Given Ezekiel's priestly background we are not surprised by this statistic, but it is noteworthy that only 5 of the uses of דם in the book of Ezekiel refer literally to the blood of sacrifices, all of them within chapters 40–48.[78] Much more commonly blood is used as a metaphor. Sometimes it represents the violence of YHWH's judgement upon a nation, especially seen in conjunction with pestilence (5: 17; 14: 19; 28: 23; 38: 22). More interesting to us, however, are the numerous occasions on which Ezekiel uses blood imagery to represent the sins of the people, most often the sins of social injustice. We find blood paired with words for offences against social justice in several cases. Ezekiel 7: 23 reads: 'Because the land is full of bloody crimes [משפט דמים] and the city is full of violence', and 9: 9 proclaims: 'the guilt of the house of Israel and Judah is exceedingly great; the land is full of blood (דמים), and the city full of injustice'.

This is a metaphor for social ills which Ezekiel uses again and again.[79] Most commonly the phrase שפך דם expresses the violence in Jerusalem (16: 38; 18: 10; 22: 3, 6, 9, 12, 27; 23: 45; 24: 7, 8; 33: 25; 36: 18). This expression regularly refers to murder in the Hebrew Bible, and is a serious charge.[80] In Ezekiel's oracles the image sometimes may refer literally to murder, but often seems to express a more general violence and lawlessness in society. In the allegories of chapters 16 and 23 the crime is actually given a cultic context, since the blood which the women have shed is that of their own children sacrificed to idols.

In the Hebrew Bible the greatest concern for blood comes from within the priestly tradition, perhaps because so much of the priestly task involved the manipulation of blood. It is blood's

---

[78] Ezek. 43: 18, 20; 44: 7, 15, 19.
[79] Elsewhere in the prophets it appears at e.g. Mic. 3: 10; Hos. 4: 2, but nowhere is the emphasis as consistent as in Ezekiel.
[80] Cf. B. Kedar-Kopfstein, 'דם', in *TDOT*, iii. 242.

quality of life which gives it atoning power in sacrifice (Lev. 17: 11), and this atoning power makes it one of the most important elements of the cult.[81] To the priests all blood that is shed, whether human or animal, belongs to God and must be disposed of properly. 'For your lifeblood I will surely require a reckoning; of every beast I will require it and of man; of every man's brother I will require the life of man.' (Gen. 9: 5). The theology of the divine image is brought into play to explain the need for shed blood to be avenged: 'Whoever sheds the blood of man, by man shall his blood be shed; for God made man in his own image.' (Gen. 9: 6). In the Holiness Code all blood is powerful, even that of animals: someone who slaughters an animal in the wrong place without due regard to cultic practice is guilty of blood guilt: 'He has shed blood; and that man shall be cut off from among his people' (Lev. 17: 4).[82] The eating of blood is forbidden and any animal that is killed away from the sanctuary must have its blood poured out and covered with dust (Lev. 17: 10–13). Thus within the priestly system it would appear that the shedding of any blood is a particularly dangerous offence, and we can see how Ezekiel's emphasis on bloodshed as a metaphor for social violence fits into the prophet's cultic concerns. Julie Galambush explains further:

Ezekiel's emphasis on Jerusalem's bloodiness is directly related to his concern over Yahweh's abandonment of the Jerusalem sanctuary. Control over the lifebearing power of blood is central to the priestly purity system, since the correct or incorrect handling of blood determines the cleanliness or defilement of the sanctuary, and therefore Yahweh's ability to dwell within it. All shed blood is to be ritually offered, preferably at the sanctuary itself; improperly shed blood pollutes the altar, and this pollution can only be removed by the blood of the sin offering (or in some cases not at all).[83]

In fact the shedding of human blood would appear to be one of the things for which there is no remedy, at least according to Numbers 35: 33–4, which deals with murder:

You shall not thus pollute [חנף] the land in which you live; for blood pollutes the land, and no expiation can be made for the land, for the blood that is shed in it, except by the blood of him who shed it. You shall

---

[81] Both the Deuteronomic and priestly traditions make the association of blood with life explicit (Deut. 12: 23; Gen. 9: 4; Lev. 17: 11).

[82] The expression שפך דם is the same one found throughout Ezekiel.

[83] Galambush, *Jerusalem in the Book of Ezekiel*, 103.

not defile (טמא) the land in which you live, in the midst of which I dwell; for I the LORD dwell in the midst of the people of Israel.

Here we find made explicit the connection between bloodshed and defilement, which seems to be at the root of Ezekiel's choice of this metaphor for violence in society.

A second and related use of blood imagery in Ezekiel is as a metaphor to represent guilt. A good example of this can be found in chapter 35: the oracle against Edom. Edom's crimes are perpetual enmity towards Israel and betrayal, and 35: 6 follows their proclamation with: 'therefore, as I live, says the Lord GOD, I will prepare you for blood and blood shall pursue you; because you are guilty of blood,[84] therefore blood shall pursue you.' There can be no question that guilt is the issue; as Reventlow says 'דם heißt hier in ganz allgemeiner Bedeutung: »schwere Schuld«'.[85] The sense that blood actively pursues the offender is unique here in Ezekiel, but the notion of blood guilt is also to be found at 16: 38; 22: 4; 23: 37, 45 in the context of the bloody crimes of Jerusalem.

In chapters 3, 18, and 33 the word דם is used in the context of a sinner's responsibility for his own death. In the watchman passages we find it in the expression which determines whether the prophet is held responsible for the death of a sinner or not. 'His blood I will require at [the prophet's] hand' (3: 18, 20; 33: 6, 8). If the prophet is not to be held responsible (because the sinner has been warned and remains unrepentant) we find the phrase 'his blood shall be upon himself' (33: 4, 5).[86] This expression also appears at 18: 13, where the climax to the description of the wicked man reads: 'He has done all these abominable things; he shall surely die; his blood shall be upon himself.' Zimmerli points out that the expression דמיו בו יהיה is, according to Leviticus, 'the formula with which the persons who are to carry out a death sentence affirm that no blood guilt rests on them because the unrighteous dies on account of his own guilt'.[87] Here, in 18: 13, the

---

[84] Reading אשמה with LXX εἰς αἷμα ἥμαρτες; MT שׂנא ('you hated blood') makes poorer sense; cf. Cooke, *Ezekiel*, 382; Zimmerli, *Ezekiel 2*, 224; Wevers, *Ezekiel*, 187; Allen, *Ezekiel 20–48*, 167.

[85] Reventlow, *Wächter über Israel*, 144; cf. Zimmerli, *Ezekiel 2*, 235.

[86] Reventlow considers this an expression of guilt drawn from cultic law, which he translates, 'Seine Verschuldung komme über ihn.' See his 'Sein Blut komme über sein Haupt', *VT* 10 (1960), 319–20.

[87] Zimmerli, *Ezekiel 1*, 384. Cf. 2 Sam. 3: 27–8, where David denies responsibility for the death of Abner using this formula.

effect of this idiom drawn from cultic law is to emphasize the guilt of the sinner. He is introduced with Ezekiel's stock phrase as a שֹׁפֵךְ דָּם ('shedder of blood' (18: 10)). This description is amplified by the list of cultic, social, and sexual crimes which he commits, and the example ends with the use of the blood-guilt formula, an image 'which places the responsibility clearly on the offender rather than Yahweh'.[88] In these passages in chapters 3, 18, and 33 we find another distinctive use of the imagery of blood which is drawn from the language of the cultic laws and used to represent the sin and responsibility of the house of Israel.

Ezekiel shares the priestly concern that blood should not be eaten (Gen. 9: 4 ff.; Lev. 17: 10 ff., 14 ff.; 19: 26), and treats it as a serious crime on the same level as bloodshed and idolatry. Ezekiel 33: 25 lists the crimes of those left in the land: 'You eat flesh with the blood [עַל הַדָּם], and lift up your eyes to your idols, and shed blood; shall you then possess the land?' A number of scholars have suggested emending עַל הַדָּם here to עַל הֶהָרִים, after the model of 18: 6 and 22: 9.[89] However, there is no textual support for this, and Zimmerli is probably correct to retain the reading found in the Masoretic text, since it makes good sense in the light of Ezekiel's concern over the shedding of blood.[90] Consumption of blood appears again in Ezekiel 39, where we find the prediction that the birds and beasts will come to eat the flesh and drink the blood of Israel's enemies, in horrifying contrast to the prohibition of chapter 33 (39: 17–19).

One of the most powerful figures in Ezekiel's judgement speeches is the personification of Jerusalem as 'the bloody city' (עִיר הַדָּמִים: 22: 1–4; 24: 6–15). Ezekiel takes up this image, which had previously been applied to Nineveh by the prophet Nahum (3: 1), and in both cases adapts it to his own more cultic concerns. In 22: 1–4 the prophet is called to judge the 'bloody city' and declare her תּוֹעֵבוֹת. These abominations are explained first in terms of shedding blood and defilement by idols (22: 3–4), then in the mixture of social, ritual, and sexual offences in verses 6–12, which reflect both violence in society and its guilt.[91] The shedding

---

[88] Matties, *Ezekiel 18*, 78.

[89] e.g. Cooke, *Ezekiel*, 368; Eichrodt, *Ezekiel*, 460–1; Wevers, *Ezekiel*, 180; Fohrer, *Ezechiel*, 187.

[90] Zimmerli, *Ezekiel 2*, 199. Cf. also Allen, *Ezekiel 20–48*, 150.

[91] Zimmerli suggests that as a symbol this shows 'how closely in priestly thinking crimes of blood, the sins of social oppression, and ritual disorder come together, which the

of blood provides a catch-phrase for the whole oracle, and is applied to sins like slander and bribery, which apparently have little to do with murder. It is possible that the phrase למען שפך דם refers to the crime of judicial murder, but in the context of a broad list of sins even that should be seen as a symbol of violence and injustice in society. Reventlow points out that we should not be surprised by the use of שפך דם here: 'Der Anstoß verschwindet, wenn man das שפך דם (vgl. Lev. 17: 4) als Anrechnungsformel kultischer Vergehen erkennt, deren Anwendungsbereich die Verstöße gegen Leib und Leben längst überschritten hat.'[92] For him bloodshed is used to express the guilt associated with capital offences, and he would explain 'bloody city' as 'Stadt der (aus der Kultgemeinschaft ausschließenden) Kapitalvergehen', and that שפך דם in 22: 6, 8, and 12 carry the sense 'so daß sie in schwere Schuld gerieten'.[93] It is probably going too far to divorce the phrase from actual offences and use it only as an expression of guilt, but Reventlow is right to see the cultic community as the context in which the crime of bloodshed is extended to represent more generally the sins and guilt of the people.

The image of the 'bloody city' appears again in 24: 6–14, where Ezekiel's poem about a pot of boiling meat moves into a harsh condemnation of Jerusalem which links bloodshed and uncleanness by the image of a rusty pot. The image the prophet develops here is apparently that of a temple vessel which is so corroded or encrusted with filth that it is ceremonially unclean and can no longer be used: the only thing to be done with it is to melt it down for scrap.[94] The identification of the filth with uncleanness is made in 24: 11, where טמאה parallels חלאה, and the point is hammered home in verse 13: 'For your depraved uncleanness, because I tried to cleanse you but you would not be cleansed from your uncleanness, you shall no longer be cleansed until I assuage my fury

modern mind holds apart . . . Thus "bloodguilt" in the priestly understanding becomes a comprehensive category of guilt' (*Ezekiel 1*, 456).

[92] Reventlow, *Wächter über Israel*, 102.

[93] Ibid. 102–3; see also his 'Sein Blut', 320.

[94] Greenberg provides the alternatives 'verdigris' and 'filth' as a translation of the Hebrew word חלאה. He favours the latter, but proposes that 'the difficulty may be resolved by assuming that *ḥel'a* denotes any distasteful soiling and foulness' (*Ezekiel 21–37*, 499). J. L. Kelso's earlier suggestion that the word literally means 'disease' is perhaps less likely, but if it were correct might make חלאה another term like the צרעת of Leviticus 13–14 which can defile both humans and inanimate objects ('Ezekiel's Parable of the Corroded Copper Caldron', *JBL* 64 (1945), 392).

against you.'[95] Verses 6–8 make clear that the rust or corruption of the pot is a symbol for the blood shed by the city of Jerusalem. 'The uncleanness of the city consists in the shedding of innocent blood.'[96] Verse 24: 7 makes a direct connection with Leviticus 17: 13—the command to cover spilled blood with earth: 'For the blood she has shed is still in the midst of her; she put it on the bare rock, she did not pour it upon the ground to cover it with dust.' This blood is crying out for atonement but will receive none from the citizens of Jerusalem. Eichrodt correctly points out that Ezekiel 'does not mean to suggest that those in power in Jerusalem might have protected themselves against God's curse by taking a few ritual precautions'.[97] Rather we have here another example of Ezekiel's use of ritual imagery to describe sins that are not in themselves ritual.

Ezekiel clearly shares the priestly concern for the correct manipulation of blood, which in many contexts has significant power. He takes a number of images drawn from the cultic understanding of blood and applies them to the state and behaviour of the house of Israel. Blood, and especially the shedding of blood, is his favourite image for violence in society, and this choice of image is another example of the ritualization of ethics to be found in this book. Ezekiel uses blood to emphasize the guilt of the hated Edomites, but most often it shows the guilt of the city of Jerusalem, whose crimes have earned her the title 'city of blood'. Many of the images which Ezekiel uses are not unique, but the degree of concentration on blood as a symbol of violence and of pollution is unparalleled elsewhere in the Hebrew Bible: this concentration is a highly distinctive feature of the prophet's style and theology. It shows his deep attachment to the temple and cult as symbols for explaining the present exiled state of the people, and, like the other ritual elements which are so prominent in his message, represents his characteristic contribution to prophetic ethics.

---

[95] My translation, following Greenberg, *Ezekiel 21–37*, 496, 503.
[96] Zimmerli, *Ezekiel 1*, 500.
[97] Eichrodt, *Ezekiel*, 339.

## Female Blood

We have not yet exhausted Ezekiel's use of the symbol of blood. Nahum used the image of the bloody city in the context of a per-sonified attack on Nineveh as a woman (Nahum 3), and both the metaphor of Jerusalem as a woman and the image of female bloodiness are taken up and developed considerably in Ezekiel's prophecy. The main thrust of Julie Galambush's work is to examine this metaphor of the city as YHWH's wife, which is most obvious in the allegorical chapters 16 and 23. Galambush makes a strong case that the use of feminine imagery, not only in these chapters but also elsewhere in the book, serves to give the city 'an implicitly female persona'.[98] This female persona provides the occasion for a further development of Ezekiel's ritualism, since within the priestly purity system the discharge of uterine blood by women at birth, menstruation, and on any other occasion was considered defiling.[99] Within Ezekiel's specific and more general characterization of the city as a woman, female blood is highly in evidence as an image for severe impurity and sin.

At the beginning of chapter 16 the baby Jerusalem is left abandoned and unwashed, 'wallowing in her blood' (16: 6, 22). This blood is the blood of her birth, which is a major pollution according to Leviticus 12.[100] Thus from the very beginning we associate Jerusalem with uncleanness. When YHWH adopts and marries the girl, he cleanses her, washing off her blood (16: 9). It is possible that this is 'in the telescoped vision of the allegory, her birth blood that still clung to her'.[101] Others have suggested that it is menstrual blood, since the girl has passed puberty.[102] It is per-haps most likely that the two forms of uncleanness have coalesced in the mind of the author; both forms of blood are defiling and would require purification.[103] The gifts which YHWH gives to Jerusalem she uses in the service of adultery, and despite her cleansing she cannot keep free of the pollution caused by blood

[98] Galambush, *Jerusalem in the Book of Ezekiel*, 2.
[99] See esp. Lev. 12 and 15.
[100] The plural דמים follows normal priestly terminology for female discharges of blood (Lev. 12: 4; 15: 19; 20: 18); see Greenberg, *Ezekiel 1–20*, 275.
[101] Greenberg, *Ezekiel 1–20*, 278.
[102] Cf. Cooke, *Ezekiel*, 163; Eichrodt, *Ezekiel*, 199.
[103] Galambush, *Jerusalem in the Book of Ezekiel*, 94. Cf. M. Malul, 'Adoption of Foundlings in the Bible and Mesopotamian Documents: A Study of Some Legal Metaphors in Ezekiel 16: 1–7', *JSOT* 46 (1990), 97–126.

but sacrifices her own children to idols. Galambush suggests how
Ezekiel continues to use the defiled purity of the female body to
express the crimes of the city:

Ezekiel exploits fully the unique ability of the female body to exhibit not
only the defilement of adultery, but also every type of blood pollution,
from menstruation and childbirth to murder . . . At birth she is left in the
unclean blood of her mother's womb. Upon reaching puberty, she
apparently remains in the impurity of her unwashed menstrual blood,
until washed by her husband. Finally she incurs blood guilt through the
murder of her own children.[104]

Thinking of the importance of blood in the temple theology,
Galambush believes that the uterus of the woman Jerusalem is
symbolic of the temple within the city, which has been defiled by
adulterous infidelity and by its own unclean blood. This may seem
rather far-fetched, but we need only look at 23: 20 to be reminded
that Ezekiel is capable of using the most explicit sexual metaphors, and it does seem to fit remarkably well with the importance
Ezekiel lays on both purity and the temple. Moreover, there can
be no question that he elsewhere employs images of female
defilement to express the state of the people, as is clear from the
appearance of menstrual uncleanness in 7: 19–20 and 36: 17.

The term which Ezekiel uses in these cases is נדה, which is the
normal priestly word for the uncleanness of menstruation. A
woman's regular monthly flow of blood therefore made her
unclean and a source of defilement, and the detailed priestly legislation concerning this is found in Leviticus 15: 19–33.[105] A woman
who is menstruating is unclean for seven days and can communicate uncleanness to those who touch her and everything upon
which she sits or lies. If a man has intercourse with her in this
condition he takes on the same seven-day impurity. In Ezekiel and
the Holiness Code sexual relations with a menstruating woman is
a serious crime (Ezek. 18: 12; 22: 10; Lev. 18: 19) and is extremely
threatening to the continued existence of the community, and
even in Leviticus 15, where the impurity is less serious, there is a
connection made with the survival of the community. 'Thus you
shall keep the people of Israel separate from their uncleanness, lest
they die in their uncleanness by defiling my tabernacle that is in

---

[104] Galambush, *Jerusalem in the Book of Ezekiel*, 102.
[105] For a discussion of parallels in ancient and primitive societies and of the rationale
behind it see Milgrom, *Leviticus 1–16*, 763–8, 948–53.

their midst' (Lev. 15: 31). What made it so abominable is not entirely clear, but may have been the juxtaposition of blood, the life force, with its flow, a sign of death.[106]

As has proved the case with uncleanness and blood, Ezekiel is not unique in using the image of menstruation as a metaphor or symbol of sin and rejection: the נדה in particular takes on a further range of meaning connected more generally with severe uncleanness, which seems to carry a moral significance as well. In Leviticus 20: 21 it appears in a declaratory formula which has nothing to do with menstruation: 'If a man takes his brother's wife it is impurity [נדה הוא]; he has uncovered his brother's nakedness; they shall be childless'.[107] It is in this metaphorical sense that Ezekiel uses the expression first in 7: 19–20:

They cast their silver into the streets, and their gold is like a נדה . . . Their beautiful ornament they used for vainglory, and they made their abominable images and their detestable things of it; therefore I will make it a נדה to them.

Bettenzoli has suggested that in fact the two uses of the word are unconnected: 'Dieser terminus findet sich in Ez 7, 20 und in der nachexilischen Literatur als Synonym von *ḥt'h* bzw. von kultischer Sünde. Die zweite Bedeutung von *ndh* im Sinn von *Menstruation* wird hier nicht berücksichtigt: sie hat mit der ersten Bedeutung kaum Berührung und wird vorwiegend von P gebraucht.'[108] But there seems no good reason to draw such a sharp distinction. In general, it is characteristic of the prophet that he extends the symbolic range of ritual concepts to include a broader ethical dimension. Moreover, the image is used in another text which probably comes from the early exilic period within an explicit characterization of Jerusalem as a sinful and shamed woman (Lam. 1: 8, 17).[109] Given Ezekiel's widespread use of blood meta-

---

[106] Cf. Galambush, *Jerusalem in the Book of Ezekiel*, 104. Alternatively it may have something to do with the association of blood and semen, as Milgrom suggests: 'It may be the loss of both life-giving semen and genital blood that evoked the utmost horror of the legislator' (*Leviticus 1–16*, 941).

[107] This is the same sort of formula as זמה הוא (Lev. 18: 17; 20: 14: sexual relations with both a mother and her daughter) or תועבה הוא (Lev. 18: 22: homosexuality).

[108] Bettenzoli, *Geist der Heiligkeit*, 80.

[109] See I. W. Provan, *Lamentations*, NCB (Grand Rapids, Mich., and London, 1991), 44–5, for discussion of the text; also K. M. O'Connor, 'Lamentations', in C. A. Newsom and S. H. Ringe (eds.), *The Women's Bible Commentary* (Louisville, Ky., 1992), 180. Also similar is Isa. 64: 5–6, where the sinful people is compared to a בגד עדים: a garment polluted by menstrual blood.

phors and female metaphors it is hardly surprising that Ezekiel takes up menstrual blood with some rhetorical force.

Here, in 7: 19–20, the area of life to which the metaphor is applied would appear to be idolatry and the temple. The gold and silver which the people of Jerusalem possess have been turned into idols. Galambush interprets verse 21 as referring to temple holy things:

Yahweh's threat to make 'it' like a *nddh* to the people is further explained in v 21. He will give 'it' to foreigners who will 'profane' (*ḥll*) it. The referent of 'it' is unclear at this point. Because gold and silver are temple sancta the verb 'profane' could be used of them . . . 'It' could also refer to the temple itself, in which case Yahweh's threat to make it 'like a menstruant' would be especially severe. The temple was not only protected from contact with the unclean, but was the place where blood was employed as a purifying agent.[110]

Thus what makes it so severe is that menstrual blood is the wrong sort of blood for the temple. As Howard Eilberg-Schwartz comments, 'blood has different meanings depending upon how it originates and from whom it comes'.[111] The blood of sacrifices is legitimate in the temple, where it is used as an offering to YHWH and for purification (Ezek. 43: 18, 20; 44: 7, 15, 19), whereas menstrual blood is irretrievably unclean and defiling.

While 7: 19–20 refers to cultic sins using the image of menstrual defilement, the second use of the theme in this way is more general in application, and sets together two different kinds of blood, the blood of the menstruating woman and the bloodshed which is symbolic of violence in society (36: 17–18):

Son of man, when the house of Israel dwelt in their own land, they defiled it by their ways and their doings; their conduct before me was like the uncleanness of a woman in her impurity [כטמאת הנדה]. So I poured out my wrath upon them for the blood which they had shed in the land (הדם אשר שפכו על־הארץ), for the idols with which they had defiled it.

Cooke considers that the image of the נדה is used here as 'a figure for idolatry', as it was in 7: 19–20, and certainly idols do feature in the second half of verse 18.[112] On the other hand Eilberg-Schwartz relates the shedding of menstrual blood only to the

---

[110] Galambush, *Jerusalem in the Book of Ezekiel*, 133.
[111] H. Eilberg-Schwartz, *The Savage in Judaism: An Anthropology of Israelite Religion and Ancient Judaism* (Bloomington, Ind., 1990), 179.          [112] Cooke, *Ezekiel*, 389.

bloodshed of verse 18 and sees here a metaphor for murder: 'Women's bleeding is symbolic of violent bloodshed and God's revulsion over such acts is equated with Israel's purported reaction to menstrual blood.'[113] Surely the most natural way to read the passage is to see the menstrual uncleanness as referring to both kinds of sin, cultic and social. In the first instance it describes the people's 'way' (דֶּרֶךְ), a very general term for their conduct. In the following verse this is exemplified by both bloodshed and idolatry.

Why should the impurity associated with menstrual blood play such an important part in Ezekiel's imagery? In the first place it is part of that general concern with pollution and purity that Mary Douglas has shown is symptomatic of a society whose identity is under threat. Douglas develops this idea further in her discussion of the body: she argues that the ways in which people in any given society use their bodies (such as the rituals they perform, the foods they eat, the sexual mores they adopt) will be representative of broader aspects of that society's social structure: 'The body is a model which can stand for any bounded system. Its boundaries can represent any boundaries which are threatened or precarious.'[114] Indeed, like other ritual actions, bodily taboos bespeak their actors' commitment to that society's common set of norms for behaviour and belief.[115] Her argument works well applied to ancient Israelite dietary regulations, whose observance is a mark of membership or non-membership of the community. Regardless of whether we accept Douglas's own classificatory scheme for understanding the abominations of Leviticus,[116] she has successfully shown that the concern to regulate what enters the body expresses a communal desire to keep firm boundaries around the Israelite community.[117]

---

[113] Eilberg-Schwartz, *Savage in Judaism*, 181.

[114] Douglas, *Purity and Danger*, 138.

[115] M. Douglas, *Implicit Meanings: Essays in Anthropology* (London, 1975), 63.

[116] For a recent treatment of this subject with full discussion of various theories and bibliography see W. Houston, *Purity and Monotheism: Clean and Unclean Animals in Biblical Law*, JSOTS 140 (Sheffield, 1993).

[117] Cf. Grabbe's discussion in *Leviticus*, 58–9. Douglas's insights are taken up and developed in Eilberg-Schwartz's *Savage in Judaism*. Another important study of the ancient world that focuses on this issue is P. Brown, *The Body and Society: Men, Women, and Sexual Renunciation in Early Christianity* (NY, 1988). Brown shows that an increasing emphasis on bodily continence and sexual asceticism in the early church was symptomatic of a broader Christian rejection of the civic ideals of the classical (and therefore pagan) city.

As well as what goes into the body, the fluids that come out of a body play an important symbolic role in many cultures, and Douglas draws a connection directly with ancient Israel:

When rituals express anxieties about the body's orifices, the sociological counterpart of this anxiety is a care to protect the political and cultural unity of a minority group. The Israelites were always in their history a hard-pressed minority. In their belief all the bodily issues were polluting, blood, pus, excreta, semen, etc. The threatened boundaries of their body politic would be well mirrored in their care for the integrity, unity and purity of their physical body.[118]

She may be criticized for presenting Israelite thought as too monolithic, and there were undoubtedly groups and periods in Israel's history to which such a scheme would not apply. But it is particularly at the time of the exile that Israel's status as a threatened minority becomes most apparent, and it is, therefore, no surprise that in Ezekiel, the prophet of the exile, the horror of menstrual blood gains a symbolic prominence it did not have before.

While accepting her general theory of the body as a mirror of society, Eilberg-Schwartz has criticized Douglas's view of Israelite fluid symbolism, and argues that the symbolism of menstrual blood is more concerned with the internal ordering of Israelite society than with the setting up of boundaries against the outside world.[119] He outlines the opposition between the blood of circumcision which is symbolic of life, fertility, and the propagation of the community, and the blood of menstruation, which is symbolic of death and uncontrollability. In particular, he relates this to the subordinate position of women in ancient Jewish society: 'Clearly, the gender of blood signifies other kinds of differences, such as the opposition between covenant, righteousness, and wholeness on the one hand, and sin, indecency, and death on the other. One might summarize this by saying that menstruation is everything that circumcision is not.'[120] In broader terms he relates the opposition between the blood of circumcision and that of menstruation to the opposition between life and death, and connects this with

---

[118] Douglas, *Purity and Danger*, 148.

[119] Eilberg-Schwartz, *Savage in Judaism*, 179 ff.

[120] Ibid. 181. Douglas makes the point herself when she points out that belief in the danger of menstruation often functions 'to assert male superiority', and to act as a coercive force to make women conform to a set social pattern (*Implicit Meanings*, 62).

the priestly concern that the Jewish community should be fruitful and ensure its continuance: a task which of course cannot be achieved without the compliance of women, and requires a degree of control over their sexual relationships. Women are, in a sense, marginal characters in the male and thoroughly patriarchal community of exiles, and yet they are powerful because they promise the perpetuation of that community.

We may, therefore, see in the particularly strong dangers associated with female blood a perceived threat to the existence of Jewish society. Even if bodily imagery does reflect internal rather than external boundaries, the community is only maintained by its members' commitment to this one of a number of possible social groupings, and we have suggested that as part of the experience of exile there must have been a considerable pressure to assimilate to the local population in Babylonia. Thus it seems artificial of Eilberg-Schwartz to treat ancient Judaism as an enclosed social system, lacking contact with the outside. His logic fails, for if the opposition between menstrual blood and the blood of circumcision can represent the opposition between covenant and sinfulness, it also must represent the distinction between inside and outside. Moreover, if the concern with the impurity of women's bleeding reflects a fear of women's uncontrollability, this may represent the fear that women will leave the community. Certainly the presentation of the city of Jerusalem throughout the book of Ezekiel, of which the symbol of menstrual uncleanness is part, consistently emphasizes the rejection, the 'otherness', of the woman. Galambush comments: 'Jerusalem is defined as the defiled and defiling other.'[121] We may add that where that 'otherness' is defined it is in her Canaanite descent (16: 3, 45) and in the many foreign lovers whom she takes (16: 25–31; 23: 11–18). We might point out that these allegories in fact refer to men, and are metaphors for male sin.[122] However, for the imagery to work requires the acceptance by Ezekiel's community of an ideology in which women are little more than chattels.

---

[121] Galambush, *Jerusalem in the Book of Ezekiel*, 125.

[122] Allen (*Ezekiel 20–48*, 51) and Eichrodt (*Ezekiel*, 333) maintain that the whole substance of the allegory is metaphorical. Zimmerli, more plausibly in view of 23: 48, sees a genuine warning to 'individual women in their moral and social conduct' (*Ezekiel 1*, 492). See also K. P. Darr, 'Ezekiel', in Newsom and Ringe (eds.), *The Women's Bible Commentary*, who writes: 'the original imagery's inclusiveness has collapsed into a threat intended for women alone' (189).

The concept of harlotry has meaning only within an ideology that views women's bodies as the property of men . . . The divine husband's superiority over his nation-wife . . . lends legitimacy to the human husband's superiority over his wife, who, following this model, is subservient to him and totally dependent on him. Through messages about gender relations encoded in these texts, men are taught to exert their authority and women are taught to submit.[123]

Despite the fact that the primary reference of the adulterous allegories is political (the prophet uses them to condemn Judah's involvement with idolatry and foreign alliances), the need for women to remain within the boundaries of the community is made clear in 23: 46–8:

For thus says the Lord GOD: 'Bring up a host against them, and make them an object of terror and a spoil. And the host shall stone them and despatch them with their swords; they shall slay their sons and their daughters, and burn up their houses. Thus will I put an end to lewdness in the land, *that all women may take warning and not commit lewdness as you have done.*

The warning to real women is the sting in the tail of an oracle which has up to that point been an allegory of male behaviour. But it is clear that women's sexual freedom would pose a threat to the community of exiles. If women were to have sought husbands or lovers outside the community (or, perhaps more plausibly, their fathers were to have married them to outsiders), then it might have proved increasingly difficult to maintain a distinctively Jewish culture and identity.[124] While Ezekiel contains little explicit criticism of marriage with outsiders, the fear of Israelite women mixing with foreign men present in chapters 16 and 23 complements the imagery of the נדה elsewhere in the book, and thus it is likely that the portrayal of menstrual blood as unclean and uncontrollable does reflect the fears of the exiles that they will lose the clear boundary between themselves and the outside world. The

---

[123] J. C. Exum, 'The Ethics of Biblical Violence Against Women', in J. W. Rogerson, M. Davies and M. D. Carroll R (eds.), *The Bible in Ethics: The Second Sheffield Colloquium*, JSOTS 207 (Sheffield, 1995), 258–9.

[124] This is certainly one of the more obvious forms which a pressure to assimilate might take, as Causse recognized: see *Du Groupe ethnique*, 191–2. He had already argued that women gained a higher status and level of independence in the diaspora communities than previously (*Du Groupe ethnique*, 189–90 n. 4); if this view were correct, then Ezekiel might be reacting against the expression of that independence in relationships with Gentiles.

uncleanness associated with uterine bleeding, then, like all the language of purity in Ezekiel, has its original significance in the world of the Jerusalem temple. But again the prophet has creatively transformed the temple symbolism to be of relevance in the community of exiles.

## Conclusion

In the previous chapter we saw how important the maintenance of the state cult is in determining the fate of Jerusalem, and also how this particular issue reflects the typical moral concerns of the Jerusalem élite who formed the bulk of the deportees. For such people the state cult was perhaps the principal symbol of monarchy, national independence, and autonomy, and we might imagine that in the aftermath of defeat its power to maintain community would be highly limited. However, in Ezekiel this is far from the case. We have seen that Ezekiel expands the scope of ritual language in his application of it to many aspects of Israel's moral life, and, as the orbit of impurity broadens to include not only the sanctuary but also the people and the land, we cannot forget that it is the temple and its cult which provides the concepts and language which are being applied. Neusner affirms this:

The temple supplied to purity its importance in the religious life. As the temple signified divine favour, and as the cult supplied the nexus between Israel and God, so purity, associated so closely with both, could readily serve as an image either of divine favour or of man's loyalty to God. From that fact followed the assignment of impurity to all that stood against the temple, the cult, and God: idolatry first of all.[125]

This is true even when Israel found itself without a temple: between 587 and 515 BCE, and after 70 CE. In such a situation the concern for purity demonstrates the vitality of the temple as a symbol not only of divine favour, but also of the idea of nationhood, a common identity and common values:

When ideas of purity are removed from the physical temple itself they continue to testify to the importance of the temple for they serve to define communities which compare themselves to the Jerusalem temple, claiming to constitute a surrogate or to replace it. Or they provide

---

[125] Neusner, *Idea of Purity*, 15.

metaphors for social virtues or vices which attain transcendent importance because they can be referred back to the cult. The temple in retrospect, therefore, would turn out to be the one point in Israelite life upon
which the lines of structure, both cosmic and social, converge. Therefore
social values are going in some measure to depend for both vividness and
moral authority upon their capacity to find a place within the temple
symbolism.[126]

Again this fits the position of the book of Ezekiel: this language
of ritual, so intimately bound up with the temple and its cult, is
one of the most significant distinguishing features of Ezekiel's
prophecy. Mary Douglas writes of secular rituals: 'Ritual focuses
attention by framing: it enlivens the memory and links the present
with the relevant past. In all this it aids perception. Or rather it
changes perception because it changes the selective principles.'[127]
In some respects Ezekiel's approach to sacred ritual is doing the
same: by the constant reference to ideas of purity and cult, the
temple remains as a frame through which members of the community can express and symbolize their experience.

The ritualization of ethics which we see in the book is itself a
response to the crisis of exile which the prophet and his community were experiencing. Ezekiel's interpretation of the events of
the early sixth century often seems an overwhelmingly negative
one, as he places responsibility for the national disaster squarely
on the shoulders of the people: it is their sins which have driven
YHWH from his temple and forced him to act in judgement. Yet at
the same time the manner of Ezekiel's condemnation, with its
emphasis on cult and ritual, begins to provide a strategy for the
community's survival in exile. Even in exile, and even after its
destruction, the temple can remain the principal focal point for
the social values and aspirations of the Jewish community.

[126] Ibid. 28–9.        [127] Douglas, *Purity and Danger*, 79.

# 6

# The 'Domestication' of Ethics

In the previous chapter I argued that the huge emphasis on ritual throughout the whole of the book of Ezekiel can be seen as a strategy for survival in the straitened circumstances of exile. In the absence of the institutions of state, the memory of the temple becomes the focus for ethical reflection and discourse. This chapter will concentrate in detail on two oracles which appear to be directly addressed to the community of exiles: 14: 1–11 and 18: 1–32. In both of these oracles there are prominent themes that suggest that the range of moral options open to the group has become limited by comparison with their former life in Judah.

One of the most distinctive features of Ezekiel's prophecy, first noted by Zimmerli, is his reapplication of legal forms to theological issues, which is most evident in 14: 1–11 and chapter 18.[1] Concentration has tended to be on the theological significance of such a move; for instance, Paul Joyce shows how Ezekiel takes the legal point that individuals are responsible and reapplies this to explain the national collective crisis.[2] However, if it were the case that the community had largely lost its legal autonomy, then it might be necessary to reapply legal language theologically in order to preserve the legal traditions and the sense of moral responsibility which the application of those traditions allows. This movement of law from the judicial to the religious sphere can be seen as further evidence of the limiting of moral possibilities in the exiled community. In Ezekiel, when we see the legal traditions taken up and reapplied, the logic is similar to that involved with the temple and ritual: that which had previously been a symbol of power and autonomy is scaled down to suit the changed circumstances of the exiles in Babylon.

It is also significant that in these two key oracles in chapters 14 and 18, which are addressed specifically to the exilic situation, we find that the reapplication of legal language is combined with a

---

[1] Zimmerli, 'Eigenart', 1–26.  [2] Joyce, *Divine Initiative*, 33–60.

narrower focus of ethical content: the notion of sin takes on a more individualistic or domestic colouring than elsewhere in the book. In contrast to the majority of those oracles which are addressed to Jerusalem, here the areas of ethical decision making require no political autonomy or power. In so far as individualism is a feature of Ezekiel's discourses, it may be a response to a situation in which major communal decisions are simply no longer there to be taken.

Finally, it is in these two oracles that we find most clearly stated a call to repentance. This is a difficult subject within the book of Ezekiel, which often appears to equivocate about the possibility and even value of a response to the prophet's preaching. However, a closer examination of the texts will reveal that while repentance is not significant in the prophet's prediction of the fall of Jerusalem, nor in his promises of future restoration, it is directed towards the present experience of exile, and shows YHWH's continuing concern that his people should act rightly even in exile.

## The Exilic Focus of 14: 1–11 and 18: 1–32

The majority of Ezekiel's oracles of judgement, although delivered to the exiles, address events and circumstances in Judah and Jerusalem. However, both 14: 1–11 and 18: 1–32 appear more clearly to reflect the situation of Ezekiel's audience. For once it is the ethical behaviour of the people round about the prophet that is at issue. In 14: 1 we are told of a group of the 'elders of Israel', who have come to consult Ezekiel. This situation is repeated in 20: 1, and we are presumably to imagine the same group of men as the 'elders of Judah' to whom the vision of chapters 8–11 is addressed. And in fact the vision of the temple in chapter 8 is useful to put in context the sin of the elders in chapter 14, since in both cases elders are accused of idolatry (8: 11; 14: 3–4), but whereas in chapter 8 it is idolatry in distant Jerusalem, in chapter 14 the very men who have come to consult Ezekiel are accused. It is האנשים האלה ('these men' (14: 3)) who have committed the offence.

Ezekiel 18 does not open with a consultation in the same way as chapter 14, but with the saying 'the fathers have eaten sour grapes, and the children's teeth are set on edge' (Ezek. 18: 2), which implies that its speakers are suffering because of the actions of their predecessors, and which the majority of exegetes agree represents the opinions of the exiled community about their present unfortunate position. The saying may be 'concerning the land of Israel', but this does not detract from its exilic focus since it was, of course, events in Jerusalem that were the principal causes of the exile. As Allen comments: ' The fate of the homeland is in view, and so their own fate as displaced persons.'[3] There is, admittedly, some debate surrounding the translation of the expression that introduces the saying עַל־אַדְמַת יִשְׂרָאֵל (Ezek. 18: 1). Some, including Zimmerli and Greenberg, take עַל to mean 'in' or 'on' and see the quotation as being put in the mouth of those still in the land.[4] Such an interpretation may be suggested by its appearance in Jeremiah 31: 29 (cf. Lam. 5: 7), but even its currency within the land of Israel at the time of the exile by no means excludes the possibility that those who were exiled also saw themselves as the unfortunate victims of their fathers' mistakes. As Zimmerli writes: 'Such pregnant metaphorical sayings as Ezek. 18: 2 (= Jer. 31: 29) undoubtedly became a temptation and danger for many exiles whose ears they reached. Thus an argument with a saying current "in the land of Israel" was quite directly intended for the exiles also.'[5]

Zimmerli would prefer to see both of these oracles dated after 587 BCE, largely on the grounds that the calls to repentance of 18: 21–32 and 14: 6 belong to a second, more hopeful, phase of the prophet's ministry which did not begin until after the fall of Jerusalem.[6] On the other hand, Joyce dates chapter 18 before 587, arguing that the present location of the oracle within the book suggests it should be thought of as pre-fall material, and that the presence of the repentance theme is not necessarily a sign of hope.[7] If the presence of a repentance theme does not demand a post-fall dating for chapter 18 then the same is true of 14: 1–11. Moreover, the subject matter of these oracles—the elders' idolatry

---

[3] Allen, *Ezekiel 1–19*, 205.

[4] Zimmerli, *Ezekiel 1*, 369; Greenberg, *Ezekiel 1–20*, 325, 327; so also A. Graffy, *A Prophet Confronts his People: The Disputation Speech in the Prophets*, Analecta Biblica, 104 (Rome, 1984), 53. Those who support the translation of עַל as 'concerning' include RSV; Joyce, *Divine Initiative*, 43, 56; Allen, *Ezekiel 1–19*, 265, 270. J. S. Kaminsky translates 'concerning', but allows for possible poetic ambiguity on the part of the author (*Corporate Responsibility in the Hebrew Bible*, JSOTS 196 (Sheffield, 1995), 155).          [5] Zimmerli, *Ezekiel 1*, 377–8.

[6] Ibid., 313, 377; see also Allen, *Ezekiel 1–19*, 197, 269–70.

[7] Joyce, *Divine Initiative*, 50–60; also in favour of a pre-fall date for chapter 18 are Wevers, *Ezekiel*, 109; Greenberg, *Ezekiel 1–20*, 342.

and the injustice of present suffering—is just as appropriate to exiles of 597 as to any who arrived later. The first deportation of 597 was unquestionably a disaster for those who experienced it, and it could not have put a complete stop to their religious belief and practice. However, in the absence of external evidence, it is probably impossible to be sure about the date of these oracles. We are on firmer ground if we concentrate on their explicitly exilic orientation, which may account for some of their differences from the surrounding material: because these oracles are addressed directly to Ezekiel's own community, they share a number of characteristics which provide particularly helpful insights into the new moral world of the exiles.

## The Transformation of Legal Forms of Speech in 14: 1–11 and 18: 1–32

While evidence is limited, we can be fairly confident that the Jews exiled to Babylon had largely lost their legal autonomy. They could not have moved the whole of the pre-exilic legal apparatus which, like the temple, had provided one of the most important focuses for moral discussion (we might think of, for example, the way in which legal prescriptions are used as the basis for prophetic condemnations from Amos onwards, as well as the use of the ריב form in prophetic invective). Ezekiel, however, picks up legal forms to a degree unprecedented in prophecy, and redirects their focus towards the theological interpretation of experience. Particularly in chapters 14, 18, and 22 (but elsewhere as well) we find that language appropriate to criminal cases is reused in theological contexts. In chapters 14 and 18 especially we find the casuistic formulation of a hypothetical case (or cases) followed by a statement of verdict and/or sentence which is typical of the priestly legal collections. I should like to suggest that this shift of legal language from the genuinely legal sphere to the theological is representative of a larger shift in the community Ezekiel addresses, a shift from privilege to deprivation, in which the old institutions of Judah must be re-symbolized in order to maintain continuity of community. This is something which is most extensive in Ezekiel in the case of the temple and ritual, but which can also be seen in other legal language.

Chapter 14 was the prime example used by Zimmerli to make the case that this legal language was not extrinsic to the prophecy of Ezekiel, but was a fundamentally important part of his style.[8] There are a number of features of legal style which are to be found here. Initially the condemnation of the elders is framed in the third-person language of case-law.

Any man of the house of Israel who takes his idols into his heart and sets the stumbling block of his iniquity before his face, and yet comes to the prophet, I the LORD will answer him myself (14: 4).

The expression איש איש מבית ישראל ('any man of the house of Israel' (vv. 4, 7)) is closely paralleled by passages in the Holiness Code (Lev. 17: 3, 8, 10, 13; cf. 20: 2; 22: 18). Zimmerli sees these formulations as belonging originally to the legal discourse of the pre-exilic period, 'when settlement "in the midst (בתוך Lev 17: 8, 10, 13) of Israel" still retained its quite objective meaning'.[9] It is, however, an expression that 'undoubtedly had already become stereotyped before the beginning of the exile'.[10] Thus Ezekiel is adopting stereotypical legal discourse to describe the sin of the elders who have come to him.

Not only the description of the crime, but also the nature of the sentence itself is drawn from the sacral-legal sphere. In particular, the phrases והכרתיו מתוך עמי ('I will cut him off from the midst of my people' (14: 8)) and ונשאו עונם ('and they shall bear their punishment' (14: 10)) are drawn from the language of criminal cases. The latter is a common formula used 'to qualify decisively a sacral-legal offense'.[11] The threat of 'cutting off' is found in a variety of forms in the priestly legislation and Holiness Code as a punishment inflicted for crimes which involve a breach of the covenant.[12] On reflection it is a highly appropriate punishment to be referred to in the exiled community. Occasionally the הכרת penalty is a death penalty carried out by the community, but more often it seems that if an offender is to die, the responsibility for punishment is YHWH's. Concerning the exact role of the righteous members of the community the legislation is ambiguous, and thus the phrase here in Ezekiel is susceptible of different interpretations. Greenberg, in

---

[8] Zimmerli, 'Eigenart'.
[9] Zimmerli, *Ezekiel 1*, 303.
[10] Ibid. 303.
[11] Ibid. 305; 'Eigenart', 10–12.
[12] W. Horbury, 'Extirpation and Excommunication', *VT* 35 (1985), 17–18.

line with rabbinic tradition, considers that the community has no part in the הכירת penalty. Rather the phrase promises a 'sudden, untimely death'.[13] Zimmerli and others accept the primary sense of divinely ordained death, but see a role for the community in its expulsion or excommunication of the sinner: 'Die הכירת-Formel ist eine Bannformel, die ausdrückt, daß ein Mensch aus der Nähe Gottes ausgeschlossen und damit dem Verderben übergeben ist ... Die einzige Activität der Gemeinde, die auf jeden Fall erwartet sein wird, ist auch hier der Ausschluß aus der Mitte der gottes-dienstlich Gott nahen Gemeinde.'[14]

Whichever thesis is correct, the implication of this divinely ordained punishment is that the community is not in a position to impose the death penalty that it considers appropriate for the offence. Hence, the language Ezekiel uses to express punishment fits well a situation where the autonomy of the community is severely limited. Even within the context of the legal material, at most the sentence can only symbolize the punishment from YHWH which a sinner deserves.

Two points about crime and punishment in this oracle suggest themselves. First, we should remember that Ezekiel is not himself passing a legal judgment in court, but adapting the language of the courts to a theological purpose. Thus he is not legally empowered to act, but is only engaged in an interpretation of the actions and beliefs of his contemporaries. The forms of the court find new life in Ezekiel's prophecy to his own community of exiles, and the fact that the punishment is entirely in YHWH's hands connects with the legal logic of those whose ability to punish is constrained, and with the theocentric nature of the book as a whole. Second, it is interesting that the punishment proposed is itself reduced in scope by comparison with some of the promises of disaster we have so far encountered in the prophecies of Ezekiel. Here it is less significant that the community is not responsible for the imposi-tion of a penalty; in fact, all punishment in the book is carried out by YHWH, either directly or through his agents. Nevertheless, as the raising up of idols in the hearts of the elders is an offence on a

---

[13] Greenberg, *Ezekiel 1–20*, 250. For this interpretation of the penalty see M. Tsevat, 'Studies in the Book of Samuel', *HUCA* 32 (1961), 195–216; M. Weinfeld, *Deuteronomy and the Deuteronomic School* (Oxford, 1972), 241–3.

[14] Zimmerli, 'Eigenart', 19; cf. *Ezekiel 1*, 303–4. A similar interpretation is given by A. Phillips, *Ancient Israel's Criminal Law: A New Approach to the Decalogue* (Oxford, 1970), 28–32. See also Joyce, *Divine Initiative*, 67.

less dramatic scale than the wholesale defilement of the Jerusalem temple, so the punishment of exclusion or a sudden divine blow affecting the individual sinner is on a smaller scale than the destruction of an entire city and nation. The major sins of national life lead to military defeat and exile, while the smaller-scale sins of chapter 14 lead to the loss of individuals from the community and the threat of its disintegration.

What is the relationship between individuals and community in this passage? As Joyce points out, there is a strong emphasis on responsibility in 14: 1–11.[15] The house of Israel has become estranged from YHWH through its idolatry, and all those guilty will be cut off and will bear their punishment. The manner in which this responsibility is expressed also suggests that there is some degree of individualism in the theology of the oracle. At the very least this can be seen in the legal language which uses individual cases to exemplify the sin of idolatry and the punishment for that sin: those who are guilty are the ones to be punished. This should not surprise us given the consistent emphasis on individual responsibility in Israel's legal traditions.[16] But Joyce is also right to point out that the purpose of the individualism in 14: 1–11 is to safeguard the assembly of YHWH: the community of exiles.[17]

Zimmerli saw that the threat of destruction which Ezekiel voices is addressed not only to individual idolaters and prophets, but also to the whole house of Israel. He comments on 14: 5: 'This divine saying does not restrict itself with this threat of judgement to individual men, but shows immediately the deeper truth that this holy wrath has in mind "Israel" when speaking about the individual sinner. The "house of Israel" will be taken hold of in their hearts by the judgement against the individual sinner.'[18] Furthermore, the language of excommunication, if that is what it is, sheds light on the relation of individual and community. Joyce writes:

We may note here a paradoxical feature of all language of excommunication, namely that it involves a strong sense both of individual responsibility and also of the vital importance of community: the guilty individual is singled out for punishment, but this is for the very purpose

---

[15] Joyce, *Divine Initiative*, 66.

[16] See e.g. B. Lindars, 'Ezekiel and Individual Responsibility', *VT* 15 (1965), esp. 453–6.

[17] Joyce, *Divine Initiative*, 68. See esp. Ezek. 14: 11.

[18] Zimmerli, *Ezekiel 1*, 307.

of preserving the social unit. A similar ambivalence marks Ezek. 14: 1–11, where language about the exclusion of the sinner is closely related to concern for the ultimate preservation of the community.[19]

This relationship between individual and community fits well with Ezekiel's exiled situation. The nature of the threat towards a community of exiles is very different from that which threatens the leading citizens of an autonomous nation-state. It is the disintegration of community rather than indiscriminate military disaster that is to be feared: the integrity of the community is directly dependent on the actions and intentions of the individual members of the community, who have to relate to one another without the institutional framework of the state. The language of 14: 1–11 is such that a threat to individuals is transformed into a threat to the community. This takes place through the language of excommunication, as we have seen, but may also be seen in the language of estrangement which is so prominent in the chapter. The sinners are the house of Israel 'who are all estranged from me through their idols' (14: 5), and those who separate themselves from YHWH (14: 7). The purpose of the punishment as described is to put an end to this estrangement of God's people: it is 'that the house of Israel may go no more astray from me, nor defile themselves any more with their transgressions, but that they may be my people and I may be their God'. That YHWH is himself the guarantor and focus of community for Ezekiel is clear from his treatment of the temple, and even for the exiles he remains that focus: 'a small sanctuary' (11: 16) to them in Babylonia.

It has often been thought that Ezekiel 18 brings out more clearly than anywhere in scripture the notion of individual responsibility, by which is meant that God judges each person according to his or her merits in isolation from their contemporaries. In this chapter Ezekiel rebuts the statement 'the fathers have eaten sour grapes and the children's teeth are set on edge' with the strong statement 'the soul that sins shall die'. There follow three test cases of a righteous father, wicked son, and righteous grandson, which serve further to demonstrate the point. An emphasis on this 'moral independence of contemporary individuals'[20] has been regularly seen as Ezekiel's great contribution to Old Testament ethics: 'The responsibility and freedom of the

---

[19] Joyce, *Divine Initiative*, 68.     [20] Joyce's phrase: ibid. 35.

individual lie at the root of all moral living: to have proclaimed this as the outcome of God's justice and desire for man's recovery was Ez.'s great achievement.'[21]

However, it is far from clear that such an emphasis on the individual really is innovative. Barnabas Lindars has demonstrated that individual responsibility is clearly enshrined in both the whole Israelite legal tradition and the tradition of thinking about divine punishment. Ezekiel's innovation lies in the way he takes concepts previously applied to individuals and relates them to the whole people. The real issue is the responsibility of the generation of exiles, and in Ezekiel 18 we see 'not a new statement of the situation of the individual before God, but a new application of the ideas of individual responsibility which are already current in priestly *torah*'. Lindars goes as far as to say, 'there is no suggestion that some may repent and live, while others persist in sin and die'.[22] He is supported in this view by Joyce, who argues that 'far from constituting an argument for "individual responsibility", the purpose of the chapter is to demonstrate the collective responsibility of the contemporary house of Israel for the national disaster which she is suffering'.[23] Important for his argument is the distinction between criminal law and divine retribution:

Whereas in criminal law evidence can demonstrate that a particular individual is responsible for a particular crime, it is impossible to demonstrate a direct causal relationship between human sin and divine punishment. This is precisely because the reasoning characteristically goes the other way; adversity is interpreted as punishment for sin and then an attempt is made to identify the sin in question.[24]

Such a movement from punishment to sin allows plenty of scope for disagreements about blame like that between Ezekiel and his audience in chapter 18, and the confusion of law and retribution

---

[21] Cooke, *Ezekiel*, 196. So also von Rad, *Old Testament Theology*, ii. 230–1; Eichrodt, *Ezekiel*, 231–49, Brownlee, *Ezekiel 1–19*, 50, 284, 292. The view is widespread in recent popular commentaries: e.g. J. Taylor, *Ezekiel: An Introduction and Commentary*, Tyndale Old Testament Commentaries (London, 1969), 45; R. E. Clements, *Ezekiel*, Westminster Bible Companion (Louisville, Ky., 1996), 80–1. Cf. also the recent article by B. Uffenheimer, 'Theodicy and Ethics in the Prophecy of Ezekiel', in H. G. Reventlow (ed.), *Justice and Righteousness: Biblical Themes and their Influence*, JSOTS 137 (Sheffield, 1992), esp. 202, 219–24.

[22] Lindars, 'Ezekiel and Individual Responsibility', 466.

[23] Joyce, *Divine Initiative*, 36.

[24] Ibid. 38. See also Lindars, 'Ezekiel and Individual Responsibility', *VT* 15 (1965), 456.

is what has thrown so many interpreters off the scent. Ezekiel 18 abounds in legal language, and, as in chapter 14, this language is reapplied theologically. Thus Ezekiel takes up legal language, but he uses it to argue a point about divine retribution rather than individual culpability.

Within the chapter the test-case formula is probably the most prominent legal feature. This use of hypothetical situations ('if a man does . . . then . . .') here is reminiscent of the test case in 14: 1–11 and particularly of cases within the Holiness Code such as Leviticus 20: 9, 15. The cases are concluded with a statement of verdict and declaration of outcome. This can be either favourable or unfavourable, as McKeating neatly summarizes: 'So we have the alternatives "He is righteous" (verdict), "He shall surely live" (declaration of his fate); or "He has done all these abominable things" (verdict), "He shall surely die" (sentence).'[25] It is possible that this form reflects the statement of acquittal or condemnation in priestly criminal cases (cf. Lev. 20: 9, 15) and is therefore part of the procedure of the court which Ezekiel has adapted.[26] Alternatively its origin may be found in a temple entrance liturgy (cf. Pss. 15, 24),[27] or possibly instructions for priests which were inscribed on the doorposts of temples.[28] Whatever may be the case it seems likely that priestly law forms the background for the expressions used. The third feature which is often related to priestly law is the use of lists of sin and virtue in the three test cases. Lists are prominent elsewhere in Ezekiel as well (22: 6–12, 25–7; 33: 15, 25–6), and, while it is difficult to find an exact parallel within the priestly literature, both form and content seem closer to parts of the Holiness Code than to anything else in the Bible, which would suggest that Ezekiel is here also adapting another element of legal language.

For our perspective, what is important is that this language is taken out of its original context, be that criminal case or temple

[25] McKeating, *Ezekiel*, 53; cf. also Block, *Ezekiel 1–24*, 564–5.

[26] See Schulz, *Todesrecht*, 163–87; see also Joyce, *Divine Initiative*, 40.

[27] See G. von Rad '"Righteousness" and "Life" in the Cultic Language of the Psalms', in his *The Problem of the Hexateuch and Other Essays* (Edinburgh and London, 1966), 243–66; Zimmerli, *Ezekiel 1*, 375–7.

[28] See M. Weinfeld, 'Instructions for Temple Visitors in the Bible and in Ancient Israel', in S. Israel-Groll (ed.), *Egyptological Studies*, Scripta Hierosolymita, 28 (Jerusalem, 1982), 224–50. His examples all come from Hellenistic Egypt. For fuller discussion of the background of these forms see Matties, *Ezekiel 18*, 66–70.

entrance liturgy, and reapplied to explain the situation presupposed by the sour-grapes proverb at the beginning of the chapter:
the divine retribution being suffered by his fellow exiles. The institutional framework of temple and courts may have been lost, but
Ezekiel retains the forms appropriate to those institutions as he
addresses his audience. Joyce writes: 'Ezekiel's concern is to discuss the causes of a particular historical disaster, the defeat of the
nation and the deportations which followed it, but he advances his
argument by drawing upon analogies from the realm of criminal
law. Recognition of the reapplication of this language is the key to
the understanding of the chapter.'[29] Ezekiel's response to the exile
is the creative use of traditional forms to meet new circumstances.
Here, in both 14: 1–11 and 18: 1–32, he appropriates the symbolic
apparatus of the law and uses it to make sense of the new experience of exile. In the exile, where there is no legal autonomy, this
acts to preserve the traditions and the sense of moral responsibility
which their application allows. This theologizing of law represents
Ezekiel's response to domination in much the same way as does
his reinvention of the temple and ritual as the main focus of moral
life in exile.

## The Content of Sin and Virtue in the Exile

The majority of Ezekiel's oracles of judgement attempt to explain
and apportion responsibility for the catastrophe of the exile, and
in large measure are directed against the Jerusalem élite. The sins
for which they are condemned are largely appropriate to the
moral horizons of the upper classes in an agrarian society like
Judah. State institutions like cult and foreign policy form a central
part of his concern. For the exiles, though, however much influence they may have had back home, there is no state left to lose,
no major institutions within which to work, so the socio-political
ramifications of their sins are inevitably on a smaller scale. In the
absence of the communal institutions the moral world has become
more restricted, and the effect of this is to make moral debate
appear more individualistic than it did previously.

Despite the fact that it is no longer possible to sustain the view
that individual responsibility was Ezekiel's great moral innovation,

[29] Joyce, *Divine Initiative*, 41.

it is hard to deny that in both 14: 1–11 and 18: 1–32 there is a degree of individualistic colouring. Among the old school, C. F. Whitley argued that individual responsibility was a doctrine particularly suited to the social circumstances of exile:

Deported from their native land with its communal pattern of life and settled in different centres of Babylonia, it is doubtful if they would have survived for long as a racial entity if they did not adapt themselves to more individualistic conditions of life . . . The more the individual Israelite was encouraged to think and act for himself, the sooner could he 'make within him a new heart and a new spirit' (Ezek. 18:31) and discover the secret of personal fellowship with God.[30]

This focus on the community as a collection of individuals certainly does not do justice to the highly communal interests we have found elsewhere in the book. We have seen how Ezekiel's use of ritual language and his reapplication of legal forms of speech work not to emphasize a personal relationship with God, but principally to build up and maintain a faithful Jewish community in exile. Whitley may be wrong to read wholesale individualism into Ezekiel's oracles, but he is right to suggest that those who lived in exile experienced 'more individualistic conditions of life'. Nevertheless, such individualism as is present is forced more by circumstances than ideological innovation. Hence I prefer to use the term 'domestication of ethics', by which I mean the restriction of practical moral decision making to such areas as personal religious behaviour, or family and business relationships, which are more often than not relationships between individuals. It is, therefore, the content of sin and virtue in 14: 1–11 and 18: 1–32 which I should like to examine next: the areas of action and belief for which people are held responsible. In contrast to many of the judgement oracles elsewhere in the book, chapters 14 and 18 offer some direct insights into the dynamics of sin and ethics among the exiles.

It may be instructive to begin by comparing the treatment of the elders' idolatry in chapters 8 and 14. In chapter 8 we find the seventy 'men of the elders of the house of Israel' who offer incense to the loathsome idolatrous reliefs inside the temple. The scene forms part of the build-up of idolatry which pollutes the temple and finally drives YHWH out of it, to leave the city to its doom. In 14: 1–11, however, the exiles have no temple to defile, and so we find that their sin takes place on a different scale: they have 'taken their idols into their hearts, and set the stumbling block of their iniquity before their faces'. It is not immediately apparent from the use of the word גלולים in Ezekiel 14: 3 what is meant. As Zimmerli observes:

> The general term גלולים is used by Ezekiel in a very wide meaning for the whole sphere of things which concern non-Israelite worship and its impurity. It does not, in itself, satisfy the modern desire with its interest in religious history, for precise distinctions, and leaves the offense of the elders more veiled than plain.[31]

It is possible that Ezekiel faces a wholesale syncretism and turning towards the gods of Babylon,[32] but it does seem rather unlikely that such men would seek an oracle from Ezekiel. The elders' idolatry must have been such that they believed it to be compatible with the worship of YHWH. Might it have been the attempt to establish sacrificial worship of YHWH in Babylon, as may be implicit in chapter 20?[33] It has been suggested that we should understand the phrase על־לבם literally as referring to amulets or even tattoos.[34] Greenberg thinks that we should be more concerned with the elders' thoughts or intentions than with their cultic paraphernalia: 'when, in vs. 6, the men are urged to repent, the language is not that of 20:7, "cast away the loathsome objects before your eyes"—viz. the idols worshiped in Egypt—but "turn your faces away from your abominations"—a metaphor for disregarding what is only in the mind'.[35]

Whatever may be the exact case in 14: 1–11, it appears that, while the nature of the sin condemned is not dissimilar to that of chapter 8 (since we have idolatry in both cases), here the scale of the sin has been transformed from the national and political to something smaller, more individual and domestic. And again we should point out that the punishment at issue is more individualistic and limited than is the case in Chapters 8–11.[36] As we have seen, however, this movement is not surprising given the dramatic

---

[31] Zimmerli, *Ezekiel 1*, 306–7.

[32] Fohrer, *Ezechiel*, 76.

[33] I shall discuss this more fully later in this chapter.

[34] J. Schoneveld, 'Ezekiel 14: 1–8', *Oudtestamentische Studiën*, 15 (1969), 193–204. Cf. Greenberg, *Ezekiel 1–20*, 248; Eichrodt, *Ezekiel*, 180.

[35] Greenberg, *Ezekiel 1–20*, 248; see also Block, *Ezekiel 1–24*, 425.

[36] See discussion above, Ch. 5.

change in the deportees' situation: the domestication that we find is not so much a major shift in ideology as an adaptation to changed circumstances.

The oracle in chapter 18 has a slightly different setting. Here Ezekiel is not directly condemning his own community for specific sins as he does in 14: 1–11. Rather he is attempting to convince his audience of their complicity in the events of the current national crisis. His audience who use the sour-grapes proverb believe themselves to be suffering because of their fathers' sins: a whole generation is suffering collectively for the sins of a previous one. Ezekiel's argument is designed to force his own generation to accept responsibility for the present disaster, not as individuals, but together, as a generation: 'Although a single man is considered in each of the three test-cases, it is the cause of the nation's predicament which is being explored; the proverb blames the sins of previous generations for the sufferings of the present, and accordingly the individuals of the test-cases each represent a generation.'[37]

What is most interesting about this chapter from our perspective is, however, the nature of the test cases themselves, since the examples they provide are very unlike most of the reasons given for the national disaster previously. By contrast with many of the oracles of judgement the details of the test cases in chapter 18 do not focus on the desecration of the temple and the build-up of impurity there, nor do they address the illegitimacy of alliances with foreign powers, nor do they really address the widespread injustice which Ezekiel describes in Jerusalem society. Rather they appear to be just what they are on the surface, test cases from which one is led to draw a wider conclusion. I believe, however, that the ethical content of these test cases represents the narrower moral focus of the exiled community, which inevitably takes on a more individual or domestic colouring because it is no longer so easy to make decisions which affect more than one's immediate neighbours and family.

The first of the test cases sets out to define the righteous man:

ואיש כי־יהיה צדיק ועשה משפט וצדקה

That is: 'If a man is righteous and does justice and righteousness' (18: 5).[38] The combination of משפט ('justice') and צדקה ('righteous-

---

[37] Joyce, *Divine Initiative*, 46.     [38] My translation.

ness') is familiar from the prophets as a general expression for correct behaviour. Ezekiel's list that follows in verses 6–8 serves to fill out the content of that behaviour with concrete examples. The list is repeated with some variation of order and content in 18: 10–13 (the wicked son) and 18: 14–17 (the righteous grandson). This variation suggests that Ezekiel is not quoting a well-known set of standards, but has composed his own list.[39] The list is probably not intended to be comprehensive, since the concluding element 'walks in my statutes and is careful to observe my ordinances' (18: 9; reversed in 18: 17; cf. 18: 19, 21) not only summarizes the contents of the list in legal terms, but is also broad enough to cover any unmentioned trespasses.

The lists contain a typically Ezekielian mixture of religious and social injunctions, but are for the most part concerned with family and business morality, not with the affairs of state that have characterized the preceding chapters (esp. 16–17). As it were, some adaptation to exilic circumstances is already apparent in the examples chosen for the test cases. The righteous person is defined here not on the basis of his relationship to the major institutions of Israelite life, but as is appropriate to the straitened moral circumstances of exile, the activities by which he is declared righteous or wicked are those which are possible among the community of exiles.[40]

The first and most complete list in 18: 6–8 takes the reader through three basic areas of moral activity, religion, sexuality and social relations. We may begin with the strictly religious elements of the sin list. The righteous man:

אל־ההרים לא אכל ועיניו לא נשא אל גלולי בית ישראל[41]

That is, 'does not eat upon the mountains or lift up his eyes to the idols of the house of Israel' (18: 5, 15; cf. 18: 11, 12; 22: 9). In fact this first injunction is one of the most difficult for my case, and the majority of commentators believe that it refers not to the exile, but to worship on the high places in the land of Israel, which Ezekiel has so roundly condemned in chapter 6.[42] Ezekiel has elsewhere

---

[39] Greenberg, *Ezekiel 1–20*, 342.

[40] Eichrodt's comment is apt, if slightly overstated: 'What is enumerated by Ezekiel here is independent of any tie with the soil of Palestine or the temple of Jerusalem' (*Ezekiel*, 238–9). [41] על־ההרים=אל־ההרים cf. Ezek. 18: 15.

[42] See e.g. May, 'Ezekiel', 158–9; Wevers, *Ezekiel*, 109: Zimmerli, *Ezekiel 1*, 380; Kaminsky, *Corporate Responsibility*, 161.

shown his anger at this worship, especially in chapter 6, but also in 16, 20, and 22.[43] The phrase 'eat upon the mountains' only appears in Ezekiel, and does not seem to depend on any particular tradition, legal or prophetic. Zimmerli considers the mention here to be a backward-looking one, concerned especially with the pre-Josianic period.[44] I am not sure that the evidence of the book as a whole would support such a conclusion; Ezekiel is at pains throughout the book to stress the culpability of the present generation in all areas of life: cultic, sexual, social, and political. His attacks on all forms of cultic apostasy do not mention Josiah and his reforms and have a thoroughly contemporary edge to them.

How can we see this case as relevant to the circumstances of exile? Eichrodt, for one, wishes to retain the exilic location of the text but believes that 'such a denunciation of high-place worship would be out of place in speaking to the exiles'.[45] He therefore adopts the emendation to read here עַל־הדם ('with the blood'), in view of Ezekiel 33: 25, and presumably on the basis of the law in Leviticus 19: 26: 'You shall not eat עַל־הדם'.[46] This would be the simplest solution, and we would have instead of an activity which requires the possession of the land a more simple ritual injunction about the eating of certain kinds of food. The importance of such ritual regulations is indisputable within Ezekiel's moral scheme, as we have already seen.[47] However, the emendation is itself highly suspect. The fact that the phrase is repeated more than once in the chapter makes scribal error a rather unlikely explanation.[48] Moreover, it is at least as possible that the Leviticus text should be emended in line with Ezekiel 18 and 22, since the Septuagint reading at Leviticus 19: 26 is ἐπί τῶν ὀρέων ('on the mountains').[49] Elsewhere in Leviticus laws about eating blood take דם as a direct object with no preposition (Lev. 17: 10–16; cf. also Deut. 12: 16). Given that עַל־הֶהָרִים is well attested in Ezekiel, Matties's conclusion is appropriate:

The Ezekiel text probably stems from the common polemic against

---

[43] See discussion above, Ch. 4.

[44] Zimmerli, *Ezekiel 1*, 380; Allen, *Ezekiel 1–19*, 274.

[45] Eichrodt, *Ezekiel*, 233.

[46] Ibid. 231–3; so also Elliger, *BHS*, ad loc.; Stalker, *Ezekiel*, 159.

[47] See above, Ch. 5; for another specific example involving food we may look to Ezek. 4: 14.

[48] Cooke, *Ezekiel*, 198.

[49] Matties, *Ezekiel 18*, 163.

idolatry and the sacrificial meals accompanying it. The language belongs to an inner Ezekielian concern and is expressed in terms independent of Israel's legal traditions. It bears closest resemblance to the judgment oracles in Ezekiel 1–24 which castigate prevailing idolatrous practice.[50]

The close association of this phase with the following 'lift up his eyes to the idols of the house of Israel' may suggest that the eating on mountains is more part of Ezekiel's general condemnation of idolatry, which we have seen to be at the heart of his criticism in chapter 14. The similarity of the phrases in both chapters suggests that here, as in 14: 1–11, Ezekiel is not concerned with the large-scale desecration of the temple or widespread cultic abuse in the land of Israel, but with the no less offensive infidelity of his own community, whose crimes mirror in smaller scale the offences of the Jerusalem élite at home.

One possibility is that the conjunction of sacrificial meals and idolatry refers to the exiles' desire to erect a *bamah* for themselves, either idolatrous or Yahwistic. That such a desire was current among the exiles may be implied by the difficult verse 20: 32: 'What is in your mind shall never happen—the thought, "Let us be like the nations, like the tribes of the countries, and worship wood and stone."' The whole of chapter 20 is a response to the inquiry of the elders in Babylon for a word from YHWH on a matter which remains unclear. It seems unlikely that these elders would approach Ezekiel to ask whether to erect an idolatrous shrine, but it is not so unlikely if they wanted to begin worshipping YHWH. Eichrodt draws attention here to the similarity to 1 Samuel 8, where the Israelites' desire for a king is expressed in similar terms: 'It is a classic formula expressing the mutiny against God implicit in the plan formed by the exiles, which has met such prompt rejection.'[51] Greenberg also thinks that Chapter 20 may address the exiles' desire to worship in Babylon:

Considering the peculiar emphasis on proper and improper sites of worship (alongside the accusation of idolatry) and the iteration of the promise of the land, it seems more likely to suppose that a *bama* had either been established or proposed by the exiles. Since in concurrence with the view of Deuteronomy, Ezekiel does not distinguish between outright idolatry and disapproved modes of worshiping YHWH, he would

---

[50] Ibid. 164. See also Greenberg, *Ezekiel 1–20*, 329; Zimmerli, *Ezekiel 1*, 453.
[51] Eichrodt, *Ezekiel*, 277.

have regarded this as a continuation of apostasy. Such a heathen practice, adopted as an accommodation to living on heathen soil, might well
have stimulated the diatribe.[52]

On the other hand, Zimmerli sees 20: 32 as expressing not the
desire for sacrificial worship but the deep despair which takes
seriously the religious consequences of the destruction and scattering of the nation. The promise of a new exodus in 20: 33–44 is
intended as encouragement to those who are at a loss.[53] Nevertheless, the stress on the holy mountain and the acceptance of
offerings in 20: 40 does suggest that Ezekiel is still concerned with
the central-sanctuary law, and perhaps trying to dissuade his
fellow exiles from building a shrine of their own. If this is a satisfactory interpretation of chapter 20, then it is not unlikely that we
find a reference to such possibilities in 18: 5. Even if there is no
sense of a planned *bamah*, then it is likely that Ezekiel's treatment
of 'mountains' and of 'idols' belong together as a part of his
general criticism of idolatry (as exemplified also by 14: 1–11).
While this language has its origins in the land of Judah, as does the
sour-grapes proverb, it remains highly appropriate to the exiles,
and in either case we are dealing with sin on a more domestic
scale than we find in much of the rest of the book.

Ezekiel's list displays a more explicit concern for morality at the
level of the family or immediate community as it moves on from
religious to sexual ethics. Adultery (18: 6, 10, 15) is a crime which
threatens the disintegration of the community by striking at the
family bonds which are its basic building-blocks. Eichrodt comments that it 'must have constituted a particularly dangerous
temptation among a crowd of exiles cut off from all traditional
ties'.[54] Elsewhere Ezekiel uses it as one of the most powerful
metaphors for the behaviour of the people of Judah and Jerusalem
(Ezekiel 16; 23). Here, however, the usage is not metaphorical,
and it is clear that the integrity of the family would be of vital
importance for the maintenance of community in exile. As Albertz
writes:

Now in the exilic period not only did family piety become significant for
all of society, but for the first time the family joined the ranks of those
who handed on official religion. As the main form of social organization,

---

[52] Greenberg, *Ezekiel 1–20*, 387.          [53] Zimmerli, *Ezekiel 1*, 414–15.

[54] Eichrodt, *Ezekiel*, 239.

it representatively assumed important functions which supported the identity of the people of Judah as a whole, in that old family customs took on a new confessional quality or earlier official cultic festivals were transformed into family rites . . . Nothing makes clearer the prominent religious role which the family came to occupy after the exile than the fact that in the rather later priestly conception of history the covenant between Yahweh and Israel is not made with the people on Sinai, but with the family of Abraham (Gen. 17).[55]

The word which Ezekiel uses in 18: 6 is not the normal verb נָאַף ('to commit adultery'), but the ritual term טמא ('to defile').[56] The prophet's attachment to ritual is more evident still in the second sexual item on the list: ואל־אשה נדה לא יקרב ('he does not approach a menstruating woman'). נדה, as we have seen, is the normal priestly word for the uncleanness of menstruation.[57] In these sexual examples not only is the family (rather than the State) the locus of moral activity, but we also find an element of Ezekiel's wholesale ritualization of ethics, both of which suggest its relevance to the community of exiles.

Next the lists move on from sexual to social sins, which make up the bulk of the material, and again we find right and wrong action defined on a smaller socio-political scale than elsewhere in the book. Where they are specific they seem to belong to the realm of family and business ethics, one area in which it appears that the exiles had some competence.[58] The simplest images are the demands not to commit robbery and to feed the hungry and clothe the naked (18: 7, 12, 16), which appear to be part of a general concern for the poor and needy, with no particular tie to specific social circumstances. All the others, however, can be related to the more restricted moral world of the exiles.

איש לא יונה ('he does not oppress anyone' (18: 7, 16, cf. 18: 12)) appears to be more than a broad reference to wrongdoing. Greenberg comments: 'again in 45: 8, 46: 18, *hona* denotes specifically doing a (usually helpless) person out of his property

---

[55] Albertz, *History of Israelite Religion*, ii. 407.

[56] See discussion above, Ch. 5; Neusner, *Idea of Purity*, 14.

[57] See the discussion of female blood above, Ch. 5.

[58] See discussion above, Ch. 2. Ezekiel's designation of the place of exile as 'a land of trade', and 'a city of merchants' (17: 4; cf. 16: 29) may imply that even from an early stage the exiles were engaged in business of some kind. Indeed Barstad goes so far as to suggest that even for slaves Babylonia in this period was a 'land of opportunity' (*The Myth of the Empty Land*, 75).

(Jer. 22: 3)'.[59] The context of trade is suggested by Leviticus 25: 14: 'And if you sell to your neighbour or buy from your neighbour, you shall not wrong one another [אל־תונו איש את־אחיו].' In Ezekiel 45: 8 the prince is the specific subject, as in Jeremiah 22: 3. As Matties points out, the law here, in Ezekiel 18, 'seems . . . to evoke echoes of royal responsibility democratized'.[60] Such democratization is certainly appropriate to the exile, where the royal house has lost so much of its influence and responsibility.

In חבלתו חוב ישיב ('restores to the debtor his pledge' (18: 7; cf. 18: 12, 16)), Ezekiel alludes to laws regarding the taking of a pledge for debt, the most prominent of these being Exodus 22: 26: 'If ever you take your neighbour's garment in pledge, you shall restore it to him before the sun goes down' (cf. also Deut. 24: 6, 17).[61] This is an action which takes place in the economic rather than the political sphere, where we have to do with business relationships between individuals rather than decisions which will affect large groups of people.

The condemnation of usury in בנשך לא יתן ותרבית לא יקח ('does not lend at interest or take any increase' (18: 8, 13, 17; cf. 22: 12)). is common to all the Israelite legal traditions, the Book of the Covenant (Exod. 22: 24), Deuteronomy (23: 19–20), and the Holiness Code (Lev. 25: 35–7). Ezekiel's language seems closest to the legislation in Leviticus. This contains the same parallelism of נשך ('interest') and תרבית ('increase') and also uses the verbs לקח and נתן (as in 18: 8) Ezekiel appears to be unique among the prophets for condemning usury, but this is not surprising given his tendency to use law as a basis for his work, and again we find him reflecting legal material which is relevant to the business needs of the community.

---

[59] Greenberg, *Ezekiel 1–20*, 329.

[60] Matties, *Ezekiel 18*, 168. Although he also points to democratization in this oracle, Block goes further in suggesting that the whole set of test cases in Ezekiel 18 relates to a royal standard of 'justice and righteousness' (*Ezekiel 1–24*, 568–9), and it is certainly true that a number of the stipulations could be breached by a king or royal official. However, he is surely wrong to argue that offences such as adultery, holding on to a pledge, or taking interest would ever have been perceived as significantly more appropriate to royalty than to other people. An interesting sidelight may be shed on this by the seventh-century Yavneh-Yam ostracon, where the offender who has appropriated a worker's garment would appear to be no more exalted a person than the overseer of a work gang. For text and translation see J. C. L. Gibson, *Syrian Semitic Inscriptions*, i. *Hebrew and Moabite Inscriptions* (Oxford, 1971), 26–30.

[61] Matties points out that no priestly legislation on the pledge exists, showing that Ezekiel is dependent on a range of Israelite legal traditions to construct his lists (*Ezekiel 18*, 168).

In 18: 8, 17 we read מעול ישיב ידו משפט אמת יעשה בין איש לאיש
('withholds his hand from iniquity, executes true justice between
man and man'). Zimmerli believes that these expressions come
from the law courts, and refer to correct behaviour in judicial
cases: עול 'must be interpreted here of unlawful action in a court
of law' because of parallels in the Holiness Code, and משפט אמת
should best be translated 'true law'. As he says, 'the inculcation of
right conduct in the administration of law was already a foundation of Israel's early law'.[62] However, it is far from clear that the
expressions demand explanation in terms of the courts: they may
rather be redefined to reflect more ordinary concerns.

The word עול is used several times elsewhere in the book of
Ezekiel as a general term for wrongdoing (it summarizes the
behaviour of the wicked in 3: 20; 18: 24, 26; 33: 13, 15, 18).[63]
Whereas in Leviticus 19: 15 the expression לא־תעשו עול במשפט probably has a legal context, in Leviticus 19: 35 the same expression
applies to just measures, and therefore to 'the context of trading
relationships'.[64] The same is implied by Ezekiel 28: 18: 'by the
multitude of your iniquities, in the unrighteousness [עול] of your
trade you profaned your sanctuaries'. As for משפט אמת, that expression 'is not dependent on any legal text or tradition', but belongs to
the practice of relational obligations to fellow Israelites which are
apparent primarily in the socio-economic sphere.[65] This is in line
with Greenberg's argument:

> For the association of *'wl*, *'šh*, and *mšpt* in the two parts of this verse
> Kimhi rightly cites Lev. 19: 35 'Commit no injustice in judgment' (*l' t'św
> 'wl bmšpt*). The terms have been recombined here and, in the context of
> a layman's everyday affairs, *mšpt* bears the different sense of 'arbitration,
> decision, settlement.'[66]

Weinfeld goes further still, arguing that here and elsewhere in
scripture the expression refers 'not to the passing of a verdict in a
court', but to 'the preservation of the existence of right relationships between a man and his fellow'.[67] If this is not strictly legal

---

[62] Zimmerli, *Ezekiel 1*, 381. Similar opinions appear in Wevers, *Ezekiel*, 110; Stalker, *Ezekiel*, 160.

[63] It has a similar general sense elsewhere; see e.g. Deut. 32: 4; Ps. 7: 2–3; Prov. 29: 27; Jer. 2: 5.          [64] Matties, *Ezekiel 18*, 172; cf. also Deut. 25: 16.

[65] Matties, *Ezekiel 18*, 172.

[66] Greenberg, *Ezekiel 1–20*, 330.

[67] M. Weinfeld, *Social Justice in Ancient Israel and in the Ancient Near East* (Jerusalem, 1995), 220.

language, but the language of right relationship between individuals, then again we have an example where the activities
referred to in the Ezekiel 18 list reflect the narrower range of moral
possibilities open to Ezekiel's exiled audience.

Throughout this list of sins and virtues we have found evidence
for a shift of moral focus away from the grand, institutional sins
that have brought about the fall of Jerusalem towards a smaller,
more circumscribed moral world of exile. It must be said, however, that there is still a great deal of common ground between the
two. Throughout the book Ezekiel makes it plain that obedience
to YHWH's commandments is the fundamental moral duty of every
Israelite. Moreover, the offences of idolatry and social injustice
feature in all his ethical thinking. As we saw in the case of 14: 1–11
there is no radical discontinuity between the morality that was
appropriate in Jerusalem and that for the exile. The overall aim
which the test cases serve is to convince the exiles of their own
responsibility for the straitened circumstances in which they find
themselves. It is not surprising that Ezekiel uses some stereotypical
language which would have been as much at home in Judah as in
exile, and it is even possible that in some cases he may use examples reminiscent of the sins his audience could have committed
before their exile. But an overall shift towards exilic conditions is,
nevertheless, evident in the chapter.

I should like to illustrate this point further by drawing a comparison between chapter 18 and the one other passage in Ezekiel
in which a sin list features prominently, 22: 6–12. There are clearly great similarities between the two lists, one addressed to the
exiles about themselves, and one to the exiles about the inhabitants of Jerusalem. Greenberg comments:

> The family resemblance of the lists cannot be missed, and it supports the
> impression made of our list being Ezekiel's creation. The differences are
> accountable to the fact that our list is of virtues . . . while ch. 22 is a bill of
> indictment (hence the addition of desecration and sexual offences) . . .
> Their divergences are not such as can be accounted for by geographical
> or social conditions.[68]

When confronted with such a similar list serving a different
purpose, one might think either that this too reflects wholly the
circumstances of exile, or that I am mistaken to draw social con-

---

[68] Greenberg, *Ezekiel 1–20*, 343.

clusions from the content of these lists. Elements of 22: 6–12 certainly fit the pattern of an exilic moral world which I have proposed for chapter 18. If anything, concern for the integrity of the family is more apparent in 22: 6–12, with the dishonouring of parents (22: 7) and the addition of incest to the categories of sexual misconduct (22: 10). Aspects of bad business practice like oppression (הונה (22: 7)) and the taking of interest (22: 12) also come under attack. However, I would like to suggest that there are small but significant differences between the kinds of moral action in the lists of 18 and 22, which make the one appropriate to an exilic situation and the other to that of the city of Jerusalem. A number of the items in 22: 6–12 do seem to represent the kind of moral possibility open to those in Jerusalem, which are denied to the exiles and therefore not in 18. In particular, religious offences are mentioned which demand the presence of the temple, the royal house features prominently in the condemnation, and there are hints that much of the social criticism is directed towards abuse of the judicial process.

In the sphere of religion it is noteworthy that the mention is made of a crime which has to refer to the temple in Jerusalem: the reference to YHWH's holy things in 22: 8. The sudden change of style to the second person feminine and of subject matter to cultic regulations have led many scholars to consider this verse a late interpolation.[69] However, the similar transition of person from verse 12a to verse 12b, where no ritual is at issue, makes this un-likely.[70] Moreover, it is anachronistic to demand a strict separation of 'ritual' and 'ethics' which would have been meaningless in the sixth century BCE. We do appear to have at this point a direct con-nection with the Holiness Code, and in particular with Leviticus 19: 30, which reads את שבתתי תשמרו ומקדשי תיראו, 'You shall keep my sabbaths and reverence my sanctuary.'. The difference is that Ezekiel's concern here is not just with the sanctuary (מקדש), but more generally with the holy things or sancta (קדשים). This implies all the things connected with the temple worship, vessels, sacri-fices, and so on, as well as the sanctuary itself, and may refer to the abominations Ezekiel has described in chapter 8 and elsewhere. We should remember that the holy things are no longer there to be

---

[69] e.g. Eichrodt, *Ezekiel*, 308.

[70] Zimmerli, *Ezekiel 1*, 458; R. M. Hals, *Ezekiel*, FOTL 19 (Grand Rapids, Mich., 1988), 157.

defiled after the destruction of the temple. While the holy things
seem more appropriate to Jerusalem, one might think that the
mention of sabbath breaking might fit more neatly in the exilic
setting, where it, along with circumcision and the dietary laws,
became one of the primary distinguishing marks of Jewish identity.
But the sabbath was clearly an institution respected in pre-exilic
Israel, as Amos 8: 5 and Isaiah 1: 13 make clear. In pre-exilic
Jerusalem it seems to have been part of the temple cult and so its
mention in connection with the temple holy things is quite appropriate.[71] It is by no means necessary that the mention of sabbath
breaking implies an exilic context. Indeed, it is worth noting here
that Ezekiel only refers to sabbaths in two contexts: first, as something profaned before the exile (20: 12, 13, 16, 20, 21, 24; 22: 26; 23:
38), and, secondly, as part of the transformed worship of the new
temple (44: 24; 45: 17; 46: 1, 3, 4, 12).

A stronger argument for the relevance of the sin list to Jerusalem
rather than the exiles can be made from the social location of the
criminals in 22: 6. In the first instance the list in chapter 22 locates
its targets as the political élite of the state of Judah:

הנה נשיאי ישראל איש לזרעו היו בך למען שפך דם

That is: 'Behold, the princes of Israel in you, every one according
to his power, have been bent on shedding blood.' This first item in
the list is the only one which is directed against a specific group of
people, the ישראל נשיאי ('princes of Israel'), who come in for heavy
criticism later in the chapter as well.[72] This term probably refers to
the royal house, Zedekiah and his family, and possibly also his
predecessors.[73] The idiom of 22: 6 is hard to translate literally, but
the word זרוע ('arm') clearly refers to the strength of the rulers.[74] In
Ezekiel 30: 20–6 it is used as a metaphor for the military power of
the Egyptian and Babylonian kings, but here it seems to represent
the power that Judah's rulers have over their own community.
This abuse of power by society's leaders is reminiscent of the
prophetic critique in Micah 3: 1–12; Jeremiah 22: 13–19 and

---

[71] See e.g. Isa. 1: 13; Hos. 2: 13; 2 Kgs. 16: 17f.; Lam. 2: 6; Albertz, *History of Israelite
Religion*, ii. 408. See also the fuller discussion above, Ch. 5.          [72] Ezek. 22: 24, 27.

[73] Kessler, *Staat und Gesellschaft*, 105; Duguid, *Leaders*, 38; Wevers, *Ezekiel*, 129; Allen,
*Ezekiel 20–48*, 36; Cooke, *Ezekiel*, 201.

[74] See e.g. Authorized Version (AV), Revised English Bible (RSV), New Jerusalem Bible
(NJB). Zimmerli does retain a literal sense, translating 'See, the princes of Israel in you have
each thrust in his (powerful) arm to shed blood' (*Ezekiel 1*, 453).

Habakkuk 2: 12.[75] The final clause לִמַעַן שָׁפַךְ דָּם ('in order to shed blood') reappears in verses 9 and 12, where it appears to refer not only to 'crimes of a social nature', as Zimmerli puts it,[76] but perhaps more specifically to the crime of judicial murder. It was the princes who would have had prime responsibility for the administration of justice in Jerusalem, and who are often condemned for abusing this privilege to cause suffering or death.[77]

Other aspects of the list in 22: 6–12 seem to reflect judicial murder and therefore a legal autonomy that is lacking in chapter 18. אַנְשֵׁי רָכִיל . . . לִמַעַן שָׁפַךְ דָּם ('men who slander to shed blood') are Ezekiel's concern in 22: 9. The word רָכִיל ('slanderer') only occurs six times in the Hebrew Bible, and the most significant occurrence from our point of view is in the Holiness Code, where it appears linked with the crime of judicial murder: 'You shall not go up and down as a slanderer among your people, and you shall not stand forth against the blood of your neighbour' (Lev. 19: 16). Concern about slander is also found in Proverbs 11: 13; 20: 19 and in Jeremiah 6: 28, 9: 4 (MT 9: 3). Zimmerli considers that the parallel with Jeremiah 'shows that Ezekiel actually mentions here other well-known diseased aspects of contemporary Jerusalem'.[78]

Judicial murder appears to be the issue again in 22: 12, where the third group of statements which point out disorder in the social and economic sphere opens with an accusation of bribery: שֹׁחַד לָקְחוּ בָךְ לִמַעַן שָׁפַךְ דָּם. Ezekiel adds his refrain 'to shed blood', which suggests that he is again referring to injustice in the courts, and possibly judicial murders. The prohibition of bribery throughout the Hebrew Bible tends to appear in the context of the administration of justice.[79] So we find in Exodus 23: 6–8:

You shall not pervert the justice due to the poor in his suit. Keep far from a false charge, and do not slay the innocent and righteous, for I will not acquit the wicked. And you shall take no bribe, for a bribe blinds the officials, and subverts the cause of those who are in the right.[80]

---

[75] Kessler, *Staat und Gesellschaft*, 105.

[76] Zimmerli, *Ezekiel 1*, 467.

[77] Cf. Jer. 22: 13–19, addressed to Jehoiakim, or the story of Naboth's vineyard in 1 Kgs. 21. See Allen, *Ezekiel 20–48*, 36.                [78] Zimmerli, *Ezekiel 1*, 458.

[79] As elsewhere in the ancient Near East; see the Hymn to Shamash which contains: 'The unrighteous judge thou dost make to see imprisonment; the receiver of a bribe who perverts (justice) thou dost make to bear punishment.' (ii. 41–4; in Pritchard (ed.), *Ancient Near Eastern Texts*, 388); cf. Boecker, *Law and the Administration of Justice*, 54.

[80] Cf. also Deut. 10: 17–18; 16: 19; 27: 25; Zimmerli, *Ezekiel 1*, 458–9.

These references to the administration of justice, combined with the pointed attack on the 'princes of Israel', do seem to mark the sin list in 22: 6–12 as distinct from the list in chapter 18, despite the many similarities. In 22: 6–12, addressed to the capital city, there are elements which belong to moral decisions facing the Jerusalem élite, whereas chapter 18 consistently represents a reduced scope for moral action more appropriate to the exiled community.

Ezekiel's audience was drawn from the community of exiled Judaeans, and in 14: 1–11 and 18 we have found evidence for the ways in which ethical thinking could be adapted to suit the new circumstances in Babylon. By comparison with their previous life in Jerusalem the exiles' moral world became circumscribed, and the kinds of decision they could make more limited in scope and application. The ethical content of 14: 1–11 and 18 exemplifies this scaling down of sin and virtue to the more domestic or individual level appropriate to exile. At the same time Ezekiel's transformation of the language of criminal law to a more theological purpose shows the enduring symbolic value of the old institutions of state. The prophet creatively reforms traditions whose home is the state of Judah, so as to provide meaning and continuity for his fellow exiles, and to prevent the disintegration of the people of YHWH.

### Repentance: Converting to the Exile?

The theology of repentance poses some serious problems for the reader of Ezekiel. It is one of the areas of the book's thought which seems most inconsistent. On the one hand, the prophet clearly demands that his audience repent (14: 6; 18: 30; cf. 18: 21–32; 33: 10–20). On the other hand, it seems clear that any repentance will not avert the judgement that is promised: Ezekiel's prophecies of doom make it plain enough that there will be no reprieve for Judah. Indeed, it is likely that the prophet's demands for repentance are addressed not to the inhabitants of Judah, but to the exiles in Babylonia.[81] Surprisingly, however, repentance seems to have no direct connection with the promised restoration of temple, city, and nation, which YHWH will bring about more or less entirely on his own initiative. If there is any

---

[81] As we have seen, the clearest demands for repentance appear in 14: 1–11 and 18: 1–32, both of which belong to Ezekiel's exilic context.

benefit to the exiles in repentance, it is to be found somewhere else. The benefit may be limited to life in exile, and therefore the call to repent as Ezekiel uses it may be further evidence for the limited moral scope of the exiled community.

The theme of repentance in the prophets has drawn a number of different responses. In the first place there are those who believe that exhortation was a real and important part of a prophet's office. In all prophetic activity the prophet is attempting to change people's behaviour. Gordon Matties, for one, believes that 'the call to repentance is a fundamental facet of Hebrew moral discourse. The prophet exhorts the people not simply because he is interested in averting judgment, nor simply to guarantee salvation. Rather the exhortation serves as the basic statement of human responsibility in a cosmos characterized by order.'[82] On the other hand, however, there are many scholars who believe that future judgement was the primary message that the prophets attempted to communicate, and that exhortations and calls to repent are largely rhetorical devices which serve to bolster whatever future prediction or comment on society the prophet is making. 'Nicht moralische Erneuerung, sondern Verkündigung der Gottesgerechtigkeit war die Aufgabe der Propheten, "damit allen der Mund gestopft wird und alle Welt vor Gott dasteht" (Rom 3, 19).'[83] Given the wide divergence of opinions, it seems best to take nothing for granted about 'the' nature of prophecy or of the call to repent, but to consider each case individually on its own merits.[84]

So what is the point of the calls to repentance in the book of Ezekiel? I shall concentrate on chapter 18, since this is where the discussion centres. After the examples of the three generations

---

[82] Matties, *Ezekiel 18*, 109. See also T. M. Raitt, 'The Prophetic Summons to Repentance', *ZAW* 83 (1971), 30–49.

[83] J. Barton, 'Begründungsversuche der prophetischen Unheilsankündigung im Alten Testament', *EvTh* 47 (1987), 435; for fuller discussion see also W. H. Schmidt, *Zukunftsgewißheit und Gegenwartskritik: Grundzüge prophetischer Verkündigung*, BibS[N] 64 (Neukirchen-Vluyn, 1973); C. Westermann, *Basic Forms of Prophetic Speech* (Phil., 1967); H. W. Wolff, 'Das Thema "Umkehr" in der alttestamentlichen Prophetie', *ZThK* 48 (1951), 129–48; A. V. Hunter, *Seek the Lord! A Study of the Meaning and Function of the Exhortations in Amos, Hosea, Isaiah, Micah, and Zephaniah* (Baltimore, Md., 1982).

[84] T. Krüger, discussing the problem of whether or not judgement prophecies imply the possibility of repentance, draws a similar conclusion: 'Es ist demnach in jedem Einzelfall neu zu prüfen, ob eine prophetische Gerichtsprognose mit der Möglichkeit einer Abwendung des angekündigten Unheils oder nicht, und welche Wahrscheinlichkeit sie ihr gegebenenfalls zubilligt' (*Geschichtskonzepte im Ezechielbuch*, BZAW 180 (Berlin, 1988), 348–9).

in 18: 1–20, verses 21–32 move into a theoretical discussion of repentance which reaches its culmination in the demand:

Repent and turn from all your transgressions, lest iniquity be your ruin. Cast away from you all the transgressions which you have committed against me, and get yourselves a new heart and a new spirit! (18: 30–1)

The interpretation of this passage provides a good example of different attitudes to the call to repent. It is possible to read 18: 21–32 as a later addition to the chapter, which is not essentially connected with the discussion of the three generations,[85] but most commentators accept that it forms a natural continuation of the debate about responsibility in verses 1–20.[86] Indeed, the majority of interpreters are united in seeing it as the climax to the whole of chapter 18. Thus Stalker writes:

It is to this call that the whole chapter has been leading up. No feelings of guilt due to solidarity or to one's own sinful past need paralyse moral decision and effort. Later (36: 26) Ezekiel speaks of the NEW HEART and the NEW SPIRIT as the gift of Yahweh. Here, however, his concern is to declare that a man can, by an act of will, change his mode of life.[87]

The understanding of repentance in 18: 21–32 is in some ways dependent on the attitude taken to the rest of the chapter. Ezekiel has traditionally been seen here as the champion of individual (as opposed to communal) responsibility, and for some interpreters it is as individuals that the audience is called to turn. Ezekiel has no further hopes for the nation to do anything about its state:

Having totally given up on national repentance, having promised the annihilation of Jerusalem and the departure of God's glory from the temple, and stung by the question of God's justice in letting the innocent suffer equally with the guilty, Ezekiel opens up this substantially new teaching of repentance for the individual to show that there is hope for those who accepted the exile with faith in God's abiding Lordship and Justice.[88]

Fishbane too sees the call to repent as connected with individuals' response to their exiled situation:

---

[85]  e.g. Graffy, *A Prophet Confronts*, 58–9.
[86]  Zimmerli, *Ezekiel 1*, 374; Joyce, *Divine Initiative*, 55; Matties, *Ezekiel 18*, 45–6; Kaminsky, *Corporate Responsibility*, 161–2.
[87]  Stalker, *Ezekiel*, 161–2; cf. Zimmerli, *Ezekiel 1*, 374.
[88]  Raitt, *Theology of Exile*, 49.

In order to reject the notion of vicarious punishment and assert the principle of individual responsibility—a theological necessity if the people in exile were to assume religious responsibility for their lives—the prophet had first to stress the uniqueness of each person (and so each generation) before the law, and this he did via the apodictic legal formulation in v 4 (and v 20) and the casuistic legal formulations found in vv 5–18. He was still left with a religious problem, however, for while the first argument emphasized that there was no transfer of guilt from one generation (person) to another, nothing was said about the sinner and his own lifetime. Was a (repentant) person to be considered guilty in later years for sins committed earlier, and vice versa? Surely not, says the prophet: the Lord wants repentance and so the life of the sinner. Thus, implies the prophet, those in exile are there for their own sins and not those of their parents, and since their relationship with God is not an intractable or inherited fate they can take responsibility for it and return to YHWH.[89]

But we should challenge too individualistic a reading of this passage; just as the individual fathers and sons of 18: 1–20 are best seen as representative of the community as a whole, the test cases of 21–32 also use the examples of individuals to serve an argument about the community. In particular, the use of the phrase 'house of Israel' four times in this section (18: 25, 29, 30, 31) emphasizes the fact that 'Yahweh is not calling a few dissatisfied individuals to take note, but his people as a whole'.[90]

What is the purpose of this call to YHWH's people? Paul Joyce has presented a serious challenge to the idea that Ezekiel envisages any repentance as a real possibility for his audience. Joyce understands the main purpose of chapter 18 to be the demonstration of Israel's collective responsibility for the disaster of exile, and, for him, the call to repent serves to underline this message: it is principally a rhetorical flourish which serves to underscore the seriousness of the position of those who will not repent.[91] He also opposes the view of Zimmerli that Ezekiel 18 belongs to a new phase of the prophet's ministry beginning after the destruction of Jerusalem.[92]

---

[89] Fishbane, 'Sin and Judgment', 141–2; a similar position is outlined by H. Gross, 'Umkehr im Alten Testament: In der Sicht der Propheten Jeremia und Ezechiel', in H. auf der Maur and B. Kleinheyer (eds.), *Zeichen des Glaubens: Studien zu Taufe und Firmung: Balthasar Fischer zum 60. Geburtstag*, (Zürich and Freiburg, 1972), 19–28.

[90] Zimmerli, *Ezekiel 1*, 386. Cf. also Joyce, *Divine Initiative*, 54; K. D. Sakenfeld, 'Ez 18: 25–32', *Int* 32 (1978), 295–6. Greenberg points out the exilic nature of the community: 'Ezekiel's message was for the nation—that is the exilic continuation of the nation that he regularly calls *bet yisra'el* (vv. 25, 29–31; cf. 3: 4 with 3: 11)' (*Ezekiel 1–20*, 341).

[91] Joyce, *Divine Initiative*, 50–60.       [92] Zimmerli, *Ezekiel 1*, 377.

The sour-grapes proverb belongs as naturally to the exiles of 597 as those of 587, and the oracle's position in the book makes it likely that 'at some point relatively soon after commencing his ministry the prophet addressed the major question of the cause of the disaster, which he and his immediate audience had been experiencing to the full since 597'.[93] The question of date is especially important because the purpose of a call to repentance made prior to disaster is likely to be different from that of one made in its aftermath: if it comes alongside a wholehearted prediction of disaster it would appear less likely to offer any genuine hope. So how should we understand this call to repentance? Joyce claims that it is not implied that repentance would avert the coming disaster: it is definitely too late for that. Rather the motif has two functions, of which the first is 'to underline Israel's responsibility for the coming disaster', where 'by emphasizing the demand of Yahweh, the call to repentance underlines the fact that Israel has had every warning and is wholly to blame for the crisis which is even now engulfing her.'[94]

Joyce is probably right to see this as one aspect of the call to repentance in this passage. Elsewhere in the book a failure to repent is presupposed as part of the basis for judgement. In the historical summary of chapter 20 Ezekiel describes how the ancestors were commanded to repent and failed to do so (20: 7–8, 18–21). That the same should be true for a present, even more corrupt generation should not surprise us.[95] Some such polemical intent in 18: 21–32 is further suggested by the way that the divine justice is set against Israel's injustice: 'Hear now, O house of Israel: Is my way not just? Is it not your ways that are not just?' (18: 25). Joel S. Kaminsky argues that the call to repent not only underlines the responsibility of Ezekiel's audience, but also helps them to accept the prophet's conclusions: 'If one knows that one can repent and start anew, then it is easier to admit one's guilt. Thus the repentance motif is a carrot that is held out to the

---

[93] Joyce, *Divine Initiative*, 56. W. Zimmerli, ' "Leben" und "Tod" im Buche des Propheten Ezechiel', *ThZ* 13 (1957), 494–508.

[94] Joyce, *Divine Initiative*, 57.

[95] This may be the implication of 24: 13: 'Because I would have cleansed you and you were not cleansed from your filthiness, you shall not be cleansed any more till I have satisfied my fury upon you.' For a fuller discussion of the failure to repent in Jeremiah and Ezekiel see Raitt, *Theology of Exile*, 35–49.

people to help them admit that they are guilty and deserving of
the punishment that they have received.'[96]

But Joyce also suggests a second, more positive, function for the
call to repent: to stress what YHWH would wish for Israel under
better circumstances. Despite everything, the god still yearns for
his people's obedience: 'As we shall see, Ezekiel's God will not
in the end allow the sin of Israel to be the last word. Beyond the
disaster—and not before—the prophet looks to a new beginning
for his people, in which "life" will consist in the fullness of relationship with God in contrast to the "death" of estrangement
from him.'[97] Joyce might make more of this. There is a genuine
desire for a response on the part of the people that is more than
just the acceptance of responsibility. It is made very clear that
YHWH takes no pleasure in the death of the sinner (18: 23, 32), and
the final 'turn and live' does at least leave open the possibility that
the prophet's hearers will respond.

An examination of 33: 10–20 may help us to confirm this. Joyce
argues that this passage draws on the language of chapter 18 to
make more or less the same point as that chapter, and also that
'the immediate function of the repentance motif (vv. 11–16, 18–19)
is again to highlight the responsibility for the impending final
judgement'.[98] However, this oracle responds to a quotation which,
on its most natural reading, suggests that his audience has already
accepted responsibility for what they are suffering: 'Our transgressions and our sins are upon us, and we waste away because of
them; how then can we live?' (33: 10).[99] In this context the call to
repentance looks less like a further demand for his audience to
accept responsibility and more like the attempt to find some way
out of 'the pit of their despair and cynicism'.[100] Moreover, by contrast with chapter 18, much more is made of the case of the wicked

---

[96] Kaminsky, *Corporate Responsibility*, 166.

[97] Joyce, *Divine Initiative*, 57–8.

[98] Ibid. 144 n. 87.

[99] Joyce raises the possibility that פשעינו וחטאינו in v. 10 should be taken to refer not to
acknowledged sins but rather to undeserved punishments', pointing to the use of פשע in
Dan. 8: 12, 13; 9: 24 and of חטאת in Zech. 14: 19 (*Divine Initiative*, 144 n. 87). While חטא, like
עון, can certainly mean both 'sin' and 'punishment', the evidence that פשע ('transgression',
'rebellion') can also carry the sense of punishment is ambiguous at best, and comes from a
very late source. The more natural reading is RSV's 'transgressions and sins', which makes
clear that this is a confession of guilt.

[100] Lemke, 'Life in the Present and Hope for the Future', *Int.* 38 (1984), 169; Greenberg,
*Ezekiel 1–20*, 341.

man who repents than any of the other cases. Graffy argues that this stress highlights the importance of repentance: 'The lamenting exiles can change their future by returning from their sin to a life of justice and righteousness.'[101]

It would appear, then, that the call to repentance does have two functions. Not only does it serve to bolster Ezekiel's argument that his audience should accept responsibility for the disaster that has befallen them, it also expresses a genuine desire that they should amend their lives and return to YHWH. What remains unclear is the value of repentance: what would repentance do for the people who repent?

We have seen that although there is considerable use of individualistic language and individual test cases in chapters 18 and 33, their basic orientation is towards the community of Israel. This also applies to the situation in chapter 14, where we also find an explicit call to repentance. We have already shown how in 14: 1–11 the language of 'cutting off' and of estrangement are intimately linked with the maintenance of community, so that there the call to repentance has the purpose of protecting and maintaining the community of exiles. Perhaps parallel to this language of 'cutting off' is the legal vocabulary of life and death, which in the test-case verdicts has been reapplied theologically to the question of responsibility and repentance. It is also more satisfactorily seen as referring to life in community, but at issue is the nature of the community to which it refers.

Gordon Matties makes the point that Ezekiel 18 occupies a somewhat liminal point in the movement of the book, finding its place 'in the imagined world between judgement and reordering'. One of its most important functions is as a call to envision a new community which will live along the lines suggested by the legal lists of the case study. For the exiles, 'the list of laws functions as a dossier, a list of virtues that characterize the repentant ones, the ones on whom the new community will be built'.[102] In this view those who repent begin to take on the character of the restored community and indeed to anticipate a fuller restoration than is possible within the confines of exile. This is certainly true up to a point, but if the chapter provides a guide to the character of the

---

[101] Graffy, *A Prophet Confronts*, 75; see also Zimmerli, *Ezekiel 2*, 188.

[102] Matties, *Ezekiel 18*, 195; cf. also Greenberg, *Ezekiel 1–20*, 345–6; J. Blenkinsopp, *A History of Prophecy in Ancient Israel*, 2nd edn. (Louisville, Ky., 1996), 173.

restored community, it is a very incomplete guide. If we have contrasted the content of Ezekiel 18 with those oracles of judgement addressed to Jerusalem before its fall, we must also contrast it with the vision of a restored community we receive from chapters 40–48. In Ezekiel 18 there is no sense of the importance of the national institutions of sacrificial cult, priesthood, and secular leadership that we find in 40–48, nor is there reference to a return to the land, which is central to Ezekiel's vision of restoration. Ezekiel 18 fails to relate fully to the institutional and communal life of a restored Israel, and so at best provides a kind of interim ethic, or temporary vision of society.[103]

A further question that arises is whether obedience to the demands of chapter 18 can bring about a restoration, and many commentators would answer this in the affirmative. Matties, for one, sees a profound eschatological edge to the call to repent, arguing that the chapter 'is an exhortation to the people to qualify for the return, which will include both temple and land in the presence of Yahweh'.[104] Leslie Allen makes a forceful case that it points forward to another future judgement beyond the judgement of Jerusalem: 'A coming event of relative but serious judgement was to constitute a serious divine roadblock that need pose no fear for the righteous but would bar the apostate . . . It is to this roadblock that the future prospect of death refers.'[105] The implication, as Allen argues, is that 'life' in chapter 18 must be life in the land. This is odd, given that the connection between life and land is far from explicit in the text: nowhere in 18: 1–32 is life defined as having anything to do with the land. Repentance may bring about a divine acquittal, but the implications of that acquittal are left unexplained and the content of life is never spelt out, one way or another. Although it is true that in 20: 38 YHWH promises that he will purge all Israel's rebels in the wilderness before they can enter the land, elsewhere in the book the oracles of restoration consistently present Israel's future as YHWH's unconditional gift to an undeserving people.[106] Since so little to be found elsewhere in the book links repentance with restoration, it is possible that what chapter 18 offers is something other than a fully restored life in the land of Israel.

---

103 See also Janzen, *Old Testament Ethics*, 167–9.
104 Matties, *Ezekiel 18*, 186.
105 Allen, *Ezekiel 1–19*, 270.
106 For fuller discussion see Ch. 7.

Zimmerli is more subtle in his approach to the problem than Allen, and may point a way forward. He does argue that 'life' in all its fullness must include restoration to the land. However, he makes the important form-critical point that 'the promise of life, like the preceding description of the demands of righteousness and the declaratory affirmation, stems from the sphere of the sanctuary and all that goes on there'.[107] 'Life', in the context of Ezekiel 18, belongs to the linguistic world of the temple and its worship. We have already seen that Ezekiel repeatedly reapplies cultic language in the absence of the temple itself, adapting concepts and images drawn from the cult to provide a moral and religious framework for life in exile. Indeed, we may question, in the light of the 'small sanctuary' of 11: 16, whether the blessing of the sanctuary was completely absent from Ezekiel's understanding of the present situation.[108] As Joyce puts it, 11: 16 'provides a positive, if qualified, statement of divine blessing in exile, and not merely an essentially negative preamble to the promise of physical restoration from exile'.[109] Traditional Jewish exegesis of this verse sees in the small sanctuary a reference to the institution of the synagogue, and the Targum to 11: 16 reads: 'Because I scattered them in the countries, therefore I have given them synagogues, second only to My Holy Temple.'[110] While the suggestion of actual synagogues is historically unrealistic, we should nevertheless reckon with the possibility of some sort of cultic life in which YHWH remained the focus of the exiles' worship and thus, to some extent, their communal life. Admittedly the divine presence in Babylonia does not equal or replace a full cultic life in Jerusalem, but the small sanctuary must imply the possibility of some sort of 'life' for the exiles.

If, then, we consider that the language of life and death has its setting in the cultic community, this does not demand that the nation's restoration is the likely divine response to repentance.

---

[107] Zimmerli, *Ezekiel 1*, 382.

[108] Ibid. 382. The Hebrew expression מעט מקדש is ambiguous: מעט may be understood as referring either to duration (e.g. New International Version's sanctuary 'for a little while') or to degree (e.g. AV's 'little sanctuary'). Certainty is probably impossible but, with Paul Joyce, I am persuaded that degree is the more likely option: P. M. Joyce, 'Dislocation and Adaptation in the Exilic Age and After', in J. Barton and D. J. Reimer (eds.), *After the Exile: Essays in Honour of Rex Mason* (Macon, Ga., 1996), 55–6; so also Cooke, *Ezekiel*, 125; Eichrodt, *Ezekiel*, 145; Greenberg, *Ezekiel 1–20*, 186. In either case the מקדש מעט is clearly something available to those who are currently in exile.

[109] Joyce, 'Dislocation and Adaptation', 56.

[110] Levey, *Targum of Ezekiel*, 41.

Georg Fohrer's comment on 18: 21–32 seems more accurately to express Ezekiel's position: 'man kann auch in Babylonien 'leben', d.h. ein vollwertiges, langes und glückliches Dasein führen, wenn man sich nur innerlich wandelt und dem Willen Gottes gemäß lebt. Nicht die äußere Situation, sondern das Verhalten in ihr entscheidet'.[111] Fohrer's interpretation of the passage is perhaps too individualistic, but he is correct in pointing out that Ezekiel wants to show that God is still concerned with the moral behaviour of his people, even once their tie with the land and its institutions has been severed by the exile. The situation is closely paralleled by part of Solomon's prayer in 1 Kings 8:

> If they sin against thee . . . and thou art angry with them, and dost give them to an enemy, so that they are carried away captive to the land of the enemy, far off or near; yet if they lay it to heart in the land to which they have been carried captive, and repent, and make supplication to thee in the land of their captors . . . then hear thou in heaven thy dwelling place their prayer and their supplication, and maintain their cause and forgive thy people who have sinned against thee, and all their transgressions which they have committed against thee; and *grant them compassion in the sight of those who carried them captive, that they may have compassion on them.* (1 Kgs. 8: 46–50)

The content of 'compassion' is left open, but it looks as if repentance will bring blessing in exile rather than a return from exile, and this also appears to be the case in Ezekiel 18: 21–32. That such an open interpretation is closer to the mark is perhaps confirmed by the fact that 14: 6, the other explicit call for the exiles to repent, is equally vague about the result of that repentance.[112]

As we examine the calls to repent in the book, it begins to seem that repentance is something Ezekiel sees as possible within the confines of the exiled community, and that perhaps the calls for repentance are to be understood straightforwardly. At the very least, 14: 1–11 and 18: 1–32 suggest that the exiles continue to have moral responsibility for their lives. As Matties puts it, 'the human community can engage in responsible moral discernment and

---

[111] Fohrer, *Ezechiel*, 104.
[112] Block comments that 'it opens the door just a crack to a new future for the immediate audience. What that future will be like the prophet cannot contemplate until the judgment has passed' (*Ezekiel 1–24*, 429). As we have seen, the oracle's focus is more on the penalties for disobedience than the prize of obedience.

transformation'.[113] However, no direct connection is made between repentance and YHWH's action in restoration. Rather, as Fohrer suggested, it seems to offer the possibility of a life led in exile. We have argued that although the argument of 18: 1–20 may be a general one attempting to force his generation to accept responsibility, nevertheless in the specific examples used it reflects the new lifestyles of the exiles, and the possibilities open to them. Might not the same be the case with 18: 21–32? The general discussion of repentance both highlights the seriousness of the wrong choices made by this generation and offers a genuine way forward.

It is highly significant that the two most unequivocal calls for repentance come in chapters 14 and 18 which, as I have shown previously, can be seen as most directly reflecting the present situation of the exiles. In these chapters more than anywhere else in the book we can find a scaled-down notion of sin: the elders who take their idols into their hearts in chapter 14, and the range of circumscribed moral possibilities which provides the examples for the test cases of chapter 18. It is also worth noting that in chapter 33, the other main discussion of repentance, examples from the lists of chapter 18 are chosen to characterize the repentant man: 'yet if he turns from his sin and does what is lawful and right, if the wicked restores the pledge, gives back what he has taken by robbery and walks in the statutes of life, committing no iniquity; he shall surely live, he shall not die' (33: 14–15). If the lists in chapter 18 reflect a scaled-down notion of sin and virtue in the exiled community, here we find much the same thing, and again repentance appears. And it is in this context of moral 're-scaling' that both repentance and Ezekiel's so-called individualism may be explained. Robert Carroll makes some interesting general comments on repentance:

The theology of repentance is an obscure and difficult matter. It had its roots in prophecy, particularly in the idea of broken and mended relationships and metaphors of going astray and returning. Because human relationships could be restored after breaches of trust, it was posited of the deity that he would forgive and restore the community which returned from its infidelity with foreign cults to the proper worship of Yahweh. The difficulty with this extended metaphor is that not only is it grounded in anthropomorphic (metaphorical) language

[113] Matties, *Ezekiel 18*, 59.

but, further, it only makes sense when applied to dealings between individuals or families. It loses substantive meaning when applied to a whole community.[114]

For Carroll there is something inevitably individualistic about the notion of repentance, and he makes the important connection between individuals and families. By contrast with the arena of national politics, moral decision making is inevitably more 'individualistic' because of the smaller number of individuals involved and the more intimate nature of their relationships. Thus it seems possible that for Ezekiel repentance is a concept which functions at the level of the domestic day-to-day life of the exiles more than at the national-political level. McKeating puts it in terms of the distinction between criminal law, which controls the test cases, and family law, which controls the notion of repentance:

If one is thinking of the law administered by magistrates and judges, then the idea that the penitent offender should go unpunished seems unthinkable; but if one is thinking in terms of the authority wielded by the paterfamilias over his household, such an idea is much more easily credited. Ezekiel may be thinking of a legal situation such as that presupposed in Deut. 21: 18–21, the Law of the Rebellious Son. In such a situation as that described in Deuteronomy 21 a parent would, surely, seize on any evidence of a genuine change of heart as a reason for not carrying out the sentence.[115]

Whereas in the formal legal setting the repentance of a guilty party can have no effect on the verdict, within the closer relationships of the family there is always the desire to reward a change for the better. Thus it may be that the call to repentance in Ezekiel itself forms part of the evidence for the more limited, domestic scope of the exiles' moral world. I would hesitate to make too strong a case, since moral exhortations feature in all kinds of prophetic literature,[116] but it nevertheless seems more than a coincidence that so many 'domestic' features cluster in the two chapters 14 and 18, which do appear to be among the most directly relevant to the social situation of the exiled community.

---

[114] R. P. Carroll, *From Chaos to Covenant: Uses of Prophecy in the Book of Jeremiah* (London, 1981), 80.

[115] McKeating, *Ezekiel*, 85.

[116] It is necessary to treat each of the prophets on his own terms; cf. above, 203.

## Conclusion

We have seen that a distinction is to be drawn between the 'large-scale' sins which bring about the exile and the 'smaller-scale' morality open to the exiles. Two different moral worlds both seem to be present within the book, one centred upon the land and politics, the other on exile and the domestic world. As Ezekiel predicts and explains the fall of Jerusalem, the national and communal sphere is to the fore: he does condemn the nation as a whole, but the burden of his criticism falls upon the king and the political élite, including such named individuals as Jaazaniah ben Shaphan (8: 11) or Pelatiah ben Benaiah (11: 1–13). These are individuals capable of making communal decisions: decisions, that is, which affect the community as a whole, principally through the national institutions of state and temple. These institutions provide, as it were, symbolic mediation between YHWH and his people: in Ezekiel's view the temple especially is the guarantee of the nation's survival. Therefore the crimes of the political class which affect these communal symbols directly have far-reaching communal effects. At a more practical level these institutions are symbolic of national independence: their destruction by an invading army signals the end of that independence, and for the élite the loss of the world of decision making with which they are familiar.

Ezekiel's community in exile have already experienced this loss, and their situation before 587 in some ways anticipates that of the whole nation after the disaster. Only moral actions on a more individual, domestic scale are possible, and these actions of individuals seem no longer to affect YHWH's relationship with the land. As we shall see when we examine Ezekiel's oracles of salvation, national restoration now requires YHWH's action alone: communal repentance is not possible, perhaps because the key communal institutions are no longer accessible. Yet, at the same time, on the more domestic scale of relations between individuals and families, repentance remains an option, and one which YHWH wills for his people. Ezekiel is not neutral about the moral behaviour open to the exiles: he clearly distinguishes what is acceptable from what is not. And, as 33: 13–16 shows that the content of repentance is not far removed from the lists of virtues in chapter 18, we see that Ezekiel is, in the end, concerned with exhortation as well as with explaining the ongoing disaster of exile. The house of Israel never ceases to be YHWH's people, even when they have no outward and visible signs of his favour. He retains an interest in their well-being and their obedience.

YHWH's interest even extends as far as restoration to the land, but the hallmark of Ezekiel's restoration is divine initiative. Without access to the communal institutions it would appear that the people of Israel cannot themselves shape their communal future, but remain morally passive in the face of the promised action of God. In the final part of this study I shall examine the shape of the prophet's future hopes, again concentrating on the moral world that this seems to reflect. The very hope for salvation, which grows in force as the book progresses, may be seen as further evidence that the prophet's hearers are suffering from oppression from which they seek an escape.[117] But it is interesting that salvation is left very much in the hands of God. Paul Joyce has drawn attention to the dichotomy between responsibility and grace in Ezekiel, and relates both of these to the maintenance of YHWH's honour.[118] The people's sins demand that YHWH punish them, but their loss of land and nation is just as much an embarrassment to him, so he must act to restore his people and his reputation. The people themselves take no action to bring about the revival of their fortunes, but are rather YHWH's pawns. There may be some connection between this movement from responsibility to passivity and the actual social circumstances of the exiles, who have gone from being people of some importance, with a wide range of moral possibilities open to them, to people for whom the relationships of individuals, family, and business form the whole of their moral perspective.

---

[117] See e.g. Weber, *Sociology of Religion*, 107.
[118] Joyce, *Divine Initiative*, 89–129.

# 7

# From Responsibility to Passivity

Thus far we have examined two ethical 'strategies for survival' in the book of Ezekiel which reflect the social situation of the Babylonian exiles. Both the ritualization and the domestication of sin and virtue can be seen as a response to their new and smaller moral world. In a situation where large-scale decisions of policy can no longer be taken, new rules for behaviour develop that enable the community to survive and maintain its distinctiveness and cohesion, and the old symbols are adapted to new circumstances. The third area I shall examine is the place of hopes for salvation in Ezekiel's theology and ethics. In particular I shall concentrate on two aspects: first, the way in which hopes for the future in fact have a 'cash value' in the present, serving as another strategy for the survival of the community in exile; and, secondly, the shift from moral responsibility to moral passivity on the part of the people that accompanies the new note of hope in Ezekiel's prophecy.

## The Shift from Judgement to Salvation

Most of our examination of Ezekiel has focused upon the oracles of judgement that dominate the first half of the book. The prophet expresses YHWH's fierce anger at the people of Judah and Jerusalem for their sin and infidelity and predicts the disasters of military defeat, exile, and the destruction of city and temple. Despite this enormous emphasis on the guilt and responsibility of the people and on the terrible fate that awaits such sinners, we find in the book of Ezekiel a dramatic shift from judgement to salvation. Especially in the latter chapters of the book (Ezek. 34–48), and after the announcement of the actual fall of the city that confirms his predictions of doom (33: 21–2), the prophet proclaims a release from exile and a restoration of Israel. This vision of restoration is centred on a return to the land of Israel: YHWH will gather the exiles from all the places where they have been scattered, and they will live in peace and prosperity in the land of Israel. The people's relationship to YHWH will be secure again and, although there are considerable modifications in detail, he will reinstate the institutional framework of nation, ruler, and temple.

This immense shift in Ezekiel's theology was noted by the rabbis who divided the book into two parts: 'the book of Ezekiel begins with doom but ends with consolation'.[1] It is not surprising, however, that such a dramatic change of tone within the book has led a number of scholars to question the authenticity of all Ezekiel's oracles of restoration. Thus Siegfried Herrmann came to the conclusion on traditio-historical grounds that, 'mit hoher Wahrscheinlichkeit in dem uns vorliegenden Ezechiel-Buch *nichts* enthalten ist, was als Heilserwartung des exilierten Propheten angesehen werden kann'.[2] Nevertheless, the majority of recent interpreters do accept that oracles of salvation formed part of the original message of the prophet Ezekiel.

Important here is the continuity of style and theology between oracles of judgement and restoration. Zimmerli points out, for example, that in its mode of experience and language the vision of dry bones in 37: 1–14 is 'clearly Ezekielian', and argues that 'if . . . we can ascribe to the prophet's proclamation the massive promise for the future in 37: 1–14, then we must hold out the possibility that other elements in the salvation promised in the book of Ezekiel come from the prophet's own hand'.[3] He sees room for hope at all stages in Ezekiel's prophetic career, arguing that on the basis of 11: 14–21 we cannot exclude the possibility of

---

[1] Babylonian Talmud: *Baba Bathra*, 14b. Greenberg comments that 'the tannaitic bipartition of the book into dooms and consolations has served to explain an otherwise enigmatic statement in Josephus (*Antiq.* 10. 5. 1. [79]) that Ezekiel 'left behind him in writing two books' (*Ezekiel 1–20*, 3).

[2] S. Herrmann, *Die prophetischen Heilserwartungen im Alten Testament, Ursprung und Gestaltwandel*, BWANT 5 (Stuttgart, 1965), 290 (Herrmann's italics). More recently Clements has advanced a similar opinion: 'The area of elaboration and addition to Ezekiel . . . shows a very marked emphasis in the direction of affirming ultimate return, restoration and salvation for Israel. Without wishing to return to the rather wooden critical dogma that all preexilic prophecy was prophecy of judgement and doom, nevertheless this viewpoint does contain a substantial truth' ('Chronology of Redaction', 286).

[3] W. Zimmerli, 'Plans for Rebuilding After the Catastrophe of 587', in W. Brueggemann (ed.), *I am Yahweh* (Atlanta, Ga., 1982). 112.

salvation preaching before 587. Even the hope in chapters 40–48, which show the clearest evidence of additional elements, 'cannot with certainty be denied to the prophet himself'.[4] In a similar vein Paul Joyce points out numerous connections between the vocabulary of Ezekiel 36: 16–38 and the 'primary' material that is more oriented towards judgement.[5] Besides these stylistic features both Joyce and Thomas Raitt have pointed out theological connections between the oracles of judgement and of salvation: Joyce highlights the motif of the vindication of YHWH's name,[6] and Raitt draws attention to the rigorous nature of the oracles of salvation, which so often focus back on the preceding judgement.[7]

As we have pointed out before, it is often difficult to distinguish between primary and secondary material because of the homogeneity of the Ezekiel tradition, but such editing as there was seems to have been largely completed before the end of the exile, since there is so little correspondence between the book's hope and the reality of post-exilic Judah. As Greenberg writes of chapters 40–48, 'Wherever Ezekiel's program can be checked against subsequent events it proves to have had no effect', and this view is shared by many scholars who are less conservative in their approach to the text.[8] Thus it seems probable that in the majority of oracles of salvation we find the words of Ezekiel or his exilic editors, and we may therefore see in them a response to exilic conditions.

Early sociological interpreters of the Hebrew Bible such as Weber and Causse were quick to point out that the principal importance of exilic hopes for salvation was not in relation to the future of Israel, but these hopes were largely concerned with the preservation of a community in the present, among the exiles. Weber sees the exiles' hope of restoration as an important part of the transformation of Judaism into a religious community:

---

[4] Zimmerli, *Ezekiel 1*, 62, 65.

[5] Joyce, *Divine Initiative*, 117.

[6] Ibid. 116.

[7] Raitt, *Theology of Exile*, 126.

[8] M. Greenberg, 'The Design and Themes of Ezekiel's Program of Restoration', *Int.* 38 (1984), 208. Wevers considers that the book's editing took place during the exile, and writes: 'Since there is no evidence that the traditions represented in chapters 33–48 show any awareness of the post-exilic Temple or of the conditions in Judah after the return, it would seem likely that [the editor] did his work before the end of the sixth century' (*Ezekiel*, 29).

The pressing emotional timeliness of the eschatological expectation was all-decisive. There was indeed great need for it in Exile . . . Thirst for revenge and hope were the natural mainsprings of all conduct of the believers, and only that prophecy which offered hope to all to see these passionate expectations still fulfilled during their lifetime could give religious cohesion to the politically destroyed community.[9]

The use of dramatic future hopes as a focus of communal solidarity is typical of so-called 'millenarian' groups, and in many respects Ezekiel's picture of hope shares common ground with millenarian eschatology. While originally connected with Christian interpretations of the book of Revelation, the term now has a wider application in the sociology of religion, and the sociologist Yonina Talmon provides a definition: 'religious movements that expect imminent, total, ultimate, this-worldly collective salvation'.[10] The definition is broad enough that a vast range of different groups from different periods and geographical areas is covered by it, but despite their many differences the millenarian groups often share similar patterns of hope and of social experience. Within Biblical Studies much of the attention given to millenarian groups has been as part of the study of apocalyptic literature rather than prophecy, and the post-exilic period in particular. Most influential has been Paul Hanson's division of the post-exilic world into priestly pragmatists and apocalyptic visionaries: his analysis of the visionaries as being marginalized groups within post-exilic Judah rests substantially on the sociology of millenarian sects.[11] More recent work has developed his approach

[9] Weber, *Ancient Judaism*, 334. Causse put a similar value on the eschatology of the exilic prophets; see *Du Groupe ethnique*, 201–15; S. T. Kimbrough comments that for Causse, 'the persistence of the myth of the establishment of Israel kept alive the idea of *kol yisrael*': S. T. Kimbrough, *Israelite Religion in Sociological Perspective: The Work of Antonin Causse*, Studies in Oriental Religions, 4 (Wiesbaden, 1978), 75.

[10] Y. Talmon, 'Millenarian Movements', *Archives Européenes de Sociologie*, 7 (1966), 159. D. L. Smith, with the Babylonian exile in view, defines them slightly more narrowly: 'Sociologically, millennialism is most widely defined in terms of mass movements that, while experiencing social uprooting or confusion, seek solace in a religious-oriented prediction that the catastrophic changes precede better social conditions' (*Landless*, 50).

[11] Hanson, *Dawn of Apocalyptic*, esp. 210 ff. where he discusses the work of Mannheim, Weber, and Troeltsch. Of equivalent importance is the work of O. Plöger, *Theocracy and Eschatology* (Oxford, 1968). Plöger also draws a picture of the post-exilic period as marked by an increasing division between the priestly establishment and marginalized apocalyptic sects. The picture is developed in much recent work, including, e.g., R. R. Wilson, 'From Prophecy to Apocalyptic', *Semeia*, 21 (1981), 79–95; Albertz, *History of Israelite Religion*, ii, esp. 437–597; R. P. Carroll, *When Prophecy Failed: Reactions and Responses to Failure in the Old Testament Prophetic Traditions* (London, 1979), 204–13.

in some respects and challenged it in others, and in particular it is questionable whether a millenarian eschatology is an essential part of apocalyptic literature.[12] Philip Davies helpfully suggests that biblical scholars should cease talking about 'apocalyptic communities' on the basis of the genre, but instead use the more commonly accepted sociological category of 'millenarian communities'.[13]

Ezekiel, with the possible exception of the Gog prophecy in chapters 38–9, is not an apocalyptic text; nevertheless, because of the unequivocal hope of salvation and the group nature of the exiles' experience it may be appropriate to make comparisons with millenarian movements. By comparison with later eschatological material its hope might seem quite muted and pragmatic, but by contrast with the previous message of judgement and, indeed, the present status of the exiles, Ezekiel's promises of salvation appear extravagant and unrealistic, amounting to nothing less than the complete reversal of their communal misfortune.

Talmon suggests that two important aspects of the millenarian hope are that it is both this-worldly and collective, and this is certainly true of Ezekiel. For all the discussion of individualism in Ezekiel's theology, it is important to note that the promised restoration, like the judgement, is a communal one. In almost all the salvation oracles we find the theme of gathering the people from the places where they have been scattered and returning them to the land (11: 17; 20: 34, 41; 28: 25; 34: 13; 36: 24; 37: 21; 38: 12; 39: 27–8). The very notion of gathering a scattered people into one place implies that the prophet's vision is more communal than individual. Moreover, the hope focuses on Israel's return to the land from which they had been exiled, and its reconstitution as the people of YHWH. Attention has often been drawn to the prominent place that the land plays in the book of Ezekiel, and in particular to the expression אדמת ישראל, which occurs only in this book (17 times throughout both judgement and salvation oracles). Greenberg writes of the phrase that it 'evokes the earth of the cultivated homeland lived on by Israel', and is 'particularly poignant in the mouth of an exile'.[14] The reoccupation of this land

---

[12] For fuller discussion and critique see P. R. Davies, 'The Social World of the Apocalyptic Writings', in R. E. Clements (ed.), *The World of Ancient Israel: Sociological, Anthropological and Political Perspectives* (Cambridge, 1989), 251–71; S. L. Cook, *Prophecy and Apocalypticism: The Postexilic Social Setting* (Minn., 1995).

[13] Davies, 'Social World', 253.

[14] Greenberg, *Ezekiel 1–20*, 145.

is a communal one, which according to 36: 8–10, 33–8 will involve the renewal of both agricultural and urban land. Indeed, a central plank of the vision of restoration is the revitalization of the old communal institutions that had been lost in YHWH's judgement: the re-establishment of a united Israel comprising both North and South (37: 15–28); the renewal of some form of monarchy (34; 37; 40–48); and, of course, YHWH's provision of a new temple and cult at the centre of the restored community (37; 40–48). However much these new institutions may differ from the old flawed ones, they are presented as the symbols around which the people of Israel (or at least the returning exiles) will construct their communal and national identity.

In addition to repopulation and restored economic and social life, Ezekiel promises a renewed relationship with YHWH. This renewed relationship is not expressed in individual terms, but most commonly by using the so-called 'covenant formula' (*Bundesformel*). This is always expressed in plural form, addressing all the members of the people of Israel together:

והיו־לי לעם ואני אהיה להם לאלהים

That is: 'and they shall be my people and I will be their God'.[15] To think of covenant in this context may be misleading if we are led to think that the formula implies a relationship with obligations on both sides. The phrase occurs in the Bible in connection with covenants both conditional and unconditional, and its emphasis is not upon the terms of the covenant but, as Raitt says, 'more likely it is to do with the presupposition of covenant (election) or the goal of covenant (communion with God)'.[16] In Ezekiel it always refers to the future, and in particular to the unconditional restoration of an ideal bond between God and people.[17] Both Fohrer and Raitt consider that this new relationship we see in Ezekiel is more inward and personal than institutional and formal, with Fohrer especially thinking of the new community as made up of transformed individuals: 'So bildet sich das neue Volk Jahwes als eine heilige Gemeinde, weil und nachdem die Einzelmenschen erneuert worden sind und nunmehr zusammen

---

[15] 11: 20; so also in 14: 11; 37: 23, 27; cf. 34: 24. Ezek. 36: 28 adopts the second-person-plural form.

[16] Raitt, *Theology of Exile*, 198.

[17] See Greenberg, *Ezekiel 1–20*, 254.

eine Gemeinschaft bilden, die in enger Beziehung zu Jahwe steht.'[18] There may be something to this, given the covenant formula's occurrence in proximity to the language of new heart and spirit (11: 19–20; 36: 26–8), but the important factor in the new community is not that it is a collectivity of transformed individuals, but that it is the reconstituted people of YHWH. The focus of all the covenantal language in Ezekiel's salvation oracles is communal rather than individual.[19]

The idea of a people of Israel was intimately linked with possession of the land, and the devastation of Judah and scattering of its citizens posed a serious threat to that link. Equally it threatened to sever the powerful symbol of relationship between the people and their national deity. Ezekiel's oracles of salvation address these threats to Jewish identity in that they promise, on the one hand, the physical reconstitution of the land and people of Israel, and, on the other, the revitalizing symbol of a restored relationship with YHWH, which is outside Israel's power to damage. It is certainly plausible to think of this shared future hope as one of the possible mechanisms for survival and resistance in exile. In our previous discussion we have examined the uses of myth and of ritual in defining social borders and maintaining group identity.[20] Bruce Lincoln points out that such a focus on community need not be restricted to stories about its past and actions in the present, but is equally to be found in communal projections of the future. 'There are other myths, and extremely important ones, that are not set in the past but in the future, a mythic future that—like the mythic past—enters discourse in the present always and only for reasons of the present'.[21] It is a common feature of movements that resist colonial domination that they hold out a hope of restoration to their previous way of life, or perhaps an idealized and transformed version of their previous way of life.[22] In Ezekiel's

---

[18] Fohrer, *Ezechiel*, 62.

[19] I shall return to discuss covenantal language later in this chapter.

[20] See above, Ch. 5.

[21] Lincoln, *Discourse and the Construction of Society*, 38.

[22] Much of the anthropological research has concerned Native American movements. See esp. B. Barber, 'Acculturation and Messianic Movements', *American Sociological Review*, 6 (1943), 663–9; R. Linton, 'Nativistic Movements', *American Anthropologist*, 45 (1943), 230–40; A. F. C. Wallace, 'Revitalization Movements', *American Anthropologist*, 58 (1956), 264–81. Broader comparative studies include V. Lanternari, *The Religions of the Oppressed: A Study of Modern Messianic Cults* (London, 1963); B. R. Wilson, *Magic and the Millennium: A Sociological Study of Religious Movements of Protest Among Tribal and Third-World Peoples* (NY, 1973). The phe-

construction of the future we can see a similar resistance to the colonizing power that expresses the response of a dominated minority. My aim here is not to argue that the presence of hopes for salvation in any Hebrew Bible text demands that the text was produced during the exile, but rather that, given what we know about the experience of exile, it appears to be a highly appropriate context for such hopes. Thus expressions of hope for salvation in known exilic texts like Ezekiel can legitimately be interpreted as the community's response to the rigours of exile.

Certainly many of the explanations that are commonly suggested for the rise of millenarian expectations fit well the position of Ezekiel and the exiles.[23] The hope for salvation has long been explained, at least in part, as arising out of situations of deprivation. Weber writes: 'Since every need for salvation is the expression of some distress, social or economic oppression is an effective source of salvation beliefs, though by no means the exclusive source.'[24] Talmon supplements this by suggesting that it is not only a simple situation of deprivation that provokes a millenarian response, but '*multiple deprivation*, that results from the combined effect of poverty, low status, and lack of power'.[25] The hope of salvation is particularly compelling for such people: 'Being at the bottom rung of the social ladder on so many counts, they are attracted to the myth of the elect, and to the fantasy of a reversal of roles which are important elements in the millenarian ideology.'[26]

It would appear that a millenarian response is all the more likely if there is a sudden and dramatic crisis in the life of the community; if the experience of deprivation is intensified by the experience of disaster. Michael Barkun has pointed out that

nomenon is a highly complex one, and I do not wish to suggest that a hope of restoration must necessarily involve the attempt to retain culture, only to show that there are many cases where this does in fact occur.

[23] Because there are so many variations it is difficult to say what is absolutely typical, but nevertheless a number of elements seem to repeat themselves in the majority of cases.

[24] Weber, *Sociology of Religion*, 107. Also influential have been K. Mannheim, *Ideology and Utopia* (London, 1936) and E. Troeltsch, *The Social Teaching of the Christian Churches* (NY, 1931).

[25] Talmon, 'Millenarian Movements', 181 (her emphasis); this is the principal theme of Lanternari's *Religions of the Oppressed*; see also e.g. Linton, 'Nativistic Movements', 234–5; Barber, 'Acculturation', 664–5. There is discussion of deprivation in relation to biblical texts in, e.g., Wilson, 'From Prophecy to Apocalyptic', 84–5.

[26] Talmon, 'Millenarian Movements', 181.

deprivation is not a sufficient condition: there are many cases of very deprived groups who have not been prone to millennialism. In his study of the phenomenon he has argued for the priority of *disaster*. 'It is the very cause of the millenarian commitment itself. Men cleave to hopes of imminent worldly salvation only when the hammerblows of disaster destroy the world they have known and render them susceptible to ideas which they would earlier have cast aside.'[27] Thus far the Judaean exiles fit the profile well: they have suffered the sudden disaster of war and the destruction of their homes; they have been catapulted into a new life in Babylonia, where they have lost the power and influence that they had previously.

This transformation may be significant, since a further explanation of the origins of millenarianism is to be found in the notion of relative deprivation, that is, 'a negative discrepancy between legitimate expectation and actuality',[28] or, as Talmon puts it, 'a markedly uneven relation between expectations and the means of their satisfaction'.[29] The inability to fulfil traditional expectations will have been a significant factor among the Jewish exiles, removed from their previous occupations and spheres of influence, and, even if their economic situation was not as straitened as I have proposed, there will have been a dramatic reduction of scope for action and decision making in exile.

Deprivation and relative deprivation, however, may not be such good indicators of the propensity for millennial belief as has been commonly thought. In his recent work *Prophecy and Apocalypticism*, Stephen Cook has re-examined the post-exilic social situation and, strongly challenging the Hanson-Plöger orthodoxy, argues that apocalyptic beliefs could arise as easily within central groups holding power as within marginalized conventicles. In particular, he highlights Ezekiel 38–9, Zechariah 1–8, and Joel as proto-

---

[27] M. Barkun, *Disaster and the Millennium* (New Haven, Conn., 1974), 1; Talmon, 'Millenarian Movements', 181; Barber, 'Acculturation', 664–5.

[28] D. F. Aberle, 'A Note on Relative Deprivation Theory', in S. Thrupp (ed.), *Millennial Dreams in Action: Essays in Comparative Study* (The Hague, 1962), 209.

[29] Talmon, 'Millenarian Movements', 182. C. Y. Glock broadens the description of deprivation to include a number of different kinds that may produce different responses: economic deprivation, social deprivation, organismic deprivation, ethical deprivation, and psychic deprivation. See Glock, 'The Role of Deprivation in the Origin and Evolution of Religious Groups', in R. Lee and M. W. Marty (eds.), *Religion and Social Change* (NY, 1964); a similar argument appears in C. Y. Glock and R. Stark, *Religion and Society in Tension* (Chicago, Ill., 1965).

apocalyptic texts belonging to central priestly groups in Judah. A significant part of this project is a critique of the sociological work on deprivation as a source of millenarian group activity.

Fundamental to Cook's critique is the existence of a number of what he calls 'nondeprived millennial groups', all of which drew members from the élites of their societies, and who were therefore not suffering any economic or social deprivation.[30] Thus, he concludes, oppression and poverty are neither sufficient nor even necessary conditions for millennialism to arise within a given group. Moreover, he finds the concept of relative deprivation inadequate because of its vagueness and inability to predict when a movement will arise, and because of its reductionism in treating millennialist religious ideas as a pathological effect that must have a material cause in social and economic distress.[31] As an alternative he proposes that we concentrate on the whole world-view of millenarian groups, admitting that there are a number of features which may vary significantly between groups, and accepting 'that a change in worldview can take place among many kinds of groups, even among groups in power who do not feel resentment like those in a setting of deprivation'.[32] Cook's broadening of perspective is to be welcomed, and indeed opens up new possibilities for explaining the origins of the apocalyptic literature, but in both his sociological analysis and some of his biblical exegesis he attempts to push his case further than it will go.

In the first place, despite the occurrence of millenarian dreams among non-deprived groups, it is clear that the phenomenon is considerably more common among subordinate groups of one kind or another, for whom it is natural to hope for a transformation of their situation. This is well expressed by James Scott, in a study not of millennialism but of the politics of subordinate groups such as slaves and peasants. He states:

The millennial theme of a world turned upside down, a world in which the last shall be first and the first last, can be found in nearly every major

---

[30] These include, among others, Savonarola's movement to revitalize Florence in the late fifteenth century; Geronimo de Mendieta's Franciscan millennialists who held episcopal, governmental, and economic power in the Spanish New World; the seventeenth century Jewish movement led by Sabbatai Sevi; and the Irvingite Catholic Apostolic Church in nineteenth century Britain, whose leadership especially came from the upper class. For fuller discussion see Cook, *Prophecy and Apocalypticism*, esp. 35–40.

[31] Ibid. 40–1.

[32] Ibid. 50.

cultural tradition in which inequities of power, wealth and status have been pronounced . . . Most traditional utopian beliefs can, in fact, be understood as a more or less systematic negation of an existing pattern of exploitation and status degradation as it is experienced by subordinate groups . . . Given their position at the bottom of the heap, it is little wonder they should have a class interest in utopian prophecies, in imagining a radically different social order from the painful one they experience.[33]

Nevertheless, in agreement with Cook, there is a wide awareness on the part of sociologists that deprivation is not in itself enough to provoke a millenarian response; there have been so many examples of deprived groups whose dreams have not found expression in the form of a millenarian group that there must be other predisposing factors besides deprivation. Thus Barkun suggests that disaster or crisis is the key, and Talmon suggests further that factors such as social isolation, significant social transition, and especially the experience of powerlessness or political helplessness are often accompanied by a growth in millenarian activity.[34]

An important factor is that, while there is not always severe economic deprivation to be found, it is extremely rare to find millenarian movements that do not have a background in some sort of disruption of an accepted pattern of life. Even some of Cook's examples of non-deprived millennial groups can be seen as responding to some kind of crisis or situation of alienation. For example, the Savonarolan movement in Florence, which, admittedly, was largely composed of members of the upper class, nevertheless arose in a period when Florence was threatened by war and outside influence to an unaccustomed degree.[35] The Florentine nobles may have sought remedy for their uncertainty in millennial hopes. Cook recognizes this, and provides a theoretical framework into which any given group can be placed. Besides a group being central or peripheral within its own society, the conditions in which it develops may be endogenous, entirely within one cultural tradition, or exogenous, where groups arise in a situation of contact between cultures.[36] In the latter case the millennialists will

---

[33] Scott, *Hidden Transcripts*, 80–1.

[34] Talmon, 'Millenarian Movements', 184–5.

[35] For a full treatment see D. Weinstein, *Savonarola and Florence: Prophecy and Patriotism in the Renaissance* (Princeton, NJ, 1970).     [36] Cook, *Prophecy and Apocalypticism*, 55–74.

represent either the dominant culture or, more normally, the subordinate culture. Thus Cook accepts the possibility that groups that are central or power-holding in respect of their own small-scale community may yet be dominated by outside, colonial forces. This is indeed the situation he presupposes for the formation of Ezekiel 38–9. However, he does not take into account the possible frustration and perceived deprivation on the part of the secondary élite, who must cede ultimate power to another, more dominant group.

Moreover, as he argues against the importance of deprivation, he takes little account of the widespread recognition that millennialism has appeared in all levels of society, and that it is rarely the most underprivileged of the underprivileged who seek refuge in millenarian sects: 'members of the deprived stratum who are somewhat better off are often more able to take stock of their situation, to react and reorganize'.[37] This was one of Weber's significant insights into the nature of religious sects; he argued that those at the very bottom of the social ladder were less likely to develop a salvation religion than members of the middle classes.[38] As Talcott Parsons explains in his introduction to the translation of Weber's *Sociology of Religion*: 'Above all, he is concerned to show that prophetic movements have not been primarily movements of economic protest, motivated mainly by the economic interests of the disadvantaged classes. Middle classes of various types . . . have been very prominent.'[39] Cook is in danger of turning Weber into a straw man, since when Hanson claims him as an authority for his idea that eschatology is a function of deprivation, and Cook attacks him as the source of Hanson's theory they are both failing to do justice to Weber's actual position, which is perhaps closer to Cook than he recognizes.

Cook's survey and evaluation of current theories of millennialism is thorough and useful, and he demonstrates his case that eschatological expectations and millenarian groups are not limited to the lower strata of society, but can be found in power-holding groups. However, in setting out his case he risks giving the impression that deprivation, frustration, and crisis are never

---

[37] Talmon, 'Millenarian Movements', 186–7.
[38] Weber, *Sociology of Religion*: particularly relevant are chapter 6, 'Castes, Estates, Classes, and Religion', and chapter 7, 'Religion of Non-Privileged Classes'.
[39] T. Parsons, 'Introduction' to Weber, *Sociology of Religion*, p. xli.

significant factors in the rise of millennialism. While it is certainly true that the presence of all of these elements cannot be guaranteed to produce a millenarian response, nevertheless the overwhelming majority of millenarian groups that have been studied have been to some degree deprived, threatened, or marginalized.

Cook's work is important not only for its attention to theory but also because it deals with the social context of at least part of the book of Ezekiel: the first biblical text that Cook examines is the Gog prophecy in Ezekiel 38–9. This section of the book has a number of features that scholars have seen as proto-apocalyptic. Most obvious is the radical eschatology: the prophecies picture a great future battle in which YHWH defeats his enemies and restores 'peace with honour' to his people. Whilst the motif of divine agency is typical of the Ezekiel tradition as a whole, here it is expressed more forcefully and with more bizarre imagery than elsewhere. Secondly, the section exhibits a moral dualism in which there is a final battle between good and evil, in which Gog and his allies represent 'the antithesis of heavenly power'.[40] There is also present the dualism between present distress and future salvation that is more in keeping with the rest of the book. The Gog prophecy is particularly unusual in that it, as Cook points out, 'looks two stages beyond the present'.[41] It presupposes a situation where the exiles have already been gathered together in the land (38: 8, 14); only after this can the final apocalyptic battle be fought. Such a scheme is very surprising since it seems to reverse Ezekiel's normal order of things. Moreover, it appears to disrupt the connection between the end of chapter 37, which introduces the restored temple, and chapters 40–48, which spell out that restoration.[42]

This combination of features has led many scholars to propose that chapters 38–9 are a very late apocalyptic addition to the book.[43] Hanson, while placing Ezekiel himself on the priestly and pragmatic side of his division, sees the book of Ezekiel as a battleground for the rival interpretations of visionaries and Zadokites. The Gog prophecy is a visionary contribution: 'As the Zadokites

---

[40] Cook, *Prophecy and Apocalypticism*, 92.
[41] Ibid. 94.
[42] See e.g. Stalker, *Ezekiel*, 260.
[43] Cooke, *Ezekiel*, 407–8; Eichrodt, *Ezekiel*, 519; R. Ahroni, 'The Gog Prophecy and the Book of Ezekiel', *HAR* 1 (1977), 1–27; Blenkinsopp, *History of Prophecy*, 178.

advanced their cause by inserting into the Book of Ezekiel a polemical statement against the Levites (Ezekiel 44), so too the visionaries laid claim to the authority of Ezekiel by inserting Ezekiel 38–9.'[44] On the other hand, the section shows numerous linguistic and thematic connections with the rest of the book of Ezekiel, not only in the priestly language it displays, but also in the unconditional salvation that it offers to the Israelites. While much of 38–9 is yet more overstated and even bizarre than Ezekiel's other prophecies of salvation, there is enough kinship to lead Zimmerli to believe that we have a genuine kernel of Ezekiel's prophecy at the heart of it: 'the basic text is in no way stylistically different from what is usual elsewhere in Ezekiel, but rather in many respects corresponds to it'.[45] Cook makes a thorough examination of the language of the two chapters and demonstrates a very substantial continuity of idiom, concluding that Ezekiel 38–9 'clearly belongs to the mainstream of the Ezekiel priestly tradition'.[46] As usual, the homogeneity of the Ezekiel tradition makes it difficult to tell exactly where the prophet stops and his interpreters take over.

Cook's main thesis about Ezekiel 38–9 is that it demonstrates the presence in one source of both apocalyptic or visionary eschatology and central priestly notions of holiness and the sanctity of Jerusalem. He draws attention to the presence of cultic terminology and argues that because it is linked with the Holiness Code central priests must have produced it.[47] He finds further evidence for this in the imagery of Jerusalem as a bulwark against the nations, which draws on traditions of the inviolability of Zion.[48] He locates the social context of at least the core of the passage as that of Ezekiel and his disciples in the Babylonian exile. However, for Cook, this context of exile leaves no room for deprivation theory in explaining the proto-apocalypticism of the Gog prophecy, since the experience of exile was a wholly positive one for the priestly élite: 'Ezekiel and his disciples, having gone into exile from central posts in Jerusalem, were among the leaders

---

[44] P. D. Hanson, 'Israelite Religion in the Early Postexilic Period', in Miller, Hanson, and McBride (eds.), *Ancient Israelite Religion*, 502.
[45] Zimmerli, *Ezekiel 2*, 302. So Wevers, *Ezekiel*, 201.
[46] Cook, *Prophecy and Apocalypticism*, 103.
[47] Ibid. 105.
[48] Ibid. 107.

of the exiled Israelites. In fact, Ezekiel's continuing school provided the theological basis for the program of the late-exilic
Zadokite leadership.'[49] He quotes favourably Hanson's suggestion
that Ezekiel is in large measure the literature of a pragmatic,
Zadokite leadership of the exiled Judaeans, and concludes: 'Thus,
in contradiction to deprivation theory, those at the center of
society wrote proto-apocalyptic literature.'[50] Moreover, he argues
that although the Ezekiel group's situation is 'central in terms
of its own society, but . . . dominated by another culture', this
experience of domination has little effect, and 'there is no evidence in the book of Ezekiel that this social context involved any
suffering or oppression for Ezekiel and the priestly élite'.[51]

Cook is right to point out the many linguistic and thematic connections between Ezekiel 38–9 and the rest of the book.[52] As we
have seen, the promise of total and unconditional salvation,
expressed using priestly terminology, is absolutely characteristic of
the rest of the book. (One might make the case that the people
are marginally less passive in 38–9, since they are required to clear
up the weapons and corpses of YHWH's enemies after the great
battle.) It is therefore a mistake to treat the eschatology of 38–9 as
massively different from that which is to be seen in the rest of
Ezekiel. There is more continuity than discontinuity and, therefore, throughout all the prophecies of salvation we find a dramatic
unconditional promise that is not out of keeping with the hope of
a typical millenarian group. What is more, it is clear that this
group has substantial priestly interests.

What is not at all clear is that the mere presence of priestly
language and ideas demands that the texts were produced by
'priestly officials' whose programmes 'upheld the established
order of society'.[53] Certainly before the exile the priests of the

---

[49] Cook, *Prophecy and Apocalypticism*, 108.

[50] Ibid. 108.

[51] Ibid. 109–10.

[52] If anything, he makes perhaps too strong a distinction between the eschatological
hope of the Gog prophecy and that of the other prophecies of salvation. In particular, he
suggests that the previous prophecies of salvation are in some sense incomplete, and do
not effect a real reversal of the situation of exile, whereas the Gog prophecy does provide
some sort of final solution. However, in a number of cases outside chs. 38–9 we see the
systematic reversal of the experience of disaster—in the restoration of the mountains of
Israel in 36: 8–15, in the resuscitation of the corpses of Israel in chapter 37, and in the
culminating point of the book: the return of YHWH to the temple which he had previously
abandoned to destruction (43: 1–9).        [53] Cook, *Prophecy and Apocalypticism*, 213.

Jerusalem temple formed part of Judah's upper class, and will have had more access to political power than the mass of the population, but this does not itself guarantee any real measure of control over Judaean society. On the contrary, that was the role of the king and his chosen officials, some of whom might be priests, but many of whom were not. Our examination of cultic politics in pre-exilic Judah showed that the temple hierarchy, like the upper class in general, was not monolithic, but that priests might support different political factions in much the same way as prophets or members of the nobility.[54] While Cook's ability to see that apocalyptic writing need not be bound to any particular social context is admirable, where the priests are concerned he falls into the same trap as Hanson, in assuming that all those who practise a similar occupation must share the same political outlook. As we have seen, Ezekiel's critique of Judaean society and religion looks more like that of a political opposition.[55] Priestly language is as much a feature of the oracles of judgement as of salvation, and since the oracles of judgement are very definitely not there to support the established order of Jerusalem society, why should this suddenly become the case when the same terminology is used in oracles of salvation?

In many respects, Cook's argument seems to read the experience of the later period back into the earlier—because a priestly class was dominant in the post-exilic period, then it must also have been dominant in the exile (not to mention before the exile). Moreover, since Ezekiel shares many characteristics with post-exilic priestly literature he too must have been a leader within the dominant group. But this is all too simple. The very fact that so little of Ezekiel's so-called programme of restoration was in fact put into practice after the exile should make us pause before we imagine that his ideas were the most influential among those competing for power in the Second Temple period. The profound differences between his legislation and that of the Priestly Code and even the Holiness Code are at least as important as the similarities. Greenberg points out: 'The second temple had one or two features that recall Ezekiel's, but too little is known of the differences between Ezekiel's temple and the last stage of Solomon's to assert that it was owing to Ezekiel's influence that

---

[54] See above, Chs. 1, 3, 4.
[55] An élite faction, admittedly, but nevertheless not one holding power.

such features occur. In everything relating to the temple personnel and rituals the law of Moses superseded those of Ezekiel.'[56]

Robert Wilson also argues against the tendency to regard
Ezekiel as some sort of central representative of Jerusalemite
prophetic and priestly traditions, pointing out his close ties with
Deuteronomy and Jeremiah. These he believes to be the representatives of a more marginal or peripheral Ephraimite tradition.
Such eclectic and individual views, combined with evidence for
strong opposition among the exiles, make it unlikely that Ezekiel
was a 'central prophet' amongst them: 'Rather, the evidence suggests that he was a peripheral prophet whose views were largely
rejected by the orthodox Zadokite community.'[57]

Cook's explanation of Ezekiel as a non-deprived and central
figure is rather insecure. He even admits that 'Ezekiel may have
been a recognized leader in the exile, but he was not listened to
by his contemporaries'.[58] Cook accepts that Ezekiel was a member of a dominated community in Babylonia, that the members of
his own community ignored him, and that his message was only
in part taken up in the post-exilic constitution. If this is the case,
at what point does it become untenable to see the prophet as
representative of a powerful millennial group, the government-in-
waiting of Persian Judah?

It is better to think of Ezekiel not as the conscious architect of
the post-exilic community, but as a prophet intensely concerned
with the situation of exile in which he found himself, and which
showed few empirical signs of coming to an abrupt end. We have
examined the circumstances of Ezekiel's community and drawn
the conclusions that, although they may have begun as members
of a privileged élite, the experience of deportation was for them a
considerable drop in status, and one which was intended by the
Babylonian rulers to be a constant reminder to the deportees of
their subordinate position. However little economic hardship they
suffered, there will have remained a vast discrepancy between
their experience as members of the Jerusalem élite and their new
expectations as exiles. But despite this, as one time members of an
élite, they will have retained skills and abilities that formed part of
their education and training, especially literacy and the possession

---

[56] Greenberg, 'Program of Restoration', 208.
[57] R. R. Wilson, *Prophecy and Society in Ancient Israel* (Phil., 1980), 285.
[58] Cook, *Prophecy and Apocalypticism*, 110 n. 114.

of their cultural heritage. It is therefore hardly surprising that in the straitened circumstances of exile they should draw upon the old order to provide a symbolic apparatus for resistance and community maintenance. In fact, what we have seen throughout the book of Ezekiel is not political and religious conservatism, but a profound and creative transformation of the old priestly orthodoxies into forms which are relevant to the life of the exiles. We have described the ritualization of ethics and the domestication of legal forms, and indeed the content of ethical decision making as strategies for community survival in exile, and it seems far more likely that what hope there is in the book of Ezekiel serves similar ends, rather than the practical construction of a new state in the land of Israel.

Cook is right to point out that Ezekiel's community both shows evidence of central symbolism and belongs to a group dominated by foreign rulers, but he fails to capitalize on this insight in the interests of drawing closer connections between Ezekiel 38–9 and the post-exilic Zechariah 1–8 and Joel. The presence in Ezekiel's oracles of salvation of central symbols from the pre-exilic order and the temple cannot be understood apart from the context of exile, and is best explained by the fact that it was from the political classes of Jerusalem and Judah that the exiles were drawn.

## The Shift from Responsibility to Passivity

We have seen throughout the judgement oracles in Ezekiel that YHWH's action against Israel is a punishment for sin. It is presented not as the random behaviour of a capricious deity, but as the only coherent response to appalling wrongdoing. The immense pressure of sin drives YHWH to abandon his sanctuary, his city, and his people, bringing upon them a terrible retribution in the shape of Nebuchadnezzar and his armies. Ezekiel does not question YHWH's justice in this action: the population of Judah and Jerusalem are held wholly responsible for the disaster. While their sin is often depicted as infecting the whole of Judahite society, we have seen that Ezekiel's more concrete examples focus mainly on sin within the institutions of state such as the temple cult and foreign policy.[59] From this we have drawn the conclusion

[59] See above, Chs. 3 and 4.

that Ezekiel's condemnation is directed principally against the Jerusalem élite, and is addressed to them in language and symbols with which they are familiar.

We have already demonstrated that the centrality of Jerusalem in Ezekiel's oracles of judgement is not incommensurate with its relevance to the community of exiles. Significantly, it seems likely that they believed that events in Jerusalem could affect their position in Babylonia, and it is widely accepted that many of the exiles hoped for a speedy return to Jerusalem and an end to the exile. Jeremiah 28–9 suggests that there were those both in Jerusalem and among the exiles who expected their fortunes soon to be reversed, and Jeremiah is presented as insisting that there will be no escape for Jerusalem, and a lengthy exile for those in Babylonia.[60] Ezekiel's attack on the prophets in chapter 13 likewise condemns them for encouraging a false confidence in Jerusalem's ability to survive (13: 10–16).

Furthermore, in 12: 21–5 and 26–8 we find two oracles that address similar concerns. The first of these two disputation speeches replies to the proverb 'the days grow long, and every vision comes to naught' by proclaiming that YHWH's word will soon be performed. The second saying that Ezekiel contests is similar in content: 'the vision that he sees is for many days hence, and he prophesies of times far off'. Again the response is the same: 'None of my words will be delayed any longer, but the word which I speak will be performed.' The first of these two proverbs is spoken 'concerning the land of Israel'[61] and may address those in Jerusalem, but the second saying is spoken by the 'house of Israel', who should probably be seen as the community of exiles, especially since it specifies a single prophetic figure that must be Ezekiel himself. The burden of both oracles is that Ezekiel's words of doom will soon be fulfilled, and that it will affect both communities alike.[62]

Not only will the exiles be affected by the coming disaster, since it will confirm the permanence of their exile, but they also share in the responsibility, as Ezekiel condemns them alongside those in

---

[60] Cf. McKane, *Jeremiah XXVI–LII*, pp. cxxxiv–cxl.

[61] Or 'in the land of Israel'; see discussion of עַל־אַדְמַת יִשְׂרָאֵל above, pp. 220–1.

[62] Graffy (*A Prophet Confronts*, 58–9) suggests that 12: 26–8 refer to Ezekiel's oracles of hope, not of judgement, but the context does not support this and it is widely agreed that the message is one of doom in both cases: e.g. Greenberg, *Ezekiel 1–20*, 230–321; Wevers, *Ezekiel*, 84, Zimmerli, *Ezekiel 1*, 283.

Judah. There is certainly a degree of dichotomy between Judah
and the exile: it is clear from 11: 14–21 and 33: 23–9 that both
before and after the fall of Jerusalem Ezekiel placed a higher value
on the exiles than on those remaining in the land, but this does
not mean that the exiles are absolved from responsibility for the
disaster, nor do they occupy the moral high ground. By contrast
with Jeremiah 24, where the exiles of 597 are the 'good figs' which
YHWH will cherish, Ezekiel never represents the community of
exiles as intrinsically good, or as deserving of better treatment by
YHWH. Their status is far more ambiguous. In the saying of 11: 15
the inhabitants of Jerusalem make their claim on the land that
the exiles have left behind with a sharp condemnation: 'They
have gone far from the LORD.'[63] The distance is not only physical
but also moral; as Graffy comments, 'the quotation loads all guilt
on the shoulders of the exiles'.[64] YHWH's response refutes the
Jerusalemites' claim to possession by promising a restoration of
the land, confirming that if Israel has a future it lies with the exiles.
He also goes some way to dismiss the idea that the exiles are
distant from him, by proclaiming himself to have been a 'small
sanctuary' to them in exile.[65] However, the response also makes
plain that YHWH had imposed their exile upon them as a punishment: 'Certainly I removed them far off among the nations;
certainly I scattered them among the countries (11: 16).'[66] Rather
than denying that the exiles were guilty at all, the emphasis here
implies that they are suffering a punishment decreed by God, and
therefore necessarily a just punishment. Even YHWH's presence
with them is not wholly good. Greenberg notes that the small
sanctuary is a statement of deprivation as well as one of nearness,
when he comments that 'his presence among the exiles is but a
shadow of what it was formerly'.[67]

Equally ambiguous is YHWH's presence in Babylonia in the
opening chapters of the book. The tendency among scholars has
been to see the initial vision of chapter 1 as a positive sign for the

[63] RSV: reading רָחֲקוּ (perfect) for MT רַחֲקוּ (imperative): so Elliger, *BHS*, ad loc.; Cooke,
*Ezekiel*, 124; Zimmerli, *Ezekiel 1*, 229; Wevers, *Ezekiel*, 79; Graffy, *A Prophet Confronts*, 50.
[64] Graffy, *A Prophet Confronts*, 50.
[65] See discussion above, p. 210.
[66] My translation of the Hebrew כי הרחקתים בגוים וכי הפיצותים בארצות. The force of כי here
is emphatic: see Zimmerli, *Ezekiel 1*, 261–2; F. Horst, 'Exilsgemeinde und Jerusalem in Ez
8–11: Eine literarische Untersuchung', *VT* 3 (1953), 336.
[67] Greenberg, *Ezekiel 1–20*, 186.

exiles that God has not abandoned them but can be with them
even at a distance from Jerusalem. Ralph Klein may serve as a
representative example: 'The new combination of images and
words makes evident that Yahweh is not limited to heaven, to the
Jerusalem temple, but that he in all the fullness of his divine
majesty, is available to the prophet and to the exilic people.'[68]
This assumption that the divine presence is a blessing for the
exiles is very widely held.[69] However, in a recent article Leslie
Allen has argued that the opening vision in Ezekiel is, in fact,
threatening to the exiles.[70] Allen argues that the storm and throne
imagery of the vision fits YHWH's anger and judgement much
better than it fits his consolation, and that in the context of
Ezekiel's call to preach disaster the vision has a negative thrust.
Robert Wilson also points out that the vision is ominous, because
it suggests that YHWH may have abandoned his dwelling-place in
Jerusalem, which, of course, is what ultimately happens in the
vision of chapters 8–11.[71] However, as the prophecies unfold we
see that the vision is a prelude not only to judgement and disaster
but also to ultimate salvation and restoration, so perhaps the most
we can say initially is that the divine presence is ambiguous: 'The
significance of God's dwelling among the exiles is not yet clear, for
up to this point there has been no verbal communication between
God and the prophet. God's presence may mean reassurance for
the exilic community, but it may also mean judgment.'[72]

When YHWH does speak to Ezekiel, at first it is the message of
judgement that is to the fore; the exiles' responsibility is confirmed
by the account of Ezekiel's call. The prophet's initial commissioning defines those to whom he is sent as rebels against YHWH: 'Son
of man, I send you to the people of Israel, to a nation of rebels,
who have rebelled against me; they and their fathers have transgressed against me to this very day' (2: 3). As the call narrative
develops we find that the expression בית מרי is repeated six times
to stress the people's rebelliousness (2: 5, 6, 8; 3: 9, 26, 27). This

---

[68] Klein, *Ezekiel: The Prophet and his Message*, 26–7.

[69] So e.g. C. H. Toy, *The Book of the Prophet Ezekiel* (NY, 1899), 96; Fohrer, *Ezechiel*, 2–14;
Zimmerli, *Ezekiel 1*, 140; Hals, *Ezekiel*, 6.

[70] L. C. Allen, 'The Structure and Intention of Ezekiel 1', *VT* 43 (1993), 145–61. See also
J. Rosenberg, 'Jeremiah and Ezekiel', in R. Alter and F. Kermode (eds.), *The Literary Guide
to the Bible* (London, 1987), 196, who describes it as a 'state of emergency'.

[71] R. R. Wilson, 'Prophecy in Crisis: The Call of Ezekiel', *Int* 38 (1984), 125.

[72] Wilson, 'Prophecy in Crisis', 125.

phrase, which is highly characteristic of Ezekiel's description of his audience, initially refers not only to the exiles in Ezekiel's immediate surroundings, but also to those still in the land.[73] However, as the call narrative progresses it is made clear that his message is primarily addressed to his own community in Babylonia: '"And go, get you to the exiles, to your people, and say to them, 'Thus says the Lord GOD'; whether they hear or refuse to hear"' (3: 11). Zimmerli notes that the expression 'rebellious house' does not occur in these verses, and asks:

Could this be because Yahweh's threat was more restrained in the sending to the exiles, who had already experienced the divine judgement, than where the prophet addressed all Israel, of which the remnant in Jerusalem had still not experienced that judgement?[74]

It may be that the exiles have already begun their punishment, but this does not make them less rebellious. Throughout the prophet's commissioning it is made clear that the people to whom he is sent, the rebellious house, will not listen to his words, and will oppose him. As Wilson notes, the divine encouragement to persevere in the face of opposition makes more sense if the prophet's opponents are his fellow exiles.[75] Moreover, that an accusation of rebellion is made against the exiles is confirmed by the recurrence of the motif in 12: 1–16. Here the prophet is addressed as follows: 'Son of man, you dwell in the midst of a rebellious house, who have eyes to see, but see not, who have ears to hear, but hear not, for they are a rebellious house' (12: 2–3). In this case Zimmerli admits that 'the group of exiles in which Ezekiel lives is . . . regarded as representative of the whole people whose character it embodies'.[76] If this is true of Ezekiel's audience in chapter 12 there is no good reason why it should not also be true from his commissioning. It does also seem to be the sense of בית המרי where it occurs in the introductions to oracles in 17: 12 and 24: 3.[77] The exiles are responsible for what has become of themselves thus far, and continue to share in the prophet's

---

[73] Zimmerli, *Ezekiel 1*, 132.

[74] Ibid. 138; Wevers makes a similar argument (*Ezekiel*, 48).

[75] Wilson, 'Prophecy in Crisis', 127.

[76] Zimmerli, *Ezekiel 1*, 269. Further confirmation can be found in 12: 9, where the rebellious house ask the prophet what he is doing. Those asking the questions must belong to the prophet's community in exile. See also Cooke, *Ezekiel*, 129, Wevers, *Ezekiel*, 100.

[77] See also 12: 9, 25.

criticism along with the inhabitants of Judah. As the book progresses they play a subordinate role to Jerusalem, but a few
oracles deal with their situation. We have seen that at least one of
the purposes of chapter 18 is to demonstrate that the punishment
that this generation is suffering in exile has been justly deserved.[78]
Chapter 20, with its long historical retrospect, seems to include
the exiles among those transgressors whose sins built up to such an
intolerable level.[79]

Finally, even the ultimate destiny of the exiles in a restored land
of Israel serves to confirm their guilt and responsibility for the
exile. In a number of oracles of restoration we find a motif of
remembrance and responsibility. The people who are restored do
not take pleasure in their own righteousness but are required to
remember their past sins and loathe themselves:

And you shall know that I am the LORD, when I bring you into the land
of Israel, the country which I swore to give to your fathers. And there
you shall remember your ways and all the doings with which you have
polluted yourselves; and you shall loathe yourselves for all the evils that
you have committed. (20: 42–3)

The people are to be shamed and humiliated by their restoration:
'Be ashamed and confounded for your ways, O house of Israel'
(36: 32).[80] In all these cases it is the exiles who are restored and who
therefore acknowledge responsibility for the evil that happened to
them.[81]

Throughout the book of Ezekiel, therefore, it is made plain that
the exiled Judaeans whom Ezekiel addresses are held morally
responsible for the fate that has befallen them, and they share
in the condemnation of Jerusalem which causes the ultimate
destruction of the city. The fall of Jerusalem is the responsibility of
its people and their leaders, and Ezekiel's own community does
not escape this condemnation. Human actions have brought

---

[78] See discussion above, pp. 185–7.

[79] We might think especially of YHWH's refusal to let the elders inquire of him in 20: 3–4,
31.

[80] The motif of shame is most developed in 16: 53–63. For fuller treatment see M. S.
Odell, 'The Inversion of Shame and Forgiveness in Ezekiel 16: 59–63', *JSOT* 56 (1992),
101–12.

[81] It is perhaps worth noting that another feature of millenarian groups that sociologists
have recognized is 'a deep sense of guilt or responsibility for the plight in which the followers find themselves' (M. B. Hamilton, *The Sociology of Religion: Theoretical and Comparative
Perspectives* (London, 1995), 88).

about the destruction of state and temple—of the main institutional symbols of nationhood and independence. Where judgement is concerned we can in fairness speak of 'human initiative' and 'divine response'!

Human initiative brought about disaster and exile: can human initiative return Israel to the land? The short answer is 'no'. The restoration of Israel to the land is seen wholly as YHWH's action, done for his own sake not that of his people, and without any action on their part to provoke it. We have seen that there are scholars like Matties who believe that the call to repentance is at the heart of all prophetic speech.[82] In this case, surely repentance is required as a prelude to restoration. I have already examined repentance in Ezekiel and, I hope, demonstrated that while it does play a part in the prophet's vision, it does not enter into YHWH's relationship with the land of Israel. YHWH desires repentance and right behaviour from his people, but this operates only at the level of the exiled community and within the limited moral world of that community. Neither individual nor communal repentance is seen to be the precondition for restoration. If the limited scope of repentance is a shift away from broader communal or national notions of responsibility, then the shift to complete passivity can be seen in Ezekiel's treatment of restoration.[83] YHWH restores Israel for his own sake alone, and irrespective of the repentance of the people. If anything is required at all, then the precondition for restoration is the mere acceptance that the disaster which has happened is the will of YHWH. M. E. Andrew makes this point: 'The harsh condition demanded of the exiles is that they recognize that only by accepting the destruction of their only hope for the future can there be any possibility of restoration.'[84] He sees Ezekiel himself as a model for the exiles' acceptance of their fate. The prophet shows how to accept judgement in his symbolic actions, and especially in his reaction to his wife's death in chapter 24. As he cannot mourn for his wife so they cannot mourn for Jerusalem, but must see in the fall of the city the only seed of future hope. Andrew may be right in seeing this emphasis in

---

[82] Matties, *Ezekiel 18*, 109; see above, p. 203.

[83] Carroll describes the similar move in Jer. 31: 31–4 as 'a counsel of despair' and 'the prophetic loss of nerve brought on by 587' (*When Prophecy Failed*, 64).

[84] M. E. Andrew, *Responsibility and Restoration: The Course of the Book of Ezekiel* (Dunedin, 1985), 29.

Ezekiel, but the acceptance of responsibility is still a far cry from active repentance and participation in the restoration. In the oracles of salvation YHWH is the only significant actor: the people are passive recipients of his grace, and occasional collaborators in his project of rebuilding a nation and a name for himself. What is interesting is the way that this theological shift from responsibility to passivity mirrors the social experience of the exiles as we have seen it—a shift from positions of social responsibility and power to a new world in which there is far less scope for influential decision making and action.

As a preliminary to our examination of this shift, it is worth returning briefly to the sociology of millenarian groups. Yonina Talmon points out that while many such movements are pre-political or non-political, a number are what she calls 'post-political':

> The collapse of an entire political system by a crushing defeat and the shattering of tribal or national hopes have sometimes led to widespread millenarism [*sic*]. It is the sense of blockage—the lack of effective organization, the absence of regular institutionalized ways of voicing grievances and pressing claims, that pushes such groups to a millenarian solution. Millenarism is born out of great distress coupled with political helplessness.[85]

Such a theoretical situation is very similar to that faced by the people of ancient Judah, and the eschatological hope of Ezekiel and the other exilic prophets grew out of this change of fortunes. Furthermore, the position of the Jewish exiles as a dominated élite may be parallel to the common 'prominence of members of a frustrated secondary élite among the leaders of millenarian movements'.[86] This describes perfectly the position of priests like Ezekiel in the exile, who retained some of the authority of their calling without the practical possibility of carrying it out.

Bryan Wilson may also shed some light on the shift from responsibility to passivity in Ezekiel's oracles in his discussion of 'revolutionist' responses to cultural contact. Revolutionism, in Wilson's explanation, is the hope of a divinely wrought overturning of the world order, and is the closest of his seven sectarian responses to that seen in the future hopes of the book of Ezekiel:

---

[85] Talmon, 'Millenarian Movements', 185.
[86] Ibid. 187.

Believers may themselves feel called upon to participate in the process of overturning, but they know that they do no more than put a shoulder to an already turning wheel and give an earnest of faith: the outworking of the prophesied cataclysm and subsequent restoration is essentially the doing of supernatural agencies. Men have no hope except from a new dispensation and the creation of such a new order is the intention of god or the gods.[87]

Wilson describes a number of phases of the revolutionist response to cultural contact with dominating outsiders, using evidence drawn mostly from the Native American experience. He suggests that the level of passivity in the programmes of millennial groups varies with their ability to make any impact on their position. Thus, 'in the early stages of culture contact, whilst resistance is still feasible, revolutionist religious orientations appear as prophecies of encouragement of military enterprise'.[88] Such an activist stance may be visible in the prophecies of those whom Jeremiah and Ezekiel condemned for their support of Zedekiah's rebellious attitude to Babylon. Wilson, however, goes on to describe a second stage of passive revolutionism, which develops when activism has ceased to be an option: 'When warfare has failed, revolutionist responses become more totally religious: reliance is now placed entirely on supernatural action . . . Visions of a trans- formed society and especially of a restored society, constitute the revolutionist response.'[89] This again fits the position of Ezekiel's community in exile, and even makes a fair summary of the prophet's message of unconditional salvation.

Daniel L. Smith points out a similar pattern in his study of the use of folklore as a mechanism for survival among communities of exiles, which concentrates on the 'diaspora hero' story. Stories of heroes who overcome the adversity facing an exiled community represent a projection of the values and aspirations of the tellers in story form.[90] Smith discusses not only stories of heroes like Daniel and Esther, but also 'Messianic' figures such as the servant in Second Isaiah. He points out that the move from suffering to redemption is important in the scheme of the Messiah and the

---

[87] Wilson, *Magic and the Millennium*, 23.
[88] Ibid. 272.
[89] Ibid. 272.
[90] Smith, *Landless*, 85 ff., 153–64; cf. R. D. Abrahams, 'Some Varieties of Heroes in America', *Journal of the Folklore Institute*, 3 (1966), 341–62; L. Lombardi-Satriani, 'Folklore as a Culture of Contestation', *Journal of the Folklore Institute*, 11 (1974), 99–121.

servant, but that equally important is another theme, that of *humiliation and restoration:* 'The social importance of this theme . . . is not properly understood apart from its exilic roots in a captive, powerless, low status minority and the hope and resistance that the existence of the hero as social type persistently encourages'.[91] All this is rather speculative, and will not account for all the complexities of Jewish Messianism, but it is also suggestive of a similar pattern in Ezekiel. According to this the 'hero' of the book of Ezekiel would be YHWH himself, who is first humiliated by both the sin of his people and by the abject state in which they are left after he punishes them, but who then acts powerfully to restore his people and thereby his own reputation.

In all Ezekiel's oracles of restoration YHWH's powerful action is in the foreground. He demonstrates his power by restoring the nation which has shamed him first by its sins and then by the defeat at the hands of Nebuchadnezzar which he himself imposed on it. He acts for his people, gathering them from where they are scattered, bringing them into the land of Israel, and making them prosper there. Paul Joyce, in his chapter 'The Radical Theocentricity of Ezekiel', has convincingly demonstrated that throughout the book YHWH's power and reputation are paramount. The characteristic recognition formula 'You (they) shall know that I am YHWH' echoes around the oracles of judgement and of deliverance. This knowledge that 'I am YHWH' can be rather cryptic and mysterious, and sometime its full import is unclear, but in every case 'the theocentric focus is unambiguous'.[92] Equally important is the explicit concern for his name and reputation that dominates all YHWH's actions, and especially those where he acts to deliver his people Israel.[93] Nowhere else in the Bible is it made so clear that it is not out of love, duty, or forgiveness that YHWH restores Israel, but solely for the sake of his own reputation.

We may contrast the vision of Jeremiah with that of Ezekiel on this point. There is much in common between these two prophets

---

[91] Smith, *Landless,* 170.

[92] Joyce, *Divine Initiative,* 94. He goes on to write that 'the concern that it should be known that "I am Yahweh" is at times so pressing that the specific recipients of this revelation fade into relative obscurity and it becomes unclear precisely who is being addressed—in such cases we are forcefully reminded that the focus is upon the God who is known rather than upon those by whom he is known'.

[93] Joyce, *Divine Initiative,* 97–103.

of the early sixth century, and there are particularly close parallels between the salvation oracles. Both offer a promise of return, blessing, and prosperity to the Jewish exiles, but even where the same literary and linguistic motifs appear there is a significant difference in tone, and in the characterization of the deity. We read in Jeremiah, for example:

Behold, I will gather them from all the countries to which I drove them in my anger and my wrath and in great indignation; I will bring them back to this place, and I will make them dwell in safety. And they shall be my people and I shall be their God. I will give them one heart and one way, that they may fear me for ever, for their own good and for the good of their children after them. I will make with them an everlasting covenant, that I will not turn away from doing good to them; and I will put the fear of me in their hearts, that they may not turn from me. I will rejoice in doing them good, and I will plant them in this land in faithfulness, with all my heart and with all my soul. (Jer. 32: 37–41)[94]

Now certainly there is a great deal of divine grace operative in this oracle, and YHWH is presented as almost the sole actor to restore the people, but Ezekiel's oracles display far less genuine concern for the people. We may compare, for example, Ezekiel 36: 22–4, 31–2, where it is made explicit that YHWH acts not for the sake of his people but for himself alone:

It is not for your sake, O house of Israel, that I am about to act, but for the sake of my holy name, which you have profaned among the nations to which you came. And I will vindicate the holiness of my great name, which has been profaned among the nations, and which you have profaned among them; and the nations will know that I am the LORD, says the Lord GOD, when through you I vindicate my holiness before their eyes. For I will take you from the nations, and gather you from all the countries, and bring you into your own land . . . Then you will remember your evil ways and your deeds that were not good and you will loathe yourselves for your iniquities and your abominable deeds. It is not for your sake that I will act, says the Lord GOD; let that be known to you. Be ashamed and confounded for your ways, O house of Israel.

---

[94] There is an even stronger contrast to be drawn between Ezekiel's tone and that of Jer. 31: 20: 'Is Ephraim my dear son? Is he my darling child? For as often as I speak against him, I do remember him still. Therefore my heart yearns for him; I will surely have mercy on him, says the LORD' (cf. also Hos. 11: 8–9). However, it is significant that even where Jeremiah presents a picture that is closer in spirit to Ezekiel, the latter prophet retains a harder edge (cf. also Jer. 31: 31–3, which mentions forgiveness and YHWH's forgetting of Israel's sin).

As Zimmerli says of this oracle, 'Ezekiel is devoid of all soft-hearted features and warm-hearted loves'.[95] YHWH's honour and holiness is the only real focus of the passage, and indeed of nearly all the oracles of judgement and restoration in the book.

Whereas the focus on human responsibility has been important in explaining the events of the disaster, the exiled people play very little part in their own restoration: YHWH's action and power is in the foreground. This point is made clearer by the use of language in these oracles. In 34: 11–15, part of the allegory of the shepherds and sheep, the first oracle of salvation opens with the hugely emphatic הנני־אני ודרשתי את־צאני ('behold I myself, I will seek out my sheep'). It continues with a relentless series of first person singular verbs:

I will seek them out [ובקרתים] . . . I will seek out [אבקר] my sheep . . . and I will rescue them [והצלתי אתהם] and I will bring them out [והוצאתים] . . . and I will gather them [וקבצתים] . . . and I will bring them [והביאתים] . . . and I will tend them [ורעיתים] . . . I will tend them [ארעה אתם].

It closes with another pair of emphatic אניs:

אני ארעה צאני ואני ארביצם נאם אדני יהוה

That is: 'I myself will tend my sheep, and I myself will make them lie down, says the Lord YHWH' (34: 15). Again, throughout chapter 37 there is a similarity of diction amongst the oracles of salvation addressed to the people, which all begin with the emphatic הנה אני (37: 5, 12, 19, 21). These oracles do not make any demands on the audience, but promise them unconditionally a return to their land.[96] Zimmerli makes a fascinating point when he draws attention to a later Jewish interpretation of 37: 1–14 which seems unwilling to accept that such an unconditional offer is really meant:

The fragment of the Palestinian Targum . . . which in the resurrection event leaves at least one dead body lying on the ground and has God's angel reply to a question about that body, 'For interest and surcharge he has lent (his money), therefore he is not honest (enough) to receive life along with his brothers', has undoubtedly quite rightly been aware of the unprecedented nature of such a proclamation, but has wrongly tried to soften it.[97]

---

[95] Zimmerli, *Ezekiel 2*, 247.
[96] Raitt, *Theology of Exile*, 106–8.
[97] Zimmerli, *Ezekiel 2*, 265. The fragment has been published by A. Diez-Macho, 'Un segundo fragmento del Targum Palestinense a los Profetas', *Biblica*, 39 (1958), 198–205.

It is not quite fair of Zimmerli to say that the promise of unconditional salvation is entirely unprecedented, since, as Joyce points
out: 'It must be acknowledged that the Old Testament as a whole
is marked by reluctance to speak of divine favour as deserved.
Even in Deuteronomy, a book characterized by moral exhortation with rewards promised for right conduct, the notion that
blessings enjoyed by Israel are merited is corrected.'[98] But, as he
continues, 'it is in Ezekiel that the conviction that divine favour is
undeserved is articulated more consistently than anywhere else in
the Old Testament'.[99]

In fact it is made clear in Ezekiel that even the people's ability
to respond to YHWH's grace is something which the god himself
empowers or enables. Chapters 11 and 36 use the language of a
new heart and a new spirit in connection with the restoration.

A new heart I will give you and a new spirit I will put within you, and I
will take out of your flesh the heart of stone and give you a heart of flesh.
And I will put my spirit within you and cause you to walk in my statutes
and be careful to observe my ordinances. (Ezek. 36: 26–7; cf. 11: 19–20)

The key words in this promise—לב ('heart') and רוח ('spirit')—
both have a wide range of possible meanings, but are commonly
associated with thinking and moral decision. Aubrey Johnson
writes of the heart that 'it is here that a man's character finds its
most ready expression',[100] and Ezekiel is here predicting a transformation of the character of his people, so that they can begin to
act rightly. Joyce has shown that in these passages the words לב
and רוח seem to have closely similar meanings, and refer to the
seat of thought and particularly of moral judgement: 'Indeed it
seems that the "new heart" and the "new spirit" both refer primarily to the gift of a renewed capacity to respond to YHWH in
obedience.'[101] Perhaps one could go further, and suggest that the
language of spirit serves to intensify the role that YHWH plays in
the transformation of his people, as Zimmerli proposes when he
compares Ezekiel 36 with Jeremiah 31: 'Jer 31:31 ff had referred to

[98] Joyce, *Divine Initiative*, 99.
[99] Ibid. 99.
[100] A. R. Johnson, *The Vitality of the Individual in the Thought of Ancient Israel* (Cardiff, 1949),
85.
[101] Joyce, *Divine Initiative*, 111. Such a renewed capacity to respond is also the theme of
Deut. 30: 6 and Ps. 51, both of which are probably to be dated in the exilic period; see
Joyce, *Divine Initiative*, 120–1.

the putting of the law in the human heart. Ezek 36: 27 speaks of putting the spirit there and in this way goes beyond Jer 31 and allows Yahweh to participate directly in man's new obedience.'[102] It is important to realize that here, even as he enables his people to be obedient, YHWH does not lose interest in the moral nature of his people's actions. The statutes and ordinances remain to be observed, but the restoration does not depend on the people's initiative in obeying them. In contrast to the call for repentance in chapter 18 which also uses the image of the new heart to examine responsibility, in the restoration passages the image is one of God himself providing his people with the moral will to carry out his commands in a way that they were conspicuously incapable of previously. Raitt describes this motif as 'the refusal to compromise away the necessity of moral preconditions, even if those moral preconditions are fulfilled by God as an arbitrary act of his divine prerogative'.[103] There is clearly a tension between restoration and the call to repent, but rather than jump to the conclusion that the two different images of a new heart represent different redactional strata in the book or belong to different periods of the prophet's ministry, I would argue that they are responses to different situations. The call for repentance in chapter 18 is set within the context of the moral possibilities that genuinely face the exiles, whereas in 11 and 36 the restoration is something that is well out-side the scope of their capabilities and must be left to their God.

It is not only in the context of the new heart and spirit that we find YHWH providing the will for his people to act properly; the idea is expressed again in 37: 23.[104] Here YHWH promises that after he has returned Israel to the land as one nation they will no longer defile themselves by their actions, but 'I will save them from all the backslidings in which they have sinned'. One has the sense that the god achieves right action on the part of his people only by doing himself what is required on their behalf. This is powerfully taken up in much Christian theology of atonement, but YHWH's action in Ezekiel has a harder edge to it than most Christian presentations of grace. One theologian who was in accord with the spirit of Ezekiel was John Calvin, who found here support for his doctrine of total depravity. He argues in his commentary on Ezekiel that the very need of a new heart and spirit suggests that

---

[102] Zimmerli, *Ezekiel 2*, 249.     [103] Raitt, *Theology of Exile*, 179.
[104] See ibid. 183.

the human soul is 'so corrupt that its depravity may be called death and destruction, so far as rectitude is concerned', and, moreover, that 'in our good works nothing is our own', but they are entirely the work of God within us.[105] Calvin well conveys the strength and power of God in these passages, but his rather individualistic interpretation obscures the fact that this is a communal restoration—the whole people of YHWH is to be restored.

The unconditional nature of Israel's salvation is emphasized in the few oracles which speak of a covenant as part of the restoration. Covenant is not a major theme in Ezekiel's oracles of judgement or of deliverance. The covenant between YHWH and his people is alluded to in the marriage of YHWH to Jerusalem in 16: 8, and 17: 13–19 makes a considerable play on Zedekiah's covenant with Nebuchadnezzar and YHWH's covenant with Israel.[106] It also appears in two oracles of deliverance which describe the reconstitution of the people, where, unlike Jeremiah, Ezekiel does not refer to a '*new* covenant', but to a 'covenant of peace' (ברית שלום) (34: 25; 37: 26)) and to an 'eternal covenant' (ברית עולם (37: 26)). We commented above that the 'covenant formula' in Ezekiel did not refer to an imposition of new obligations upon Israel, and this is also the case with the prophet's explicitly covenantal language, which appears in oracles that express a restoration without condition.[107] Thus in 34: 25 we find the expression ברית שלום in a context of rebuilding and restoration: 'I will make with them a covenant of peace and banish wild beasts from the land, so that they may dwell securely in the wilderness and sleep in the woods.' It has often been pointed out that the language of this oracle is extremely close to that of Leviticus 26, and seems particularly dependent on the introductory section, Leviticus 26: 3–6, which details the benefits that will follow obedience.[108] But whereas in Leviticus 26 the

---

[105] J. Calvin, *Commentaries on the First Twenty Chapters of the Book of the Prophet Ezekiel*, tr. T. Myers (Edinburgh, 1849); see esp. i. 373–80, where Calvin comments on 11: 19–20.

[106] The references to breaking, remembering, and establishing the covenant in 16: 59–63 are commonly adjudged late additions to the oracle, made under the influence of the priestly school. See e.g. Zimmerli, *Ezekiel 1*, 353; Eichrodt, *Ezekiel*, 216; Wevers, *Ezekiel*, 103; even the relatively conservative Cooke suggests that these verses are 'an appendix added after Ezekiel's time' (*Ezekiel*, 180).

[107] See above, p. 221.

[108] There is a very clear table of comparison and discussion in D. Baltzer, *Ezechiel und Deuterojesaja: Berührungen in der Heilserwartung der beiden großen Exilspropheten*, BZAW 121 (Berlin, 1971), 150–6. See also Bettenzoli, *Geist der Heiligkeit*, 140–1; Zimmerli, *Ezekiel 2*, 220; Allen, *Ezekiel 20–48*, 163, who rightly points out that 'the borrowing is not slavish but creative'.

promise is conditional upon obeying the commandments and a list
of curses will follow upon disobedience, in Ezekiel 34 the covenant
of peace is entirely unconditional. 'What in Lev. 26: 5bβ, 6 is the
reward of human obedience appears here as YHWH's free gift to his
people.'[109] The unconditional nature of the covenant is so striking
that it has provoked some strong reactions from commentators.
M. E. Andrew suggests translating ברית here as 'promise', arguing
that 'it is clear from this context that *berit* is a promise, for Yahweh
says that he will remove wild beasts and the people will dwell
safely; he lays an obligation on himself but not on the people, only
saying what he will do for them'.[110] Moshe Greenberg goes so far
as to argue that in the ברית שלום we do not have a reference to the
covenantal relationship between YHWH and his people at all: 'The
covenant of 34: 25 is correctly understood not as the grand bond
between God and people, but as a specific assurance of everlasting
physical security in the land'.[111] However, given the close connection with the explicitly covenantal framework of Leviticus 26, it
is better to see this as something new, certainly, but still a reference
to the genuine bond between YHWH and Israel. This is confirmed
by the appearance of a variation on the covenant formula that
concludes the oracle: 'And they shall know that I, the LORD their
God, am with them, and that they, the house of Israel, are my
people' (34: 30).

The covenant of peace reappears in Ezekiel 37, again in the
context of an unconditional promise of restoration, which this
time contains allusions to a wide range of covenantal traditions.[112]
The restored people will fulfil the requirements of the Mosaic
covenant: 'They shall follow my commandments and be careful to
observe my statutes' (37: 24). They will occupy the territory
promised in the patriarchal covenants: 'They shall dwell in the
land where your fathers dwelt that I gave to my servant Jacob' (37:
25a). Their political organization will be in accordance with the
Davidic covenant: 'and David my servant shall be their prince for
ever' (37: 25b). This picture of restoration leads into the promise
of the covenant of peace, and this is in turn illuminated by its

---

[109] Zimmerli, *Ezekiel 2*, 220.

[110] Andrew, *Responsibility and Restoration*, 173.

[111] Greenberg, *Ezekiel 1–20*, 303.

[112] Raitt, *Theology of Exile*, 204–5, for whom the section is 'like a veritable fugue of
election motifs'.

qualification as an eternal covenant (עולם ברית (37: 26)). This expression, which occurs regularly in priestly material concerning the promise to the patriarchs (Gen. 9: 16; 17: 7, 13, 19: 1 Chr. 16: 17 = Ps. 105: 10), also appears in relation to the house of David (2 Sam. 23: 5). Thus Ezekiel appears to be drawing on a range of covenantal traditions, but emphasizing those that stress the unconditional and permanent nature of Israel's restored relationship with YHWH.

There is an occasional sense of collaboration with YHWH, which is expressed in the hope for a renewed monarchy and in the obligations that remain upon the Israelites after their restoration. Ezekiel contains prophecies of a coming Davidic ruler who will rule over the people with justice, but on the whole, Messianism is a very muted theme in the book.[113] Ezekiel 17: 22–4 is a supplement to the allegory of the cedar in 17: 1–21, that develops the image by promising a replanting of the royal tree in the land of Israel, a 'noble cedar' which will bear fruit and provide shade for the animals and birds. We should note, however, that it is YHWH who does the replanting. Ezekiel 34: 23 promises a Davidic shepherd for the sheep of Israel: 'And I will set up over them one shepherd, my servant David, and he shall feed them and be their shepherd.' The royal figure does not act to help YHWH restore Israel to the land; his rule appears more like one of the beneficial results of YHWH's action, and he is clearly a subordinate and servant. As Fohrer writes: 'Der menschliche Hirt steht nicht neben, sondern unter dem göttlichen Hirten—als Unterhirt unter dem Oberhirt.'[114] Ezekiel 37: 24–6 follows the promise of a nation united from South and North (37: 15–23) with a recapitulation of the theme of royal shepherding: 'My servant David, shall be king over them, and they shall all have one shepherd . . . and David my servant shall be their prince for ever.' In this case again little is made of the power and responsibility of the Davidic figure. Indeed, YHWH calls him 'my servant', which marks not only a

---

[113] The word משיח does not appear in the book, and the theme is one which some scholars believe entirely secondary (e.g. McKeating, *Ezekiel*, 105–9). For recent and thorough discussions see D. I. Block, 'Bringing Back David: Ezekiel's Messianic Hope', in P. E. Satterthwaite, R. S. Hess, and G. J. Wenham (eds.), *The Lord's Anointed: Interpretation of Old Testament Messianic Texts* (Carlisle, 1995), 167–88, and P. M. Joyce, 'King and Messiah in Ezekiel', in J. Day (ed.), *King and Messiah in Israel and the Ancient Near East: Proceedings of the Oxford Old Testament Seminar*, JSOTS 270 (Sheffield, 1998), 323–37.

[114] Fohrer, *Ezechiel*, 196.

special relationship with his god, but also a clearly subordinate status. Block summarizes well:

Remarkably, he plays no part in the restoration of the nation. He neither gathers the people nor leads them back to their homeland. Unlike other prophets, Ezekiel makes no mention of the messiah as an agent of peace or of righteousness, these being attributed to the direct activity of God. The messiah's personal presence symbolizes the reign of Yahweh in the glorious new age.[115]

Whereas even Second Isaiah makes much of the role of a human deliverer in the person of Cyrus (Isa. 44: 28; 45: 1), Ezekiel's restoration is totally the work of YHWH himself.

In chapters 40–48 the נשׂיא, or 'prince', is given a prominent position within the restored community and the renewed cult, and a majority of scholars see him as in some way a continuation of the Davidic dynasty.[116] There has been a great deal of discussion of whether he is an 'apolitical' or 'depoliticized' figure with little real power,[117] or a vital and effective leader within the new constitution.[118] We should note that even if he is an exalted figure he is nonetheless subordinate to YHWH. Indeed, it has been suggested that this subordination (and, by contrast with the pre-exilic kings, reduced independence) is implicit in the choice of the word נשׂיא rather than מלך to describe him: 'das Wort *naśi*' läßt den Gedanken an absolutische, tyrannische Macht nicht aufkommen'.[119] If there is an exalted royal figure in these chapters it is none other than YHWH himself. As Joyce points out: 'The theme of God's kingship is particularly important because of the discernible pattern whereby the downgrading of human royal rule in

---

[115] Block, 'Bringing Back David', 183; cf. also Lemke, 'Life in the Present', 180. A similar case of mere collaboration with YHWH can be seen in the aftermath of Gog's defeat, where the people cleanse the land by clearing up the fallen weapons and burying the dead (Ezek. 39: 9–16). Even here, though, we should remember that it is YHWH who has single-handedly fought and won the battle.

[116] See e.g. Duguid, *Leaders*, 50; J. D. Levenson, *Theology of the Program of Restoration in Ezekiel 40–48*, HSM 10 (Missoula, Mont., 1976), 66–7. Tuell's proposal that he is the Persian governor of the province of Yehud has not won widespread support.

[117] In *Program of Restoration*, 57–101, Levenson describes Ezekiel's Messianic ideal as a leader who is YHWH's 'puppet', an apolitical king who, by contrast with his sinful predecessors, is 'shorn of the structural temptation to commit abuses' (67).

[118] Duguid, like Levenson, sees the prince as limited by comparison with past monarchs, but makes more of the actual powers that remain—the prince's 'privileged role within the cult and within society' (see *Leaders*, 43–57).

[119] Lang, *Kein Aufstand*, 180.

Ezekiel mirrors the upgrading of the royal sway of God. As one decreases the other increases, and vice versa.'[120] Moreover, as was the case in Ezekiel 34 and 36, the prince is very much a limited functionary: he does not assist YHWH in the process of restoration, but is one of the gifts which follow it.

The vision of restored Jerusalem in chapters 40–48 does seem different, and shows a much more active participation in YHWH's work: the community is maintained by the actions of the priests, the prince, and the people. There is far more concern with laying down prescriptions for the ordering of life within a restored Israel. Perhaps the more practical possibilities within the city reflect a different social context, in which genuine social organization seemed more of a possibility. Hanson, in particular, bases much of his distinction between the pragmatic Ezekiel and the visionary Second Isaiah on the importance of the temple and its institutions in Ezekiel's vision of the future:

central to the concern of Ezekiel is the rebuilding of the temple, while in Second Isaiah the temple barely receives mention. In many other respects as well the contrast could be drawn between the pragmatic priest Ezekiel concerned with laying the basis for the continuation of pre-exilic structures in the post-exilic era and the visionary prophet boldly announcing Yahweh's creation of a new order which would supplant the structures of the past.[121]

It is generally agreed that these chapters contain the greatest amount of secondary elaboration in the book of Ezekiel, and there is a case to be made that these more practical proposals represent a later filling out of the original vision. Thus Steven Tuell argues that although it has a substantial early exilic core, Ezekiel 40–48 taken as a whole is 'the religious polity of the Judaean restoration', most probably completed during the reign of Darius I (521–486 BCE).[122] In particular, the original has been supplemented by legal

---

[120] Joyce, 'King and Messiah', 335. A similar argument is made by Stevenson (*Vision of Transformation*, 109–23). Carroll, in a discussion of Isaiah 33: 17–22, points out that, while after 587 hopes for a just king became less realistic, 'dissonance caused by the loss of the monarchy could be reduced by transforming hopes about the king into beliefs about the divine king's protection of community and city' (*When Prophecy Failed*, 149). This may account for some downgrading of the human king.

[121] Hanson, *Dawn of Apocalyptic*, 234. A similar pragmatism is attributed to Ezekiel by Greenberg, 'Program of Restoration', 182–3.

[122] Tuell, *Law of the Temple*, 14. A similar suggestion is made by J. G. Gammie, who thinks that 'the external occasion and stimulus for the gathering together of Ezekiel 40–48

regulations which accord well with the realities of Persian rule over Judah. For example, the state-sponsored temple cult is to be seen in the context of Persian support of local cults; the נשיא is to be understood as the Persian governor, and the borders of the land in 47: 15–20 are seen roughly to correspond with the actual borders of the Province of Aber-Nahara.

In many respects Tuell makes a persuasive case, and from our point of view it is significant that for him the legal material—the practical requirements of the community—is post-exilic, whereas the exilic core lacks such a prescriptive emphasis. Nevertheless, he does not deal satisfactorily with all of the major disjunctions between Ezekiel 40–48 and the reality of the Persian period. If the Persian king is the ultimate sponsor of the new cult and society, it is surprising that he is not more obviously present within the vision, where YHWH is the only significant actor.[123] That the term נשיא could be used for the Persian governor lacks support from elsewhere in the Bible or other sources, and draws an unlikely contrast between the Davidic figure of chapters 34 and 36, and the related language in 40–48. Moreover, the absence of the high priest from Ezekiel's vision seems to make an exilic date at least as plausible as one following the restoration, when such a figure was always in place. We should not go so far as to attribute the whole of the temple vision to the prophet himself, but it seems likely that the exilic core takes up rather more of 40–48 than Tuell recognizes.

It can certainly be argued that the core of the vision, which goes back to Ezekiel himself, shares the same emphasis on divine grace and human passivity as the restoration oracles earlier in the book. The form of the vision presents Ezekiel with the restored temple, land, and community as a divine *fait accompli*, without demanding that he go and put it into practice. In particular, despite the detailed plans for the temple buildings, there is no sense that it requires to be built by human hands. 'What 40–48 contains in the way of new planning is imbedded in the proclamation of an

---

may well have come from the Persian bureaucracy and governmental pressure to show the need and plan for imperial assistance in rebuilding in the provinces' (*Holiness in Israel*, OBT (Minn., 1989), 53).

[123] We might again contrast Ezekiel's silence here with the exaltation of Cyrus in Second Isaiah.

impending divine deed that does not lie in the hands of human planners.'[124]

The visionary nature of the prophecy is evident from the degree to which mythological or theological symbols have pride of place in the shape of the new land. To characterize the place where the city is set as 'a very high mountain' (40: 2) immediately brings into play the myth of the sacred mountain. Although the term 'Zion' is never used (perhaps because of unfortunate associations with the monarchy), the influence of Zion theology is evident. The mountain is to be seen as the centre not only of Israel, but of the whole cosmos, it is the dwelling place of YHWH, and as such the place through which he both blesses the land and reveals himself to his people.[125] The motif of abundant fertility present in 34: 25–7 is taken up here by the astonishing image of a great river flowing from the temple (47: 1–13). In verses 6–7 Ezekiel discovers the Judaean wilderness now full of trees, and the river flows on into the Rift Valley, powerful enough to make the Dead Sea fresh and teeming with life.[126] Block emphasizes the priority of divine grace in this vision: 'The revitalization of the landscape is not achieved through human ingenuity, technology, or effort; it is the result of YHWH's lifting of the curse and replaces it with his blessing.'[127] Despite his concern for a 'realistic' interpretation of the vision as a whole, Tuell recognizes that with the highly schematized divisions of the land in chapters 47 and 48 'we . . . are in the realm, not of real estate, but of religious doctrine'.[128]

Even the detailed description of the temple may belong within a visionary tradition. Susan Niditch, in a fascinating article, has treated Ezekiel's temple vision on the analogy of the Tibetan Buddhist mandala—'a symbolic representation of the sacred

---

[124] Zimmerli, 'Plans for Rebuilding', 115. He continues: 'For example, the new sanctuary, described first in its architectural form, is not demanded imperatively as an accomplishment of postexilic temple architects. Rather it is shown in a vision to the prophet as the work which Yahweh himself has mysteriously formed, and it is measured and explicated by the other-worldly figure of "man" sent by Yahweh' (115–16). See also Eichrodt, *Ezekiel*, 542.

[125] See esp. Levenson, *Program of Restoration*, 7–24.

[126] The imagery is reminiscent of both creation narratives: river and trees seem to reflect the myth of Eden, while the verb used of the swarming fish (שרץ) is the same as that of Gen. 1: 20–1 (cf. Levenson, *Program of Restoration*, 26–34; Block, *Ezekiel 25–48*, 694–5).

[127] Block, *Ezekiel 25–48*, 701–2.

[128] Tuell, *Law of the Temple*, 173.

realm or cosmos'.[129] In the Buddhist mystical tradition such mandalas are used as a focus of mystical concentration, through which
'the successful visionary is transported to see and participate in the
sacred realm'.[130] Such mandalas often take the form of model
buildings, and highly detailed instructions for their design exist in
the Tantric literature, which are suggestive of Ezekiel 40–48.
Niditch suggests that we should not see Ezekiel 40–48 as simply a
set of architectural plans, but as a complex symbolic vision of the
cosmos as it should be:

> The vision's images, reported in words, form pillars and courtyards, and
> constitute a world; its images are real and have a reality as does the
> mandala . . . The temple imaginings thus make perfect sense in the work
> of the priest-seer-mystic. This imagining does not take place, moreover,
> in a moment of mere ordinary, mundane thinking about plans for recon-
> struction; rather, such a vision is part and parcel of the experience of
> Ezekiel as visionary and central to it.[131]

The description of the temple is less a blueprint to be acted upon
than it is, as Levenson puts it, 'public testimony to the nature of
God'.[132]

This must call into question the pragmatic conservatism that
Hanson and others have seen in the book of Ezekiel. Indeed, it is
intriguing to notice that in his introduction to *The Dawn of
Apocalyptic* Hanson, in order to distinguish the early visionary
Second Isaiah from his later apocalyptic successors, makes the
following comments:

> While a more lofty, cosmic quality is discernible in the prophecy of
> Second Isaiah, yet his message is replete with historical references which
> bind his message to the mundane sphere. Cyrus, who serves as the
> surrogate of the anointed of Israel, will be Yahweh's instrument of
> deliverance; Babylon will be the object of Yahweh's wrath; the city of
> Jerusalem will be the home to which the delivered will return.[133]

---

[129] S. Niditch, 'Ezekiel 40–48 in Visionary Context', *CBQ* 48 (1986), 208–24; cf. also
(with slightly more limited scope) S. S. Tuell, 'Ezekiel 40–42 as Verbal Icon, *CBQ* 58 (1996),
649–64. Tuell sees this early section of the Temple Vision as 'the report of an ascent to
the heavenly temple', through which its audience could be given access to the reality and
presence of YHWH (649).

[130] Ibid. 212.

[131] Ibid. 213–14.

[132] Levenson, *Program of Restoration*, 16.

[133] Hanson, *Dawn of Apocalyptic*, 25.

None of these mundane features forms part of Ezekiel's promises for the future—in each respect he is more 'visionary' than the archetypal visionary prophet. As we have seen, Ezekiel requires no human historical deliverer; YHWH alone will restore Israel to the land; the oppressor Babylon is not dignified with even a single oracle predicting her downfall; finally, the new city is never, in fact, named as Jerusalem. At the very end of the book the city receives the new name יהוה שמה ('YHWH is there' (Ezek. 48: 35)). The new city is as full of vision and promise as the rest of Ezekiel's images of restoration. Despite its details and regulations for life in the land, it does not present these as a demand the people must fulfil for YHWH to return. Rather the new system which will not allow the abuses of the past to continue is all part of YHWH's gracious gift to his people. They remain passive recipients of his bounty.

## Conclusion

As we have examined the shape and movement of the book of Ezekiel, we have seen that it displays a dramatic shift from judgement to salvation: the people will be restored to the land they have lost and will live with new and better institutions than those they had before. This shift is not a late, alien addition to the book's theology, but belongs to the exilic context of the prophet himself and his earliest editors. Alongside this movement from judgement to salvation, we have also seen a shift from moral responsibility to moral passivity on the part of the exiles. Although the people are clearly blamed for the disasters that have befallen them, when Ezekiel speaks of restoration the initiative is all with YHWH, and repentance is not made a prerequisite for the recovery of the land. While at a more domestic and individual level moral decisions remain to be made, when we look at the major institutions of land, temple, and rulers, renewal is entirely in YHWH's hands.[134] This seems a highly appropriate response of a group of people who remain interested in such institutions, but no longer retain the political power to influence them. Such a movement is by no means unparalleled in the study of millenarian movements, as we

---

[134] It is, of course, sin in these areas of activity that has been the main cause of disaster; see above, Chs. 3 and 4.

have seen from the work of Talmon and Wilson. It is, I think, significant that God takes control in precisely those areas of moral life in which the people, and especially the exiled élite, had failed so spectacularly, and in which they, as exiles in Babylonia, no longer had any practical stake. This suggests that the theocentricity and human passivity evident in Ezekiel can be related to the social circumstances of the exiles. Decisions and actions which might realistically bring about a national restoration no longer form part of their moral world. The passivity of the people mirrors their social and political impotence as exiles in Babylon, and the promise of salvation can itself be seen as an expression of powerlessness.

I do not wish to suggest that the Babylonian exile is the only social context to which oracles of salvation are appropriate. But the experience of a dramatic loss of status and power, which we see among the deported Jews, is certainly an experience of social and economic oppression such as Weber and the sociologists of millennialism describe. The theological sophistication of Ezekiel's oracles may be rooted in the élite origins of the exiled group, and thus the combination of social distress and the need for salvation with the powerful symbolic tools of Jerusalem theology has its end-product in the uncompromisingly theocentric oracles of restoration. These oracles could provide a focus for the hopes and aspirations of the exiles, and therefore a significant source of strength and common purpose in the struggle to maintain a distinctively Jewish community.

# Conclusion

## Ezekiel and the Ethics of Exile

This study of ethics in Ezekiel began by outlining an approach to the study of ethics in ancient Israel, concentrating on the historical and sociological task of describing the ideals and practice of the ancient communities which formed the Hebrew Bible. In particular, I suggested that the social circumstances of any human group are highly significant in determining the range of moral possibilities that are open to its members. Moral agents do not act independently of the world in which they live, and the ways in which they choose to act will be influenced and constrained by their different economic resources and levels of political influence, different cultures and world-views. We should therefore pay attention to these social factors if we are to draw a more complete picture of the moral life of ancient Israel.

To test the value of this approach requires attention to specific texts and situations, and to that end the rest of the study has concentrated on one period, that of the Babylonian exile, and on one text, the book of Ezekiel. Ezekiel provides a particularly interesting example because of the unusual situation of exile in which the prophet and his audience found themselves, and I have attempted to show that many of the book's most distinctive ethical ideas can be explained as a response to the experience of deportation.[1] In the aftermath of the surrender of Jerusalem in 597 BCE Nebuchadnezzar of Babylon deported King Jehoiachin of Judah, and alongside him a substantial proportion of the most powerful people in ancient Judah, the ruling élite and their retainers. For these people deportation meant an immediate and dramatic drop in status, since it is likely that many of them were deployed as con-

---

[1] Despite various attempts to challenge this setting, it remains the most likely context for Ezekiel's oracles: see Ch. 2, pp. 41–50.

struction workers or farmers in parts of the Babylonian Empire that needed redevelopment.

Part of the reason for the seventy years of relative disarray in Ezekiel studies is the obvious dual focus of the book. Ezekiel's ministry is ostensibly set in exile; the framework makes that clear, along with a few of the oracles of judgement and most of the expressed hopes for restoration. At the same time, in much of its content, and especially most of its oracles of judgement, the book clearly addresses Jerusalem and its inhabitants. Scholarly attempts to account for this dual focus have included theories of pseudepigraphy, of a Jerusalem ministry for the prophet, and of complex redactional developments in both Babylon and Jerusalem. Such theories, however, ignore one of the most common aspects of the life of any exile or community of exiles: they remain passionately interested in home. Greenberg's point about Ezekiel's community continues to have weight:

> the hearers of the prophet were, in fact, Jerusalemites who identified themselves with their fellow citizens in every way. If there is any anomaly in Ezekiel's addressing Jerusalem from the exile, it is no greater than the anomalous contemporaneity of two Jerusalemite communities hundreds of miles apart at this juncture of history.[2]

This idea that there can be Jerusalemites in two different places at once is crucial for understanding the moral world of Ezekiel and the exiles. There are in fact two distinct sets of social circumstances which are relevant to their moral interests and moral formation. The first is the old world of home, with its relative wealth, privilege, and status, the second is the new world of exile. As exiles, therefore, Ezekiel's community could belong to two different realms of moral possibility. The first of these is the moral world of the Jerusalem political élite, the second the more limited moral world of exile in Babylonia. However, because the exiles were themselves drawn from the Jerusalem élite they can be one and the same people, to whom both sets of circumstances are appropriate.

If these exiles were drawn from Judah's political classes, then before the disaster of exile they would have been in a position to make decisions affecting major communal institutions, and thus the Judaean community as a whole. Chapters 3 and 4 examined

---

[2] Greenberg, *Ezekiel 1–20*, 17.

some ways in which Ezekiel reflects these élite moral horizons, concentrating particularly on the content of the prophet's oracles of judgement. In those oracles that foretell the fall of Jerusalem, the moral issues that exercise him most are those that belong to the arena of Judah's institutions of state, and foreign relations and the correct maintenance of the state cult are particularly prominent.

On the political side, Ezekiel's primary interest is foreign policy. This is most visible in the elaborate allegories of chapters 16, 17, 19, and 23, all of which are critical of Judah's relationships with foreign powers. The condemnation of alliances is especially vivid and grotesque in chapters 16 and 23, where Jerusalem is portrayed as a woman whose voracious sexual appetite drives her to take lovers from among the nations. More explicitly political are chapters 17 and 19, in which Ezekiel condemns King Zedekiah for his political faithlessness in rebelling against Babylon. The criticism of foreign policy and the prophet's attacks on injustice in society are directed towards not only the king, but also his advisors and a wider political stratum within the society of ancient Jerusalem.

In ancient agrarian societies like Judah the line between religion and politics is very narrow, and throughout the history of Israel and Judah state religion is a major concern of the political classes. As one faction is ousted and another takes power, a different religious ideology becomes dominant, and alongside any changes in religious ideology come changes in cultic practice. Although Ezekiel's criticism is often very general, whenever he provides detailed examples of cultic apostasy to explain the fall of Jerusalem it is not the 'popular religion' of the Judaean peasant class that he attacks, but a wilful failure on the part of the élite to keep the state cult within the bounds of orthodoxy. The prophet's lengthy diatribes against sin in the religious sphere show a special concern to promote cult centralization and to root out idolatry, and appear to draw heavily on the theological and political programme of the Josianic reform. As was the case with his more secular politics, we find that if specific individuals or groups of people are mentioned as responsible for the cultic improprieties, they too are normally drawn from the political élite.

Ezekiel's own background as a priest may go a long way to explain the range of moral concerns which dominate his oracles of judgement, and it is no surprise that cultic apostasy is central among the reasons he gives for the fall of Jerusalem. However, the prophet's criticism is not restricted to the most obviously priestly interests but also takes in a range of other issues, most prominently international politics. As we have seen, upper-class political factions might contain members drawn from a variety of backgrounds, including religious professionals like Ezekiel alongside more secular figures. The combination of issues suggests that the moral world to which the majority of Ezekiel's oracles of judgement belong is that of the Jerusalem élite, which the exiles who formed his audience had only recently left behind.

This moral world is familiar to us from the writings of the other classical prophets, perhaps especially Isaiah and Jeremiah, who were based in Jerusalem and had some access to the royal court. Ezekiel's participation in these debates is by no means unique. Indeed, there is need for more serious general study of the role of prophets in politics, which attempts to relate their demands for social justice to their more obviously élite interests in foreign policy and religious orthodoxy. Accusations of injustice in pre-exilic prophetic texts may be more expressive of the political struggle between different upper-class factions than of conflict between oppressed and oppressors. Moreover, the religious orientation of material in the Hebrew Bible may sometimes mask the fact that arguments about cult and theology take place within the context of an élite political culture where divine legitimation is a necessary adjunct to political power.

Ezekiel's most characteristic contributions to prophetic ethics, however, belong to a different moral world, that of the Babylonian exile. Their new status as a dominated minority within the huge Babylonian empire brought little or no political autonomy to Judah's former élite and posed serious threats to their communal identity. They were no longer able to participate in the main areas of Jerusalem's political and religious life, but had been marginalized by both their distance from the capital and the lack of resources available to them. The scope for action open to them was thus sharply circumscribed, and it was really only in the more limited spheres of family, business, and immediate community that they could make moral decisions. Chapters 5, 6, and 7 considered the evidence for adaptation to this new moral world.

Ezekiel's ethical distinctiveness is seen perhaps most clearly in the high priority the prophet places on ritual. Among the prophets his vocabulary is most influenced by priestly theology, and this is evident in the degree to which terms like טמא and חלל permeate the book. Also typical of priestly concerns is the way in which blood provides the principal vehicle for his metaphors of guilt and social injustice. Both violent bloodshed and unclean menstrual blood are used effectively to symbolize the state of Jerusalem. Ezekiel's ritualization of ethics served to extend the symbolic language of the Jerusalem temple beyond the strictly priestly sphere and enabled the old institution to remain central to the community's social values and aspirations. In the exiled situation in which there was no temple, the use of regulations for purity which have their significance only within the context provided by the temple—one of the most powerful symbols of nationality and identity—has the purpose of providing stability and a focal point for resistance.

Chapter 6 addressed the reduced moral horizons of life in exile, where it was no longer possible to make decisions affecting the institutions of state. In particular, two key oracles that do not directly address the fall of Jerusalem (14: 1–11 and 18: 1–32) demonstrate an increasing 'domestication' of sin and virtue that moves the focus of ethical interest away from these national institutions and towards the individual and the family. A distinctive feature of Ezekiel's prophecy is his reapplication of legal forms to theological issues, which is most evident in 14: 1–11 and chapter 18. Where the community was faced with very limited legal autonomy, the reapplication of legal language in theological contexts might preserve not only the legal traditions themselves but also the sense of moral responsibility which the application of those traditions allowed. There is a similar logic to that involved in the ritualization of ethics: what had once been symbolic of power and autonomy in Jerusalem is reinvented to suit the new situation of the deportees in Babylon. Significant also is the fact that both 14: 1–11 and 18, oracles addressed specifically to the exilic situation, display a rather narrower focus of ethical content. In contrast to the majority of those oracles which are addressed to Jerusalem, here the areas of ethical decision making require no political autonomy or power. Such domestication of ethics can be seen as a response to a situation in which major communal decisions are simply no longer there to be taken. Finally, it is in these two oracles that the call to repent is most clearly stated. Repentance presents a substantial problem to the interpreter of Ezekiel, since the book often appears to equivocate about the possibility and even the value of a response to the prophet's preaching. However, a closer examination of the texts reveals that while repentance is not significant in the prophet's prediction of the fall of Jerusalem, nor in his promises of future restoration, it is directed towards the present experience of exile, and shows YHWH's continuing concern that his people should act rightly.

Chapter 7 examined the place of future hope in Ezekiel's theology and ethics. In the aftermath of the fall of Jerusalem, Ezekiel's prophecies display a dramatic shift from judgement to salvation. These promises of a communal future have their real value in the present: oracles of salvation could provide a focus for the hopes and aspirations of the exiles, and therefore a significant source of strength and common purpose to maintain a distinctively Jewish community. At the same time, the new note of hope in Ezekiel's prophecy is accompanied by an equally dramatic shift from moral responsibility to moral passivity on the part of the people. Although the people are clearly blamed for the disasters that have befallen them, when Ezekiel speaks of restoration the initiative is all with YHWH, and repentance is not made a prerequisite for the recovery of the land. Human behaviour is seen first to provoke, and then to result from, divine action: in particular, YHWH's people become less and less responsible for what happens to them at the level of their communal, national existence. This movement from responsibility for judgement to passivity in the face of restoration can be seen to mirror the actual social circumstances of the exiles, who have been transported from positions of power and influence in Jerusalem to become small-time servants of Babylonian agricultural policy.

Again, these elements in Ezekiel's ethics cannot be explained only as a result of the prophet's priestly background or attachment to certain theological traditions; they also arise as a response to the specific social experience of exile. It is important to stress that the new moral world whose contours we have found delineated in the book is not *merely* a passive reflection of changed material circumstances. Certainly the new emphases we have seen represent the reduced scope for action and more limited 'moral horizons' of life in Babylonia. But they can also be seen as powerful strategies for survival among the exiles, providing both a degree of continuity with the past and a significant impetus for the maintenance of a distinct and socially cohesive Jewish community.

The experience of exile carries with it an inevitable tension between past and present, old life and new life. The notion of a dual moral world has provided a model for exploring this tension as it appears in Ezekiel's ethics. Such a scheme will always emphasize certain themes and issues at the expense of others, and there are undoubtedly some parts of the book that are more resistant to the model than others. The inhabitants of both moral worlds are one and the same people, and it is perhaps artificial to divide so sharply something that they may in certain respects have experienced as continuous. Furthermore, complexities and inconsistencies remain in the text, which may best be explained as the result of the editorial history of the book, and its use and reapplication in the rather different social circumstances of the Jerusalem community in the Persian period. Indeed, it is striking that the very afterlife of 'the exile' as a religious theme within Judaism shows at least one significant parallel with what we have found in the book of Ezekiel. For rather as Ezekiel takes the past reality of the Jerusalem temple and transposes it to the realm of the symbolic, so we find that the exile itself is transformed into one of the defining symbols of Jewish identity in the Persian period and beyond.[3]

To apply the model of a dual moral world to the prophet's work will not solve all the problems of the book of Ezekiel. Nevertheless, it has provided a useful heuristic device with which to examine the prophet's ethics, and we have found a considerable degree of consistency in its application. Moreover, it has confirmed my initial hypothesis that we cannot understand the moral concerns and priorities of the book of Ezekiel (or, for that matter, those of any other biblical book) without paying careful attention to the distinctive social circumstances in which it arose. This study, then, is offered in the hope that it has helped not only to shed light upon some of the idiosyncrasies of this awkward yet compelling book, but also to break some new ground for further work on the ethics of the Hebrew Bible.

---

[3] See esp. the various perspectives in the volume of essays edited by Grabbe, *Leading Captivity Captive.*

# BIBLIOGRAPHY

ABERLE, D. F., 'A Note on Relative Deprivation Theory', in S. Thrupp (ed.), *Millennial Dreams in Action: Essays in Comparative Study* (The Hague, 1962), 209–14.

ABRAHAMS, R. D., 'Some Varieties of Heroes in America', *Journal of the Folklore Institute*, 3 (1966), 341–62.

ACKERMAN, S., *Under Every Green Tree: Popular Religion in Sixth Century Judah*, HSM 46 (Atlanta, Ga., 1992).

ACKROYD, P. R., *Exile and Restoration*, OTL (London, 1968).

—— 'The History of Israel in the Exilic and Post-Exilic Periods', in G. W. Anderson (ed.), *Tradition and Interpretation* (Oxford, 1979), 320–50.

AHLSTRÖM, G. W., *Royal Administration and National Religion in Ancient Palestine* (Leiden, 1982).

—— *The History of Ancient Palestine from the Palaeolithic Period to Alexander's Conquest*, JSOTS 146 (Sheffield, 1993).

AHRONI, R., 'The Gog Prophecy and the Book of Ezekiel', *HAR* 1 (1977), 1–27.

ALBERTZ, R., *A History of Israelite Religion in the Old Testament Period*, 2 vols. (London, 1994) = English translation of *Religionsgeschichte Israels in alttestamentliche Zeit* (Göttingen, 1992).

ALBRIGHT, W. F., *Archaeology and the Religion of Israel* (Baltimore, Md., 1956).

—— 'The Seal of Eliakim and the Latest Preexilic History of Judah, with Some Observations on Ezekiel', *JBL* 51 (1932), 77–106.

ALLEN, L. C., *Ezekiel 20–48*, Word Biblical Commentary, 29 (Waco, Tex., 1990).

—— 'The Structure and Intention of Ezekiel 1', *VT* 43 (1993), 145–61.

—— *Ezekiel 1–19*, Word Biblical Commentary, 28 (Dallas, Tex., 1994).

ANDREW, M. E., *Responsibility and Restoration: The Course of the Book of Ezekiel* (Dunedin, 1985).

AVIGAD, N., 'New Light on the Na'ar Seals', in F. M. Cross (ed.), *Magnalia Dei: Essays on Bible and Archaeology in Memory of G. Ernest Wright* (Garden City, NY, 1976), 294–300.

BALTZER, D., *Ezechiel und Deuterojesaja: Berührungen in der Heilserwartung der beiden großen Exilspropheten*, BZAW, 121 (Berlin, 1971).

BARBER, B., 'Acculturation and Messianic Movements', *American Sociological Review*, 6 (1943), 663–9.

BARKUN, M., *Disaster and the Millennium* (New Haven, Conn., 1974).

BARR, J., 'Semantics and Biblical Theology—A Contribution to the

Discussion', in *Congress Volume: Uppsala 1971*, SVT 22 (Leiden, 1972), 11–19.

BARRICK, W. B., 'High Place', *Anchor Bible Dictionary*, iii. 197.

BARSTAD, H. M, *The Myth of the Empty Land: A Study of the History and Archaeology of Judah During the 'Exilic' Period*, Symbolae Osloenses Fasc. Suppl. 28 (Oslo, 1996).

——'The Strange Fear of the Bible', in L. L. Grabbe (ed.), *Leading Captivity Captive: 'The Exile' as History and Ideology*, JSOTS 278 (Sheffield, 1998), 120–7.

BARTON, J., 'Understanding Old Testament Ethics', *JSOT* 9 (1978), 44–64.

——'Begründungsversuche der prophetischen Unheilsankündigung im Alten Testament', *EvTh* 47 (1987), 427–35.

——'Approaches to Ethics in the Old Testament', in J. Rogerson (ed.), *Beginning Old Testament Study*, 2nd edn. (London, 1998), 114–31.

——*Ethics and the Old Testament* (London, 1998).

BECKER, J., 'Ez 8–11 als einheitliche Komposition in einem pseudepigraphischen Ezechielbuch', in J. Lust (ed.), *Ezekiel and his Book: Textual and Literary Criticism and their Interrelation*, BETL 74 (Leuven, 1986), 136–50.

BECKING, B., and KORPEL, M. C. A. (eds.), *The Crisis of Israelite Religion: Transformation of Religious Tradition in Exilic and Post-Exilic Times*, OTS 42 (Leiden, 1999).

BEGG, C. T., 'The Identity of the Princes in Ezekiel 19: Some Reflections', *ETL* 65 (1989), 358–69.

BELL, C., *Ritual: Perspectives and Dimensions* (NY and Oxford, 1997).

BENDIX, R., *Max Weber: An Intellectual Portrait* (London, 1960).

BERRY, G. R., 'Was Ezekiel in the Exile?', *JBL* 49 (1930), 83–93.

BERTHOLET, A., and GALLING, K., *Hesekiel*, HAT 13 (Tübingen, 1936).

BETTENZOLI, G., *Geist der Heiligkeit: Traditionsgeschichtliche Untersuchung des QDŠ-Begriffes im Buch Ezechiel*, Quaderni di Semitistica, 8 (Florence, 1979).

BICKERMAN, E., 'The Babylonian Captivity', in W. D. Davies and I. Finkelstein (eds.), *The Cambridge History of Judaism*, i (Cambridge, 1984), 342–58.

BIRCH, B. C., *Let Justice Roll Down: The Old Testament, Ethics, and Christian Life* (Louisville, Ky., 1991).

BLENKINSOPP, J., *Ezekiel*, Interpretation (Louisville, Ky., 1990).

——'Temple and Society in Achaemenid Judah', in P. R. Davies (ed.), *Second Temple Studies*, JSOTS 117 (Sheffield, 1991), 22–53.

——*A History of Prophecy in Ancient Israel*, 2nd edn. (Louisville, Ky., 1996).

BLOCK, D. I., 'Bringing Back David: Ezekiel's Messianic Hope', in P. E.

Satterthwaite, R. S. Hess, and G. J. Wenham (eds.), *The Lord's Anointed: Interpretation of Old Testament Messianic Texts* (Carlisle, 1995), 167–88.

——— *The Book of Ezekiel: Chapters 1–24*, NICOT (Grand Rapids, Mich., 1997).

——— *The Book of Ezekiel: Chapters 25–48*, NICOT (Grand Rapids, Mich., 1998).

BOARDMAN, J., EDWARDS, I. E. S., *et al.* (eds.), *The Assyrian and Babylonian Empires and other States of the Near East, from the Eighth to the Sixth Centuries B.C.*, The Cambridge Ancient History, 2nd edn., vol. iii, pt. 2 (Cambridge, 1991).

BOECKER, H. J., *Law and the Administration of Justice in the Old Testament and the Ancient Near East* (London, 1980) = English translation of *Recht und Gesetz im Alten Testament und im Alten Orient* (Neukirchen, 1971).

BOTTERWECK, G. J., and RINGGREN, H. (eds.), *Theological Dictionary of the Old Testament* (Grand Rapids, Mich., 1974– ) = English translation of *Theologische Wörterbuch zum Alten Testament* (Stuttgart, 1970– ).

BROWN, P., *The Body and Society: Men Women, and Sexual Renunciation in Early Christianity* (NY, 1988).

BROWNE, L. E., *Ezekiel and Alexander* (London, 1952).

BROWNLEE, W., ' "Son of Man Set Your Face": Ezekiel the Refugee Prophet', *HUCA* 54 (1983), 83–110.

——— *Ezekiel 1–19*, Word Biblical Commentary, 28 (Waco, Tex., 1986).

BUDD, P. J., *Numbers*, Word Biblical Commentary, 5 (Waco, Tex., 1984).

CALVIN, J., *Commentaries on the First Twenty Chapters of the Book of the Prophet Ezekiel*, tr. T. Myers (Edinburgh, 1849).

CARLEY, K. W., *Ezekiel Among the Prophets: A Study of Ezekiel's Place in Prophetic Tradition*, SBT, 2nd series, 31 (London, 1975).

CARNEY, T. F., *The Shape of the Past: Models and Antiquity* (Lawrence, Kan., 1975).

CARROLL, R. P., *When Prophecy Failed: Reactions and Responses to Failure in the Old Testament Prophetic Traditions* (London, 1979).

——— *From Chaos to Covenant: Uses of Prophecy in the Book of Jeremiah* (London, 1981).

——— *Jeremiah: A Commentary*, OTL (London, 1986).

——— 'The Myth of the Empty Land', *Semeia*, 59 (1992), 79–93.

——— 'Deportation and Diasporic Discourses in the Prophetic Literature', in J. M. Scott (ed.), *Exile: Old Testament, Jewish and Christian Conceptions*, Journal for the Study of Judaism, Supplement Series, 56 (Leiden, 1997), 63–85.

——— 'Exile! What Exile?', in L. L. Grabbe (ed.), *Leading Captivity Captive: 'The Exile' as History and Ideology*, JSOTS 278 (Sheffield, 1998), 62–79.

CAUSSE, A., *Les Dispersés d'Israël: les origines de la Diaspora et son rôle dans la formation de Judaïsme* (Paris, 1929).

—— *Du Groupe ethnique à la communauté religieuse: le problème sociologique de la religion d'Israël* (Paris, 1937).

CAZELLES, H., '587 ou 586?', in C. L. Meyers and M. J. O'Connor (eds.), *The Word of the Lord Shall Go Forth: Essays in Honor of David Noel Freedman in Celebration of his Sixtieth Birthday* (Winona Lake, Ind., 1983), 427–35.

CHANEY, M. L., 'Systemic Study of the Israelite Monarchy', *Semeia*, 37 (1986), 53–76.

—— 'Debt Easement in Israelite History and Tradition', in D. Jobling, P. L. Day, and G. T. Sheppard (eds.), *The Bible and the Politics of Exegesis: Essays in Honor of Norman K. Gottwald on his Sixty-Fifth Birthday* (Cleveland, Ohio, 1991), 127–40.

CHILDS, B. S., *Biblical Theology in Crisis* (Phil., 1970).

—— *Biblical Theology of the Old and New Testaments* (London, 1993).

CLEMENTS, R. E., 'The Ezekiel Tradition: Prophecy in a Time of Crisis', in R. J. Coggins, A. Phillips, and M. Knibb (eds.), *Israel's Prophetic Tradition: Essays in Honour of Peter Ackroyd* (Cambridge, 1982), 119–36.

—— 'The Chronology of Redaction in Ez 1–24', in J. Lust (ed.), *Ezekiel and his Book: Textual and Literary Criticism and their Interrelation*, BETL 74 (Leuven, 1986), 283–94.

—— *Ezekiel*, Westminster Bible Companion (Louisville, Ky., 1996).

COGAN, M., *Imperialism and Religion: Assyria, Judah and Israel in the Eighth and Seventh Centuries B.C.E.*, SBLDS 19 (Missoula, Mont., 1974).

—— 'Judah under Assyrian Hegemony: A Reexamination of Imperialism and Religion', *JBL* 112 (1993), 403–14.

COGAN, M., and TADMOR, H., *II Kings*, Anchor Bible, 11 (New York, 1988).

COGGINS, R. J., 'The Origins of the Jewish Diaspora', in R. E. Clements (ed.), *The World of Ancient Israel: Sociological, Anthropological and Political Perspectives* (Cambridge, 1989), 163–81.

COLE, S. W., *Nippur in Late Assyrian Times, c.755–612 BC*, State Archives of Assyria Studies (Helsinki, 1996).

COLLINS, R., *Three Sociological Traditions* (NY, 1985).

COOGAN, M. D., 'Life in the Diaspora: Jews at Nippur in the Fifth Century BC', *Biblical Archaeologist*, 37 (1974), 6–12.

—— *West Semitic Personal Names in the Murašu Documents*, HSM 7 (Missoula, Mont., 1976).

COOK, S. L., *Prophecy and Apocalypticism: The Postexilic Social Setting* (Minn., 1995).

COOKE, G. A., *A Critical and Exegetical Commentary on the Book of Ezekiel*, ICC (Edinburgh, 1936).

CROSS, F. M., *Canaanite Myth and Hebrew Epic: Essays in the History of the Religion of Israel* (Cambridge, Mass., 1973).

DALLEY, S., 'Foreign Chariotry and Cavalry in the Armies of Tiglath-Pileser III and Sargon II', *Iraq*, 47 (1985), 31–48.
——'Nineveh, Babylon and the Hanging Gardens: Cuneiform and Classical Sources Reconciled', *Iraq*, 56 (1994), 45–58.
DANDAMAEV, M. A., *Slavery in Babylonia from Nabopolassar to Alexander the Great (626–331 B.C.)* (DeKalb, Ill., 1984).
——'Babylonia in the Persian Age', in W. D. Davies and I. Finkelstein (eds.), *The Cambridge History of Judaism*, i (Cambridge, 1984), 326–42.
——'Neo-Babylonian Society and Economy', in J. Boardman, I. E. S. Edwards, *et al.* (eds.), *The Assyrian and Babylonian Empires and other States of the Near East, from the Eighth to the Sixth Centuries B.C.*, The Cambridge Ancient History, 2nd edn., vol. iii, pt. 2 (Cambridge, 1991), 252–75.
DARR, K. P., 'The Wall Around Paradise: Ezekielian Ideas About the Future,' *VT* 37 (1987), 271–9.
——'Ezekiel', in C. A. Newsom and S. H. Ringe (eds.), *The Women's Bible Commentary* (Louisville, Ky., 1992), 183–90.
——'Ezekiel Among the Critics', *Currents in Research: Biblical Studies*, 2 (1994), 9–24.
DAVIES, P. R., 'The Social World of the Apocalyptic Writings', in R. E. Clements (ed.), *The World of Ancient Israel: Sociological, Anthropological and Political Perspectives* (Cambridge, 1989), 251–71.
——*In Search of 'Ancient Israel'*, 2nd edn., JSOTS 148 (Sheffield, 1995).
DAVIS, E. F., *Swallowing the Scroll: Textuality and the Dynamics of Discourse in Ezekiel's Prophecy*, JSOTS 78 (Sheffield, 1989).
DAY, J., 'Asherah in the Hebrew Bible and Northwest Semitic Literature', *JBL* 105 (1986), 385–408.
——*Molech: A God of Human Sacrifice in the Old Testament*, University of Cambridge Oriental Publications, 41 (Cambridge, 1989).
DIEZ-MACHO, A., 'Un segundo fragmento del Targum Palestinense a los Profetas', *Biblica*, 39 (1958), 198–205.
DIJK-HEMMES, F. VAN, 'The Metaphorization of Woman in Prophetic Speech: The Case of Ezekiel 23', in A. Brenner (ed.), *A Feminist Companion to The Latter Prophets* (Sheffield, 1995), 244–55; first printed in A. Brenner (ed.), *On Gendering Texts* (Leiden, 1993), 167—76. An earlier draft of this essay is found in *VT* 43 (1993), 162–70.
DIJKSTRA, M., 'Goddess, Gods, Men and Women in Ezekiel 8', in B. Becking and M. Dijkstra (eds.), *On Reading Prophetic Texts: Gender-Specific and Related Studies in Memory of Fokkelien van Dijk-Hemmes*, Biblical Interpretation Series, 18 (Leiden, 1996), 83–114.
——'The Valley of Dry Bones: Coping with the Reality of Exile in the Book of Ezekiel', in B. Becking and M. C. A. Korpel (eds.), *The Crisis of Israelite Religion: Transformation of Religious Tradition in Exilic and Post-Exilic Times*, OTS 42 (Leiden, 1999), 114–33.

DOMMERSHAUSEN. W., 'חלל I', *TDOT*, iv. 409–17.

DONNER, H., 'The Separate States of Israel and Judah', in J. H. Hayes and J. M. Miller (eds.), *Israelite and Judaean History*, OTL (Phil., 1977), 435–88.

DOUGLAS, M., *Purity and Danger: An Analysis of Concepts of Pollution and Taboo*, paperback edn. (Harmondsworth, 1970).

——*Natural Symbols: Explorations in Cosmology*, 2nd edn. (London, 1973).

—— *Implicit Meanings: Essays in Anthropology* (London, 1975).

DRIVER, S. R., *Introduction to the Literature of the Old Testament*, 2nd edn. (Edinburgh, 1891).

DUGUID, I. M., *Ezekiel and the Leaders of Israel*, SVT 56 (Leiden, 1994).

DUTCHER-WALLS, P., 'The Social Location of the Deuteronomists: A Sociological Study of Factional Politics in Late Pre-Exilic Judah', *JSOT* 52 (1991), 77–94.

——*Narrative Art, Political Rhetoric: The Case of Athaliah and Joash*, JSOTS 209 (Sheffield, 1996).

EDELMAN, D., 'Biblical Molek Reassessed', *JAOS* 107 (1987), 727–31.

EICHRODT, W., *Ezekiel: A Commentary*, OTL (London, 1970) = English translation of *Der Prophet Hesekiel*, ATD 22 (Göttingen, 1965–6).

EILBERG-SCHWARTZ, H., *The Savage in Judaism: An Anthropology of Israelite Religion and Ancient Judaism* (Bloomington, Ind., 1990).

EISENSTADT, S. N., *The Political Systems of Empires* (NY, 1963).

EPHʿAL, I., 'The Western Minorities in Babylonia in the 6th–5th Centuries BC: Maintenance and Cohesion', *Orientalia*, 47 (1978), 74–90.

——'On the Political and Social Organization of the Jews in the Babylonian Exile', *ZDMG suppl.* 5 (1980), 106–12.

EWALD, H., *Die Propheten des Alten Bundes*, ii (Stuttgart, 1841).

EXUM, J. C., 'The Ethics of Biblical Violence against Women', in J. W. Rogerson, M. Davies, and M. D. Carroll R (eds.), *The Bible in Ethics: The Second Sheffield Colloquium*, JSOTS 207 (Sheffield, 1995), 248–71.

FEIST, U., *Ezechiel: Das literarische Problem des Buches forschungsgeschichtlich betrachtet*, BWANT 138 (Stuttgart, 1995).

FELDMAN, E., *Biblical and Post Biblical Defilement and Mourning: Law as Theology* (NY, 1977).

FINEGAN, J., 'The Chronology of Ezekiel', *JBL* 69 (1950), 61–6.

FINLEY, M. I., *The Ancient Economy* (London, 1985).

FISHBANE, M., 'Sin and Judgment in the Prophecies of Ezekiel', *Int* 38 (1984), 131–50.

FOHRER, G. *Die Hauptprobleme des Buch Ezechiel*, BZAW 72 (Berlin, 1952).

——*Ezechiel*, HAT 13, 2nd edn. (Tübingen, 1955).

FREEDMAN, D. N., *et al.* (eds.), *The Anchor Bible Dictionary*, 6 vols. (New York, 1992).

FREEDY, K. S., and REDFORD, D. B., 'The Dates in Ezekiel in Relation to Biblical, Babylonian and Egyptian Sources', *JAOS* 90 (1970), 462–85.

FRYMER-KENSKY, T., 'Pollution, Purification, and Purgation in Biblical Israel', in C. M. Meyers and M. J. O'Connor (eds.), *The Word of the Lord Shall Go Forth: Essays in Honor of David Noel Freedman in Celebration of his Sixtieth Birthday* (Winona Lake, Ind., 1983), 399–414.

GADD, C. J., 'The Harran Inscriptions of Nabonidus', *Anatolian Studies*, 8 (1958), 31–92.

GALAMBUSH, J., *Jerusalem in the Book of Ezekiel: The City as Yahweh's Wife*, SBLDS 130 (Atlanta, Ga., 1992).

GAMMIE, J. G., *Holiness in Israel*, OBT (Minn., 1989).

GARSCHA, J., *Studien zum Ezechielbuch: eine redaktionskritische Untersuchung von Ez 1–39*, Europäische Hochschulschriften, 23 (Bern and Frankfurt, 1974).

GASTER, T. H., 'Ezekiel and the Mysteries', *JBL* 60 (1941), 289–310.

GEERTZ, C., *The Interpretation of Cultures* (NY, 1973).

GESE, H., *Der Verfassungsentwurf des Ezechiel (Kap. 40–48) traditionsgeschichtlich untersucht*, BHT 25 (Tübingen, 1957).

GIBSON, J. C. L., *Syrian Semitic Inscriptions*, i. *Hebrew and Moabite Inscriptions* (Oxford, 1971).

—— *Canaanite Myths and Legends* (Edinburgh, 1978).

GISPEN, W. H., 'The Distinction between Clean and Unclean', OTS 5 (1948), 190–6.

GLOCK, C. Y., 'The Role of Deprivation in the Origin and Evolution of Religious Groups', in R. Lee and M. W. Marty (eds.), *Religion and Social Change* (NY, 1964), 24–36.

GLOCK, C. Y., and STARK, R., *Religion and Society in Tension* (Chicago, Ill., 1965).

GORMAN, F. H., jun., 'Ritual Studies and Biblical Studies: Assessment of the Past; Prospects for the Future', *Semeia*, 67 (1994), 13–36.

GOTTWALD, N. K., *All the Kingdoms of the Earth: Israelite Prophecy and International Relations in the Ancient Near East* (NY, 1964).

—— 'A Hypothesis about Social Class in Monarchic Israel in the Light of Contemporary Studies of Social Class and Social Stratification', in N. K. Gottwald (ed.), *The Hebrew Bible in its Social World and Ours* (Atlanta, Ga., 1993), 139–64.

—— 'Social Class as an Analytic and Hermeneutical Category in Biblical Studies', *JBL* 112 (1993), 3–22.

GRABBE, L. L., *Leviticus*, Old Testament Guides (Sheffield, 1993).

—— (ed.), *Leading Captivity Captive: 'The Exile' as History and Ideology*, JSOTS 278 (Sheffield, 1998).

—— 'The Exile under the Theodolite: Historiography as Triangulation', in L. L. Grabbe (ed.), *Leading Captivity Captive: 'The Exile' as History and Ideology*, JSOTS 278 (Sheffield, 1998), 87–90.

GRAFFY, A., *A Prophet Confronts his People: The Disputation Speech in the Prophets*, Analecta Biblica, 104 (Rome, 1984).

GRAYSON, A. K., *Assyrian and Babylonian Chronicles* (Locust Valley, NY, 1975).

GREENBERG, M., 'Ezekiel 17 and the Policy of Psammetichus II', *JBL* 76 (1957), 304–9.

—— 'Prolegomenon', in C. C. Torrey, *Pseudo-Ezekiel and the Original Prophecy, and Critical Articles*, KTAV edn. (NY, 1970), pp. xi–xxix.

—— *Ezekiel 1–20*, Anchor Bible, 22 (Garden City, NY, 1983).

—— 'The Design and Themes of Ezekiel's Program of Restoration', *Int* 38 (1984), 181–208.

—— 'What are Valid Criteria for Determining Inauthentic Matter in Ezekiel', in J. Lust (ed.), *Ezekiel and his Book: Textual and Literary Criticism and their Interrelation*, BETL 74 (Leuven, 1986), 123–35.

—— *Ezekiel 21–37*, Anchor Bible, 22A (NY, 1997).

GROSS, H., 'Umkehr im Alten Testament: In der Sicht der Propheten Jeremia und Ezechiel', in H. auf der Maur and B. Kleinheyer (eds.), *Zeichen des Glaubens: Studien zu Taufe und Firmung: Balthasar Fischer zum 60. Geburtstag* (Zürich and Freiburg, 1972), 19–28.

HAAG, H., 'חמס', in *TDOT* iv. 478–87.

HALPERIN, D. J., *Seeking Ezekiel: Text and Psychology* (University Park, Penn., 1993).

HALS, R. M., *Ezekiel*, FOTL 19 (Grand Rapids, Mich., 1988).

HAMILTON, M. B., *The Sociology of Religion: Theoretical and Comparative Perspectives* (London, 1995).

HANSON, P. D., *The Dawn of Apocalyptic: The Historical and Sociological Roots of Jewish Apocalyptic Eschatology*, 2nd edn. (Phil., 1979).

—— 'Israelite Religion in the Early Postexilic Period', in J. M. Miller, P. D. Hanson, and S. D. McBride (eds.), *Ancient Israelite Religion: Essays in Honor of Frank Moore Cross* (Phil., 1987), 485–508.

HARFORD, J. B., *Studies in the Book of Ezekiel* (Cambridge, 1935).

HASEL, G. F., 'Sabbath', *Anchor Bible Dictionary*, v. 849–56.

HAYES, J. H., and HOOKER, P. K., *A New Chronology for the Kings of Israel and Judah* (Atlanta, Ga., 1988).

HEIDER, G. C., *The Cult of Molek: A Reassessment*, JSOTS 43 (Sheffield, 1985).

HERNTRICH, V., *Ezechielprobleme*, BZAW 61 (Giessen, 1932).

HERRMANN, J., *Ezechiel*, KAT 11 (Leipzig, 1924).

HERRMANN, S., *Die prophetische Heilserwartungen im Alten Testament, Ursprung und Gestaltwandel*, BWANT 5 (Stuttgart, 1965).

HOLLADAY, J. S., jun., 'Religion in Israel and Judah under the Monarchy: An Explicitly Archaeological Approach', in J. M. Miller,

P. D. Hanson, and S. D. McBride (eds.), *Ancient Israelite Religion: Essays in Honor of Frank Moore Cross* (Phil., 1987), 249–99.

HOLLADAY, W. L., *Jeremiah 2*, Hermeneia (Phil., 1989).

HÖLSCHER, G., *Hesekiel: der Dichter und das Buch*, BZAW 39 (Giessen, 1924).

HORBURY, W., 'Extirpation and Excommunication', *VT* 35 (1985). 13–38.

HORST, F., 'Exilsgemeinde und Jerusalem in Ez 8–11: Eine literarische Untersuchung', *VT* 3 (1953), 337–60.

HOSSFELD, F. L., *Untersuchungen zu Komposition und Theologie des Ezechielbuches*, FB 20 (Würzburg, 1977).

HOUSTON, W., *Purity and Monotheism: Clean and Unclean Animals in Biblical Law*, JSOTS 140 (Sheffield, 1993).

——' "You Shall Open your Hand to your Needy Brother": Ideology and Moral Formation in Deuteronomy 15: 1–8', in J. W. Rogerson, M. Davies, and M. D. Carroll R (eds.), *The Bible in Ethics: The Second Sheffield Colloquium*, JSOTS 207 (Sheffield, 1995), 296–314.

HOWELL, S. (ed.), *The Ethnography of Moralities* (London, 1997).

HOWIE, C. G., *The Date and Composition of Ezekiel*, JBLMS 4 (Phil., 1950).

HUGHES, J., *Secrets of the Times: Myth and History in Biblical Chronology*, JSOTS 66 (Sheffield, 1990).

HUMPHREY, C., 'Exemplars and Rules: Aspects of the Discourse of Moralities in Mongolia', in S. Howell (ed.), *The Ethnography of Moralities* (London, 1997), 25–47.

HUNTER, A. V., *Seek the Lord! A Study of the Meaning and Function of the Exhortations in Amos, Hosea, Isaiah, Micah, and Zephaniah* (Baltimore, Md., 1982).

HURVITZ, A., *A Linguistic Study of the Relationship between the Priestly Source and the Book of Ezekiel: A New Look at an Old Problem*, CahRB 20 (Paris, 1982).

JACOBSEN, T., 'Toward the Image of Tammuz', *History of Religions*, 1 (1962), 189–213.

JANSSEN, E., *Juda in der Exilzeit*, FRLANT 69 (Göttingen, 1956).

JANZEN, W., *Old Testament Ethics: A Paradigmatic Approach* (Louisville, Ky., 1994).

JENSON, P. P., *Graded Holiness: A Key to the Priestly Conception of the World*, JSOTS 106 (Sheffield, 1992).

JOHNSON, A. R., *The Vitality of the Individual in the Thought of Ancient Israel* (Cardiff, 1949).

JOYCE, P. M., *Divine Initiative and Human Response in Ezekiel*, JSOTS 51 (Sheffield, 1989).

——'Synchronic and Diachronic Perspectives on Ezekiel', in J. C. de Moor (ed.), *Synchronic or Diachronic? A Debate on Method in Old Testament*

*Exegesis*, Oudtestamentische Studiën, 34 (Leiden, 1995), 115–28.

—— 'Dislocation and Adaptation in the Exilic Age and After', in J. Barton and D. J. Reimer (eds.), *After the Exile: Essays in Honour of Rex Mason* (Macon, Ga., 1996), 45–58.

—— 'King and Messiah in Ezekiel', in J. Day (ed.), *King and Messiah in Israel and the Ancient Near East: Proceedings of the Oxford Old Testament Seminar*, JSOTS 270 (Sheffield, 1998), 323–37.

KAISER, W. C., jun., *Toward Old Testament Ethics* (Grand Rapids, Mich., 1983).

KAMINSKY, J. S., *Corporate Responsibility in the Hebrew Bible*, JSOTS 196 (Sheffield, 1995).

KAUFMANN, Y., *The Religion of Israel* (London, 1961).

KAUTSKY, J. H., *The Politics of Aristocratic Empires* (Chapel Hill, NC, 1982).

KEDAR-KOPFSTEIN, B., 'דם', in *TDOT*, iii. 234–50.

KELSO, J. L., 'Ezekiel's Parable of the Corroded Copper Caldron', *JBL* 64 (1945), 391–3.

KENNETT, R. H., *Old Testament Essays* (Cambridge, 1928).

KESSLER, R., *Staat und Gesellschaft im vorexilischen Juda vom 8. Jahrhundert bis zum Exil*, SVT 47 (Leiden, 1992).

KIMBROUGH, S. T., *Israelite Religion in Sociological Perspective: The Work of Antonin Causse*, Studies in Oriental Religions, 4 (Wiesbaden, 1978).

KLEIN, R. W., *Ezekiel: The Prophet and his Message*, Studies on Personalities of the Old Testament (Columbia, SC, 1988).

KNIGHT, D. A., 'Introduction: Ethics, Ancient Israel, and the Hebrew Bible', *Semeia*, 66 (1994), 1–8.

—— 'Political Rights and Powers in Monarchic Israel', *Semeia*, 66 (1994), 93–117.

KNOPPERS, G. N., 'The Vanishing Solomon: The Disappearance of the United Monarchy from Recent Histories of Israel', *JBL* 116 (1997), 19–44.

KOCH, K., 'Der Spruch, "Sein Blut bleibe auf sein Haupt"', *VT* 12 (1962), 396–416.

—— 'Is There a Doctrine of Retribution in the Old Testament?', in J. L. Crenshaw (ed.), *Theodicy in the Old Testament* (London, 1983), 57–87 = English translation of 'Gibt es ein Vergeltungsdogma im Alten Testament?', *ZThK* 52 (1955), 1–42.

KOPYTOFF, I., 'Slavery', in A. R. Beals, B. Spiegal, and S. Fyler (eds.), *Annual Review of Anthropology* (Palo Alto, Calif., 1982).

KOTTSIEPER, I., ' "Was ist deine Mutter?" Eine Studie zu Ez 19,2–9', *ZAW* 105 (1993), 444–61.

KOVACS, B., 'Is there a Class Ethic in Proverbs?', in J. L. Crenshaw and J. T. Willis (eds.), *Essays in Old Testament Ethics: J. Philip Hyatt In Memoriam* (NY, 1974), 171–89.

KRÜGER, T., *Geschichtskonzepte im Ezechielbuch*, BZAW 180 (Berlin, 1988).

KUHRT, A., *The Ancient Near East c.3000–330 B.C.*, 2 vols. (London, 1995).

KUTSCH, E., 'Das Jahr der Katastrophe: 587 v.Chr', *Biblica*, 55 (1974), 520–45.

LANG, B. *Kein Aufstand in Jerusalem: Die Politik des Propheten Ezechiel*, SBB (Stuttgart, 1978).

——*Ezechiel: Der Prophet und das Buch*, EdF 153 (Darmstadt, 1981).

——*Monotheism and the Prophetic Minority: An Essay in Biblical History and Sociology* (Sheffield, 1983).

——'Street Theater, Raising the Dead and the Zoroastrian Connection in Ezekiel's Prophecy', in J. Lust (ed.), *Ezekiel and his Book: Textual and Literary Criticism and their Interrelation*, BETL, 74 (Leuven, 1986), 297–316.

LANTERNARI, V., *The Religions of the Oppressed: A Study of Modern Messianic Cults* (London, 1963).

LARSEN, M. T., 'The Tradition of Empire in Mesopotamia', in M. T. Larsen (ed.), *Power and Propaganda: A Symposium on Ancient Empires*, Mesopotamia, 7 (Copenhagen, 1979), 75–103.

LEE, D., and NEWBY, H., *The Problem of Sociology* (London, 1983).

LEMCHE, N. P., *Ancient Israel: A New History of Israelite Society* (Sheffield, 1988).

LEMKE, W. E., 'Life in the Present and Hope for the Future', *Int* 38 (1984), 165–80.

LENSKI, G., *Power and Privilege: A Theory of Social Stratification* (NY, 1966).

LENSKI, G., and LENSKI, J., *Human Societies: An Introduction to Macrosociology*, 4th edn. (NY, 1982).

LEVENSON, J. D., *Theology of the Program of Restoration of Ezekiel 40–48*, HSM 10 (Missoula, Mont., 1976).

LEVEY, S. H. (tr.), *The Targum of Ezekiel*, The Aramaic Bible, 13 (Wilmington, Del., 1987).

LEVINE, B., *In the Presence of the Lord: A Study of Cult and Some Cultic Terms in Ancient Israel*, SJLA 5 (Leiden, 1974).

LINCOLN, B., *Discourse and the Construction of Society: Comparative Studies of Myth, Ritual, and Classification* (NY, 1989).

LINDARS, B., 'Ezekiel and Individual Responsibility', *VT* 15 (1965), 452–67.

LINTON, R., 'Nativistic Movements', *American Anthropologist*, 45 (1942), 230–40.

LIVERANI, M., 'The Ideology of the Assyrian Empire', in M. T. Larsen (ed.), *Power and Propaganda: A Symposium on Ancient Empires*, Mesopotamia, 7 (Copenhagen, 1979), 297–317.

LOHFINK, N., 'The Cult Reform of Josiah of Judah: 2 Kings 22–23 as a Source for the History of Israelite Religion', in J. M. Miller, P. D.

Hanson, and S. D. McBride (eds.), *Ancient Israelite Religion: Essays in Honor of Frank Moore Cross* (Phil., 1987), 459–75.

LOMBARDI-SATRIANI, L., 'Folklore as a Culture of Contestation', *Journal of the Folklore Institute*, 11 (1974), 99–121.

LOWERY, R. H., *The Reforming Kings: Cults and Society in First Temple Judah*, JSOTS 120 (Sheffield, 1991).

LUTZKY, H. C., 'On "the Image of Jealousy" (Ezekiel viii 3, 5)', *VT* 46 (1996), 121–5.

MCKANE, W., *Prophets and Wise Men* (London, 1965).

—— *Jeremiah I–XXV*, ICC (Edinburgh, 1986).

—— *Jeremiah XXVI–LII*, ICC (Edinburgh, 1996).

MCKAY, H. A., *Sabbath and Synagogue: The Question of Sabbath Worship in Ancient Judaism*, Religions in the Graeco-Roman World, 122 (Leiden, 1994).

MCKAY, J. W., *Religion in Judah under the Assyrians 732–609 B.C.*, SBT, 2nd series, 26 (London, 1973).

MCKEATING, H., 'Sanctions Against Adultery in Ancient Israelite Society, with some Reflections on Methodology in the Study of Old Testament Ethics', *JSOT* 11 (1979), 57–72.

—— *Ezekiel*, Old Testament Guides (Sheffield, 1993).

MALAMAT, A., 'Jeremiah and the Last Two Kings of Judah', *PEQ* 83 (1951), 81–7.

—— 'The Last Kings of Judah and the Fall Of Jerusalem', *IEJ* 18 (1968), 137–56.

—— 'The Twilight of Judah in the Egyptian–Babylonian Maelstrom', in *Congress Volume: Edinburgh 1974*, SVT 28 (Leiden, 1975), 123–45.

—— 'The Last Years of the Kingdom of Judah', in A. Malamat and I. Eph'al (eds.), *The Age of the Monarchies: Political History, World History of the Jewish People: Ancient Times*, iv/1 (Jerusalem, 1979), 205–21.

MALUL, M., 'Adoption of Foundlings in the Bible and Mesopotamian Documents: A Study of Some Legal Metaphors in Ezekiel 16: 1–7', *JSOT* 46 (1990), 97–126.

MANN, M., *The Sources of Social Power*, i. *A History of Power from the Beginning to AD 1760* (Cambridge, 1986).

MANNHEIM, K., *Ideology and Utopia* (London, 1936).

MATTIES, G. H., *Ezekiel 18 and the Rhetoric of Moral Discourse*, SBLDS 126 (Atlanta, Ga., 1990).

MAY, H. G., 'The Departure of the Glory of Yahweh', *JBL* 56 (1937), 309–21.

—— 'The Book of Ezekiel', in G. A. Buttricke, *et al.* (eds.), *The Interpreter's Bible*, vi (NY and Nashville, Tenn., 1956), 41–338.

MEEKS, W. A., *The Moral World of the First Christians* (London, 1986).

MESSEL, N., *Ezechielfragen* (Oslo, 1945).

MILGROM, J., 'The Priestly Doctrine of Repentance', *RB* 82 (1975), 310–27.

—— *Cult and Conscience: The Asham and the Priestly Doctrine of Repentance*, SJLA 18 (Leiden, 1976).

—— *Studies in Cultic Theology and Terminology*, SJLA 36 (Leiden, 1983).

—— 'Rationale for Cultic Law: The Case of Impurity', *Semeia*, 45 (1989), 103–9.

—— *Leviticus 1–16*, Anchor Bible, 3 (NY, 1991).

MITCHELL, T. C., 'Judah until the Fall of Jerusalem (c.700–586 B.C.)', in J. Boardman, I. E. S. Edwards, *et al.* (eds.), *The Assyrian and Babylonian Empires and other States of the Near East, from the Eighth to the Sixth Centuries B.C.*, The Cambridge Ancient History, 2nd edn., vol. iii, pt. 2 (Cambridge, 1991), 371–409.

—— 'The Babylonian Exile and the Restoration of the Jews in Palestine', in J. Boardman, I. E. S. Edwards, *et al.* (eds.), *The Assyrian and Babylonian Empires and other States of the Near East, from the Eighth to the Sixth Centuries B.C.*, The Cambridge Ancient History, 2nd edn., vol. iii, pt. 2 (Cambridge, 1991), 410–60.

MULLO WEIR, C. J., 'Aspects of the Book of Ezekiel', *VT* 2 (1952), 97–112.

NELSON, R. D., *The Double Redaction of the Deuteronomic History*, JSOTS 18 (Sheffield, 1981).

NEUSNER, J., *The Idea of Purity in Ancient Judaism*, SJLA 1 (Leiden, 1973).

NICHOLSON, E. W., *Preaching to the Exiles: A Study of the Prose Tradition in the Book of Jeremiah* (Oxford, 1970).

NIDITCH, S., 'Ezekiel 40–48 in Visionary Context', *CBQ* 48 (1986), 208–24.

NOBILE, M., 'Lo sfondo cultuale di Ez 8–11', *Antonianum*, 58 (1983), 185–200.

NOTH, M., *The History of Israel* (London, 1958) = English translation of *Geschichte Israels*, 2nd edn. (Göttingen, 1958).

—— 'The Jerusalem Catastrophe of 587 BC and its Significance for Israel', in *The Laws in the Pentateuch and Other Essays* (Edinburgh, 1966), 260–80 = English translation of 'Die Katastrophe von Jerusalem im Jahre 587 v.Chr und ihre bedeutung für Israel', in M. Noth, *Gesammelte Studien zum Alten Testament*, 2nd edn. (Munich, 1960), 346–71, originally published as 'La Catastrophe de Jérusalem en l'an 587 avant Jésus-Christ et sa signification pour Israel', *RHPR* 33 (1953), 82–102.

OATES, J., 'The Fall of Assyria (635–609 B.C.)', in J. Boardman, I. E. S. Edwards, *et al.* (eds.), *The Assyrian and Babylonian Empires and other States of the Near East, from the Eighth to the Sixth Centuries B.C.*, The Cambridge Ancient History, 2nd edn., vol. iii, pt. 2 (Cambridge, 1991), 162–93.

O'CONNOR, K. M., 'Lamentations', in C. A. Newsom and S. H. Ringe (eds.), *The Women's Bible Commentary* (Louisville, Ky., 1992), 178–82.

ODED, B., 'Judah and the Exile', in J. H. Hayes and J. M. Miller (eds.), *Israelite and Judaean History*, OTL (Phil., 1977), 435–88.

——*Mass Deportations and Deportees in the Neo-Assyrian Empire* (Wiesbaden, 1979).

ODELL, M. S., 'The Inversion of Shame and Forgiveness in Ezekiel 16: 59–63', *JSOT* 56 (1992), 101–12.

——'You Are What You Eat: Ezekiel and the Scroll', *JBL* 117 (1998), 229–48.

OLYAN, S., *Asherah and the Cult of Yahweh in Israel*, SBLMS 34 (Atlanta, Ga., 1988).

OTTO, E., *Theologische Ethik des alten Testaments*, Theologische Wissenschaft 3/2 (Stuttgart, 1994).

OTZEN, B., 'Israel under the Assyrians', in M. T. Larsen (ed.), *Power and Propaganda: A Symposium on Ancient Empires*, Mesopotamia, 7 (Copenhagen, 1979), 251–61.

PARSONS, T., 'Introduction', in M. Weber, *The Sociology of Religion* (London, 1965).

PATTERSON, O., *Slavery and Social Death* (Cambridge, Mass., 1982).

PFEIFFER, R. H., *Introduction to the Old Testament*, 3rd edn. (NY, 1941).

PHILLIPS, A., *Ancient Israel's Criminal Law: A New Approach to the Decalogue* (Oxford, 1970).

PLEINS, J. D., 'Poverty in the Social World of the Wise', *JSOT* 37 (1987), 61–78.

PLÖGER, O., *Theocracy and Eschatology* (Oxford, 1968) = English translation of *Theokratie und Eschatologie*, WMANT 2 (Neukirchen, 1959).

POHLMANN, K.-F., *Ezechielstudien: Zur Redaktionsgeschichte des Buches und zur Frage nach den altesten Texten*, BZAW 202 (Berlin, 1992).

——*Der Prophet Hesekiel/Ezechiel Kapitel 1–19*, ATD 22/1 (Göttingen, 1996).

PONS, J., 'Le Vocabulaire d'Ez 20: Le prophète s'oppose à la vision deutéronomiste de l'histoire', in J. Lust (ed.), *Ezekiel and his Book: Textual and Literary Criticism and their Interrelation*, BETL 74 (Leuven, 1986), 214–33.

PRITCHARD, J. B. (ed.), *Ancient Near Eastern Texts Relating to the Old Testament*, 3rd edn. (Princeton, NJ, 1969).

PROVAN, I. W., *Lamentations*, NCB (Grand Rapids, Mich., and London, 1991).

RAD, G. VON, *Old Testament Theology*, 2 vols. (London, 1962, 1965) = English translation of *Theologie Des Alten Testaments*, 2 vols. (Munich, 1957, 1960).

——' "Righteousness" and "Life" in the Cultic Language of the Psalms', in G. von Rad, *The Problem of the Hexateuch and Other Essays* (Edinburgh and London, 1966), 243–66 = English translation of ' "Gerechtigkeit" und "Leben" in der Kultsprache der Psalmen', in *Festschrift für Alfred Bertholet* (Tübingen, 1950), 418–37.

RAITT, T. M., 'The Prophetic Summons to Repentance', *ZAW* 83 (1971), 30–49.

——*A Theology of Exile: Judgment/Deliverance in Jeremiah and Ezekiel* (Phil., 1977).

READE, J., 'Ideology and Propaganda in Assyrian Art', in M. T. Larsen (ed.), *Power and Propaganda: A Symposium on Ancient Empires*, Mesopotamia, 7 (Copenhagen, 1979), 329–43.

RENZ, T., *The Rhetorical Function of the Book of Ezekiel*, SVT 76 (Leiden, 1999).

REVENTLOW, H. G., *Wächter über Israel: Ezechiel und seine Tradition*, BZAW 82 (Berlin, 1962).

——'Sein Blut komme über sein Haupt', *VT* 10 (1960), 310–27.

RINGGREN, H., *Israelite Religion* (London, 1966) = English translation of *Israelitische Religion* (Stuttgart, 1963).

ROBINSON, H. Wheeler, *Two Hebrew Prophets: Studies in Hosea and Ezekiel* (London, 1948).

RODD, C. S., 'New Occasions Teach New Duties? 1. The Use of the Old Testament in Christian Ethics', *ExpT* 105 (1994), 100–6.

ROOKER, M. F., *Biblical Hebrew in Transition: The Language of the Book of Ezekiel*, JSOTS 90 (Sheffield, 1990).

ROSENBERG, J., 'Jeremiah and Ezekiel', in R. Alter and F. Kermode (eds.), *The Literary Guide to the Bible* (London, 1987), 184–206.

ROWLEY, H. H., 'The Book of Ezekiel in Modern Study', *BJRL* 36 (1953/4), 146–90.

SAKENFELD, K. D., 'Ez 18: 25–32', *Int* 32 (1978), 295–300.

SANDERSON, S. K., *Social Evolutionism: A Critical History* (Oxford, 1990).

——*Social Transformations: A General Theory of Historical Development* (Oxford, 1995).

SCHMIDT, W. H., *Zukunftsgewißheit und Gegenwartskritik: Grundzüge prophetischer Verkündigung*, BibS[N] 64 (Neukirchen-Vluyn, 1973).

SCHONEVELD, J., 'Ezekiel 14. 1–8', *Oudtestamentische Studiën*, 15 (1969), 193–204.

SCHULZ, H., *Das Todesrecht im Alten Testament: Studien zum Rechtsformen der Mot-Jumat-Sätze*, BZAW 114 (Berlin, 1969).

SCOTT, J., *Stratification and Power: Structures of Class, Status, and Command* (Oxford, 1996).

SCOTT, J. C., *Domination and the Arts of Resistance: Hidden Transcripts* (New Haven, Conn., 1990).

SEITZ, C. R., *Theology in Conflict: Reactions to the Exile in the Book of Jeremiah*, BZAW 176 (Berlin, 1989).

SHANKS, H. (ed.), *Ancient Israel: A Short History from Abraham to the Roman Destruction of the Temple* (London, 1989).

SIMIAN, H., *Die theologische Nachgeschichte der Prophetie Ezechiels: Form- und traditionskritische Untersuchung zu Ez 6; 35; 36*, FB 14 (Würzburg, 1974).

SMITH, D. L., *The Religion of the Landless: The Social Context of the Babylonian Exile* (Bloomington, Ind., 1989).

—— 'The Politics of Ezra', in P. R. Davies (ed.), *Second Temple Studies*, JSOTS 117 (Sheffield, 1991), 73–97.

SMITH, J., *The Book of the Prophet Ezekiel: A New Interpretation* (London, 1931).

SMITH, M., *Palestinian Parties and Politics that Shaped the Old Testament* (NY, 1971).

—— 'The Veracity of Ezekiel, The Sins of Manasseh, and Jeremiah 44: 18', *ZAW* 87 (1975), 11–16.

SMITH-CHRISTOPHER, D. L., 'Reassessing the Historical and Sociological Impact of the Babylonian Exile (597/587–539 BCE)', in J. M. Scott (ed.), *Exile: Old Testament, Jewish and Christian Conceptions*, Journal for the Study of Judaism, Supplement Series, 56 (Leiden, 1997), 7–36.

SOGGIN, J. A., *Introduction to the Old Testament*, 3rd edn. (London, 1989).

—— *An Introduction to the History of Israel and Judah*, OTL, 2nd edn. (Valley Forge, Pa., 1993).

SPEISER, E. A., 'Background and Function of the Biblical *Nāśî*'', *CBQ* 25 (1963), 111–17.

SPIECKERMANN, H., *Juda unter Assur in der Sargonidenzeit* (Göttingen, 1982).

STALKER, D. M. G., *Ezekiel: Introduction and Commentary* (London, 1968).

STEVENSON, K. R., *The Vision of Transformation: The Territorial Rhetoric of Ezekiel 40–48*, SBLDS 154 (Atlanta, Ga., 1996).

STOLPER, M. W., *Entrepreneurs and Empire: The Murašû Archive, The Murašû Firm, and Persian Rule in Babylonia* (Istanbul, 1985).

TALMON, Y., 'Millenarian Movements', *Archives Européenes de Sociologie*, 7 (1966), 159–200.

TAYLOR, J. B., *Ezekiel: An Introduction and Commentary*, Tyndale Old Testament Commentaries (Leicester, 1969).

TAYLOR, J. G., *Yahweh and the Sun: Biblical and Archaeological Evidence for Sun Worship in Ancient Israel*, JSOTS 111 (Sheffield, 1993).

THOMPSON, T. L., 'The Exile in History and Myth: A Response to Hans Barstad', in L. L. Grabbe (ed.), *Leading Captivity Captive: 'The Exile' as History and Ideology*, JSOTS 278 (Sheffield, 1998), 101–18.

TOORN, K. VAN DER, *Sin and Sanction in Israel and Mesopotamia: A Comparative Study*, SSN, 22 (Assen, 1985).

TORREY, C. C., *Ezra Studies* (Chicago, Ill., 1910).

—— *Pseudo-Ezekiel and the Original Prophecy*, Yale Oriental Series Researches, 18 (New Haven, Conn., 1930).

Toy, C. H., *The Book of the Prophet Ezekiel* (NY, 1899).
Troeltsch, E., *The Social Teaching of the Christian Churches* (NY, 1931).
Tsevat, M., 'Studies in the Book of Samuel', *HUCA* 32 (1961), 195–216.
Tuell, S. S., *The Law of the Temple in Ezekiel 40–48*, HSM 49 (Atlanta, Ga., 1992).
——'Ezekiel 40–42 as Verbal Icon, *CBQ* 58 (1996), 649–64.
Turner, B. S., *Status* (Milton Keynes, 1988).
Uffenheimer, B., 'Theodicy and Ethics in the Prophecy of Ezekiel', in H. G. Reventlow (ed.), *Justice and Righteousness: Biblical Themes and their Influence*, JSOTS 137 (Sheffield, 1992), 200–27.
Ussishkin, D., 'Royal Judean Storage Jars and Private Seal Impressions', *Bulletin of the American Schools of Oriental Research*, 223 (1976), 1–14.
Vaughan, P. H., *The Meaning of 'bamâ' in the Old Testament: A Study of Etymological, Textual and Archaeological Evidence*, SOTS, Monograph Series, 3 (Cambridge, 1974).
Vaux, R. de, *Ancient Israel: Its Life and Institutions* (London, 1961) = English translation of *Les Institutions de l'Ancien Testament* (Paris, 1960).
Voltaire, F. M. A. de, *The Complete Works of Voltaire*, xxxv. *Dictionnaire philosophique, ii*, sous la direction de Christiane Mervaud (Oxford, 1994).
Wallace, A. F. C., 'Revitalization Movements', *American Anthropologist*, 58 (1956), 264–81.
Weber, M., *Ancient Judaism* (NY, 1952) = English translation of *Gesammelte Aufsätze zur Religionssoziologie*, iii. *Das antike Judentum* (Tübingen, 1921).
—— *The Sociology of Religion* (London, 1965) = English translation of 'Religionssoziologie', from *Wirtschaft und Gesellschaft: Grundriss der verstehenden Soziologie*, 4th edn. (Tübingen, 1956).
—— *Economy and Society: An Outline of Interpretive Sociology* (Berkeley, Calif., 1978) = English translation of *Wirtschaft und Gesellschaft: Grundriss der verstehenden Soziologie*, 4th edn. (Tübingen, 1956).
Weidner, E. F., 'Jojachin, König von Juda, in babylonischen Keilschrifttexten', in *Mélanges Syriens offerts à Monsieur René Dussaud*, ii (Paris, 1939), 923–35.
Weinfeld, M., *Deuteronomy and the Deuteronomic School* (Oxford, 1972).
—— 'Instructions for Temple Visitors in the Bible and in Ancient Egypt', in S. Israel-Groll (ed.), *Egyptological Studies*, Scripta Hierosolymita, 28 (Jerusalem, 1982), 224–50.
—— *Social Justice in Ancient Israel and in the Ancient Near East* (Jerusalem, 1995).
Weinstein, D., *Savonarola and Florence: Prophecy and Patriotism in the Renaissance* (Princeton, NJ, 1970).

WEIPPERT, H., *Palästina in vorhellenistische Zeit*, Handbuch der Archäologie, Vorderasien II, Band i (Munich, 1988).

WEISSBACH, F. H., *Das Haupteiligtum des Marduk in Babylon* (Leipzig, 1938).

WESTERMANN, C., *Basic Forms of Prophetic Speech* (Phil., 1967). = English translation of *Grundformen prophetischer Rede*, BEvTh 31 (Munich, 1960).

WEVERS, J. W., *Ezekiel*, NCB (Grand Rapids, Mich., and London, 1969).

WHITELAM, K. W., *The Just King: Monarchical Judicial Authority in Ancient Israel*, JSOTS 12 (Sheffield, 1979).

—— 'The Defence of David', *JSOT* 29 (1984), 61–87.

—— 'Israelite Kingship: The Royal Ideology and its Opponents', in R. E. Clements (ed.), *The World of Ancient Israel: Anthropological, Sociological and Political Perspectives* (Cambridge, 1989), 119–39.

—— *The Invention of Ancient Israel: The Silencing of Palestinian History* (London, 1996).

WHITLEY, C. F., *The Exilic Age* (London, 1957).

WILKIE, J. L., 'Nabonidus and the Later Jewish Exiles', *JTS*, NS, 2 (1951), 36–44.

WILLIAMSON, H. G. M., *Ezra, Nehemiah*, Word Biblical Commentary, 16 (Waco, Tex., 1985).

WILSON, B. R., *Magic and the Millennium: A Sociological Study of Religious Movements of Protest Among Tribal and Third-World Peoples* (NY, 1973).

WILSON, R. R., *Prophecy and Society in Ancient Israel* (Phil., 1980).

—— 'From Prophecy to Apocalyptic', *Semeia*, 21 (1981), 79–95.

—— 'Prophecy in Crisis: The Call of Ezekiel', *Int* 38 (1984), 117–30.

—— 'Ethics in Conflict: Sociological Aspects of Ancient Israelite Ethics', in S. Niditch (ed.), *Text and Tradition: The Hebrew Bible and Folklore* (Atlanta, Ga., 1990), 193–213.

—— 'Sources and Methods in the Study of Ancient Israelite Ethics', *Semeia*, 66 (1994), 55–63.

WISEMAN, D. J., *Nebuchadrezzar and Babylon* (Oxford, 1983).

—— 'Babylonia 605–539 B.C.', in J. Boardman, I. E. S. Edwards, *et al.* (eds.), *The Assyrian and Babylonian Empires and other States of the Near East, from the Eighth to the Sixth Centuries B.C.*, The Cambridge Ancient History, 2nd edn., vol. iii, pt. 2 (Cambridge, 1991), 229–51.

WOLFF, H. W., 'Das Thema "Umkehr" in der alttestamentlichen Prophetie', *ZThK* 48 (1951), 129–48.

WRIGHT, C. J. H., *Living as the People of God: The Relevance of Old Testament Ethics* (Leicester, 1983).

WRIGHT, D. P., 'The Spectrum of Priestly Impurity', in G. A. Anderson and S. Olyan (eds.), *Priesthood and Cult in Ancient Israel*, JSOTS 125 (Sheffield, 1991), 150–82.

—— 'Holiness (OT)', *Anchor Bible Dictionary*, iii. 237–49.

WRIGHT, D. P., 'Unclean and Clean', *Anchor Bible Dictionary*, vi. 729–41.

WUTHNOW, R., *Meaning and Moral Order: Explorations in Cultural Analysis* (Berkeley, Calif., 1987).

ZADOK, R., *The Jews in Babylonia during the Chaldean and Achaemenian Periods according to the Babylonian Sources* (Haifa, 1979).

——'Onomastic, Prosopographic and Lexical Notes', *BN* 65 (1992), 47–64.

ZIMMERLI, W., 'Die Eigenart der prophetischen Rede des Ezechiel: ein Beitrag zum Problem an Hand von Ezech. xiv 1–11', *ZAW* 66 (1954), 1–26.

—— ' "Leben" und "Tod" im Buche des Propheten Ezechiel', *ThZ* 13 (1957), 494–508.

—— 'The Special Form- and Traditio-Historical Character of Ezekiel's Prophecy', *VT* 15 (1965), 515–27.

—— 'The Message of the Prophet Ezekiel', *Int* 23 (1969), 131–57.

—— 'Deutero-Ezechiel?', *ZAW* 84 (1972), 501–16.

—— *Ezekiel,* Hermeneia, 2 vols. (Phil., 1979, 1983) = English translation of *Ezechiel,* 2 vols (Neukirchen, 1969).

—— 'Plans for Rebuilding after the Catastrophe of 587', in W. Brueggemann (ed.), *I am Yahweh* (Atlanta, Ga., 1982), 111–33 = English translation of 'Planungen für die Wiederaufbau nach der Katastrophe von 587', *VT* 18 (1968), 229–55.

# INDEX OF AUTHORS

# INDEX OF BIBLICAL REFERENCES